FRANCIS OF ASSISI AS ARTIST OF THE SPIRITUAL LIFE

An Object Relations Theory Perspective

Andrew T. McCarthy

University Press of America,® Inc.
Lanham · Boulder · New York · Toronto · Plymouth, UK

Library of Congress Control Number: 2010929879
ISBN: 978-0-7618-5250-6 (paperback : alk. paper)
eISBN: 978-0-7618-5251-3

To my children and wife

CONTENTS

Acknowledgments

As this text attempts to indicate, so much is possible with a supportive family environment. My central argument is that Francis indeed had a "good-enough mother." The two mothers that I am most familiar with far exceed this description. I owe so much to Carla McCarthy the mother of my children who has carried a preponderance of the family burden to allow me to follow a dream. My own mother, Kathleen McCarthy, presented me with a world full of possibilities, a long line of strong maternal personalities, and the imagination with which to dream. Envisioning a possibility is often not enough. From my father, Andrew McCarthy, I learned that pursuit of a dream requires faith on many levels but in particular in one's own abilities. To my children, who still have difficulty explaining what their father does all day, I owe a return to some level of normalcy. Andrew, Kristjana, Kieran, Justin, and Juliana are the inspiration for the direction this project has taken. Each has a unique perspective on reality, and I suspect all have the ability to make reality more meaningful. As Francis learned from the Benedictines so have I. Dr. Raymond Studzinski, O.S.B. gave direction and shape to the inquiry that I first brought to my scholarly endeavors, but it has been his personal encouragement that helped me see this project through to completion. All good things to each of you!

Warm thanks are extended to Regis Armstrong, OFM, Cap. and Ilia Delio, OSF for giving me the confidence to move ahead with this project. I also want to thank Samantha Kirk at University Press of America for her support and guidance in the process of advancing this work to publication. Appreciation is extended to New City Press for permission to use material from *Francis of Assisi: The Early Documents*. The same is extended to St. Anthony Messenger Press for permission to use material from *St. Francis of Assisi: Writings and Early Biographies: English Omnibus of Sources for the Life of St. Francis*. Additional appreciation goes to Cengage Learning for permission to use material from *Playing and Reality*. For rights to print text from *Bernard of Clairvaux*, I thank Paulist Press, and I also thank International Universities Press for rights to print material from *The Play of the Imagination: Toward a Psycho-Analysis of Culture*.

CHAPTER ONE
PURPOSE AND INTRODUCTION

Purpose

"Who is this person? What can we know of him or her? What should we make of this information?" These are questions that might be asked about a potential friend, a business rival, or the subject of a media report. Place the person in the distant past, at the center of a religious movement that still has reverberations today, and the task of understanding the meaning of his or her life becomes even more complex. The thorough study of an influential religious figure, eight hundred years in the grave, involves numerous challenges and calls for many avenues of approach. Such is the case with St. Francis of Assisi (c. 1182-1226). He left behind only a limited number of personal writings. The more voluminous writings about him must be traversed carefully, with a mind wary of the social, political, and ecclesiastical forces at work behind them.

Many authors have attempted to present a full depiction of Francis. While these efforts have often been edifying, they have not been complete. There simply is not enough reliable information about him to put together a precise portrait of his life. What can be achieved, instead, is a series of focused studies of specific areas of his life, applying more recent analytical theories or techniques to interpret the data that is available. Joining together several such studies cannot lead to the perfect image. It just does not exist! But, like a mosaic that is missing many pieces, retaining those that remain will allow one to view dimly the splendor of the original work.[1] The present volume is but a single piece.

It has already been suggested that the first two questions are an ongoing source of frustration: "Who is this person?" and "What can we know of him or her?" The potential of the third question gives this study an overarching purpose and influences the specific approach chosen: "What should we make of this information?" The assertion here is that Francis saw the world in a different fashion from other people apparently observing the same scene. Furthermore, it seems that he was able to extend this way of seeing, at least in some degree, to others. The driving impetus of this work, then, is to bring to the present-day-world a desperately needed example of seeing differently, but little will be said about contemporary applications, for this is not the immediate focus of this endeavor. It should merely be understood that a study of the past is of negligible value if it is not in some way related to the advancement of the future.

The observation that Francis sees differently has led to the selection of his imagination as the narrow focus of this work. The imaginative dimension of his life and writings will be investigated from a psychodynamic viewpoint. To ask how one can know Francis better through the workings of his imagination and what can be known of his imagination, one might want to begin with a definition of imagination proper. In reviewing the literature on imagination, it becomes clear that no truly adequate definition exists. Imagination is a compelling topic that has received its fair share of scholarly attention ranging back to the early Greek philosophers. However, in all its history, imagination has not even held to a fixed position in the categorical hierarchy of the workings of the human mind. Views have ranged widely over the type of faculty it should be considered or whether it should even be considered a faculty. It is the difficulty of studying the machinations of the mind, wherein the imagination is active, that limits the possibility of setting a definition that declares the full scope and functional range of the imagination. For this reason, any attempt to study imagination should begin by understanding the term *imagination* to refer more to a description than a definition. In this work, which is concerned primarily with the imagination's religious dimension, imagination will be described as: the mental process that enables us to regard reality, ourselves, and God in such ways that invite or repel response, action, and connection.[2]

From the description adopted, it is clear that imagination does not yield the same results in each person. As an *enabling process* it will work only to the extent that it is used, or is even capable of being used. All people do not seem to have the same ability to use their imaginations. The description also indicates that there may be more than one way to regard and respond to reality, ourselves, and God. From this it should be obvious that the given description of imagination can support the contention that Francis sees differently. The choice of the selected description of imagination must eventually be more fully justified to uphold this claim, but first more should be known about Francis. In this introductory chapter his life will be observed from the viewpoint of a near contemporary. Then, to place in perspective the use of a psychological theory to investigate a historic person, some of the approaches taken by scholars who observe such a subject through the lens of psychology will be considered. This will first allow for a greater familiarity with Francis and also clarify the method for studying his imaginative activity.

In the second chapter the context is set for Francis' imagination. In a quick race across philosophical history some of the highlights of the development of the imagination, leading up to Francis' time, come under review. From this the extent of the influence of the intellectual tradition on Francis' imagination will be estimated. A weaker connection here would suggest a greater amount of uniquely creative imagination on Francis' part. Francis will also be compared with others of his time who were recognized for their ability to grasp the popular imagination. Since this study of Francis concentrates on the way he expresses a series of relationships involving himself, God, other humans, and the rest of created reality, examples of writings will be offered from two religious figures whose spirituality often shared a similar concern for relationality. Aelred of Rievaulx (1110-1167) and Bernard of Clairvaux (1090-1153) provide texts that represent the use of imagination by other religious leaders in a period of renewal and transition. Alongside a contextualization of the imagination as it emerged in Francis' day, the imagination can be regarded according to its more modern understanding. This endeavor will be carried out in Chapter Three where contributions made in the areas of philosophical, sociological, religious, and psychological approaches to imagination will be examined. This will not be an exhaustive review, but it will serve as a basis for identifying features the chosen psychodynamic theory of imagination holds in common with the general body of recent literature on imagination, as well as highlighting those features which make the theory unique.

The fourth and fifth chapters offer an understanding of the primary theory to be used as a tool for scrutinizing the works of Francis' imagination. At this point a brief introduction to this theory is in order as a prologue to reviewing other outlooks on imagination in the preceding chapter. Psychoanalytic Object Relations Theory (ORT) is a contemporary development of Freudian psychoanalytic theory. The field of contributors to the theory is wide enough that it is necessary to select from the writings of only a limited number of theorists. These include D.W. Winnicott, Paul Pruyser, John McDargh, and Ana Maria Rizzuto. The selection of these authors is made largely on their interest in the individual's ability to imaginatively form an inner psychic world as the basis for inter-relationship with the external world. In each case there is also a keen awareness of connections between religion and the imagination.

The Object Relations Theory psychoanalytic perspective will throw light on the significance of Francis' relationships with other people, aspects of reality, and God as reflected in his writings. According to this theory, in our coming to terms with our separateness in early life, we link internally created mental representations of an element, whether it is of a person, activity, concept, or object, with an actual element in the external or shareable world. This process occurs in what has been called transitional space. The comfort with which the infant has learned to operate in this psychic space, that links yet holds separate the internal and external world, ultimately determines the richness of the adult's imaginative creativity and ability to appreciate the imaginative work of others. Within the transitional space, internal object representations fashioned out of previous experiences are brought into a creative synthesis with data from the external world to yield an imaginatively unique view of an aspect of the external world. Francis' maternal orientation and rich perception of the sacred-in-the-world are just the first indications that he was well able to make use of the transitional space in his imaginative activity.

In the search for distinctiveness in Francis' imagination there could be no claim that ORT only applies to the workings of this particular saint's imagination. The beauty of the theory is that it offers a respectable near-universal influence in an age when anything claimed as universal is viewed with suspicion. At the heart of the theory is the infant-mother relationship. While not every infant has had a meaningful relationship with a mother or significant care-giver, ORT recognizes that the vast majority of people in this world have had a relationship with Winnicott's broadly defined "good-enough mother."[3] The point to be argued in Francis' situation is that he seems to have made the best of this relationship as indicated by his imaginative activity.

In Chapter Six, Chapter Seven, and Chapter Eight the significant amount of theory, previously discussed, will be brought to bear on a selection of Francis' writings. Francis' genius is encountered in the richness of the spiritual creativity found in his compositions. To fully comprehend this it might help to begin viewing him as an artist of the spiritual life. The application of object relations theory to his writings will shed light on his ability to craft a vision of the world that sees a spiritual dimension of reality intertwined with the ordinary people, material, and events of everyday existence. As a master artist, Francis' talent does not end on the "canvas" but extends to the studio of life where others are guided to fully engage their own imaginations and craft a spiritual way of *being* in the style their master provides in his writings. Through his texts Francis will be shown to have left a method for developing a spiritually imaginative way of seeing.

The final chapter, Chapter Eight, will also clarify the originality of Francis' imagination. A summary reflection will be made of the justification for the claim that Francis' imagination, as seen in his writings, is a uniquely powerful example of original creativity as understood from an ORT perspective. From this it will be possible to envision Francis as an individual: who was no longer able to embrace the existing way of viewing the world, who burst into a new and more meaningful mode of perception, and who ultimately extended this vision to others who also would never again be able to rest contently in their previous conception of reality.

Turning now to the most well known text on the saint's life, Francis is introduced by someone who knew his culture, environment, and closest friends. It is an introduction that many people do not get beyond, and it sculpts in stone an impression they often retain for better or worse.

A First Introduction to Francis

Thomas of Celano's *Vita Prima* or First Life of Francis of Assisi was an early attempt to capture a portrait of Francis in writing. The narrative of his conversion process provides the most pertinent preface to his psychological development. According to Thomas, Francis emerges from a deficient upbringing. He was reared "proud of spirit [to arrogance], in accordance with the vanity of the age."[4] Of his parents, Thomas claims they "seek to educate their children from the cradle on very negligently and dissolutely."[5] Such a description carries on to the age of 25:

> Indeed, he outdid all his contemporaries in vanities and he came to be a promoter of evil and he was more abundantly zealous for all kinds of foolishness. He was the admiration of all and strove to outdo the rest in the pomp and vainglory, in jokes, in strange doings, in idle and useless talk, in songs, in soft and flowering garments, for he was very rich, not however avaricious but prodigal,

not a hoarder of money but a squanderer of his possessions, a cautious business man but a very unreliable steward. On the other hand he was a very kindly person, easy and affable, even making himself foolish because of it."[6]

Thomas depicts Francis' life as lacking in purposeful direction until he is brought low by illness, following which he determines quite impulsively to set out on an adventure of conquest with a local nobleman. "Francis, who was flighty and not a little rash, arranged to go with him."[7] Having a dream that suggests good fortune in his future is not enough to keep Francis on this path. Just as spontaneously as he decides for the adventure, he abandons these plans and directs his attention to God. Francis begins to spend time in isolation with a single friend. "He often took him to remote places...," however, upon reaching a particular cave, Francis "would enter the grotto, while his companions would wait for him outside; and filled with a new and singular spirit, he would pray to his father in secret."[8] After this he starts to speak using symbolism, "in an obscure manner," for example he mentions taking "a more noble and more beautiful spouse than you have ever seen, and she will surpass all others in beauty and will excel all others in wisdom."[9]

The various elements of Francis' conversion are brought to a new turning-point as he sells expensive cloth and a horse and seeks to donate the proceeds to a local church. To avoid the wrath of his father, from whom he had obtained the dispensed items, Francis hides in a tiny pit for a month. Here, he is sustained as if in a womb, where he was "filled with a certain exquisite joy of which till then he had had no experience; and catching fire there-from, he left the pit and exposed himself openly to the curses of his persecutors."[10] The violence of this birthing process comes at the hands of his father who returns him to another womb of sorts, imprisoning him in the family home. Lady Pica, his mother, recognizes that the time of confinement must come to an end, as well as the primary attachment he has to her. "She was moved by motherly compassion for him [maternal instinct], and loosening his chains, she set him free."[11] As with each birth, a mother knows her time has arrived and a child nakedly enters a territory that it has not known but must make its own. Francis, driven before the bishop by a father who sees no other option, repudiates his relationship to the family by a symbolic relinquishment of the clothing they had provided him. This brings to an end the central story of Francis' conversion as taken in brief from Thomas of Celano's *The First Life of Saint Francis by Thomas of Celano*. Thomas has more to say about the formation of a religious order around Francis' charism and the many miracles that have been attributed to the saint, but these events offer a less focused insight into the development of Francis' personality. In any case, it is Francis' writings in the later years that will give the strongest evidence of his imagination, not what other people have attributed to him.

This conversion description is not as moving as St. Augustine's. The most notable difference is that Augustine gives the intimate details of his own experience. Francis' experience is captured second hand. In fact it comes filtered through the hagiographical tradition of the church's first thousand years. One might see through conventions that require a saint to be pure and set aside from birth or deformed in character, yet, by the grace of God, reformed. Many saints have recognized their purpose after a sudden illness or injury, and Francis was not the first to gain the attention of birds during a sermon or even to tame a ferocious beast, as some of his miracle accounts would claim. Thomas has brought the hagiographical records of both Anthony of the Desert and Martin of Tours into the life of Francis. To be fair, Francis' chronicler could have recognized the patterns of the earlier saints' lives in Francis' own story. It might even be conceivable that Francis sought to mold the understanding of his own life according to these well-known forerunners. This could never be known for certain, but there is another pattern that is recognizable in the account that has intentionally been woven together above. There are certain features that Thomas has attributed to Francis' young life and personality. These aspects, which are also associated with an Object Relations Theory understanding of a highly imaginative personality, will be briefly pointed out now.

If Thomas is offering an accurate depiction, the indulgence with which Francis' parents raised him suggests that his many needs in infancy were more than adequately met. His effort "to outdo the rest in the pomp of vainglory, in jokes, in strange doings, in idle and useless talk, in songs," indicates a playful disposition.[12] We also heard about his generosity and his spontaneous behavior with the sudden decisions about an adventure. He was given to dreaming, and he was both able and eager to spend time alone. His inner musings broke forth in symbolic expression, and if we are not reading too deeply into his story, Francis was able to break the symbiotic bond with the care-giving unit, his family, that both nurtured him and offered him a particular worldview or perspective on reality.

Taken alone, this data would suggest that Francis meets the general criteria of someone who is able to piece together a view of reality that is both imaginatively creative and meaningful in a shared or common way. Unfortunately this data cannot stand by itself. There is no assurance that these personality elements did not belong to Anthony or Martin, or to any other influential saint. For that matter, it is not clear that much of Thomas' personality and youthful development is not present in this account. A hagiographer will project a certain amount of his or her own experience into the experience of the subject.[13] A cross-comparison with other early accounts of Francis' life might alleviate the uncertainty. Thomas was not the only one to write about Francis from a familiar vantage point. Some of his earliest followers, Leo, Angelus, and Rufino are associated with *The Legend of the Three Companions* and *The Assisi Compilation*.[14] Pulling in their remembrances might add to what is known about Francis, but there is still the dilemma scholars of hagiography have been aware of since Hippolyte Delehaye first started debunking the myth of originality in the *vitae* or saints' lives.[15] Given the questionable unreliability of first and second hand accounts emerging from the thirteenth century, the present work seeks to know something of Francis on a more solid basis. Since Thomas' data can only be taken as suggestive of an imaginative personality in Francis, it must be supported by data that is more firmly linked to the actual person of the saint. This confirmation will be sought in Francis' own writings in chapters six through eight.

At the Crossroads of Franciscan Studies, Spirituality, and Psychology

The previous section is a first step in answering the question: "Who is this person?" Francis is seen through the eyes and words of Thomas of Celano. The range of difficulties to be encountered in answering the question, "What can we know of him or her?" has also been broached. Francis is available to modern day readers, but not without some effort on their part and not completely in the stories that claim to portray him. It is the texts most broadly accepted among Franciscan scholars as reflecting Francis' own words and thoughts that offer the best access to Francis the person. On this basis, the answer to the question, "What should we make of this information?" can be pursued critically. What discipline, then, can be applied to interpret the data available on Francis?

Viewing the expanse of literature, Franciscan Studies have been carried out through three primary methods: literary/critical, spiritual/devotional, and historical. Examples of the first category include the Quaracchi Friars' *Analecta Franciscana*, Kajetan Esser's *Die Opuscula des Hl. Franziskus von Assisi: Neue textkritische Edition*, Marion Habig's *St. Francis of Assisi: Writings and Early Biographies: English Omnibus of Sources for the Life of St. Francis*, and *Francis of Assisi: Early Documents* by Regis Armstrong et al.[16] In the second category, spiritual/devotional literature, it is clear that the life and story of Francis has incited no small number of works. These range from the sentimental to brilliant endeavors to set Francis' message of peace and fraternity over against contemporary predicaments that call for engagement emanating from a solid spiritual foundation. One illustration of this category, that is not strictly sentimental but rather thoroughly meditative, is Murray Bodo's *Francis: The Journey and the Dream*.[17] Although it could arguably be placed in a category of its own, Leonardo Boff's *Saint Francis: A Model for Human Liberation* is also included under the heading spiritual/devotional, since it is notably an exemplar of spirituality directed toward action.[18] The third category, historical works, has benefited from a recent publishing trend that adds significantly to the number of titles falling under this grouping. Taking advantage of an expanded knowledge of the culture and community of medieval Assisi and Italy, the following works locate Francis firmly in his historical period: the *Francis of Assisi* volumes written respectively by Michael Robson, Chiara Frugoni, and Adrian House, as well as Donald Spoto's *Reluctant Saint*.[19]

The present work's contribution to a greater understanding of Francis will cross over and take from two of these categories in pursuing a distinctive discipline that can be called academic spirituality. Using an interdisciplinary methodology, this work will depend on the products of the literary critical field to delve into Francis' own writings, and it will use the historical works for a deeper insight into the content and activity of creative imaginations in Francis' period.

More should be said about the discipline of academic spirituality. A well recognized proponent of this area of study is Sandra Schneiders. Speaking of the Christian branch of the discipline, she calls it "that field-encompassing field which studies Christian religious experience as such."[20] Clearly, the *experience* of greatest interest here is Francis' imaginative activity as expressed in his writings. At another point, Schneiders identifies the object of Christian spirituality as "transformative religious experience."[21] If Francis' imaginative activity can be shown to form or transform his relationships with God, others, and all of created reality, than it is an apropos subject for study within the discipline of academic spirituality. The specific choice of a psychological theory in pursuit of understanding Francis' transformative experience would equate to Schneiders' "problematic discipline," one which "allows better access to the experiential aspect of the object under investigation."[22] The concept of a "problematic discipline" is one that expands the understanding of an experience through its interpretive function.[23] The application of psychology, in this case, will also meet a hermeneutical exigency of the discipline of spirituality through which it "seeks to interpret the experience it studies in order to make it understandable and meaningful in the present without violating its historical reality."[24]

As a further location of the present work, it should be seen in its similarity to and difference from a branch of historical studies called "psychohistory." This discipline uses the insights of psychology to draw more out of what can be known of the past. There is one branch of psychohistory that is directed toward specific historical participants; this branch is called "psychobiography." While it may seem that a study of a historical figure, such as Francis, using a psychological theory, fits into this category, it is not a very good fit. A review of several psychobiographies, whose subjects are religious figures and whose authors are noted scholars, will delineate the distinction standing between the present effort and these others. In this process, various elements from the life of the religious figure will be shown to have some significance in any psychological lens.

One of the earliest entrants into the field of psychobiography with an interest in a religious figure was Erik Erikson. His *Young Man Luther* is a pioneering effort that deserves attention for its deep look into the life of an influential and controversial person at a key waypoint in history.[25] Erikson focuses on critical moments in Martin Luther's early life, in particular on crises, to discern his overall psychological development. Central among these are a thunderstorm that drove young Luther (age 21) to commit himself to a monastic vocation, and a later occasion, during the so-called "Revelation in the Tower" incident in which the meaning of a Scripture passage came to him with sudden clarity.[26] Then, there is also the "Fit in the Choir," which is described as a demonic, raving possession. It occurred at a moment in Luther's life when he was struggling against and denying his father's occupational intentions for him.[27]

An interesting study might compare Francis' conversion process, from a psychological angle, with that of Luther.[28] In each case the father's influence adds great tension to the spiritual transition and may even trigger it. Erikson describes the elder Luther as a brutal man who made up for his own shortcomings by physically and verbally belittling his family.[29] In Francis' situation, the anger of his father, Pietro Bernardone, can be viewed as the result of the pain, frustration, and embarrassment that his son's occupational carelessness brings about. This anger is, nonetheless, not evident until later in Francis' life as suggested by the indulgence observed in Francis' upbringing, according to Thomas of Celano.[30] An area where Francis and Luther diverge is in their relationships with their mothers. It has been suggested, and this point will continue to be argued, that Francis' relationship with his mother was good or "good-enough." According to Erikson, Luther gained some degree of trust from his early association with his mother but was driven out of this stage at a far too tender age.[31] One, perhaps telling, cause of this mistrust is Luther's memory of siblings crying themselves to death in light of their mother's inattention.[32] This weak relationship may allow Erikson to dismiss maternal influence far too easily. He does go on to offer the helpful suggestion that evidence for a subject's relationship with his or her mother can be gleaned from later dealings with and perceptions of women.[33] However, Erikson is far more attuned to the paternal influence, and this should not be surprising, since Luther's father is a more recognizable factor in the critical events that fit Erikson's own theory of human development in response to life's various crises.[34] Connected with Erikson's theory is the exploration of an individual's identity formation. As Erikson uncovers Luther's identity he is engaged in developing a thorough personality profile. This may be the necessary chore of psychobiography, but it is an attempt that will be avoided in the present work where a single element, Francis' imagination, will be examined.

W.W. Meissner has produced a similar work on the inner psychological world of Ignatius of Loyola entitled *Ignatius of Loyola: The Psychology of a Saint*.[35] Meissner has learned from many of the pitfalls Erikson encountered, yet he seeks to achieve a comparable result, a complete personality profile. The concluding chapter is described as a psychoanalytic portrait of Ignatius. True to his school of traditional Freudian Psychoanalysis, Meissner draws attention to the various drives that could be seen to influence Ignatius' development. Using terminology that includes some ORT phrases Meissner claims, "Life, therefore, begins in a state of primary narcissism in which libido resides in the as-yet undifferentiated self. Differentiation of self from the external world brings with it the capacity to direct libido to external objects or conversely the self as object."[36] In fact, much of Meissner's analysis seems driven by a diagnosis of phallic narcissism in the period from Ignatius' youth to the age of thirty.[37] On the other hand, Meissner does leave plenty of room for the nurture factor in the nature and nurture equation of Ignatius' human development. In the introduction he expresses that his understanding of a saintly personality entails the integration of nature and grace.[38] Grace can be taken to be God's nurturing touch.

Meissner's methodology is more apparent when he explains, "The biographer is on safer ground when he starts with what is known about the background or development of his subject and applies it to its determinable consequences in later and historically relevant contexts."[39] To this end, he relates likely psychological influences and developments to indications that these have played out in his subject's advanced personality formation. This approach, looking at developmental background, can support the endeavors of a therapist, but, then, a therapist can get more confirming feedback from a live client than Meissner can from Ignatius. For his part, where the resulting analysis is not clear, Meissner is able to show that two conflicting personality aspects are in a struggle to influence the situation with potentially unpredictable results and the opportunity for grace to play a role.[40]

Meissner's subject lived at a much later period in history than Francis, but Meissner takes the trouble to trace Ignatius' lineage back to the twelfth century to expose any family personality traits. He also considers some of Ignatius' written documents, including the Jesuits' *Constitution* and the *Spiritual Exercises*. A distinction can be drawn, here, between Ignatius' imaginative activity in the meditative *Exercises* that center on a spiritual battle and Francis' imaginative activity as seen in some of his less complicated but no less meditative works like the *Expositio of the Lord's Prayer* and the *Canticle of the Creatures*. These clearly show a focus on integration and harmony rather than on conflict. When Francis does use conflict terminology actual violence is noticeably absent.

Francis' influence is not altogether lacking on the later saint. Meissner tells us that an image of Francis "stirred" Ignatius' "imagination on the sickbed of Loyola."[41] Like Francis, Ignatius' psychological functioning is reoriented by a traumatic event that enables him to begin seeing the world differently.[42] Perhaps less like Francis is Meissner's portrayal of Ignatius where it includes relationships with women more as objects than subjective influences.[43] Meissner does, however, consider the impact of Ignatius' maternal relationship, and he makes room for the positive contribution of a caring wet nurse as a substitute for the saint's deceased mother.[44] A fair amount of Ignatius' development is attributed to this surrogate maternal relationship as well as several other associations Ignatius has with women. Meissner identifies the saint's connection with his "spiritual daughters" as an unconscious attempt to make up for his lost mother.[45] An issue that might bear some consideration is that Ignatius intentionally keeps these women out of the order, while Francis, whose maternal relationship was more firm, welcomes Clare.[46]

How does Meissner make any sense of the numerous analytical conclusions he draws from his study of Ignatius? He ultimately brings the psychological source of the saint's holiness down to a case of identity transformation due to an internalization and integration of a value system, made possible by the complex interaction of ego and superego.[47] To avoid conclusively diagnosing Ignatius as suffering from some physiological disorder, he determines that, even if such were the case, grace would not be prevented from operating in him, and, in fact, it could even use such conditions.[48]

Much of Meissner's data on Ignatius' life, both interior and exterior, is based on the biographical details obtained from the saint by Gonsalvez da Camara.[49] There are similar accounts of Francis' life, but as I have indicated, these are hagiographical in nature with the attendant likelihood that the details of Francis' life were altered, rearranged, added to, and taken away from, in order to fit the form of a saint's life or *vita*. Francis' own writings have few biographical details, and so we are left with little information to construct a broad personality description but ample data to observe his imaginative activity.

Even with the amount of information Meissner is able to bring together on the life of Ignatius he considers his task daunting. As significant challenges, he raises the difficulty of entering into another historical period and the dangers of what one would bring to that period. The scholar can easily approach the life of a historical figure with a predetermined model or image of how that person should be seen.[50] Therapists are well aware of a related concern called counter-transference. When this occurs, one person *transfers* some of his or her own characteristics, or characteristics he or she would like to have, onto another person. If this phenomenon should transpire, it is easy to imagine the ensuing image taking on an idealized form. Meissner goes into great detail to indicate his awareness of these and other, less significant, hazards of the psychobiographer's task.[51] Many of these problems are sidestepped by concentrating on just one aspect of personality and relying on the subject's own writings. In any case, Meissner's admonitions should be heeded that "the psycho-biographical approach cannot reach very far beyond the conjectural," it does not offer a "simple causal explanation," it "adds to other explanations in history; it is no substitute for them."[52]

The third and final scholar whose work considers a historic religious figure from the perspective of psychology is Jean Leclercq. His book, entitled *A Second Look at Bernard of Clairvaux*, is an attempt to bypass some of the common themes of hagiography in search of a more realistic or humanly grounded holy person.[53] The *second look* is clearly intended to be through a psychological lens. The title of the French publication of this work describes it as a psychohistory.[54] Leclercq takes a very interesting approach to the use of psychology in its application to a historical figure. He enlists the services of a team to provide the more technical analyses. Specifically, he relies on the expertise of a psychoanalyst, a psycholinguist, several psychologists, and a medical doctor.[55] The advantages of this broad field of deep knowledge, however, can easily be lost in an effort to integrate every member's input. It is difficult to pin down a single theory that is consistently being used to give order to the details of Bernard's interior life, and, consequently, there is a limited extent to which aspects of the saint's personality are reflected upon.[56]

A significant amount of data attended to by the team consists of written signs of repression, anger, aggressiveness, and in particular the need for dominance.[57] Using examples from Bernard's writings in the context of spiritual direction, Leclercq claims that Bernard himself was psychologically astute. The saint's method of leading others to reflect on their own attitudes and motivations might almost seem underhanded but is creative and imaginative.[58] While it would be difficult to ignore the acumen with which Bernard judges human nature, Leclercq seems to reach too far when commenting, "Perhaps, Bernard detected in him someone strongly marked by some sort of Oedipus Complex."[59] Attributing, to Bernard, recognition of a complicated set of interpersonal attachments may be a more tenable assertion.

A sense of Bernard's type of imagination and its contents begins to emerge under Leclercq's probing. He highlights Bernard's emotions as an access to the saint's psychological functioning, and the deepest of his feelings are expressed through images.[60] Leclercq also finds that Bernard's monastic foundation, Clairvaux, has greater meaning than just a residence, a place of fellowship, and a place of prayer. The monastery is the living image of his project of meaning.[61] Since a comparison of Bernard and Francis' imaginative activity in the light of Object Relations Theory will involve maternal imagery, Leclercq's thoughts on the subject in reference to Bernard may be useful. He notes that much of Bernard's consideration of familial relationships is drawn from his work on the *Song of Songs*.[62] Early in his description of the saint, Leclercq peers through one of the traditional hagiographic conventions. Where Bernard's mother has a dream of his future religious status, Leclercq recognizes the significance of a mother's desire for her own meaning being lived out in her child.[63] Meissner, and more so Erikson, concentrate a weighty paternal influence on the religious figure's development, but Leclercq is willing to see a mother's sway. He goes on to point out the role fulfilled by some other mother figure, most prevalently the Virgin Mary, as compensation for the mother-love that is left behind upon *leaving the world*.[64]

Leclercq observes that Bernard struggled with his ability to find the right words to express himself.[65] This difficulty can be explained as the effort to give some form of concrete articulation to his world of symbolic imagery. Elsewhere Leclercq realizes that the saint speaks and writes within two orders, the real and the symbolic, and "realism is always subordinated to symbolism."[66] What is not clear is the amount of symbolic imagery that can be attributed to Bernard's raw imagination and the amount that comes out of the biblical way of seeing reality that would have been common to anyone coming through medieval monastic formation. As partial answer, Leclercq finds the source of Bernard's impetus to be an application of Scripture to his own experiences coupled with "the vigor of his psyche, the rigor of his art, and the loftiness of his religious inspiration."[67]

When Leclercq endeavors to pull his portrait of Bernard together, he is left with the formidable undertaking of unifying some very divergent characteristics. He has to show the integration of elements as distinct as domineering and obeisance traits. He gently diagnoses the coexistence of great passion in conjunction with a "sublime ideal."[68] Leclercq seems to suggest that it is the transformation of this passion, with aggression as its servant, which is ultimately at the service of holiness in the life of Bernard.[69] But it is just these traits, in their raw form, that reflect the "absolute nature of his character." [70] And it is the absolute and unswerving nature of his character, for instance, the need to be agreed with, which could present the greatest obstacle to Bernard's creative imagination. The effective use of such an imagination demands a greater openness to the possible ways of seeing or perceiving in any situation.

Before leaving this review of several eminent scholars who have contributed to the discipline of psychohistory and psychobiography, it should be noted that Leclercq's theories on the application of psychology to an earlier time in history extend beyond his work on Bernard.[71] Bearing in mind modern approaches to historical writings, he laments the possibility of causing: "'the agony of the text,'" in which it is "emptied of its primitive significance, or smothered under a heap of alien interpretations for which it was merely a pretext."[72] Even so, what is to be made of any ancient writing if a reader does not bring some modern experience to it? A book read simply for its access to the past is read, at very least, with nostalgic inclination, and an older text read without some relationship to a contemporary context is one that has lost its meaning in a bygone era. Leclercq shows his awareness of these issues when it comes to psychology.

He comments, "History without psychology ceases to be human: psychology applied to the past heedless of any historical method would be very shaky."[73] All in all, he is very positive about the prospect of engaging history with psychology in an effort to achieve *understanding*. By this term he means "an effort to interpret men of the Middle Ages, and this, not according to a society, cultural elements, and theories of men belonging to other ages and milieu, but according to the trans-cultural human facts which psychological sciences permit us to perceive."[74] Again, the point must be taken that one of the most identifiable trans-cultural or nearly universal "human facts," is the presentation of reality to an infant by a maternal caregiver. This is a basic tenet of ORT that affords a degree of confidence in proceeding with the present study of the imaginative activity of Francis of Assisi.

On a final note, Leclercq reiterates the aspect of medieval life that binds Francis' imagination to the common imagination and provides Bernard with an outlet and boundary for his. The author explains, "The most important factor in this culture is the Bible, with the specific vocabulary and imagination which it fashions in those who are receptive to its influence and allow it to penetrate them by constantly listening to it, committing it to memory, and referring to it."[75] What Leclercq does not point out is that everyone in medieval society did not receive the same level of exposure to Scripture indicated here. From his depiction, only those engaged in the monastic lifestyle would have benefited to the fullest extent from this kind of imaginative formation. It is fair to claim that most other people would have supplemented Biblically inspired imagination with additional sources, including the products of their own creative imaginations. Leclercq is, however, largely correct in asserting that, "It is impossible to interpret the representations, images, and reflexes of medieval Christians without bearing in mind this intermediary which then stood between spontaneous drives, archetypes, and all other depth factors and the expression of them in a basically Biblical literature."[76]

Summary

This chapter has headed down various, and at times seemingly unrelated, paths. On final consideration it should be clear, however, that all these paths do lead to a necessary initial location of this work. As such the motivation and objective of this endeavor were conveyed. Francis of Assisi is to be more fully understood in a single psychologically explicable aspect of his personality, his imagination. It is an imagination that will be seen to enable him to fashion a spiritual view of the world through the transformation of existing religious imagery into new and original creations. In this chapter, Francis was also introduced to the reader through the eyes of Thomas of Celano. The impression given by Thomas was revealed to be not so much a false depiction but as questionably unreliable by itself. Its primary value was as a call for more substantiate-able evidence and as an initial ORT view of his youthful development. The type of study that follows this path was located in the emerging academic discipline of spirituality after comparing and contrasting it with other methods for studying Francis. In an effort to relate but not identify this study of a historical figure's imagination with works in a genre entitled "psychobiography," three examples of this latter literature were reviewed with an eye toward depicting their more wide-ranging and less tenable scope, in addition to learning from their insights and missteps. It should be clear that the aim of this work is to apply Object Relations Theory to Francis of Assisi's writings as a psychological theory capable of revealing the richness of the workings of his spiritually imaginative way of viewing reality.

Notes

1. This technique is used on many of the earthquake and war damaged mosaics and frescoes salvaged in Italian churches. The missing or unrecoverable portions are filled in with plain plaster. In some cases the majority of a wall or ceiling is plastered in with only the smallest remnant of the original work visible.

2. This description of imagination was worked out in dialogue with Dr. Raymond Studzinski, O.S.B. of The Catholic University of America. It is to Dr. Studzinski that I owe much of my own deep interest in the psychodynamic element of the human spirit.

3. D.W. Winnicott, *Playing and Reality* (London: Tavistock, 1971), 10. Winnicott describes this person as one who "adapts" to the infant's needs. As an at-home father writing this in between his infant son's waking hours, I am well aware that circumstances might warrant the use of a more generic term, however, since this volume is concerned with an individual raised under a mother's care the maternal reference will be primarily used.

4. Thomas of Celano, *The First Life of Francis of Assisi*, in Marion Habig, ed. *St. Francis of Assisi: Writings and Early Biographies: English Omnibus of Sources for the Life of St. Francis.* (Quincy, IL: Franciscan University Press, 1991), 229. At times comparisons will be made with the more recent translations found in Regis J. Armstrong, J.A. Wayne Hellmann, and William J. Short, eds. *Francis of Assisi: Early Documents.* Vol. 1, *The Saint* (New York: New City Press, 1999). See page 182. Unless identified as *Francis of Assisi: Early Documents: The Saint,* anything attributed to Francis will be taken from Habig, *Omnibus of Sources.*

5. Francis of Assisi, *Omnibus of Sources,* 229.

6. Ibid., 230.

7. Ibid., 232.

8. Ibid., 234.

9. Ibid., 235.

10. Ibid., 238.

11. Ibid., 240; see also Francis of Assisi, *Francis of Assisi: Early Documents,* : *The Saint,* 192.

12. Ibid., 230.

13. Hippolyte Delehaye cautions about the use of hagiographic material as biographical. He describes the *vita* or life of a saint as an accrual of previous saints' stories, local secular legends, some fact, and imaginative stories. See: Hippolyte Delehaye, *The Legends of the Saints,* trans. Donald Attwater (New York: Fordham University Press, 1962).

14. Regis J. Armstrong, J.A. Wayne Hellmann, and William J. Short, eds. *Francis of Assisi: Early Documents.* Vol. 2, *The Founder* (New York: New City Press, 2000), 62, 113.

15. Delehaye, 7, 16.

16. *Legendae S. Francisci Assisiensis: Saeculis XIII et XIV Conscriptae.* Analecta Franciscana sive Chronica aliaque varia documenta ad historiam fratrum minorum spectantia, X (Ad Aquas Claras: Florentiae: Collegium S. Bonaventurae, 1895-1941); Kajetan Esser, ed., *Die Opuscula des hl. Franziskus von Assisi: Neue textkritische Edition* (Grottaferrata: Spicilegium Bonaventurianum XIII, 1976); Marion A. Habig, ed., *St. Francis of Assisi: Writings and Early Biographies: English Omnibus of Sources for the Life of St. Francis,* Franciscan University Press: Quincy, IL, 1991; Regis J. Armstrong, J.A. Wayne Hellmann, and William J. Short, eds. *Francis of Assisi: Early Documents.* Vol. 1, *The Saint.* Vol. 2, *The Founder.* Vol. 3, *The Prophet* (New York: New City Press, 1999-2001).

17. Murray Bodo, *Francis: The Journey and the Dream* (Cincinnati: St. Anthony Messenger Press, 1988).

18. Leonardo Boff, *Saint Francis: A Model for Human Liberation*, trans. John W. Diercksmeier (New York: Crossroad, 1985).

19. Michael Robson, *St. Francis of Assisi: The Legend and the Life* (New York: Continuum, 1997); Chiara Frugoni, Francis of Assisi (New York: Continuum, 1999); Adrian House, *Francis of Assisi: A Revolutionary Life* (Mahwah, NJ: Hidden Spring, 2001); Donald Spoto, *Reluctant Saint: The Life of Francis of Assisi* (New York: Viking Compass, 2002).

20. Sandra M. Schneiders, "Theology and Spirituality: Strangers, Rivals, or Partners?," *Horizons* 13, no. 2 (1986): 268. See also: Sandra M. Schneiders, "The study of Christian Spirituality: Contours and Dynamics of a Discipline," *Christian Spirituality Bulletin* 6, no. 1 (1998); Sandra M. Schneiders, "Religion and Spirituality: Strangers, Rivals, or Partners?" *The Santa Clara Lectures* 6, No. 2 (2000).

21. Schneiders, "The Study of Christian Spirituality: Contours and Dynamics of a Discipline," 3.

22. Ibid., 4.

23. Schneiders, "Theology and Spirituality: Strangers, Rivals, or Partners?" 273.

24. Schneiders, "The Study of Christian Spirituality: Contours and Dynamics of a Discipline," 3.

25. Erik H. Erikson, *Young Man Luther: A Study in Psychoanalysis and History* (New York: Norton and Co., 1962). On his psychobiography see also: Donald Capps, Walter H. Capps, and Gerald Bradford, ed., *Encounter with Erikson: Historical Interpretation and Religious Biography* (Santa Barbara: Scholars Press, 1977); Homans, Peter, ed. *Childhood and Selfhood: Essays on Tradition, Religion and Modernity in the Psychology of Erik H. Erikson.* Lewisburg PA: Bucknell University Press, 1978.; Mel Albin, ed., *New Directions in Psychohistory: The Adelphi Papers in Honor of Erik H. Erikson* (Lexington MA: Lexington Books, 1980).

26. Erikson, *Young Man Luther*, 38, 201.

27. Ibid., 24.

28. It could be noted with some interest that Francis' life must have been a topic of discussion in the Erikson household. Erikson's wife, Joan Mowat-Erikson, wrote a book on Francis' life from the perspective of four women. Two of the women were actually in his life, his mother and Clare, and the other two women were actualized in his life, the Blessed Mother and Lady Poverty. See: Joan Mowat Erikson, *Saint Francis et His Four Ladies* (New York: W.W. Norton and Co., 1970).

29. Ibid., 66-67.

30. There is another theory that claims Francis was at the center of an inheritance battle. Richard Trexler finds that Francis' renunciation of his familial legal status was the result of a maneuver by his stepfather, Pietro, to ensure control of a family fortune that moved according to his wife's direct bloodline. Richard C. Trexler, *Naked Before the Father: The Renunciation of St. Francis of Assisi* (New York: Peter Lang, 1989), 105.

31. Erik Erikson, 255.

32. Ibid., 72.

33. Ibid., 73.

34. Erik H. Erikson, *Identity and the Life Cycle* (New York: WW Norton and Co., 1980). See also: Henry W. Maier, *Three Theories of Child Development: The Contributions of Erik H. Erikson, Jean Piaget and Robert R. Sears, and Their Application* (New York: Harper&Row, 1965); Robert Coles, *Erik H. Erikson: The Growth of His Work*

(Boston: Little Brown, 1970); Eugene J. Wright, *Erikson, Identity and Religion* (New York: Seabury Press, 1982).

35. W.W. Meissner, *Ignatius of Loyola: The Psychology of a Saint* (New Haven: Yale U.P., 1992).

36. Ibid., 378.

37. Ibid., 41.

38. Ibid., ix.

39. Ibid., xix.

40. Ibid., 378.

41. Ibid., 399.

42. Ibid., 41.

43. Meissner points out the importance of displacing the libidinal energy of the saint's sexual drives. Ignatius had among other displacements "the vision of our Lady." See Meissner, 241-242. While it would be deceptive to deny the reality of any saint's human desires, I think a theory, such as ORT, that calls on the powerful attachment to meaningful object representations provides a more realistic explanation of a mature person's sexuality without reinforcing the notion that other persons exist simply as an outlet for an instinctual drive.

44. Ibid., 9.

45. Ibid., 271.

46. On a negative note, Francis was not able to imagine an alternative state of religious life than the cloister for Clare, or he was unable to influence the imagination of others on this point.

47. Ibid., 399.

48. Ibid., 271. Meissner does mention psychosis and a limbic disorder as concerns, although confirming such a diagnosis would be next to impossible given the inability to assess him on any other grounds beyond written statements.

49. Ibid., xxiv.

50. Ibid., ix-x, xvii.

51. For a more in depth discussion of the problems to be contended with by anyone applying psychological theory to a non-living subject see Meissner's introduction: Meissner, i-xxix.

52. Meissner, *Ignatius of Loyola*, xvi, xv.

53. Jean Leclercq, *A Second Look at Bernard of Clairvaux*, trans. Marie-Bernard Saïd (Kalamazoo: Cistercian Publications, 1990).

54. Jean Leclercq, *Nouveau visage de Bernard de Clairvaux: approches psychohistoriques* (Paris: Editions du Cerf, 1976).

55. Leclercq, *A Second Look at Bernard of Clairvaux*, 1.

56. For more on the challenges of psycho-history in general see: Paul J. Archambault, "Augustine's Confessions: on the uses and limits of psychobiography, in *Collectanea Augustiniana* (New York: Peter Lang, 1990); Jean Marc Charon, "Psychohistoire et Religion: perspectives, defies et enjeux," *Religiologiques* 2 (Oct 1990); Thomas A. Kohut, "Psychohistory as History," *American Historical Review* 91, no. 2 (Apr 1986). David E. Stannard, *Shrinking History: On Freud and the Failure of Psychohistory* (Oxford: Oxford University Press, 1980). It should be noted that Leclercq's effort in this field gained less attention than Erikson's.

57. Leclercq, *A Second Look at Bernard of Clairvaux*, 29-31, 38.

58. Ibid., 72.

59. Ibid., 63.

60. Ibid., 87, 34.

61. Ibid., 38.

62. Ibid., 109. Although the imagery in the Song of Songs or Super Canticus reflects a conjugal relationship, the sense of its fruitful nature should not be overlooked. In the following chapter, excerpts from this lengthy series of sermons will be used as examples of Bernard's imaginative activity.

63. Ibid., 10, 12.

64. Ibid., 13.

65. Ibid., 17.

66. Ibid., 125.

67. Ibid., 56.

68. Ibid., 143.

69. Ibid., 145.

70. Ibid., 100.

71. Jean Leclercq, "Modern Psychology and the Interpretation of Medieval Texts," *Speculum: A Journal of Medieval Studies* 48 (1973). In this article the author claims that few texts from the Middle Ages are directly psychological, but many include elements of human experience.

72. Jean Leclercq, "Psycho-History and the Understanding of People," *The Hanoverian* 6 (1975): 7.

73. Ibid., 6.

74. Ibid., 8.

75. Ibid.

76. Ibid., 9.

CHAPTER TWO
INFLUENCES ON THE FORMATION OF
MEDIEVAL IMAGINATIONS

Even among the most influential religious personalities in history there is no completely original imagination. Each imagination except perhaps that of a madman or madwoman can be shown to have some formative influence from an earlier imagination or even school of imagining. While this study argues for the essential connection between a creative imagination and its foundation in the developmental period of healthy early infancy, it is also clear that the imagination is receptive to ongoing formation. Raymond Studzinski finds that the imagination is open to external influence for better or worse. Since this is the case, appropriate effort can be made to "tutor" the imagination within a given social-religious tradition.[1]

Francis' imagination was certainly affected by his family, his community, and his Catholic religion. His encounter with a larger world during business trips with his father and his evolving interest in Scripture are likely to have had some of the greatest impact. But, this chapter is not an attempt to trace all the influences that impacted upon Francis' imagination. Such is beyond the scope of this work and beyond the scope of the information that is available on Francis' life. Instead, the present chapter will seek to put several of the possible influences on Francis' imagination into perspective. These will include theoretical developments of the imagination, popular influences, and the impact of two near contemporaries.

Imagination: A History of Theories

To set the stage for studying Francis' imagination it would be helpful to look at the theoretical understanding of the imagination leading up to his time. However, attempting to portray Francis' imagination as the result of a progressive development of a theory of imagination would be a disservice to the uniqueness of his imagination; it would also be misleading to suggest that Francis added to or advanced a philosophical theory of imagination. A review of some of the most identifiable theories of imagination in the time frame preceding Francis' era will begin to indicate just how much Francis' imagination differs in quality, style, and content from the types of imagination suggested by these theories, and also where there are similarities. Succeeding sections of this chapter will present examples of imaginative activity from two near contemporaries of Francis who were well schooled in the imaginative techniques common to a monastic/intellectual background. Noting other possible ways of imagining will not sustain a claim for originality on Francis' part; however, it will help to establish just where his imaginative activity is unique. Such unique imaginative activity would be any imaginative act that does not consciously link an image with its concept, meaning, or original manifestation in a manner known to the imaginer to have been done in the exact same manner before.

To maintain focus on the time frame surrounding Francis' life it would be expedient to consider only the most significant theories on the imagination formulated during the Middle Ages. Unfortunately, there is some difficulty in this approach. Murray Bundy opens the chapter on medieval imagination in his book *The Theory of Imagination in Classical and Medieval Thought* with the statement, "There is no consistent medieval theory of imagination." [2] It seems that he is in large part correct. Throughout this period the penchant for relying on the authority of the "fathers" has resulted in a re-presentation of earlier theories especially the one put forward by Augustine (354-430) and those who influenced him. There were certainly imaginative movements that became popular during the Middle Ages, but these were driven more by literary and theatrical styles than a formal theory. The rise of secular romantic poetry for courtly entertainment was one such movement that will be discussed below.

Classical Theories of Imagination

Bundy's book is notably aged but not terribly dated. [3] He treats the early history of theories of imagination more comprehensively than many more recent works which tend to be interested in modern theoretical developments. In his survey of classical theories, Bundy emphasizes the struggle classical philosophers mounted to specify the relationship between the operation of the imagination and the levels of reality associated with or depicted by the imagination. He finds that the question of a material reality existing in some kind of relationship with a non-material reality began to play a role in discussions amongst the Pre-Socratic philosophers. [4] This is a pertinent issue for a study of imagination from an Object Relations Theory perspective since the imagination can play an intermediary role between the physical world and the interior (non-material) conception of it. These early philosophers were interested in the connections between the stimulation of the senses, the sense impression made, and the image formed, as well as any truth-value carried by the image. [5]

The philosopher whose thought is most typically and sometimes unfairly associated with identifying a profound dualism between the material and immaterial world is Plato. He is credited with the idea that the phenomenal world stands as an image of the ideal, non-material, world. [6] Accordingly, the imagination directed toward this ideal world is able to reproduce a likeness of an otherwise unavailable original. Plato's view of imagination, however, is not simply a reproductive conception; imagining the highest form yields an expression of an idea or, better yet, of the ideal.[7] Imagination could, therefore, also be considered a creative activity. Bundy goes on to suggest that Plato saw imagination as bringing to perception a distant ideal.[8] This is recognition of the transcendent capacity of the imagination, but unfortunately many of Plato's followers left his conception ungrounded in human experience. They held so tightly to his interest in immateriality that the dualism thus established had little regard for insights drawn from the material world of sensation, the world from which the imagination draws so much of its content.

The term most frequently used by Greek philosophers to refer to the current notion of imagination is *phantasia*. A more recent work on classical approaches to imagination begins with a consideration of *phantasia* as it evolves in Plato's writing. In Gerard Watson's *Phantasia in Classical Thought*, he observes that in the *Teaetetus*, the concept of judgment is associated with *phantasia* as a kind of perception in contrast with *phantasia* as sensation.[9] In the *Philebus* Plato connects memory with *phantasia* since "judgment is made on the basis of memory and *aisthēsis*."[10] Watson contends that in this work of Plato's, memory involves a conservation of sensation and perception.[11] Ultimately this conservation is described as paintings of judgments made in the soul, even though the term *phantasia* is not used directly with this notion.[12] In the *Timaeus*, Watson finds the clearest use of the notion of two levels of reality based on an unchanging world sometimes available to the intellect and a changing world more widely encountered by or through *phantasia*.[13] For the former world *knowledge* is described as "a 'likely' account" and for the latter world "as opinion."[14]

In an earlier work Watson more succinctly traces the relationship between classical conceptions of imagination as a way of knowing in a sense impression-based world and a higher way of knowing that has access to a deeper reality of truth.[15] He claims that Plato considered knowledge derived by *phantasia* to be inferior to intellectual forms of knowledge, although *phantasia* was viewed as the basis for most types of knowledge and therefore could not be completely discounted.[16] In his more recent work Watson seeks to justify a more respectable position for *phantasia* in Plato's writings even when the exact term is avoided.[17] Another perspective on Platonic thought holds that Plato deemed *phantasia* something from which one must be purified.[18] While Plato is recognized for identifying imagination as a way of *knowing*, his association of imagination with the possibility of deception and the most rudimentary ways of *knowing* place this capacity at an undeserved disadvantage when it comes to *knowing* in a more profound or spiritual sense.

Much of Aristotle's view of imagination can be found in his opposition to Platonic dualism. Bundy notes a greater degree of immanence in Aristotle's conception of the relationship between material and immaterial reality. The sense world, or world of appearance, is not a distant expression of an otherwise unfathomable immaterial reality.[19] In Aristotle's theory, the material world, nature, embodies or provides substance for a deeper insight into the perfect (immaterial) form.[20] Imagination, when applied to the material world, does not attempt to reproduce nature. As Bundy states, the ever-dynamic movement of nature necessitates that imaginations "seek to imitate the method of nature."[21] In other words, the imagination must capture and present the manner in which nature is structured and operates. Bundy's description of this activity has the imagination linking a series of perceptions of a very present material reality in an effort to formulate a universal perception of a more immanent concept which is the *ideal* informing all of reality.[22]

Watson also views Aristotle's approach to *phantasia* as a direct response to Plato's notions on the subject.[23] In De *Anima* he finds that Aristotle described this concept of imagination as "a movement which comes about in beings that perceive of things of which there is perception and because of an actual perception."[24] In *De Insomniis* Watson reveals a further explanation of perception as Aristotle attempted to unify his theory. The philosopher noted that "actual perception is an alteration of some sort.... Sensible objects produce sensation in us, and the effect remains even in sense organs that have ceased to perceive."[25] The primary distinction between Plato's position and Aristotle's position centers on the relationship between the perception and actual thought or judgment. According to Watson, Aristotle held perception as a bridge to "proper knowledge," but not a directly or always associated aspect of it.[26] Watson concludes that, for Aristotle, phantasia "is simply involved in the process of supplying the material on which the mind builds judgments."[27] This shift in emphasis from Plato's closer linkage between perception and judgment places a greater concern on the truth of a perception. Aristotle feared that in Plato's theory a false perception could cause a true judgment or belief. While Watson finds that Plato did not connect the two as a simultaneous and therefore necessary occurrence, Aristotle's suspicion carried on.[28]

Aristotle's conception of imagination, nonetheless, sets it as the hinge-pin holding material and immaterial reality in close relationship. Bundy claims that his views had a greater influence over medieval thinkers than Plato's theorizing simply because Aristotle was easier to comprehend.[29] In any instance, Thomas Aquinas' (1225-1274) popularization of Aristotelian thought brought it to fashion after Francis' life. Additionally, surviving Platonic views of imagination ensured that imagination would be considered deficient as a means of access to greater truths and meaning. Some form of intellectual contemplation would be held as the most reliable or only path to the most profound and meaningful knowledge. Another philosophical school would add greater suspicion to the activity of the imagination. Noting that a *phantasm* could be false or contain logical errors, the Stoic philosophers greatly mistrusted imagination.[30]

Medieval Theories of Imagination[31]

James Mackey proposes that the imagination made the Christian revolution possible. He suggests that Jesus sought "to introduce the reign of God, to release in this world—this and no other—a power which would change it utterly and for the best. And it is no accident that he adopted for this purpose the aid of imagination."[32] Francis, like Jesus, was adept at moving people to employ their imaginations, but Jesus, like Francis, did not leave a theory of imagination. It was up to a rhetorician and philosopher converted to Christianity to align a theory of imagination with Christian faith. It was both the rhetorical tradition and neo-platonic thought that under-gird Augustine's approach to Christianity. Douglas Kelly observes that imagination in early Roman oratorical practice was concerned primarily with evoking memory.[33] A reading of Augustine's *Confession* exemplifies how significant memory was in his writing. For Augustine and other rhetoricians during the early Christian centuries, memory was not limited to recalling facts and figures to mind; it had a deeper purpose.[34] The goal of the rhetorical art is to convince others of one's position in an argument. To this end, memory was used to manipulate the emotions. According to Bundy, *phantasia* was associated with the presentation of images in a manner that elicits emotional response. He calls this activity a "function of the reproductive phantasy."[35] At the same time, thinkers of this period separated *phantasia* from a simple representation of previous experience. Bundy points out Apolonius' view: "For imitation can only fashion what it has seen; but phantasy what it has never seen."[36] In Christian usage, *phantasia* as memory was most commonly engaged to bring to mind the events in the life of Christ and previous generations of believers.

The other significant influence on Augustine's thought came from Neo-Platonism, particularly the views of Plotinus (204-269). For Plotinus, reality was arranged in tiers from the archetypal or highest level down through successive spheres to the material world. The imagination has no direct participation in the higher spheres, although these do express their virtues through a series of successive emanations. In each case, the lower sphere is an image of its next higher sphere, and in this fashion the material world is able to bear some sense of the ideal of the higher reality.[37] John Dillon identifies imagination's involvement in this process where Plotinus explained that, "imagination has consciousness of what is external to it; for it allows that which has the image to have knowledge of what it has experienced."[38] Bundy describes the perceptual product of this type of imagining as "a kind of memory-image of a higher type of mental activity."[39] The human soul, as intelligent, is able to recognize the ideal of higher reality in nature when the soul retains and applies its higher sphere memory-image to the material world via the imagination.[40] Noting a not-so-enthusiastic view of physical reality, Bundy finds that, for Plotinus, nature "has little significance, save as individual souls, informed from above, attach to it a meaning, are able to see in it the image of a higher reason, the result of a creative activity."[41] Approaching physical reality with more excitement for the possibilities it holds, Object Relations Theory offers a surprisingly similar appraisal of the imaginative activity of meaning-making.

When Watson takes up Plotinus' understanding of *phantasia* he recognizes two nearly opposing approaches. *Phantasia* is viewed with suspicion due to its connection to the body and lower appetites which hold back the movement of the soul.[42] At the same time, *phantasia*, in an Aristotelian fashion, might be an aide to perceiving in the higher world.[43] Even if this vision is only fleeting, Plotinus suggested that when a "phantasia of what is now past remains present," this is memory.[44] But memory is not only a bridge to the higher reality. Plotinus indicated that the higher soul must use, or, rather cut off, memory in such a way that one achieves a "'happy forgetfulness'" of the lower world.[45] In a more platonic moment Plotinus called a *phantasia* found in the soul either a judgment or an opinion, both of which refer to intellectual or discursive activity.[46] Plotinus added that a feature of *phantasia* in some way "helps to formulate both sense-perception and acts of thought."[47]

One of the first contributions to the theory of imagination that has been attributed to Augustine is the term *imagination* itself.[48] Watson, however points out that the elder Pliny (23-79) used it earlier; what Augustine did was to give "it currency in the Latin West."[49] In his derivation of the word *imaginatio* from *imago* or image, Augustine was able to divest the use of this concept from its pagan implications associated with the term *phantasia*. The result of this expansion in terminology is the connection of negative, bad, or evil aspects of imaginative activity with *phantasia*, or fantasy, and association of the most positive aspects with imagination.

According to Bundy, Augustine made a very clear division between the most immediate image, one grasped by the senses, and the type best described as the result of reproductive imaginative activity, an image held by an inner vision.[50] Watson calls the sense-based vision "corporeal vision," which leaves an image in a higher form of vision called *visio spiritualis*."[51] This latter form, no longer, if ever, dependent on the senses, is the memory-type of imagination for which Augustine is a noted proponent. There is another type of imaginative activity that he identified in a synthesis of Neo-Platonic, Aristotelian, and Stoic thought. This is the creative imagination. Based on the fact that one can produce a false *phantasm* or image by an act of will, Augustine clarified the possibility of forming an image with no basis in prior experience or reality.[52] The Stoic influence on his thought tempered this notion with the moral concern that one has responsibility for one's images in light of the control that it is possible to apply to them.[53]

Augustine's Neo-Platonic influence is seen in his insistence that reason alone reaches to the greatest heights of encounter with the divine.[54] This is a third kind of vision that Watson transliterates as intellectual vision.[55] The intellectual vision does not depend on either of the lower visions for its activity, but *visio spiritualis* does rely on intellectual vision to verify the truth or falsity of its images.[56] Such a lofty assessment of a power not reliant in some degree on the senses or the physical world ensures the continuous influence of the platonic spirit-matter dualism over the approach to imaginative activity.

The significance Augustine gave the imagination for its involvement in acts of memory far out-shadowed any importance Boethius (470-524) allowed to the imagination in his *Consolation of Philosophy*. Bundy notes a stronger preference for the capacity of the reasoning powers in Boethius' thought. The philosopher even identified a level of reasoning that is higher than reason itself; he called it *intelligentsia*.[57] Kelly observes the medieval tendency to locate imagination within a hierarchy of cognition.[58] The origins of this tendency are found with the early Greek philosophers, but they are clearly a significant element in Boethius' thoughts. Boethius began with the senses that discern form as it is in matter. Then comes imagination that discerns form absent of matter, and following which is reason that goes on to consider the universality of a form's particulars.

At the highest level of cognition is understanding, or *intelligentsia*, that attends to form in its most simple state.[59] According to this theory, reason gives order to the perception of form derived by the imagination. Watson points out that according to Boethius: *"Imaginatio* itself is something not complete."[60] The imagination almost seems to perform a basic mechanical operation in a much more complex process. Any knowledge attributable to the senses and imagination was considered limited at best since these capacities could not move past knowing in relationship to the physical world.[61]

Moving more centrally into his discussion of imagination in the Middle Ages, Bundy contends, "There was, on the whole, little place in the theories of vision for a power capable of giving physical expression to spiritual truths."[62] More interest during this time was given over to empirical efforts to show the relationship between God and humanity.[63] While various moderate mystics respected the value of imagination, most philosophers leaned toward systems of hierarchies and subordinations--evidence of Aristotelian influence.[64] Bundy goes on to explain that the majority of medieval thinkers on imagination categorized imagination with sense impressions, not with formal thoughts or ideas.[65] This dissection further ensured that imagination would not be connected with knowing in any deeper intellectual or spiritual sense. When it comes to the area of faith, Francis will be seen to move in the opposite direction.

An early forerunner of the science of psychiatry sought to associate various aspects of mental cognition with different regions of the brain. Avicenna (980-1037) developed a physiological schema typical of this effort. The senses and the imagination first work through sense material at the front of the head, passing their product to the middle head where either intellect takes control in a process of cogitation, or the animal virtues guide the product into an imaginative recombination process. The result in this case are images, albeit, less trustworthy images. If the sense impressions had followed the route of cogitation, they might end up in the back of the head where a higher form of memory occurs than the simple memory of sense impressions as found in the front.[66] Bundy identifies several other philosophers who employed similar concepts, but what seems most typical of them all is that imagination is seen as a lower level of memory.[67] It gathers and passes on rudimentary sense stimuli or impressions that have yet to be worked on by powers of reason. Today, with Object Relations Theory, it is clear that a powerful and meaningful imaginative activity is going on prior to, and even in the absence of, the application of judgments and determinations by reason. In fact, as subsequent pages will show, and contrary to most medieval belief, all thought depends directly on imaginative activity.

Popular Influences on Medieval Imaginations

Leading up to the period of Francis' life, it is possible to observe three important influences on the formation of imagination for various people of the Middle Ages. Many of the philosophical trends, that have been discussed so far, came to affect the understanding and use of the imagination in well-read monastic circles and perhaps a little beyond. The impact of a certain type of scriptural imagery on the imagination sustained a deep-seated awareness of the yet-to-be realized apocalypse. In addition to the monastic-philosophical imagination and the apocalyptic imagination with their religious overtones, there also existed a literary movement that facilitated the growing secular imagination. Each of these types of imagination will be considered more thoroughly as a prelude to a look at the workings of two medieval imaginations that exhibit some involvement with these influences.

Monastic, Intellectual Imagination

Throughout his written works, Aelred of Rievaulx shows an interesting and varied use of the imagination. Examples of this usage will be considered in the next section. Presently, it will be of value to take note of his theoretical views on the imagination to exemplify the influence of an intellectual understanding of the imagination as it existed in certain monastic circles. Aelred's text, *Dialogue on the Soul*, contains some very clear references to the manner in which the imagination operates, but it might be misleading to call these specifically "his views." According to the introduction C.H. Talbot put together for his translation of this work, Aelred equated the imagination with one of the three highest faculties of the soul. The three-part conception of the soul, as well as many of the statements about imagination-as-memory, can be traced directly to Augustine.[68] The three highest faculties of the soul, the memory, intellect, and will, when directed toward God, offer the clearest indication of the soul's relationship to God.[69] This relationship, in which something from a lower sphere provides an impression or image from a higher sphere, is evidence of the continuity of classical notions through Augustine to Aelred. The latter thinker explained the necessary unity that exists between the faculties of the soul as they reveal the nature of the Trinity. He found that memory, reason, and will each have their own unique operation, "yet all their operations are inseparable"—"because they have the same substance they are one."[70] Talbot credits Bernard of Clairvaux with Aelred's way of attributing memory, reason, and will as the constituting elements of the soul.[71]

For Aelred as for Augustine before him, imagination played a role in the area of memory. As Talbot reads Aelred, the "memory is primarily a storehouse for images received through the senses."[72] Aelred wrote, "By using these senses the soul receives into itself the images of corporeal things."[73] Such a statement reminds one of the limited significance Boethius allowed imagination, but Aelred was really much closer to Augustine in his respect for imagination and the memory. This is observed with his assertion that the memory has "one supreme quality...it has the capacity of receiving God."[74] Talbot mentions one activity of the soul where this divine interaction could take place. The soul is said to enter into sleep where it is released from its physical body in order to enter an imaginary body where it has imaginary experiences that are nonetheless capable of "conveying" truth.[75] Aelred described this as an "imaginative power, in which the soul tarries while the senses are asleep."[76] The notion of a dream world along these lines reflects the authority so many people of the Middle Ages gave to dreams. The contents of such dreams and other imaginings could be both positive and negative. Aelred was not as concerned with Augustine's false *phantas-*

ma, and he certainly lost some of the Stoic suspicion regarding the imagination. He explained, "For through it [imagination] the good are often enlightened and the wicked frightened."[77]

Returning to memory as the locus of imagination, Talbot describes the interaction of the three faculties when working with an image. In Aelred's view, he sees that memory holds the images, reason releases them, and will provides the consent for such acts.[78] According to Aelred, reason decides what to do with the images that memory is gathering together. He asserted, "memory without reason would be able to retain, to distinguish, or to judge nothing except the images conveyed to it through the senses."[79] Talbot also observes, "the abstract laws of science and art are lodged in the memory;" it has a "power to hold innate ideas."[80] At one point in the text, Aelred attempted to convince his dialogue partner that there are things that he has perceived without benefit of sense impressions.[81] All in all, Aelred shared a very positive regard for the role imagination can play in the spiritual life. He salvaged it from some of the suspicion with which earlier thinkers approached imagination, and he gave it a more balanced relationship with reason, above all when describing the unity of the faculties of the soul. It is somewhat surprising, then, that he relied so heavily in his writing on imagery supplied by others. If nothing else, he is at least very aware of the use of imagination when struggling to make sense of the spiritual life, and his thoughts give evidence of the intellectual approach to the imagination that was present in at least some monasteries.

Apocalyptic Imagination

For the many people who strangely assumed that God would follow a humanly devised calendar, the not-too-distant passing of a millennial anniversary added at least a hint of uncertainty to life. For the more suspiciously minded medieval populations of Europe the arrival of the thousandth year of the Lord must have been greeted with even greater apprehension. The fact that end-time terrors were not unleashed across the earth was no reassurance to those who lived in the centuries to follow. It merely meant that divine wrath was being held in abeyance for the hope of salvation of a few more worthy souls. Given this overshadowing concern, it is no surprise that people looked to Scripture in order to make some sense of their experience and anxieties. Richard Emerson and Ronald Herzman survey the effects of this influence as it is found in medieval literature.[82] While Francis' constant message of repentance can be taken as heralding the fast advancing reign of God, he was not listed by these authors as one of "the most imaginative thinkers and poets of the high Middle Ages."[83] It is not clear whether he failed to meet their criteria based on the volume or contents of his writings, or whether he fell outside their chosen time frame. What is clear is that he influenced at least two individuals who were recognized for their own imaginative works, Bonaventure (1221-1274) and Jacopone da Todi (c. 1230-1306).[84] In fact, an entire chapter is devoted to Bonaventure's imaginative experience of Francis in which the life of the *poverello* is envisioned in apocalyptic terms.

Due to its vivid imagery, the Book of Revelation stirs the imaginations of those who read it. In some cases, especially when an original or unique imagination is lacking, this scriptural text can provide much of the contents for imaginative expression. Emmerson and Herzman point out that the Book of Revelation was used a great deal by Christians of the Middle Ages "to discover their place in salvation history."[85] Much of the biblical exegesis performed during the twelfth century aligned sequences and characters in the Apocalypse "with patterns, events, orders, or key figures of Church History."[86] The impact this process had on much of the writing during this time is indication that enough similarities were uncovered to sustain popular anticipation of the end times. When exploring the products of medieval religious imaginations in the pages and chapters to come, it will be apparent that apocalyptic concerns are present in the various approaches to the spiritual life. For Francis, they will serve as at least a backdrop for the way one envisions the interrelationship of all things.

As medieval people sought concurrence between life and text, certain terms took on multivalent symbolic meanings. Emmerson and Herzman contend that apocalyptic imagery was manipulated, and this was done to varying purposes.[87] They mention one symbolic image that is of interest to the present study, the woman. The authors observe, "In traditional Christian iconography the Woman represents the Church throughout time."[88] One interesting aspect of the kind of imagination being discussed here is its ability to see "various manifestations of evil as essentially demonic inversions of good."[89] The symbolic woman does not escape this practice. Emmerson and Herzman explain, "As the woman about to give birth traditionally represents *Ecclesia*, the fecund true Church, so in medieval exegesis the Whore of Babylon represents... the false, spiritually barren church."[90] The general avoidance of this type of inversion is one indication that Francis' imagination is not solely an offshoot of the apocalyptic imagination. As Aelred's presentation of Augustinian imagination in Trinitarian terms suggests, numerical symbolism was just as popular as figural symbolism during the Middle Ages. Emmerson and Herzman mention that representational numbers were employed to give order to all aspects of existence. This tendency will be most obvious in the imaginative activity of writers heavily influenced by the Neo-Platonic way of thinking. Francis' appreciation for the Gospel According to John might have yielded this approach, but the aspect of apocalyptic imagination that is found in Francis' work sees a clear interrelationship between the particular and the universal, between the historical and the cosmic.[91] This thinking style, less specific than numerical comparisons, is threaded throughout Francis' writings.

The Imagination of Courtly Romance Literature

In addition to the monastic philosophic, intellectual approach to imagination and the influence of the most vivid scriptural passages, a specific genre of secular writing took hold of many imaginations in the Middle Ages. For an understanding of the depth of this impact, recourse will be had to the thoughts of Jacques LeGoff and Douglas Kelly. LeGoff's views on medieval imaginative activity in general will also add to the overall knowledge of this topic. He very boldly entitles one of his books *The Medieval Imagination*.[92] The daring in this act lies in the notion of a singular imagination that can be labeled as a common attribute of the people of the time. He describes imagination as "a collective, social, and historical phenomenon."[93] The point has already been made that numerous influences come together in varying proportion to aid in the formation of any imagination. LeGoff may realize this since he mentions a social and historical aspect to imagination, but imagination is really only collective insofar as the majority of people have one. A final area of medieval life that will be shown to impact imaginations is the area that LeGoff has chosen to investigate as indicative of "the medieval imagination." Courtly Romance writings are one of the most pronounced secular developments to influence people's imaginations during Francis' time. A consideration of LeGoff and Kelly's views on this literature will make evident the way it has affected medieval imaginative activity.

Although LeGoff is very systematic in his approach to the imagination, he does not formulate any clear-cut theories of the imagination. He seems more interested in describing imaginative content. His precision is most notable where he discriminates between imagination and three related but distinct concepts. A brief review of this partition will help to specify the conception of imagination forwarded by the present study. In LeGoff's mind imagination is not to be confused with representation, symbolism, or ideology. While "imagined images are created images," representation refers to "any mental image of a perceived external reality."[94] Here he differs from the Object Relation Theory understanding that any mental image will involve a creative act on the part of the imaginer simply to form an object representation. Imagination is also not symbolism, which is when an object "makes reference to an underlying system of values."[95] The implication of this dichotomy is that imaginative activity occurs in a mental vacuum where previous experience and thought are of no consequence. And finally, imagination is not ideology which distorts a representation "by imposing upon it a conception of the world that alters the meaning of both the material 'reality' and that other reality that I am calling the imagination."[96] In many instances there would be a very fine line between the involvement of a value system or of an ideology in the imaginative process. Nonetheless, it appears that LeGoff is not intending a psychotic disjunction from reality when he speaks of ideology. Rather, he seems to be neglecting the widely accepted belief that all experience is mediated or interpreted in such a way that one's perception of material reality is never perfectly stable; it evolves, usually along a communally acceptable continuum. For the present study, it should be understood that by the time the imaginative act has been manifested, each of LeGoff's non-imaginative elements would have come into play to some extent or another.

Among the generalizations LeGoff offers for the medieval imagination, he claims that people of the middle ages "had a greater difficulty than we do in drawing a boundary between material reality and imaginary reality."[97] He explains that there was a clash between external sensibility and internal sensibility with the preference for the latter. Specifically, "Medieval Christianity was one long effort of internalization."[98] This can be viewed as a continuation of the spirit-matter conflict emerging from the platonic emphasis on immaterial reality.

LeGoff points out that the world was changing rapidly during the time he calls "the central Middle Ages."[99] Rapid social upheaval leads either to a retrenchment in things viewed as enduring or to an embrace of new possibilities. Sometimes it leads to both. In Chrétien de Troyes's *Yvain ou le chevalier au lion*, LeGoff observes a portrait of twelfth-century economic and social change.[100] Some of the value changes, which he describes as a "shifting of heaven toward earth," appear to be the very elements for which Francis' spiritual view of reality was, in one way or another, a response. LeGoff describes this as a time of "growing prosperity, improvement in physical comforts, increased consumption of pleasure goods, the emergence of profane literature… revival of the theme *carpe diem*… the transition from a distinction between *potens* and *pauper* (powerful and powerless) to one between rich and poor."[101] With society in such flux, the imagination is the one tool that can see past what is present to what is possible.

LeGoff's study looks for imaginative expressions that can be placed under the descriptive heading: marvel. By this method he touches upon two focal elements of the imagination that are pertinent to a more careful look into Francis' imaginative activity. These are the perceptions of the forest and of the body with its clothing.

It is not too difficult to understand why the medieval European forest was associated with a sense of the marvelous. A pilgrimage to modern day Assisi cannot offer half the insight into Francis' world as a trip into the mountains that Francis frequented above the city. At one spot, near a cave in which the saint was said to pray, an artist has captured the sense of wonder that gripped Francis in this place. A statue depicts him lying on the ground with some of his companions, excitedly pointing to something above them. The beauty of these woodlands could be enough to inspire Francis to an altered vision of the world around him, so it is difficult to assess how much his access to the popular secular literature of his time also influenced his way of seeing and living in connection with the forest.

Romantic literature fosters certain understandings of the wilderness that strike a chord with some of what Thomas of Celano has to say about Francis's reclusive behaviors. LeGoff notes a typical perception of the forest. It was the place of chaos and insecurity against which stood the city with its order.[102] This view is somewhat challenged when the city loses its traditional meaning through rapid social change. In Béroul's *Tristan and Isolde*, the forest was a place of the simple life.[103] LeGoff discovers that the forest is also imaginatively depicted alternatively as a paradise, a refuge, a second baptism, and as a place to confront demons.[104] Furthermore, it is a place of solitude or of learning in a manner not available through books.[105]

There is little reason to doubt that the wilderness surrounding Assisi played some part in Francis' spiritual transformation. As a place of trial, where one contends with one's own demons, the forest certainly did loom large for Francis. In addition to being a place of penitence and revelation, LeGoff adds that it was a home to those living on the fringe of society.[106] This could describe Francis, but it absolutely describes the very people that he mentions in his own words in

The Testament of St. Francis. "This is how God inspired me, Brother Francis, to embark upon a life of penance. When I was in sin, the sight of lepers nauseated me beyond measure; but then God himself led me into their company, and I had pity on them. When I had once become acquainted with them, what had previously nauseated me became a source of spiritual and physical consolation for me."[107] This one passage indicates that Francis did spend some time on the outskirts of civilization since lepers would not be permitted near towns and villages. It also makes clear that Francis underwent a trial as he came into direct contact with something that distressed him to the core of his being, the lepers, the cursed ones who dwelled not only outside society but also outside the limits of life as he knew it. The passage further discloses the transformation that occurred in the wilderness. Francis moved from sin and achieved an altered way of relating to others, a kind of new knowledge or insight.

Perhaps most important for a consideration of imagination, it must be noted that the *sickening experience turned to consolation* referred to Francis' sight of the lepers, and consequently, his transformation involved a new way of seeing, perceiving, and thus also imagining. But this theme is not Francis' alone. Le-Goff explains a typical sequence found in the courtly romances in which the character finds seclusion in the forest, confronts misery of some sort, and emerges with a profound insight.[108] In Chrétien de Troyes' *Yvain* (c.1180), Le-Goff points out an example that includes a description of a person living outside the acceptable boundaries of human life. In this case the main character is said to lurk in the forest like a savage during a period of apparent madness.[109] Did Francis conform the understanding of his own life to these imaginative paradigms? This is possible. Chiara Frugoni identifies one of de Troyes' other thematic characters, the "queen of largesse" as a compelling figure for the young Francis.[110] From the passage taken from the saint's *Testament* we can be sure that Thomas of Celano did not simply fabricate the idea that Francis abandoned society during periods of his conversion. Anthony Mockler has another theory about the poetic literature as it connects with Francis' life. He contends that the poets or *troubadours* were motivated by heretical Cathar beliefs that downplayed material aspects of life in favor of seeking a perfect level of immaterial purity. This purity in its abstract sense was imaginatively associated with the symbolic woman of noble qualities who figures so centrally in most of the poems.[111]

The second focal element of secular imaginative literature pertinent to a study of Francis is the body and that which covers it. LeGoff contends that the body was considered to be a metaphor for the world and society.[112] In Thomas of Celano's account, Francis' body certainly has a poignant symbolism that is backed up by Francis' implied and direct references to his own body. LeGoff suggests that a driving impetus to many of the story lines in romantic poetry is the conflict over inheritance between fathers, first sons, and brothers. In another curious connection that can be made to Thomas' depiction of Francis, LeGoff mentions that Yvain "strips his body of its clothing and his mind of its memory."[113] It is uncertain whether the chronicler's graphic depiction of the culmination of Francis' paternal conflict is factual, but Francis clearly discarded one form of attire for another. Through the courtly romances, he may have become aware of the association of a transformed way of life, as signified by clothing, with a transformed way of envisioning the world around him. The courtly literature was replete with instances where a rite of passage is marked by a change in clothing, and in many cases it is a knight who receives a new item of clothing to signify his heightened status.[114] If Francis did once aspire to worldly nobility, adornment in a rough mantel is certainly a realized reversal of that ambition. But then LeGoff offers the insight that the form of one's material adornment is both a sign of equality and inequality, depending upon the social caste in which one is standing. Perhaps a self-image founded upon the attire in which he entered the world was the only image that could allow Francis to adopt his transformative outlook.

Kelly studies the imaginative dimension of medieval courtly poetry as a form of rhetoric, but he makes clear the difference between the rhetorical goal of this secular literature and the rhetorical traditions of the Roman oratory. He explains that the poetic imagination of the Middle Ages was directed toward the visualization of what stood as otherwise invisible, while the earlier Roman form, that played a role in Augustine's intellectual development, was concerned with evoking memory.[115] Like the well-trained rhetoricians of an earlier age, Kelly describes the best of the courtly poets as true crafts-persons who developed a carefully systematized approach to giving expression to imaginative activity.

The primary instrument to be used by the *troubadours* was the metaphor. In medieval rhetoric the *imago* stood for a type of metaphor capable of showing the resemblance between something in the material world and its parallel entity in the invisible world. Kelly observes that the "Invention of an *imago* is *imaginatio*, the invention of a true or credible illustration in narrative, discourse, and argument."[116] He goes on to explain: "The *imago* is thus the visible correlative to the real, permanent archetype."[117] Expressing both Platonic and Aristotelian ideas, Kelly sees the poets living in a visible world that imperfectly reflects a more perfect invisible world, and it is their imaginative creativity that reflects the very existence of this otherwise unseen and unknown world. He writes, "The artist thus invents as God created."[118] These last words echo an understanding that resonates with Object Relations theorists taking note of an infant forming his or her own mental representations of objects discovered in external reality. Returning to the medieval artist, Kelly asserts, "His imagination, in its place and on its own plane, is a mirror of God's."[119] As a summary of the imaginative process he discovers at work among the romantic writers, Kelly suggests, "The archetype becomes a mental model the poet imitates by finding suitable words and bringing them together into a whole that manifests the archetype: the poet is indeed a *trouvère*, and his first responsibility is the invention of images that imitate archetypes."[120]

Is it possible that Francis was inventing images that did not simply reflect a different level of reality but rather a different way of relating within levels of reality? In any case, the influence of the courtly romances on Francis' imaginative activity is unmistakable. He shares this source of imaginative inspiration with the two religious figures whose imaginations will be probed in the following sections. Unlike these two Cistercian monks, Francis was not heavily impacted by the philosophic, theoretical approach to the imagination that attempts to understand and make use of what is going on in the imagination. Francis' imaginative writings also do not indicate a single-minded obsession with the Apocalypse, although apocalyptic concerns play a role in his adaptation of a new way of seeing. This selective review of influences on Francis' imagination now turns to a brief study of the imaginative activity of two near contemporaries of Francis.

A Comparison with Near Contemporaries

A Preface to Studying Imagination in the Writings of Bernard of Clairvaux

A brief survey of Bernard of Clairvaux's writings stands as an apt subject for comparison with those of Francis of Assisi. Bernard was known for his work with the imagination. He was the leader of a significant reform movement in the Church, and his concerns extended into the secular lives of people such that he was not willing to allow his listeners to leave God out of their daily consciousness. Perhaps the most interesting association to consider is that Bernard's mother insisted on breast-feeding him, herself.[121] This may seem to be a strange connection, but, as Aelred of Rievaulx's writings are explored in the next section, the importance of the maternal-infant relationship will be seen in a clearer light. It would be untenable to assert that Bernard's was a *good-enough mother* based solely on this one nurturing activity, but the feeding routine is certainly one of the earliest post-natal interactions a mother and child can have, and it is hence a precursor to the ongoing relationship within which Bernard was able to form his mental representations of himself and his world. A comfortable use of maternal imagery and the fact that he brought much of his family with him to the religious life are supportive of the idea that his early life began on a fairly positive note. There is no indication of avoiding some aspect of his first relationships. His interest was more a matter of wanting to order those relationships according to the divine will.

The workings of Bernard's imagination will best be laid bare by describing the purpose and then the technique behind his imaginative writings prior to exemplifying the use of his imagination in a selective examination of his writings.[122] The end toward which Bernard directed his writings can be divided into three related efforts. He sought to uphold his view of a divinely founded order. He struggled against significant threats to that order, and, ultimately, he intended to move people closer to God.

Purpose of Bernard's Writings

A penchant for order. One of the most common words used by the saint is loosely translated as *order.* G.G. Coulton observes that Bernard used the Latin term *ordo* "to emphasize the necessity of cooperation and discipline and subordination even in the struggle for personal salvation."[123] It is not surprising that this concept reflects the regimen of the monastery, but in his writings Bernard often extended his expectation of order beyond the monastery walls and into the activities of senior clerics and secular leaders. Unlike Francis, who was attempting to find a balance that would allow him and his followers to institute a new way of living within the Church, Bernard was harkening back to a long-established lifestyle. While Francis looked ahead to the unforeseeable possibilities inherent in an existence in poverty and simplicity as a means of entering into a closer relationship with Christ, Coulton finds Bernard looking back to the *Rule of Benedict*.[124] G.R. Evans concludes, likewise, that it was not a new way of life that Bernard envisioned so much as a return to an old way, to an established form of order.[125]

Order is also essential when it came to the faith that Bernard shared within the monastery. Evans maintains, "He rocked no boats."[126] Bernard was very much engaged in handing on the faith in an enlivened fashion, but distinctly not added to in any manner. Dennis Tamburello considers the saint's efforts in religious and secular spheres. He contends that Bernard was held in a specific tension between the Church's "relationship to the world and its relationship to God."[127] One way that Bernard was able to sustain this tension according to good order was to consider many aspects of the secular world as intended by God. Adriaan Bredero argues, "Bernard was tied to the old feudal-political religiosity."[128] For Bernard, order, including social order, was a sign and activity of God. If it takes a little effort to discern this order, all the better, since it is embedded in the mystery that is God's challenge to those who would see with a purer vision. Nonetheless, order has its antithesis. Bernard's writings and actions clearly show that for him, order had something to stand over and against.

Protecting order. In spite of being labeled a reformer, Bernard struggled against many challenges to the ancient order of the Church. Among other parallels between Bernard and Francis, Evans notes that both made their respective movements the religious fashion of the day.[129] While Bernard achieved this based on a concrete ideal, the *Rule of Benedict*, Francis formed his religious family around a more abstract ideal, poverty.[130] Had it not been for Francis' ultimate and unswerving reliance on the Gospel, Bernard might not have considered him to have a place within God's intended order. Evans observes, "Bernard was born at a time of experimentation in the religious life."[131] From what is known of Bernard's desire for order, new approaches to the faith were not looked upon with an approving eye. In addition to promoting the second crusade against the Moslem challengers of the faith, Bernard was involved in several other notable conflicts of an internal theological nature. Was there something in his personality that accounted for this distinction between his assertive nature and the oft described as peace-loving Francis? Jean LeClercq determines that it was a strong, controlled aggressiveness that was Bernard's primary force.[132] For whatever reason, he was involved in the scrutiny or prosecution of several people considered to be near or beyond the limits of acceptable religious life. Evans mentions Gilbert of Poitiers and Hildegard of Bingen; however, Bernard's most famous clash was with Peter Abelard.[133]

Coulton suggests that Bernard disdained the application of philosophic learning to support and defend the faith.[134] The idea was that since it is rightly ordered, the Christian faith stands on its own merits. Ewert Cousins adds a comparable idea, "He defended the autonomy of spirituality against what he thought was the destructive rationalism of Peter Abelard and the emerging scholasticism."[135] Just how did Bernard view this rationalism as a threat to order and thus a danger? According to Tamburello, Abelard held that "understanding must precede faith," and for Bernard, like Anselm (1033-1109) before him, faith preceded understanding.[136] Evans insists that their dispute was over "certainty."[137] By basing faith on understanding, which may or may not occur, Abelard introduced the element of uncertainty, which is incompatible with faith. Evans also sees a more particular difference between Bernard's intellectual approach to Christianity and that of Abelard and Gilbert of Poitiers. Both of the latter thinkers possessed a remarkable skill with words that they engaged "to enlarge technical language so that it could encompass and express ideas not put into words before."[138] This endeavor would certainly demand an active imagination. Bernard's efforts to avoid this threat to the order in which things were done and understood caused him to use his imagination in a much more restricted style.

Moving people to God. As seen in his actions and writings, Bernard's primary purpose, a goal that he clearly shared with Francis, was to move people closer to God and the promises of heaven. Bernard did this by influencing the way one visualizes one's relationship with God, and ultimately by shaping the means by which one knows God.

Luke Anderson uses the saint's own words to explain how he worked on the imagination to affect the way a relationship with God was imaginatively conceived. "He proposes to 'enlighten' the mind of his audience and to 'root our affection in God.' The 'incomprehensible' and 'invisible' will be manifested 'by means of figures;' and these images will be 'drawn from the likeness of things familiar to us.' What is 'precious' will be attained through the 'cheap.'"[139] Burcht Pranger adds a description of how seamless the process of entry into this way of seeing can be. "The fluency of the discourse is such as to present a natural unity which makes the reader forget about any possible distinction between the literal and the spiritual, the world and the monastery."[140] Envisioning a relationship with God is not enough. Bernard connected the use of images to see in a spiritual sense with the capacity to know in an epistemological sense long before imagination was revealed as essential to all knowing.[141]

When it came to epistemological approaches, Bernard was less a theologian than a mediator of a path to know God. LeClercq asserts, "The aim of ancient and medieval spiritual authors was not to provide food for reflection; rather, they sought to encourage an experience through recollections of a poetical nature."[142] In his own writing, Bernard supported the theory that he promoted experiential knowledge. He claimed to study and write about Scripture "not so much to explain words as to move hearts."[143] Tamburello takes from this that Bernard "is a person who always maintained the connection between theology and the human experience of the sacred."[144]

Although modern access to Bernard is through his written work, he showed people the way to know God most powerfully through the spoken word. Evans maintains that Bernard was more effective as a speaker than as a writer; he "liked to tell stories to make a point."[145] She adds, "Thus he taught his listeners in pictures how to defeat the vices and live in the love of God and neighbor."[146] The end purpose of all these epistemological efforts for Bernard was to know God through the image of God residing within oneself, presently seen only in an imperfect state. LeClercq describes this "restoration of the image of God in man," as the central effort of Bernard's spirituality.[147] As a way to come closer to God, it was a theme that Bernard presented and Aelred took up in detail.

Bernard's Imaginative Technique

Bernard appears to Evans as a seductive preacher.[148] This assessment suggests that he captured imaginations when he spoke. The same could be said of his writings, albeit to a lesser degree. To understand the technique that enabled Bernard to arrive at his imaginative style it would be helpful to consider his educational background, the degree of originality he brought to the process, the sources he used, and the method he employed.

Education. Bernard wrote and dictated over 3500 pages.[149] In spite of this prolific output, Evans notes that he lacked the formal education that was possible in his day. Although he was not in one of the "new schools" forming around a great master, LeClercq describes him as "a remarkable thinker and a well trained Latinist."[150] Possessing more than just an ability to write beautiful Latin, Bernard knew how to put it to good use. Evans observes that he was adept at rhetoric. She exclaims that he "orchestrates his words."[151] It is this rhetorical experience that both structures and limits the degree of originality in the workings of his imagination.

Originality. Earlier, Bernard's contempt for innovation was discussed. It should come as no shock that achieving new heights of originality in his writing did not appeal to Bernard. There is at least one positive aspect to this contained creativity. Evans notes that, "as Gregory the Great demonstrated, originality and influence do not always run together."[152] In his day, Bernard's influence far outstripped the significance of the writings that offer but a limited insight into his activities. Bernard's preaching and writing style required him to avoid novel images if and when they came to him. Evans reveals that Bernard's expressions did not seem to be new. "He appeared to his listeners to be doing exceptionally well something they had come to look for."[153] She goes on to say that he was recognized for "using the same examples again and again," but this was most likely intentional.[154] A fundamental practice of rhetoric is to use familiar and thus memorable elements.[155] This constraint and his own tendency to avoid disrupting order go far in restricting the possible sources that Bernard could draw from for the formation of his images.[156]

Sources. Anselm stands out as one of Bernard's more recent sources, but more for theological understanding than the formation of images.[157] An indirect source Bernard shared in part with Francis and Aelred is not an individual but rather a movement that was discussed in an earlier section of this chapter. As

Cousins remarks, "In his eulogies of human love, he echoed the troubadours, trouvéres, and the writers of romance."[158] It is not clear how much direct influence Bernard received from the courtly romance tradition. His family's status may have given him some exposure. The fact that he entered the monastery at the fairly late age of twenty-three also provided him the opportunity to develop a concept of the love of God that had its roots in a deeper understanding of male-female love, says Bredero.[159] In any case, the spirituality of love, to which Bernard was a significant contributor, had its beginnings in a secular movement.[160] A related detail that should not be overlooked is that Bernard's major imaginative input to this area was an expansion of the Bride and Bridegroom theme taken from the Biblical book the Song of Songs.

Evans determines that Bernard did not draw heavily from a variety of sources to form a whole; predominantly he used Scripture. She goes on to state, "Bernard had mastered the words; indeed, he had made them his own to such a degree that he could hardly write except in the words of Scripture."[161] Elsewhere she insists, "All Bernard's theological reflections, his sense of the divine, his vision of God, his heightened perception of the beauty of holiness, arise like a distillation from his study of the Bible."[162] Evans goes on to confirm that his exegetical ability was profound, but in such a way that his imagery was a re-presentation of the Bible and not a development from it.[163] All of her findings support the view that Bernard was not inclined to wander far from the given images of the Bible when it came to the workings of his own imagination. Finally, LeClercq describes Bernard's use of Scripture as "marked by *seeming* imagination."[164] A realistic conclusion is that his most imaginative activity is not found in the formation of images but in their arrangement!

A method for stirring the imagination. Object Relations Theory depicts imagination in terms of relating internal images or mental representations. Bernard also did this outwardly, as his chosen methodologies demonstrate. Anderson notes his heavy use of analogy and metaphor, both of which rely on the recognition of relationships.[165] The use of association is also present in allegorical writing. Cousins states, "In the patristic and medieval periods, allegory was looked upon not as a flight of fancy, but as a method of penetrating a deeper level of the sacred text, based on the structure of reality and the very nature of the psyche."[166]

Whether Bernard employed analogy or metaphor or allegory in his rhetorical efforts, he was involved in relating images. Even if the images were familiar, a necessary factor for rhetoric, Evans suggests that Bernard was able to move his audience through suspense.[167] Again, it is the arrangement of images that allows this. Suspense can be created by reference to the unknown, but, as was Bernard's method, it can also be achieved by suspending one's anticipation of the images to be related. Pranger explains it this way: "it is the arrangement and rearrangement of different sets of images which creates possibilities of meaning as yet unheard of, rather than the implementation of a strict and predictable procedure."[168] While Pranger allows some room for unique imaginative developments on Bernard's part, the saint really did not venture far from the "strict and predictable." Emero Stiegman has an interesting insight into an approach Bernard used that sustained order in his activity and, at the same time, let his imagination participate. He asserts that Bernard stood at the crossroads of two artistic ages, between the medieval concern for proportion and the burgeoning enlightenment focus on light. Specifically, Bernard's imagination was at work in the proportionate structure that he developed around his writing, preaching, chanting, and building, which, in turn, offered at least a limited vision of divine beauty. Whether it entailed predictability, predictability withheld briefly, or proportion, Bernard's imaginative activity appeared to be heavily reliant upon the arrangement of generally recognizable images as the following survey of his more imaginative writings will bear out.[169]

A View of Select Writings through the Lens of Imagination

The workings of Bernard of Clairvaux's imagination will be investigated with a consideration of images in his writing that exhibit some degree of originality and illustrate the way one might relate to God, fellow religious, the rest of created reality, and maternal figures. In addition, there will be examples of images that reflect one's relationship with oneself.[170] The selection of these categories, which are not equally represented in each text, will allow a more thorough comparison to Francis' imagination. This survey of Bernard's imaginative activity is not intended to be an exhaustive review. Although some of his images are developments from scriptural images, his hand will clearly be revealed in their elaboration. This process of relating images in new arrangements or using them to represent something in a style not seen before is a form of imaginative originality from the perspective of Object Relations Theory.

Bernard did not present as much of a theoretical understanding of the imagination in his writings as Aelred. At various points, however, Bernard made obvious his understanding of the imagination's connection with sense perception and memory. In his treatise *On Grace and Free Choice* it was the will and not reason that governed sense perception.[171] He declared, "In the material world, life is not identical with sense-perception."[172] This leaves the idea that there is more to be experienced in the material world than is available to the senses. In a follow-on statement Bernard remarked, "...Sense-perception is a vital movement of the body, alert and outward."[173] Here, it would seem that access to this *more* than is available to the senses requires a turn inward, where Bernard encountered the memory as it stands for imagination.

Like Augustine, Bernard considered memory to be ambivalent, neither bad nor good by nature. He assigned it as a constituent part of the soul, but at its worst, he described it as "a field rough and neglected," in the care of the wicked.[174] He meant by this that the memory, when sown with evil deeds, will persist for the wicked person beyond this life as a constant source of torment. Bernard went on in another work to portray memory more enthusiastically as something no longer required by members of the Church triumphant but a consolation to those who still struggle in grace. "And so memory [of God] is for the generations of this world; presence belongs to the kingdom of heaven. Those who are chosen already enjoy the glory of his presence there, the generation which is still on pilgrimage is comforted in the meantime by memory."[175] Given an understanding of Bernard's perspective on imagination, the spiritual life can be expressed as the visualization of one's relationships in an appropriate order corresponding to the will of God such that one's attention is directed ever upward to the experience of God's presence in heaven.

In his work *On Loving God*, Bernard clearly expressed the difficulty of concentrating one's attention and imagination on God. He confirmed that a person seeking God must imaginatively work through his or her relations with everything that is less than God prior to establishing a meaningful relationship with God. The saint exclaimed, "They wish to obtain all they want, but they are unable to reach the end of their desires. If they would only be content with reaching it all in thought and not on experiencing it! That they can easily do, and it would not be pointless, for man's mind is quicker than his senses and it sees further and the senses dare not touch anything which the mind has not already examined and approved."[176] Once a spiritually inclined person has cleared away the clutter in this manner, by adapting a new perception, Bernard offers two sets of images for the divine-human relationship.

In the first set of images there is God as artist and humanity as work of art. Bernard asks, "Why should the work of an artist not love its master, if it has the ability to do so? Why should it not love him with all its might, since it can do nothing except by his gift?"[177] When he expands upon this idea, Bernard clarifies an idea he brought up earlier when he mentioned a "vision of God which makes us resemble him."[178] This reflects the Cistercian concept of the image of God residing in each person, but he links it with the idea that the Word of God present in the individual is the source of the original and continuous relationship with God. Bernard goes on to say, "But he who made me by speaking once said a great deal more to remake me, and did miracles, and endured hardships, and not only hardship but humiliation.... In the first act he gave me myself; in the second he gave me himself; and when he did that he gave me back myself."[179]

The second set of images Bernard offers for the divine-human relationships are found in a description of the fourth degree of love, which entails a loss of self-will and human affections. Following in the trend of the individual resembling or sharing an image with God, Bernard insists:

> To love this way is to become like God. As a drop of water seems to disappear completely in a quantity of wine, taking the wine's flavor and color; as red-hot irons become indistinguishable from the glow of the fire and its original form disappears; as air suffused with the light of the sun seems transformed into the brightness of the light as if it were itself light rather than merely lit up; so, in those who are holy, it is necessary for human affection to dissolve in some ineffable way, and be poured into the will of God.[180]

In addition to these images of complete union taken from images in created reality, Bernard uses an image of a gentle breeze to reveal how this degree of love also involves a loss of concern for the flesh. He claims, "Holy martyrs received this grace.... The sensation of outward pain could do no more than whisper across the surface of their tranquility; it could not disturb it."[181]

For Bernard, inanimate elements from created reality have a place in his concept of order, but only when they are rightly ordered. He calls for the use of "restraint... to save you from making of nature's good things a way to serve the soul's enemy through lust."[182] He has an interesting way of drawing on nature imagery to express a gift-giving relationship between God and humanity. Bernard connects numerous otherwise unrelated Scriptural passages that use a similar image. One example is the flower. In the same area of text he brings together the passage "My flesh has bloomed again"(Ps 27.7), with "Our bed is strewn with flowers"(Sg 1.15), and "flowers from the field the Lord has blessed" (Gn 27.27).[183] After focusing his readers' attention on flowers with these and other passages that mention them, the saint makes clear the association he is positing between flowers and the resurrection. He writes, "His flesh was sown in death; it flowered again in the resurrection"(1Cor 15.42).[184] It is likely that by orienting this passage to the flower theme he is hoping that at each sighting of a flower his readers would be moved to contemplation of what God has given them in the resurrection of Christ. As in other uses of imagery from created reality, Bernard clearly intends the inanimate element to support the divine-human relationship. Francis makes a similar use of flowers in his writing.

Most of the images Bernard uses pertaining to the self are meant to direct the individual's awareness beyond that powerful magnet that is the self. Speaking of a person grasped by arrogance, Bernard says, "He endeavors like a wicked servant to snatch and steal away the Lord's glory for himself."[185] It is not just seeking after glory that constrains the order of relationships as Bernard would have it; self-love is another concern. Of this Bernard remarks, "But if the same love begins to get out of proportion and headstrong, as often happens, and it ceases to be satisfied to run in the narrow channel of its needs, but floods out on all sides into the fields of pleasure, then the overflow can be stopped at once by the commandment 'you shall love your neighbor as yourself'"(Mt 22.39).[186] Here he uses a Biblical admonition to form the image of a waterway system to guide uncontrolled waters and redirect love onto a higher level.

Bernard's treatise *On Grace and Free Choice* is a very dogmatic work that uses only a limited amount of imagery. It does, however add to the Cistercian notion of the divine image in the individual. Bernard exclaims, Christ "was able to reform what was deformed." Further insight into the abbot's view of the arrangement of this image-relationship between God and humanity is suggested in the title of one chapter: "Through Christ the Likeness which Properly Belongs to the Divine Image is Restored in Us."[187] In this chapter, Bernard goes on to describe a process that can heal the injury to this relationship. He writes, "Conformation means that the image fulfills in the body what form does in the world."[188] He explains more clearly that the person can "set up in himself a worthy likeness to the divine image, restoring, in fact, completely his former loveliness."[189] A point to observe in this explanation is the action required on the part of each person to attempt to achieve some degree of personal conformity to the divine image.

If the foregoing statement suggests a lack of room for the action of grace, it should be noted that this treatise is replete with descriptions of the essential participation of grace in achieving and sustaining the relationship between God and humanity. In fact, it is the will operating against grace that prevents the establishment of a true image of God in a person. Using nature imagery, Bernard explains that one can damage the relationship on one's own, but, unaided it cannot be healed. He writes simply, "It is not as easy to climb out of a pit as to fall into one."[190]

Another use of imagery from created reality suggests that the needs of the body are on a lower portion of the hierarchy of needs than the needs of the soul, which, when met, also fulfill the needs of the body. Bernard maintains, "Bread is fine, but to one who is hungry; drink delightful, but to the thirsty. To the sated, food and drink are a burden, not a joy."[191] This treatise does not have a significant maternal image, but it has two depreciating female images. Bernard uses the voice of a woman to refer to a will that is directed toward inappropriate choices. He asks, "How otherwise would a woman's voice have been sufficient to tempt a holy tongue into pronouncing unholy words, had not the will, mistress of the tongue, assented?"[192] One suspects that the will would not be described as "mistress" when making appropriate choices.

Bernard's work *On Consideration* provides less interesting imagery for the relationship with God than it does for each of the other types of relationships. As a challenge to Pope Eugenius III to guide the Church from the foundation he built with his monastic vocation, Bernard uses the image of a wounded body in this treatise to describe the pope's separated relationship with his brother monks. The abbot writes, "The fresh wound must be painful," but he wants to keep this notion of a recent injury alive, since "the member which is past feeling is all the farther from health," and "if you neglect the old wound it grows callous, and in proportion as it loses feeling it becomes incurable."[193] The idea is to keep Eugenius in touch with the values and meaning he discovered in the monastery, which Bernard views as a firm base for his governance of the Church and the perseverance of the pope's own soul.

To further anchor the pope so that he does not lose sight of his mediation between heaven and earth, Bernard uses natural images. He declares to Eugenius, "if you are to do the work of a prophet, what you want is not a scepter, but a hoe. The prophet does not rise to reign, but to root out the weeds."[194] Bernard goes on to suggest doing as God does, "imitate the Author of nature, by associating the highest and the lowest things."[195] He continues to utilize the God-as-Artist idea when he specifies, "Has not nature in the person of man bound together poor clay and the breath of life?"[196] Of course it is the higher things that instill value in the lower levels of reality such as inanimate creation.

Since *On Consideration* is written to a very particular individual, some images of the self take on a different style. It must be remembered, also, that Bernard considers Eugenius to be the recipient of an added amount of grace due to his position. To signify the degree of grace that the pope could locate within his own person, Bernard writes, "all alike share in you, all drink at the public fountain of your heart; and will you stand apart and thirst?"[197] In an effort to protect the pope's graced relationship with God, Bernard uses another unguided water image that is also found in *On Loving God*. Directing Eugenius away from the things of the world Bernard warns, "The flowing stream hollows out a channel for itself; similarly temporal things coursing through the mind eat away the conscience."[198] In one of the most direct reference to the pope's relationship to his own self, Bernard uses a construction image. He says, "if you know not yourself, you will be like a man building without a foundation, and will succeed not in rearing an edifice, but in making a ruin."[199]

There are two very strong sets of maternal images found in *On Consideration*. Bernard's prologue contains some of the most recognized of these. Speaking to Eugenius he writes, "Love knows no lord; it recognizes a son even in the robes of office."[200] He adds, "though I no longer act as a mother to you, I have not lost a mother's affection for you."[201] Associating his position as abbot with the role of mother goes some distance in making up for Bernard's negative female imagery in the last work reviewed, although the comparison may say something about his mental representation of his mother in contrast with all other women. The present maternal image also indicates the nature of his conception of the relationship he had with his charges in the monastic establishment. A passage that could be construed as a womb image puts this relationship on very intimate terms. He remarks, "In days gone by you were rooted in my very heart; you are not so easily to be plucked out."[202] Although these maternal images are very positive, Bernard never loses track of the fact that the mind produces images that can stand for both good and bad. He uses a web of mother and child relationships to point toward the continuity or interrelationship of character defects: "Impunity, the child of carelessness, the mother of insolence, the root of impudence, the nurse of transgression."[203] While the apparent nature of Bernard's maternal relationship is not as negative as Aelred's, Bernard's is not so clearly defined.

Bernard centers his entire treatise *On Humility and Pride* on the image of a ladder. It can be ascended by humility or, as Bernard prefers to explain, it can be descended by pride. Oddly enough, he relates the individual to God as a foot. Bernard states, "With the foot of grace planted squarely on the ladder of humility, trailing my own weak foot behind, I shall climb safely upward by holding fast to the truth."[204] This image of being gently carried from danger coordinates well with his equally tender Trinitarian expression of God in the order of Son, Holy Spirit, and Father. Bernard insists, "The first teaches us like a master. The second comforts like a friend or brother. The third embraces us as a father does his sons."[205] Each of these identifiably male-oriented images is very upbeat. Aelred uses a similar selection of three images for God, but his set is not directed toward God as Trinity, nor is his set as gentle across the board.

Another God-image that both Aelred and Bernard employ is that of doctor. Bernard first writes, "In the same way, God, the physician of souls, brings temptation upon the soul and sends tribulations."[206] In addition to portraying a positive relationship with God, Bernard goes off on an imaginative monologue with Satan to depict a bad relationship with God. Because of Satan's pride, Bernard argues, "Everyone else in heaven is standing. You alone affect to sit. You disrupt the harmony of your brothers, the peace of the whole heavenly realm, and, if it were in your power, you would disturb the tranquility of the Trinity."[207] In

Bernard's mind it is the rule of order that the devil transgresses, and, therefore, the only proper punishment is to place him in a condition of disorder. He commands Satan, "Choose for yourself a place in the air (Eph 2.2), not to sit but to hang there, so that you who have tried to shake the stability of eternity may feel the punishment of your own instability."[208] It would seem that more than anything else, God is experienced and related to in some form of order.

Images from created reality that are given in *On Humility and Pride* back up other relationships without participating in meaningful relationships themselves. Bernard uses two natural images in his opening to indicate the trepidation he feels in writing this treatise, which is only overcome by the value he sees in it. "I chose to do what I could to bring you to the fruit of my talk rather than lurk for my own safety in the harbor of silence."[209] Like the value of fruit, he assigns similar value to food in general by letting it signify love. Bernard declares, "Truly, love is sweet and pleasant food, which refreshes the weary, strengthens the weak (Is 35.3), makes the sad joyful, the yoke of Truth sweet and its burden light"(Mt 11.30).[210] Bernard's most negative inanimate image describes the eyes and ears as goats of sin: "I have rightly called them eyes and ears, for just as death entered the world through sin (Rom 5:12), so it enters the mind through these windows"(Jer 9.21).[211]

Since humility and pride both refer to the self, it is not surprising to find several creative images on this topic. Bernard contends, "Pride in the mind is a great beam which is bloated rather than heavy, swollen rather than solid, and it blocks the mind's eye and blots out the light of truth, so that if your mind is full of it you cannot see yourself as you really are."[212] The perspective from which one views oneself and one's world is central to the topic of pride and humility. Bernard speaks of people climbing "from step to step until they reach the highest peak of humility, on which, standing as though on Sion (Ps 83.6), that is, at a vantage point, they see the truth."[213] At the other end of the spectrum are those who prefer not to see themselves through the "eyes of truth."[214] Of such people, Bernard remarks, "If anything has happened which would bring contempt upon him or cast him down, he wipes it from his memory. And if he notes any good things in himself he will add them up and parade them before his mind's eye."[215] A person inclined in this way is unlikely to be relating to him or herself according to the order that leads to Truth.

The one maternal image taken from this treatise relates birth to death in an immediate sense. Bernard writes, "We are born to die because we were dying before we were born. This is the heavy burden You have laid on all your children up to this very day"(Sir 40.1).[216] Bernard sets birth in the ongoing cycle of life and death, but he has changed the arrangement to challenge his readers in the way they perceive this cycle. Birth is not the beginning of the cycle; it is simply a marker in a procession that exceeds temporal bounds. He even leaves an imaginative space in the statement since it is not clear whether it is birth or death that is the burden.

While Bernard is often engaged in fostering the relationship between himself and his brother monks, as well as among the monks themselves, his larger works are limited in their inclusion of imagery for these relationships. Several of his most readily available letters indicate that it is in his correspondence that such images are more prevalent. Also available in these letters are additional maternal images. In two of these letters Bernard associates life in the monastery with the city of Jerusalem. It is not quite clear from his writings whether he considers the monastic life to be equivalent to the theological notion of a heavenly Jerusalem, the city of God. He certainly orders his notion of Jerusalem on a higher plane then normal earthly life.

In *Letter 64: To Alexander, Bishop of Lincoln*, Bernard wrote on behalf of a monk who had recently joined his monastery. He says, "Your Philip, who wanted to go to Jerusalem, has found a shortcut and arrived there sooner than expected. He crossed this great wide sea quickly, and with a following wind he has now landed on the shore he was making for, and has dropped anchor in a safe harbor."[217] If Bernard intends the "great wide sea" to stand for one's life, then he is trying to develop the idea of the monastic life as initiation into eternal life. The "safe harbor" at the destination also gives credence to this view. Carrying on his connection between a well-ordered society and a divinely intended order, Bernard writes, "He has been made not a glorious spectator but a loyal inhabitant and enrolled citizen of Jerusalem... that free Jerusalem which is above and mother of us all."[218] His description of Jerusalem as a mother can be probed on three levels. On the highest level, Jerusalem as heaven provides an everlasting maternal relationship.[219] On a more general and earthly plane, Jerusalem can refer to the Church in her best light, and in particular, for the monks, Jerusalem could stand for their monastic home, vocation, and fraternity, seen as a combined mode of existence. Any of these views corroborate the strong and meaningful maternal image(s) held by Bernard. Another maternal image in this letter hints at a different perspective of motherhood that loosely links the maternal role with death. Bernard insists, "death will suddenly come, like the pains of a woman in labor, and they will not escape it"(1 Thes 5.3).[220] Clearly, Bernard was working with more than one maternal image while writing these passages.

While engaged in a peacemaking mission to Apulia in Campania, Bernard wrote *Letter 144: To the Brothers at Clairvaux*. In this work he identifies his brother monks with the holiest place in the city of Jerusalem. From a dream or vision he recalls, "I was able to see you who are the holy Temple of God."[221] He sets this image of holiness alongside an intimate mother-child image. Feeling his separation from the monks he despairs, "My children are snatched from my breast before it is time. Those whom I have 'begotten' in the Gospel (1 Cor 4.15) I am not allowed to rear."[222] Bernard plays carefully with this image. According to the New American Bible, Paul "fathered" his followers in the Gospel. Bernard uses a term translated as "begotten" to cover the paternal relationship in the Scripture passage, but he also adds a plausibly maternal relationship that is interrupted or thrown into disorder. The mother is not able to nurture her child. A little further down Bernard carries on the familial theme to show the relationship amongst his monks. He mentions that Pope Innocent II "has a fatherly affection for me and for all of you too. And pray for the Lord Chancellor, who is like a mother to me."[223]

This section began with Bernard's relationship with his mother. It ends with a few of his many parental images. But these are not his only images. Perhaps the one common thread running through the workings of Bernard's imagination is that of order. His family images, and specifically maternal images, indicate the place where order became important to him. While he has many meaningful images for the relationship with God, the most significant is the divine image residing in each person. Unfortunately this image is not at present in conformity with the true image of God, and thus the individual's relationship with God is out of order. The relationship among his monks is depicted as participation in a well-ordered society, either within a family or a city. In fact, existence outside the boundaries of that society is described as a wound. When inanimate creation is used in Bernard's imaginative activity, its place is simply to support the movement to higher levels of order, never to participate in them. Participation is for humanity and God alone, but humanity is meant to be in a state of motion away from itself. Images for the self involve an effort at directing the various human attachments into good order through some form of self-control, like a levy guides surging waters. In a final analysis, Bernard's imagination, where it is original, works effectively at supporting the order that is so important to him.

A Preface to Studying Imagination in the Writings of Aelred of Rievaulx

Aelred of Rievaulx has already been introduced as someone who takes an earlier theory of imagination and makes it available to the people of his time. There is, however, something more to Aelred's use of the imagination than just a borrowed idea presented in new wrappings. In business theory there is a concept known as *value added*. In observing a business process one looks to see what additional value has been given to the product as it undergoes a particular step in its production and distribution. With Aelred, knowledge of the imagination and its potential are made available to his religious family in an uncomplicated and easily embraced fashion.

The workings of Aelred's imagination stand as a valuable comparison with Francis' imaginative activity both because of the similarities and differences. Aelred brought the emerging interest in the humanity of Christ one step closer to its high point in the experience of Francis. What Francis is purported to have done with action and gesture at the crib of Greccio, Aelred achieved earlier with words in the first meditation of his *Rule of Life for a Recluse*.[224] Aelred was also very attentive to relationships. In fact, a study comparing Aelred's notions on friendship with Francis' views on fraternity might offer some support to scholars observing the flagging religious vocation rates in many countries. One point where Aelred and Francis differ is a dependence on authorities from the past for the understanding and content of the imagination. Both men rely on Scripture in their own way. This is a standard that goes far in making individual medieval imaginations mutually shareable. It is the conscious, theoretically astute use of the imagination on Aelred's part, as well as his inclusion of imagery from Augustine through Anselm that sets his imagination apart from the more primal imagination of Francis.[225] And beyond this, there is one additional area of interest that may account for a further distinction between Aelred and Francis' use of the imagination. There appears to be a profound disjunction between Aelred and his maternal object representation.

This section will introduce Aelred by a brief description of his youth and his writings followed by a more determined look at the connection between Aelred and his mother. After this, some of Aelred's spiritual writings will be explored for examples of his imaginative activity as it reveals and supports his development of the spiritual life. For Aelred, the spiritual life should be understood as the formation of one's relationship with God and with one's associates who are similarly engaged. Aelred Squire, who studies his namesake's life in detail, notes that it was relationships that sustained his religious journey.[226] However, unlike Francis, Aelred indicates little interest in any relationships with non-personal aspects of created reality.

Aelred's Youth and Formation

Marsha Dutton identifies two papal actions that set the course for Aelred's life. As a result of the Gregorian Reforms and a specific decree by Urban II, not only could priests no longer be married, but also the sons of married priests could only receive Holy Orders as Canons Regular or as monks.[227] These decisions affected the young Aelred in significant ways. In 1110 he was born into the family that had held the stewardship of the Church at Hexham for many generations. In a culture where a son's destiny is tied to his father's occupation, the loss of the family association with this church meant more than just the end of an inheritable source of income; it was also a challenge to Aelred's identity.

To add to the disruption of his formative years, Aelred was sent off to the Scottish Court at the age of 6 or 7. Brian McGuire identifies this event as the source of a significant sense of loss.[228] Nonetheless, Aelred appears to have flourished in this environment according to some estimates. He became a close associate of the royal heir, and he was eventually selected to arrange the official banquets. In this position he would have been in the midst of the political intrigue and actions of his place and time in history. As some of his historical writings demonstrate, this involvement was not something for which he had no interest. All the same, an errand that brought him into contact with the Cistercians altered his life yet again.

Aelred entered the Monastery of Rievaulx where he was eventually promoted to Novice Master. In this role he would have an opportunity to employ his imaginative capabilities as he "set before them [novices] a picture of the hidden possibilities of monastic life attractive enough to sustain their ascetic efforts and fire their enthusiasm."[229] In time he would go on to serve as abbot of this monastic establishment and influence numerous generations of monks with his imaginative approach to God.

Types of Writings

Aelred's writings fall into two categories. He produced a number of historical works in addition to the spiritual writings that are of greatest interest to this study. His historical writings are primarily biographical portraits of leading figures who he considered worthy of emulation.[230] Aelred's historical literature coincides with his continued activity beyond the monastery walls. McGuire observes a notable attachment to history on Aelred's part.[231] Like his predecessor, Bernard, he was regularly involved in affairs of state, seeking reconciliation in times of conflict.[232] In fact, as Dutton points out, Walter Daniel composed Aelred's *vita* in order to counter the growing opinion that the recently deceased Abbot of Rievaulx had put himself too much at the service of the secular world.[233]

Even a brief review of Aelred's spiritual writings makes it clear that, in spite of his efforts beyond the monastery, his heart was with his brothers, bringing them closer to the God whose love he shared with them. Squire comments that, "The list of his writings reads like a list of debts to God and men paid off over the years according to the circumstances and in the manner that each would have wished."[234] Scholars agree that Aelred puts something very personal into his writings. Amédée Hallier finds that Aelred "reveals himself, in his writings," and McGuire adds, "In terms of friendship and union among men, he remained alone in his boldness of expression and fervor of imagination."[235] Squire speaks of "the authentic Aelred, from whose imagination, long disciplined by hours of meditation and reflection, the symbols and images of scripture rise as the most adequate expression of the operative realities in his own life and experience."[236]

In their praise of Aelred's originality, both McGuire and Squire mention his imagination. In his search for a particular theological perspective in Aelred's writings, Hallier also observes a connection with the imagination. Much of his book focuses on an understanding of the individual's relationship to God as an image or likeness of God.[237] Recalling the earlier connection made between rhetoric and the imagination, Dutton finds that Aelred was clearly interested in using rhetorical techniques.[238] Amongst this wide recognition of Aelred's use of imagination to fashion his spiritual view of the world, it is possible to detect some of the distinctions that will stand between Aelred's imaginative activity and that of Francis. Squire states that Aelred's was a "disciplined" imagination, and McGuire highlights the use of his imagination to develop an appreciation for relationships among men. McGuire goes on to add that other Cistercians tended to understand relationships more in maternal terms than paternal terms. When Francis engages his more natural or uncontrived imagination the maternal tendency is evident, which is why some attention will be paid below to the nature of Aelred's relationship with his mother and the possible ramifications this presents.

Relationship with his Mother

If it is true that Aelred provides an insight into his personal life through his writings then it should be possible to perceive something of the nature of his relationship with his mother. McGuire gives a fair amount of attention to this issue since it seems to have some bearing on the kind of spiritual life that Aelred envisions for himself and his brother monks.[239] He comments on Aelred's "life-long fascination with other men in terms of their interior worlds, their intentions, and their concerns."[240] According to McGuire, Aelred shows little concern for women: "unlike some of his contemporaries, Aelred apparently did not have an elevated view of his mother. Nor did he transfer such a vision to the Virgin Mary."[241] Why is it then that women seem to have been set aside in the world Aelred observes? McGuire connects this limited presence with Aelred's early childhood development, entitling one of his chapters "An Absent Mother."[242] While there is sufficient evidence to suggest that Francis had a *good-enough mother*, the same may not have been the case for Aelred.

Based on an incident retold to Aelred by his father, mother, and brothers, McGuire contends that his mother was alive at least until he was 5 or 6.[243] The only reference that Aelred makes to his mother is found in his treatise on *A Rule of Life for a Recluse*. Writing this rule for his sister he speaks of "the evil committed by our parents."[244] McGuire claims this line "suggests that Aelred saw himself as the result of an act that in God's ordering of things should not have taken place."[245] The associated footnote in the Cistercian Publications volume also indicates that this statement refers to his parent's marriage and his father's priesthood. Aelred's strong statement could have been directed toward the illegitimacy of his parent's relationship and hence his own origins, or it could have rested on the defilement of a priesthood that he valued. In either case, such a comment supports the notion that his relationship with his mother was not well founded. As further evidence for a weak relationship, McGuire observes that the only expression of a mother's love is found in Aelred's *When Jesus was Twelve Years Old.*[246] While meditating on Mary's reunion with the lost Jesus, Aelred says to her, "Hold him fast, dearest lady, hold him fast whom you love...."[247] Could this statement, which has a moving power of its own when read in full context, be a clue to something Aelred would like to have inserted into his own childhood?

It is clear that Aelred's interior world is not completely devoid of female images. Object Relations Theory recognizes the possibility that other figures can fulfill the maternal role for an infant. This was certainly the case for Ignatius of Loyola. For Aelred, one possibility was his sister, but if he projects something of his experience of her onto his image of Mary, it is a projection of her as sister and not mother. McGuire identifies this shift of Mary's role from a mother figure to a sister figure. He says, "As a sister, she became more approachable. Aelred knew how to respect and deal with a sister, while he apparently had only a limited sense of a mother's love."[248]

In addition to McGuire's evidence for the idea that the abbot had a poor relationship with his mother, Aelred's *Sermon for the Assumption of Mary* describes the Blessed Mother like a castle with "a stout wall of chastity," a tower of charity, and a moat of humility.[249] A comparison of this imagery to the lifestyle of a recluse that he fashions for his sister is further verification of the sororal perception he had of Mary. In any instance, this is not proof that Aelred's sister filled the maternal void that McGuire indicates. The *Rule of Life for a Recluse* contains additional biographical information that substantiates a poor maternal relationship without clarifying the problem. While Aelred reveals that his sister was known to scold his miscreant behavior, a potentially parental role, he still maintains that they "were brought up by our parents."[250] How many years of upbringing this suggests is unclear. Aelred also confirms that his mother had difficulty in child bearing. She produced non-surviving premature children and stillborn children.[251] These complications leave open the possibility of her early death or an intentional distancing from the pain of potential further loss. More telling is another statement he makes in the midst of these details. He writes, "the same father begot us, the same womb bore us and gave us life."[252] Why is it that he identifies his father as "father" and his mother with the utilitarian term of "womb?"

Without specifying the involvement of Aelred's father or a brother, McGuire suggests that he formed his vision of the world on the basis of some form of male interrelationship. Noting passages in Aelred's writing that demonstrate an intense and complete bond with Jesus, McGuire asserts, "he did not suffer from an absent or silent mother. For him the primary bonds of his life were with men."[253] McGuire goes on to suggest that Aelred may have discovered a form of motherhood in Jesus.[254] Such a discovery may not have been original to Aelred, however, and, therefore, it may not be a prominent feature of his interior life. Squire explains that monks of Aelred's period sought a "complete ascesis," a linking of one's concupiscence to the Lord's flesh, generally using maternal terms. Squire attributes the first use of this terminology to Anselm.[255] Regardless of the origins of this linkage, Aelred's limited use of positive maternal imagery for any of his relationships leaves the male bond as his primary experience.

Perhaps Aelred did fashion his infantile world through interaction with men! The spiritual view of the world that he developed as a mature religious leader hints at this possibility. McGuire insists that Aelred went to Rievaulx "in order to seek out like-minded men with whom he could share his need for the love of God and the love of other men."[256] Those who know of Aelred today probably think of him foremost for his attempt to formulate a spirituality of friendship. If the imaginative, ongoing creation of one's perception of reality involves an attempt to find purpose or meaning in one's experience, Aelred uses friendship as a principal vehicle for this endeavor. McGuire points out that he seeks order in friendship, and deep friendship between men becomes idealized as a new way of seeing, the basis of community, and also a foretaste of paradise.[257]

From the foregoing discussion alone, it is obvious that Aelred's imagination is informed by a unique combination of influences. He enters deeply into a well-established lifestyle that intends to conform the imagination through rule, ritual, and reflection. He is reasonably well read, and before his vocation he commands a fairly wide-ranging view of the world. Perhaps, most significantly, as he is introduced to reality while forming it simultaneously in his interior world, something else may have happened. That trusting interactive environment where mother and child identify as actual what is otherwise only possible might have lacked a *good-enough* quality. Fortunately, this environment is sustained in some other way, and Aelred is able to develop a notable imaginative capacity as the following exploration of the workings of his imagination bears out.

A View of Select Writings through the Lens of Imagination

In this study Aelred's imaginative activity will be probed by revealing images in his writing that exhibit a degree of originality and signify the way one might relate to God, a maternal figure, fellow religious, and the rest of created reality. These categories, which are not equally represented in each text selection, will permit a more thorough comparison to Francis' imagination. This is not an exhaustive survey since his style of imagination is rich enough in its own way to possibly warrant an entire volume. Missing from this review will be the many vibrant images that can clearly be attributed to earlier sources. Examples are plentiful throughout his work, and therefore none will be highlighted below.

Some of Aelred's richest imagery is found in his treatises. In his *Pastoral Prayer* he is attempting to express the position in which he stands between God and his monks. Although he calls the brethren his family, the relationship is not one based on a creative act but on domination, more like a lower noble placed over an estate by a higher noble. Using a Gospel passage (MT 24.35) he proclaims, "And you, sweet Lord, have set a man like this over your family."[258] He goes on to explain that Jesus places him in charge of the household "to rule it well through him."[259] While viewing himself as head of a house, Aelred provides three images that he would have God take on in reference to himself. He beseeches God to see him "as a good physician sees, intent upon my healing, or else a kind master, anxious to correct, or a forbearing father, longing to forgive."[260] In each of these cases Aelred envisions himself as somehow broken and God, who is thoroughly male, as capable of reconstructing him.

Much of Aelred's most intriguing maternal imagery is contained in his meditative treatise commonly called *When Jesus was Twelve Years Old*, based on Jesus' three days of separation from his family in Jerusalem. Often Aelred's imaginative activity can be discerned in the dialogue he attributes to various characters in addition to images in the stricter sense. Early in the text he has Ivo, a fellow monk for whom the meditation was created, asking the question of a good, concerned parent: "O dear boy, where were you? Where were you hiding? Who gave you shelter?"[261] When Aelred turns his own questions toward Jesus, he begins by taking Mary's side and scolds Jesus: "You did not have compassion on your most holy Mother as she looked for you, grieved for you, sighed for you?"[262] Before Aelred turns directly to Mary with a rebuke, it should be noticed that Mary's response of looking, grieving, and sighing denotes a sense of permanent loss if not even an expression of mourning.

If there is an autobiographical hint at the nature of Aelred's relationship with his mother than it may be found in a very pointed statement that he makes to Mary: "Indeed, my Lady, if you will allow me to say so, why did you lose your dearest Son so easily, why did you watch over him with such little care, why were you so late in noticing that he was missing?"[263] Where McGuire sees loss there is also clearly a note of blame and an insight into the gentle care Aelred was known to provide the monks under his guidance as a way of making up for what he had missed out on himself. When Mary eventually finds Jesus and is instructed to "hold him fast...," Aelred also relates the absence of her child "to the greatest pain."[264] This is interesting since the words are taken in part from the *Song of Songs* which simply says, "I held him fast and would not let him go"(Sg 3.4). The originality of this image is found in the application of the additional words to an otherwise unrelated imagined encounter between Mary and her lost son and in the assertion that this loss had caused "the greatest pain." If Aelred's spirituality could be understood by this treatise alone it would be described as a spirituality of loss and restoration.

Aelred's more lengthy text, *On the Soul*, associates the individual's relationship to God with the presence of the divine image in each soul. The abbot uses a different kind of imagery to explain this imminent presence in *When Jesus was Twelve Years Old*. In words that are a forerunner to Francis' experience of Christ in each person he meets, Aelred writes, "For just as the Lord Jesus is born and conceived in us, so he grows and is nourished in us, until we all come to perfect manhood, that maturity which is proportioned to the complete growth of Christ."[265] If Aelred held the notion, common to his time, that men alone were responsible for generativity and women merely received a fertilized seed until it blossomed into a child, then this passage entrusts the complete process to him and his brother monks. A footnote to this text refers to Gueric of Igny's idea that this was a participation in Mary's maternity.[266] The earlier development of McGuire's absent-mother theory suggests this may not be the case, as does the end result of this birthing process, the monk's growth "to perfect manhood." Beyond seeing his monks as bearers of Christ, Aelred adds a fraternal connection that he would have each of them make with Jesus. Borrowing again from the *Song of Songs* he calls out, "Who will grant me to have you as my brother, sucking my mother's breast, to find you outside and kiss you"(Sg 8.1)? Has he intentionally chosen this passage for its movement away from the gentleness of the mother's presence to tenderness in each other's company? In its complete context the Biblical passage includes a return to the chamber of the mother.

Moving from the historical exposition of Jesus' loss in the temple event to its allegorical or spiritual explanation, Aelred provides more negative maternal imagery as he links the monks with "the Church of the Gentiles," those who have accepted Jesus. Here, Jesus' journey to Jerusalem is understood as his departure from the "Synagogue" to be with "the Church of the Gentiles."[267] Aelred goes on to say, "Jesus will be found by his mother, the Synagogue, as she enters the Temple, that is the Church."[268] Although a ray of hope is offered to the mother, since she enters the Temple, the allegorical association of the synagogue with the rejection of Jesus the savior and the mother with the rejection of Jesus the child further evinces the unique role Aelred's maternal image plays in his imaginative activity.

Applying the moral sense of Scripture to Jesus' loss in the Temple, Aelred provides a method to encounter God in solitude. He suggests "entering into the inner room of your heart so as to find there a cave in which after a fashion you may be buried to everything which is of the world and pray to your Father in secret."[269] This passage includes an image from nature and links it with a death image, the burial chamber. The implication that one is ultimately able to relate to God only through death stands out more powerfully than the nature image of the cave. Most of Aelred's imagery taken from the category of created reality, like the cave image, serves as a support to the more significant relationships he expresses with God, the mother figure, and his monks. Aelred attempts to draw his listener into a relationship of compassion and admiration with the infant Jesus. He writes, "If with the eyes of an enlightened mind you look at him lying in the manger, crying in his mother's arms, hanging at her breast, a little child in Simeon's arms, admire the works of his goodness."[270] True to the imaginative tradition he inherited, Aelred begins this line with an emphasis on the use of reason in the practice of intentional imagining. This passage is also another expression of the type of spiritual vision of the world found in Aelred's writings. There is an experience of separation; either Jesus is not with his mother, or if he is, the interaction lacks a symbiotic quality—he cries or he hangs. It is only when the infant is taken into a man's arms that the discomforting description stops. In the very next paragraph Aelred gives a hint at what lies behind his negative maternal imagery. He moves suddenly to a consideration of the woman who anointed Jesus' feet. He calls her a "blessed sinner" right after describing her lips as "defiled by the filth of so many sins."[271] The slightly positive connotation found in the term "blessed sinner" contrasts with the very disapproving description of her mouth. Object Relations Theory could explain this as a combination of two opposing object representations.

A beautiful meditation is included in Aelred's *Rule of Life for a Recluse*. He encourages his sister to come closer to Christ by an imaginative participation in his life. Even before Jesus' birth, when Mary meets Elizabeth, he tells his sister, "Run, I beg, run and take part in such joy, prostrate yourself at the feet of both, in the womb of the one embrace your Bridegroom, in the womb of the other do honor to his friend."[272] It might be that Aelred was offering his sister some sustaining imagery for her life in a womb-like enclosure, but he is also implying that one can relate to Christ both as a marriage partner and as a sibling who has shared the same womb. It is not only the womb image he proposes for his sister's dwelling. He speaks of the "holes in the wall of his [Jesus'] body, in which, like a dove, you may hide while you kiss them [wounds] one by one."[273] If the two dwelling images can be considered together the womb is a place of suffering, a place to hide, and also a place to encounter Jesus.

Aelred's *Dialogue on the Soul* is the source for most of what is known of his theoretical approach to the imagination, which was covered in the beginning of this chapter. Like his other theologically oriented texts, he is particularly careful in this one to avoid falling into error by relying heavily on the authority of earlier thinkers. Unfortunately, where images are utilized to better convey an understanding, he also uses the images his sources used. While this work is indicative of his awareness of the imaginary visions of others, it presents few examples of his own. At one point, in a likely autobiographical statement, he has his dialogue partner consider his own unworthiness for eternal life. But even the looming image of this personal fear is expressed in a scriptural phrase: "Dark shadows have encompassed me" (PS 55.5).[274]

Written early in Aelred's career, *The Mirror of Charity* provides a fairly scholarly, image-based description of the individual's relationship with God, but it is also the best source for an understanding of Aelred's view on relationships with created reality. The only notable reference to a maternal figure places Jesus in this role. Aelred directs his readers with exhausted spirits to "hasten to the maternal breast of Jesus in earnest, devoted prayer."[275] To explain a more theological relationship with God he bounces from biblical image to biblical image. In this manner he is able to explain, like Bernard before him, that each person is linked with God by the presence of the image of God contained within his or her soul. It is a misuse of the free choice to love true goodness that leaves this image of God disfigured.[276] In short, this text employs a substantial amount of biblical imagery at the service of a philosophical discussion of free choice as the basis of charity.

In one development on a Psalm passage (Ps 1:3), Aelred adds some of his own imagery to describe the loss of the pure image and its restoration.

> Think, I ask you, of the entire human race as a dry tree trunk, fruitless and blighted to the roots because infected by the venom of the ancient serpent; this is very justly consigned to the flames, destined for the fire, sentenced to condemnation. What follows? You show your ingratitude, useless trunk, that some twigs pruned from your dead roots are snatched from the blaze to be grafted onto a fruitful trunk like shoots and restored to their original beauty.[277]

Images from created reality, as found in this passage, are often taken from common events. Aelred has clearly had the experience of both eradicating diseased trees and grafting from one tree to another. Time spent in front of the fire made him think of the annihilation of those who lose their true image of God, and, through another aspect, the fire also reminds him of the way humanity is intended to relate to the divine. Describing the love of self, neighbor, and God as fire he explains, "these three loves are engendered by one another, nourished by one another, and fanned into flame by one another."[278] This is obviously a nearer union than the one he uses for close friendship. He mentions "the knot of a certain friendship" that held his attention earlier in life.[279] While Aelred draws on aspects from created reality to point toward the nature of relationships with other individuals and with God, the non-personal elements of created reality are always given an unmistakably subordinate role in his imaginative activity. These elements never seem to actually participate in the relationships as they sometimes do in Francis' writings. At most, they signify a relationship as do the fire or the rope mentioned previously.

Aelred explains his thoughts on the lower relationships within created reality very clearly as he addresses God.

> Creatures without reason or without sensation cannot love you; that is not their way. Of course they also have their own way, their beauty and their order, not that thereby they are or can be happy by loving you, but that thereby, thanks to you, by their goodness, form, and order they may advance the glory of those creatures who can be happy because they can love You.[280]

At most, one could say that created elements, such as animals, plants, and fire, fit into a relationship with the rest of reality only insofar as they maintain their proper place in the order of things. Aelred adds that when the proper relationship is realized each thing "tends toward its own order, seeks its own place."[281] The strongest reason he gives for segregating relationships among created elements from the higher forms of relationships between two people and between a person and God lies in his concern over attachments. Aelred expresses the idea that an attachment to something that does not allow for transcendence of the self can cause one's soul to find itself ordered according to that to which it is attached. The abbot explains, "Self-centeredness presses him downward and everything he clings to continually pushes him by its natural heaviness toward the lowest things."[282] Aelred shares this penchant for order with Bernard, and it is one reason for the lack of surprisingly unique image-associations made in their writings.

Aelred draws many of his images from his time spent preparing for the royal banquets. Regarding the spiritual life he speaks of tasting with "an inward palate," and to God he says, "You gradually became tasty to my palate."[283] Perhaps recalling scenes of unsophisticated dining he writes, "By the dreadful gnawing of the passions it tears and bloodies the poor soul."[284] Bernard also recognizes Aelred's formation in a culinary atmosphere. In a preface to Aelred's work, where the senior monk requests that he write about charity, Bernard comments that Aelred has "come to the desert not from the schools but from the kitchens."[285]

Aelred's *Liturgical Sermons* are replete with images, but as M. Basil Pennington points out, these texts are clearly less imaginative than *When Jesus was Twelve Years Old* and *A Rule of Life for a Recluse*.[286] Pennington observes that Aelred begins with a theme that brings to mind scriptural images that he is, in turn, able to relate back to the theme.[287] While reading these sermons it is possible to sense Aelred's perception of the unity of Scripture as something much more pervasive than is made obvious by homiletic styles popular today. The sermons are also an indication of how deeply medieval people entered into and even anticipated an allegorical meaning of Scripture. At one point Aelred reminds his readers, "To use the word 'thigh' for progeny is common enough in Scripture."[288] While the kind of imaginative activity involved in the sermons is not specifically original, it does require the imaginative capacity of the homilist to visualize the connections between two images in the Bible, and it also necessitates the ability of listeners to enter into an imaginative state where they can also envision and accept the associations that are put before them. Sometimes this activity demands a stretching of the imagination. In his *Sermon for the Coming of the Lord*, Aelred refers to a passage in Matthew (Mt 21:7) where clothes are placed on the ass and colt for Jesus' entry into Jerusalem. While it is suspected that most modern readers would not look past the clothes as signifying the regal nature of Christ's triumphant entry, Aelred looks further. He says, "These clothes signify the faith and the teaching of the apostles and the prophets through which the humanity of Christ, as it were, a kind of weakness, hides knowledge of the divinity."[289] In another sermon Aelred expands an image in a less drastic fashion to further exemplify his divine image in the human soul theory. *The Sermon for the Nativity of the Lord* recalls the tax census at the time of Jesus' birth. Here Aelred describes the silver coin demanded by the emperor as standing for the individual's soul. He exclaims, "Doubtless it is our soul, which bears within itself his image."[290] Then Aelred goes on to reveal the process through which the right relationship with God will be restored by way of a return of the coin with its image still discernible. "Blessed is someone who pays him his tribute, who gives him his silver coin, who restores his image to him. You see brothers, throughout the world people are racing to the officials of our emperor to be considered worthy of being registered in that glorious city on high and to give back to him his image—that is, their souls."[291]

The last work of Aelred's to be considered in this chapter is his *Spiritual Friendship*. It is modeled unabashedly on Cicero's *de amicita*, and it is recognized for its lack of allegorical interpretation.[292] These conditions limit the degree of originality in his imaginative activity where such activity can be discerned. One noteworthy image Aelred develops is that of a society, an association for common good. He uses this image to defend his belief in God's positive intention towards human friendship, and he extends the relationship of friendship to all of creation. Aelred writes, "he has left no type of being alone, but out of many has drawn them together by means of a certain society."[293] He adds, "And so even in inanimate nature a certain love of companionship, so to speak, is apparent, since none of these exists alone but everything is created and thrives in a certain society with its own kind."[294] Aelred here, again, segregates the relationships with and among elements of created reality on a lower level of their own, and, in a later chapter of the text, he assigns inanimate nature to a supporting role, as he has elsewhere. He instructs his dialogue partner to imagine himself in a world like the Garden of Eden with no other inhabitants. Then he asks him if he could enjoy the countless possibilities at his disposal.[295] In this case, the countless possibilities represent relationships with inanimate nature, which, in any instance, are not sufficient to sustain his happiness and well-being. These relationships are meant to exist as a sub-context to higher orders of relationship.

There are two final images that may share an interesting connection as this survey of Aelred's imaginative activity comes to a conclusion. Aelred advances the notion of a "mirror of friendship," suggesting that the friendship of two people is something visible in the sense that it can be reflected, but not dictated or defined.[296] Like the maternal image(s) in Aelred's interior world, the reflection is there, and it is perceptible, but it lacks the substance by which it might be embraced. A final image of relationship that Aelred offers is that of a facial expression. He observes that close friends sometimes share a likeness of expression.[297] Was Aelred looking among his brother monks for the mirror that would, in relationship, reflect back to him the face in which he first discovered that the world has meaning and value for him? And with whose face did he most naturally share his first expressions? If Aelred's unusual use of maternal imagery is a fair indication of a disjunction in his maternal relationship, who first taught Aelred to imaginatively fashion the world of which he was so much a part?

Summary

In the first section of this chapter theories of imagination are studied for their influence on medieval imaginations like those of Francis, Bernard, and Aelred. This study also provides a base from which a more advanced understanding of imagination can be developed. The second section considered various possible influences on popular medieval imaginations, while the third section delved into the imaginative activity of Bernard of Clairvaux and Aelred of Rievaulx. Bernard's imagination was recognized by the well-ordered arrangement of images, but it was somewhat constrained by a heavy reliance on known sources of imagery. The presence of maternal imagery in his writings suggested that his imagination was, like Francis', informed in part by his earliest relationship. Aelred's imagery was in many places similar to Bernard's, but his distressing use of maternal imagery indicated a period of early development that leads him to orient much of his imagery around male relationships. Is it possible that a male surrogate supported Aelred through his infancy without instilling in him a positive mental representation of a maternal figure? While no specific answer is available, attention was drawn to the critical early childhood period of imaginative formation identified by Object Relations Theory. As a final step prior to a thorough review of this theory other recent approaches to the imagination will be described in the next chapter. This effort will locate ORT in relationship with other views of the imagination and allow its unique vantage point to stand out.

Notes

1. Raymond Studzinski, "Tutoring the Religious Imagination," *Horizons* 14, no. 1 (1987).

2. Murray W. Bundy, *The Theory of Imagination in Classical and Mediaeval Thought* (Urbana: University of Chicago Press, 1927), 177. Reprints: (Urbana: Folcroft Library, 1970, 1976, 1980); (Norwood PA: Norwood Editions, 1976, 1978).

3. Note the numerous reprints. His work is also a featured source for the Northwestern University Program in the Study of Imagination and the Toronto School of Communications McLuhan Program. The majority of historical surveys of imagination theory begin with the enlightenment or the romantic period. Bundy's reach into classical thought sets his work apart. The closest work which might be considered an update to Bundy's book is Gerard Watson's *Phantasia in Classical Thought*. Watson focuses primarily on classical thinkers and admits to not discovering Bundy's book until he was nearly finished with his own. He praises it with the phrase: "I have learnt much from it." See Gerard Watson, *Phantasia in Classical Thought*, (Galway: Galway University Press, 1988), fn. 3.

4. Bundy, 11*ff.*

5. Ibid.

6. Ibid., 27.

7. Ibid., 42.

8. Ibid., 82.

9. Gerard Watson, *Phantasia in Classical Thought*, 3, 6.

10. Ibid., 7. *Aisthēsis* is the particular term that can mean both sensation and perception. Throughout his work Watson uses transliteration versus a direct attempt at translation, therefore there are very few direct quotes from the original philosophers.

11. Ibid.

12. Ibid., 7-8.

13. Ibid., 9

14. Ibid.

15. Gerard Watson, "Imagination and Religion in Classical Thought," in Religious *Imagination*, ed. James P. Mackey, 29-54 (Edinburgh: Edinburgh University Press, 1986): 29.

16. Ibid.

17. Watson, *Phantasia in Classical Thought*, 9-10

18. John Dillon, "Plotinus and the Transcendental Imagination," in *Religious Imagination*, ed. James P. Mackey (Edinburgh: Edinburgh University Press, 1986): 55.

19. Bundy, 61.

20. Ibid., 65.

21. Ibid., 81.

22. Ibid., 82.

23. Watson, *Phantasia in Classical Thought*, 15.

24. Ibid.

25. Ibid., 18, 19.

26. Ibid., 21.

27. Ibid., 26.

28. Ibid., 32.

29. Bundy, 19.

30. Ibid., 89-90.

31. Although Augustine is considered to be part of the Patristic Age, his influence on medieval theories of imagination was so profound that he will be studied in relationship to this era.

32. James P. Mackey, "Introduction," in *Religious Imagination*, ed. James P. Mackey (Edinburgh: Edinburgh University Press, 1986): 22.

33. Douglas Kelly, *Medieval Imagination: Rhetoric and the Poetry of Courtly Love* (Madison: University of Wisconsin Press, 1978), 30.

34. Watson points out that memory plays a part in Aristotle's views on *phantasia*, such that both belong to the same part of the soul. See: Watson, *Phantasia in Classical Thought*, 29.

35. Bundy, 106, 110.

36. Philostratus, *Life of Apolonius*, 2.77 in Bundy, 114.

37. Bundy, 118-119.

38. Plotinus, *Enneads*, IV.13 in Dillon, 61.

39. Bundy, 122.

40. Ibid., 128.

41. Ibid., 128.

42. Watson, *Phantasia in Classical Thought*, 96, 103.

43. Ibid., 96.

44. Ibid., 99, 101.

45. Ibid., 102.

46. Ibid., 98.

47. Ibid., 101.

48. Bundy, 158.

49. Watson, *Phantasia in Classical Thought*, 138.

50. Bundy, 158-159.

51. Watson, *Phantasia in Classical Thought*, 147. Watson describes three features of the transition from corporeal vision to *visio spiritualis*. "1) the object itself, 2)the visio which did not exist before we became aware of that object brought before the sense, and 3) the *anima intentio*, the concentration of the mind, also called the will, *voluntas...* which keeps the first two together." See Watson, *Phantasia in Classical Thought*, 139. This concept of concentrating the mind will be seen as a primary focus of many more modern approaches to imagination.

52. Bundy, 163-165.

53. Ibid., 165.

54. Ibid., 166.

55. Watson, *Phantasia in Classical Thought*, 147.

56. Ibid., 148.

57. Bundy, 176, 173.

58. Kelly, 27.

59. Ibid.

60. Watson, *Phantasia in Classical Thought*, 154.

61. Bundy, 173; Watson, *Phantasia in Classical Thought*, 153.

62. Bundy, 177.

63. Ibid., 178.

64. Ibid.

65. Ibid., 179-180.

66. Ibid., 182.

67. Watson points out that Plato made the association between the imagination and the body much earlier. In particular, he points to the role of the liver. See: Watson, *Phantasia in Classical Thought*, 11.

68. C.H. Talbot, Introduction to *Dialogue on the Soul*, by Aelred of Rievaulx, trans. C.H. Talbot (Kalamazoo: Cistercian Publications, 1981), 10-11, 23. In turn, many of these ideas can be further traced to classical sources as an earlier section of this work asserted.

69. Ibid., 10.

70. Aelred of Rievaulx, *Dialogue on the Soul*, trans. C.H. Talbot (Kalamazoo: Cistercian Publications, 1981), 78-7-, 84.

71. Ibid., 50.

72. Talbot, 13.

73. Aelred of Rievaulx, *Dialogue*, 130.

74. Ibid., 77.

75. Talbot, 15.

76. Aelred of Rievaulx, *Dialogue*, 118.

77. Ibid., 117.

78. Talbot, 13.

79. Aelred of Rievaulx, *Dialogue*, 78.

80. Talbot, 13.

81. Aelred of Rievaulx, *Dialogue*, 41.

82. Richard K. Emerson and Ronald B. Herzman, *The Apocalyptic Imagination in Medieval Literature* (Philadelphia: University of Pennsylvania Press, 1992).

83. Ibid., 22.

84. Ibid.

85. Ibid., 1.

86. Ibid., 5.

87. Ibid., 23, 41.

88. Ibid., 8.

89. Ibid., 16.

90. Ibid., 26. The authors take this comparison from Rev 12.2 and 17.

91. Ibid., 34.

92. Jacques LeGoff, *The Medieval Imagination*, trans. Arthur Goldhammer (Chicago: University of Chicago Press, 1988). While French language conventions support the use of the article in the original title, LeGoff tends to describe imaginative activity during the Middle Ages as if there was a universal imagination that everyone shared. Although some elements of each person's imagination must be capable of common expression for the sake of social interaction, universalizing the imagination is falsely restrictive of an aspect of personality that is not normally open to restriction.

93. Ibid., 5.

94. Ibid., 1.

95. Ibid.

96. Ibid.

97. Ibid., 6.

98. Ibid., 5.

99. Ibid., 10. The period runs from 1000-1400 and includes the roughly two hundred years on either side of Francis' life.

100. Ibid., 129.

101. Ibid., 70.

102. Ibid., 179.

103. Ibid., 56.

104. Ibid., 50.

105 .Ibid., 52, 54.

106. Ibid., 58, 53.

107. Francis of Assisi, *The Testament of St Francis*, in Marion Habig, ed. *St. Francis of Assisi: Writings and Early Biographies: English Omnibus of Sources for the Life of St. Francis.* (Quincy, IL: Franciscan University Press, 1991), 67.

108. LeGoff, 109.

109. Ibid., 107-108.

110. Frugoni, *Francis of Assisi: A Life*, 15.

111. Anthony Mockler, *Francis of Assisi: The Wandering Years* (New York: E.P. Dutton, 1976), 42. Mockler does not contend that Francis directly carried on any of the Cathar beliefs, nor does he maintain that the troubadours were directly involved in the advancement of these sects.

112. LeGoff, 84.

113. Ibid., 110.

114. Ibid., 150, 138.

115. Kelly, 30. Although memory refers to things no longer visible, it is distinct from the use of imagination to visualize that which was never available for visualization.

116. Ibid., 29.

117. Ibid., 30-31.

118. Ibid., 31.

119. Ibid., 32.

120. Ibid., 44. The idea of a *trouvére*, one who gathers or finds, expresses the concept of mature imaginative activity from an ORT perspective in which the person draws together mental representations, both old and recent, to give meaning and expression to a current experience.

121. Brian Patrick McGuire, *Brother and Lover: Aelred of Rievaulx* (New York: Crossroad, 1994), 28.

122. One of Bernard's most recognized works is a series of sermons on the Song of Songs. He expands the imaginative, allegorical relationship of two lovers in amazing ways. Since his imaginative development of the images contained in this series could fill many chapters by itself, I have chosen to concentrate on other, often less well known texts.

123. G.G, Coulton, *Two Saints: St. Bernard and St. Francis* (Cambridge: Cambridge University Press, 1932), 19.

124. Ibid., 103. Francis did look back to the Bible for the basis of his principles, but, as an established religious lifestyle, his approach had no single and distinctive predecessor.

125. G.R. Evans, *Bernard of Clairvaux* (New York: Oxford University Press, 2000), 9.

126. Ibid., 77.

127. Dennis E. Tamburello, *Bernard of Clairvaux: Essential Writings* (New York: Crossroad, 2000), 18.

128. Adriaan Bredero, *Bernard of Clairvaux: Between Cult and History* (Edinburgh: T and T Clark, 1996), 186. "Reformer" is an appropriate description of Bernard since he sought a return to basic principles within existing structures. Francis might arguably be called a transformer since he sought to operate outside certain structures.

129. Evans, *Bernard of Clairvaux*, 8.

130. Poverty is abstract as an ideal. As a lived non-voluntary experience, I suspect that it is all too real and concrete while the essential elements for life quickly take on an abstract quality.

131. Evans, *Bernard of Clairvaux*, 7.

132. Jean LeClercq, "Introduction," in *Bernard of Clairvaux: Selected Works*, pref. Ewert H. Cousins, trans. G.R. Evans (New York: Paulist Press, 1987), 16. Excerpts from Bernard of Clairvaux, translated by G.R. Evans, Copyright @ 1987 by Gillian R. Evans. Paulist Press, Inc., New York/Mahwah, NJ. Reprinted by permission of Paulist Press, Inc. www.paulistpress.com

133. Evans, *Bernard of Clairvaux*, 17.

134. Coulton, 2.

135. Ewert Cousins, "Preface," in *Bernard of Clairvaux: Selected Works*, trans. G.R. Evans, intro. Jean LeClercq (New York: Paulist Press, 1987), 5.

136. Tamburello, 33.

137. Evans, *Bernard of Clairvaux*, 46-47.

138. Ibid., 44.

139. Luke Anderson, "The Rhetorical Epistemology in Saint Bernard's Super Cantica," in *Bernardus Magister: Papers Presented on the Nonacentenary of the Birth of Saint Bernard of Clairvaux*, p. 95-128, ed. John R. Sommerfeldt (Spencer MA: Cistercian Publications, 1992): 96.

140. Burcht Pranger, "The Concept of Death in Bernard's Sermons on the Song of Songs," in *Bernardus Magister: Papers Presented on the Nonacentenary of the Birth of Saint Bernard of Clairvaux*, p. 85-93, ed. John R. Sommerfeldt (Spencer MA: Cistercian Publications, 1992): 86.

141. Chapter Three will cover this advent in detail. As the first section of the current chapter points out, imagination was only associated with lower forms of knowing.

142. LeClercq, "Introduction," in *Bernard of Clairvaux: Selected Works*, 30.

143. Bernard of Clairvaux, "Commentary on the Song of Songs." Full Text of St. Bernard's Commentary on the Song of Songs. Internet Archive. 28 December 2009 <http://www.archive.org/stream/StBernardsCommentaryOnTheSongOfSongs/StBernard OnTheSongOfSongsall_djvu.txt> . 16:1

144. Tamburello, 37.

145. G.R. Evans, *The Mind of St Bernard* (Oxford: Clarendon Press, 1983), 52-53.

146. Ibid.

147. LeClercq, "Introduction," in *Bernard of Clairvaux: Selected Works*, 38.

148. Evans, *Bernard of Clairvaux*, 28.

149. LeClercq, "Introduction," in *Bernard of Clairvaux: Selected Works*, 30.

150. Evans, *Bernard of Clairvaux*, 42-43; LeClercq, "Introduction," in *Bernard of Clairvaux: Selected Works*, 16.

151. Evans, *The Mind of St. Bernard*, 42-43.

152. Evans, *Bernard of Clairvaux*, 4.

153. Evans, *The Mind of St. Bernard*, 54.

154. Ibid., 61.

155. Ibid.

156. It must be clarified that Bernard's insistence on order did not preclude him from challenging what appeared to be the existing order of monastic life in his time. As a master of change, he did not seek to bring about a new way of living the monastic life, he sought a return to an existing way of carrying out that lifestyle, a strict interpretation of the *Rule of Benedict*.

157. LeClercq, "Introduction," in *Bernard of Clairvaux: Selected Works*, 35.

158. Cousins, in *Bernard of Clairvaux: Selected Works* 5.

159. Bredero, 10.

160. LeClercq, "Introduction," in *Bernard of Clairvaux: Selected Works*, 7.

161. Evans, *Bernard of Clairvaux*, 44.

162. Evans, *The Mind of St. Bernard*, 74.

163. Evans, *Bernard of Clairvaux*, 29. I argue, differently, that Bernard's images certainly came from the Bible, but he elaborated them or expanded them in such a way that they were definitely developments from Biblical imagery.

164. LeClercq, "Introduction," in *Bernard of Clairvaux: Selected Works*, 32. Emphasis mine.

165. Anderson, 116.

166. Cousins, in *Bernard of Clairvaux: Selected Works*, 10.

167. Evans, *The Mind of St. Bernard*, 68.

168. Pranger, 86.

169. Predictability and proportion are forms of order.

170. This type of image-association is not as notable in the works of Aelred of Rievaulx and will not be covered in the review of his work. This is not to say that Aelred was not concerned with issues pertaining to the development of the "self." Bernard simply uses imagery to exemplify his expressions of the self.

171. Bernard of Clairvaux, *On Grace and Free Choice*, trans. Daniel O'Donovan (Kalamazoo: Cistercian Publications, 1988), 58.

172. Ibid., 57.

173. Ibid.

174. Bernard of Clairvaux, *On Consideration*, trans. George Lewis (Oxford: Clarendon Press, 1908), v, xii, 26.

175. Bernard of Clairvaux, "On Loving God," in *Bernard of Clairvaux: Selected Works*, pref. Ewert H. Cousins, trans. G.R. Evans, intro. Jean LeClercq (New York: Paulist Press, 1987), 182.

176. Ibid., 190.

177. Ibid., 186.

178. Ibid., 184.

179. Ibid., 186.

180. Ibid., 196.

181. Ibid., 197.

182. Ibid., 192.

183. Ibid., 180.

184. Ibid.

185. Ibid., 178.

186. Ibid.

187. Bernard of Clairvaux, *On Grace and Free Choice*, 88.

188. Ibid., 89.

189. Ibid., 90.

190. Ibid., 80.

191. Ibid., 70.

192. Ibid., 97.

193. Bernard of Clairvaux, *On Consideration*, 14.

194. Ibid., II, vi, 9.

195. Ibid., II,ix,18

196. Ibid.

197. Ibid., I,v,6.

198. Ibid., IV, vi, 20.

199. Ibid., II,iii,6.

200. Ibid., 7.

201. Ibid.

202. Ibid.

203. Ibid., III.v.20.

204. Bernard of Clairvaux, "On Humility and Pride," in *Bernard of Clairvaux: Selected Works*, pref. Ewert H. Cousins, trans. G.R. Evans, intro. Jean LeClercq (New York: Paulist Press, 1987), 121-122.

205. Ibid., 117.

206. Ibid., 130.

207. Ibid., 126.

208. Ibid., 128.

209. Ibid., 102.

210. Ibid.

211. Ibid.

212. Ibid., 112.

213. Ibid., 103.

214. Ibid., 103.

215. Ibid., 132.

216. Ibid.

217. Bernard of Clairvaux, "Letter 64: To Alexander, Bishop of Lincoln," in *Bernard of Clairvaux: Selected Works*, pref. Ewert H. Cousins, trans. G.R. Evans, intro. Jean LeClercq (New York: Paulist Press, 1987), 281.

218. Ibid., 282. I would like to emphasize the connection between citizenship and a responsibility to uphold the social order. Crime, in the Middle Ages, was generally understood in terms of disturbing the peace in one form or another. Disturbing the peace was not a matter of making loud noise so much as threatening the peace of good order. In practice, justice was not the first concern of communal leaders.

219. I recognize that the idea of male-female complementarity is not easily accepted in the current day and age, however, in Bernard's time, with his interest in discovering an order for all things, balancing a masculine natured personhood with a feminine natured place/location, is not too far-fetched.

220. Ibid.

221. Bernard of Clairvaux, "Letter 144: To the Brothers at Clairvaux," in *Bernard of Clairvaux: Selected Works*, pref. Ewert H. Cousins, trans. G.R. Evans, intro. Jean LeClercq (New York: Paulist Press, 1987), 284.

222. Ibid., 284.

223. Ibid., 285. The Lord Chancellor was Aimeric at whose request Bernard wrote *On Loving God*.

224. Aelred of Rievaulx, "Treatise Concerning a Rule for a Recluse," in *Aelred of Rievaulx: Treatises*, trans. Mary Paul Macpherson (Spencer, MA: Cistercian Publications, 1971), 81ff.

225. This careful and intentional theoretically based use of the imagination is the strongest connection between Aelred and Bernard's exercise of the imagination.

226. Aelred Squire, *Aelred of Rievaulx: A Study* (London: SPCK, 1969), 99. This work is a good, broad introduction to Aelred's life.

227. Marsha Dutton, "Introduction," *The Life of Aelred of Rievaulx*, by Walter Daniel, trans. F.M. Powicke (Kalamazoo: Cistercian Publications, 1994), 8.

228. McGuire, 29-30.

229. Squire, 24.

230. Dutton, 43.

231. McGuire, 26.

232. Dutton, 30.

233. Ibid.,8.

234. Squire,151.

235. Amédée Hallier, *The Monastic Theology of Aelred of Rievaulx: An Experiential Theology*, trans. Columban Heaney (Spencer MA: Cistercian Publications, 1969), 27; McGuire, 91.

236. Squire, 3.

237. Hallier, 7.

238. Dutton, 43.

239. McGuire raises the potentially contentious question of Aelred's sexual identity without advancing a concrete conclusion. I am interested primarily in Aelred's relationship with his mother and the effect this had on the workings of his imagination. Any reading into his spiritual struggle with his sexuality should be considered in light of the grace that clearly flows through his writings.

240. McGuire, 121.

241. Ibid., 31.

242. Ibid., 34.

243. Ibid., 27.

244. Aelred of Rievaulx, "Treatise Concerning a Rule of Life for a Recluse," 92.

245. McGuire, 27.

246. Ibid., 34.

247. Aelred of Rievaulx, "The Commentary of the Venerable Aelred, Abbot of Rievaulx on the Passage from the Gospel: 'When Jesus was Twelve Years Old,'" in *Aelred of Rievaulx: Treatises*, trans Theodore Berkeley (Spencer MA: Cistercian Publications, 1971), 11.

248. McGuire, 32.

249. Aelred of Rievaulx, "Sermon for the Assumption of Mary," in *Aelred of Rievaulx: The Liturgical Sermons*, trans. Theodore Berkeley and M. Basil Pennington (Kalamazoo: Cistercian Publications, 2001), 267.

250. Aelred of Rievaulx, "Rule of Life for a Recluse," 94, 93.

251. Ibid.

252. Ibid.

253. McGuire, 37.

254. Ibid., 38.

255. Squire, 47.

256. McGuire, 67.

257. Ibid., 110; 114-115.

258. Aelred of Rievaulx, "Pastoral Prayer," in *Aelred of Rievaulx: Treatises*, trans. R. Penelope Lawson (Spencer MA: Cistercian Publications, 1971), 107.

259. Ibid., 108.

260. Ibid., 110.

261. Aelred of Rievaulx, "When Jesus was Twelve Years Old," 5.

262. Ibid.

263. Ibid.

264. Ibid., 11.

265. Ibid., 8.

266. Ibid., fn. 28.

267. Ibid., 17.

268. Ibid., 21.

269. Ibid., 29.

270. Ibid., 33.

271. Ibid.

272. Aelred of Rievaulx, "Rule of Life for a Recluse," 81.

273. Ibid., 90-91.

274. Aelred of Rievaulx, *Dialogue on the Soul*, 140.

275. Aelred of Rievaulx, *Aelred of Rievaulx: The Mirror of Charity*, trans. Elizabeth Connor (Kalamazoo: Cistercian Publications, 1990), 204.

276. Ibid., 93.

277. Ibid., 111.

278. Ibid., 224.

279. Ibid., 134.

280. Ibid., 89.

281. Ibid., 121.

282. Ibid., 207.

283. Ibid., 87, 133.

284. Ibid., 167.

285. Bernard of Clairvaux, "Preface," in *Aelred of Rievaulx: The Mirror of Charity*, trans. Elizabeth Connor (Kalamazoo: Cistercian Publications, 1990), 69.

286. M. Basil Pennington, "Introduction," for *Aelred of Rievaulx: The Liturgical Sermons*, trans. Theodore Berkeley and M. Basil Pennington (Kalamazoo: Cistercian Publications, 2001), 28.

287. Ibid., 30-31.

288. Aelred of Rievaulx, "Sermon for the Coming of the Lord," in *Aelred of Rievaulx: The Liturgical Sermons*, trans. Theodore Berkeley and M. Basil Pennington (Kalamazoo: Cistercian Publications, 2001), 82.

289. Ibid., 86.

290. Aelred of Rievaulx, "Sermon for the Nativity of the Lord," in *Aelred of Rievaulx: The Liturgical Sermons*, trans. Theodore Berkeley and M. Basil Pennington (Kalamazoo: Cistercian Publications, 2001), 92.

291. Ibid. This sermon also contains an image of poverty that is less warmly embraceable than Francis' Lady Poverty. "What a wall poverty is! How well it defends us against the pride of the world, against harmful and ruinous vanities and superfluities." Ibid., 93.

292. Douglas Roby, "Introduction," in *Aelred of Rievaulx: Spiritual Friendship*, intro. Douglas Roby, trans. Mary Eugenia Laker (Kalamazoo: Cistercian Publications, 1977), 29, 33.

293. Aelred of Rievaulx, *Aelred of Rievaulx: Spiritual Friendship*, intro. Douglas Roby, trans. Mary Eugenia Laker (Kalamazoo: Cistercian Publications, 1977), 1:53.

294. Ibid., 1:54.

295. Ibid., 3:77.

296. Ibid., 3:92.

297. Ibid., 3:131.

CHAPTER THREE
THE IMAGINATION AS VIEWED
IN CONTEMPORARY THEORIES

Object Relations Theory is not the first attempt to make sense of the part imagination plays in the drama of life.[1] This should be clear from the long history of imaginative theories and views discussed earlier. Nor is ORT the only contemporary approach to understanding this human phenomenon. Relatively recent efforts have been made to study imagination from the perspective of philosophy, other psychologies, sociology, and linguistics. In nearly each such study it is possible to note that the imagination's function is to make associations, connections, or relationships viable.

The current chapter will survey the writings of theorists who contend with the imagination and its promises and perils for humanity. These writings will come from roughly the same late twentieth century timeframe as those that represent the bulk of material on ORT to be considered in the following two chapters. In some cases theorists will refer to the endeavors of earlier writers, particularly Immanuel Kant (1724-1814). While he certainly clarified much about the philosophical dimension of the imagination, modern theories and views, often unwittingly, depend just as much, if not more, on the classical understandings of imagination.

Recent literature on imagination gives evidence of the imagination's ability to make connections, associations, and relationships in two broad areas. In the first sense, imagination is seen to link the individual with primary aspects of his or her existence. This would include experience, relationship, change, and the divine.[2] In the second sense, imagination connects contact with these fundamental realities of existence with the process of interpreting, understanding, or meaning-making. The purpose of this targeted survey is threefold. It will reveal just how much an Object Relations Theory perspective of the imagination is in continuity with other respected approaches to comprehending the workings of the imagination, and it will lay the groundwork for demonstrating just how much farther this selected theory goes in describing the actual process of developing and employing a creative imagination. Additionally, this study will further set the stage for portraying Francis as the bearer of a highly creative imagination.[3]

Imagination as Initial Point of Experience

Mary Warnock, one of the most noted theorists of the imagination, asserts that the imagination has come under an intellectual attack from the field of phenomenology. She explains that phenomenologists postulate only the existence of the perceiver and the object perceived, and no image in between.[4] A deeper appreciation for the intricacy of human psychodynamics keeps the phenomenological approach from overstepping its methodological boundaries as just one among several available techniques for comprehending the process of experiencing. The following pages will indicate that there is much more complexity to the encounter between the sentient being and his or her realm of existence. The sight of an object, the sensation of the body, and the impression in the mind do not link in some mechanical fashion to a fixed collection of interpretations, understandings, or meanings. It is true that medieval and classical scholars gave limited importance to the imagination as merely a reception point for mental images, or at best, the place where they are formed without any structure of meaning or understanding attached to them. More recently, scholars vary in the scope they will allow the imagination, but, on the whole, they see a wider role for it, beginning with the initiation of experience.

Philip Wheelwright divides the imagination into four types: Confrontative Imagination, Distancing Imagination, Archetypal Imagination, and Metaphoric Imagination.[5] The latter two types will be considered when discussing the process of meaning-making, but Confrontative and Distancing Imagination pertain to the initiatory act of experiencing. Wheelwright is among several theorists who find that the imagination works to both bring about a state of intensification and order to an experience. He describes Confrontative Imagination as a power "to intensify the immediate experience itself."[6] He goes on to say, this "imagination is active in the awareness of individual presences in their radical individuality."[7]

Students of Wheelwright recognize that intensification requires an ability to set each experience apart as exclusive.[8] Distancing Imagination further sets the experience away from "the practical aspect of things," so the experience can occur uninhibited,[9] or the object can be viewed in the fullness of its objectivity.[10] Wheelwright alternately calls Distancing Imagination: Stylistic Imagination, which "involves a hushing of ordinary compulsions, a veiling of ordinary associations, and therein makes its [imagination's] unique semantic contribution."[11] It is apparent, here, that he is referring to significant acts of the creative imagination, but it should also be made clear that he is not suggesting that the imaginative act, in its totality, occurs in a vacuum. Instead, he is pointing out the possibility of a heightened level of attention to the initial sense impression. In other words, the creative imaginer is fully open and attentive to experience.

David Tracy describes a similar initial encounter with experience in the form of a *classic*. He extends this term beyond just a classic text to include "events, images, rituals, symbols, and persons."[12] The initial experience he calls an "event of disclosure-concealment" since it provides a glimpse or makes a first impression, but it masks so much more.[13] The idea of intensity also comes into play in this view, but it is an intensification of the experiencing subject, not the experience as in Wheelwright's assertion. Tracy writes, "The artist, the thinker, the hero, the saint—who are they, finally, but the finite self radicalized and intensified?"[14] The journey of intensification, as he calls it, seems to correspond to Wheelwright's idea of un-hindering and setting the experience apart. When describing an experience of art, Tracy reveals, "I find that my subjectivity is never in control of the experience.... rather the work of art encounters me with the surprise, impact, even shock of reality itself."[15] He adds that entering into this experience requires transcending one's pure subjectivity, a "loss of self-consciousness," which opens the way for the experience to have a significant impact, to be transformative.[16] Nonetheless, Tracy does not suggest that one can have an experience completely free from any previous influence. He calls this culturally conditioned effect *preunderstanding*. But even this has a limited impact on the overall development of the experience. Tracy contends, "The preunderstanding the interpreter brings to the interpretation surely conditions, but does not determine that response."[17]

In addition to the intensification of experience, another area where contemporary theorists see imagination playing a part in the earliest advent of an experience is in the first application of order to impressions that otherwise emerge out of chaos or disorder. Tracy hints at the idea of disorder when he distinguishes between a "limit-to experience" within which ordinary insights occur, and a "limit-of experience" which necessitates the use of a creative imagination.[18] It is difficult to say whether this latter concept is an area of experiencing or an influence on experiencing, since it beckons the subject to reach beyond the known. Attempts to think or extend one's experience into this arena, beyond the limits of what one is currently able to experience, hint at the presence of the chaos or disorder that occurs outside the normal capacity to experience and apply meaning to experience.

As Tracy's title, *The Analogical Imagination*, suggests, at the heart of his view of imagination lies the linguistic technique of analogy. He explains, "analogy is a language of ordered relationships articulating similarity-in-difference."[19] It is the imagination's job to begin to see or find the similarity or order in a field of disorder, and then to connect this order with "some prime analogue."[20] The prime analogue represents a fundamental meaning by which all of reality can be interpreted.[21] In any case, without reference to a communal source of one or more central analogues, the renderings of any one person's imaginative activity would have no means of connecting with and sharing influence with any other person's imagination. Francis offers one of the clearest examples of defying disorder or chaos in his contact with the lepers. These sufferers represent death in life, an experience beyond the limits of his personal experience. The lepers also confront him with an experience of physical and human disorder. Ultimately, through the intensification of his sudden encounter with a leper, in conjunction with his Christ-centered preunderstanding, Francis is able to imaginatively perceive the lepers in a completely new light. If Francis can be said to seek meaning in the manner Tracy sets out, it can equally be said that Francis' writings represent a source of meaning in the fashion of Tracy's *classic*.

Warnock does not view the imagination as a faculty, but rather as a force. She maintains, "there is a power in the human mind which is at work in our everyday perception of the world, and is also at work in our thoughts about what is absent; which enables us to see the world, whether present or absent as significant, and also to present this vision to others, for them to share or reject."[22] She holds this view in part to refute Jean-Paul Sartre's (1905-1980) claim that perception and imagination are unrelated.[23] For her it is at the level of perception that a kind of intensification is called for. She finds that an "intensity of perceptual experience" is necessary "if we are ever to treat the objects of perception as symbolizing or suggesting things other than themselves."[24]

One possible insight into Warnock's understanding of intensification is found in her reading of David Hume's (1711-1776) views on the imagination. She reports that imagination involves the combining of weak experiences "by a principle of association, which is, however, not absolutely binding."[25] From this one could surmise that experience lacks strength, or significance, or the potential for meaning, until it is brought into a relational matrix with other experiences. Such a relational matrix could be called the imagination, or in ORT terminology, the transitional space. Warnock also mentions that the imagination "fills in the gaps in our experience."[26] Tracy, who similarly places these gaps between the experience and its meaning, has seized this idea with his descriptive phrase: an "event of disclosure-concealment."[27] His terminology suggests that an experience carries the potentiality but not the fullness of an insight. Regardless of where the gap is located, both authors point toward a so-called intensification in which experience necessarily builds on experience as a precursor to the establishment, projection, and dissemination of meaning.

Theorists can and do mean different things when they speak of experience. Whether the experience, so-to-speak, strikes the senses or the mind, it becomes more evident that it arrives at its first point of contact with the mind/body interface without a supporting context. If experience does build on experience, either the incoming sense data or the resultant mental construction lack a context until the imagination, as a matrix of experience, takes hold of them. Warnock understands the alleviation of this form of chaos in relationship to Kant's distinction between Empirical and Transcendental Imagination.[28] While the Empirical or Reproductive Imagination synthesizes a primary image from other images, impressions, and ideas, the Transcendental or Constructive Imagination, more or less, forms original images. Warnock claims that the imagination sits between the senses and the intellect, mediating and ordering the chaos of the sense data while offering content to the abstract thought of reason.[29] Based on Kant's ideas on aesthetics, she is able to say, "our pleasure in beauty is a pleasure in order, a satisfaction in our power to regulate chaos."[30] To apply order, the imagination initially presents sense data as conforming to a particular shape or form.[31] Moving beyond the given of sense data to that which is conceived wholly internally, she asserts, "Creative genius, then, consists in the ability to find expression, although inevitably not complete expression, for the ideas which are to be apprehended in, or glimpsed beyond, objects in the world."[32] Writing this prior to Tracy's concept of a "limit-of" experience, Warnock captures a similar notion.

In essence, the most creative imaginations belong to individuals who are willing to venture into the darkness beyond the comfort of order, shielded only by an imaginative faith. Francis reflects this idea with his ability to discover and promote happiness and fraternity outside the normalized securities of the world.

While some scholars show interest in the imagination as it works with objects available to direct experience by the senses, the more intriguing aspect of the imagination is its purported ability to link the individual with things, objects, or images, not within reach of the senses. Garrett Green, who describes revelatory religious experiences in terms of shifts in imaginative paradigms, goes into some detail explaining the possible sources for imaginative experience that are not initially encountered by the senses. Also working from Kant's categorization of imagination, he writes, "Imagination re-presents what is absent; it makes present through images what is inaccessible to direct experience."[33] Green elaborates on this inaccessibility of an object of imagination, pointing out that it can refer equally to things that have a real and separate existence from the representation as well as those which do not.[34] Of those objects that do subsist apart from their image, some happen to be absent and therefore not in contact with the senses. These would be directly perceived if they were present. This is a physical non-presence as opposed to a temporal non-presence. The latter such objects can be understood or expected to have existence in the natural world at some other point in time, either past or future. Memory fits in the former timeframe. Still, there is a spatial non-presence due to proximity or size. It is possible to imagine one's friend in another city or a solar system at some far reach of the universe as well as the microorganism that causes a bodily ailment. Green further proposes the actuality of logically non-present entities, particularly the soul which is not directly observable by necessity of its nature.[35] From the less trustworthy precinct of the imagination come the expressions of imaginative encounters with images that have no basis in reality. Imaginative activity directed toward the distinctly not-real includes fanciful imaginings, the stuff of pure fantasy. These can be "acknowledged departures from the real world" or deceitful misrepresentations of what is real or not real.[36]

Elaine Scarry identifies a specific experience that is not consistent with any of the scenarios depicted above since it occurs directly through the senses, yet it is also not comparable to other experiences touching on the senses. The experience in question, physical pain, induces an involuntary reaction of intensification when its onset demands most of an individual's attention. Prior to an intellectual or emotional attempt to understand it, the experience of pain also lacks meaning; it is an encounter with chaos. Bodily suffering deserves added thought, as it is something Francis was familiar with. He spent much of his life enduring exposure to the elements. He survived a considerable period of time in a medieval prison, and he faced the unmitigated pain of flesh searing red-hot metal instruments during a vision operation. In addition to being an element of Francis' personal experience, actual pain is described as initiating the activity of imagining.

Scarry demonstrates that the imagination is often able to provide an object when the world is unable.[37] She asserts, "Physical pain—unlike any other state of consciousness—has no referent content. It is not of or for anything. It is precisely because it takes no object that it, more than any other phenomenon, resists objectification in language."[38] Because there is no direct object, and therefore image, for pain, the suffering person will generally formulate one.

Often the object that causes the pain is used for this purpose, but the instrument, creature, or circumstances causing pain are not pain itself; they are merely a representation of it. Scarry remarks, "The point here is not just that pain can be apprehended in the image of the weapon (or the wound) but that it almost cannot be apprehended without it."[39] She adds, furthermore, "when physical pain is transformed into an objectifiable state, it (or at least some of its aversiveness) is eliminated."[40] Francis can be seen to both objectify and personify pain with his brother fire.

Bradford Stull, who studies Scarry's views, writes that, "language can never fully speak/write what the psychosomatic entities that we call human beings experience when they experience what we call pain."[41] He goes on to say that imagination "can be tentatively understood as linguistic manipulation of the facets of human experience, including the elements of sense reality and whatever realities there may be beyond or within the sensible world."[42] Several of Francis' writings will reveal a struggle to give meaning to pain and suffering.

Scarry's thoughts and influence reveal how the imagination confronts the experience of pain, but she also provides insight into the nature of the imagination itself. She observes, "while pain is a state remarkable for being wholly without objects, imagination is remarkable for being the only state that is wholly its objects."[43] She means by this that imagination is only experienced in reference to its objects.[44] The comparison Scarry makes between pain and imagination is this: "Physical pain, then is an intentional state without an intentional object; imagining is an intentional object without an experienceable intentional state."[45] She goes on to assert that it is pain's "objectlessness that may give rise to imagining by first occasioning the process that eventually brings forth the sea of artifacts and symbols that we make and move about in. All other states, precisely by taking an object, at first invite one only to enter rather than to supplement the natural world."[46] She adds that, "Any state that was permanently objectless would no doubt begin the process of invention."[47] In the next chapter the process of imaginative object- formation, that Scarry associates with pain, will be explained by ORT in terms of infantile discomfort and distress.

In the preceding pages, imagination has been depicted as an initial point of experience. It is where the thinking, feeling, knowing person first comes into contact with an object, image, or mental construct that calls for a next step of associating, connecting, or relating with other mental objects in the process of meaning-making. Various theorists have shown that the imagination directs primary attention onto the experience to intensify it, and cause it to stand out from the throng of chaos that is all experience, potential and actual, that still evades meaning. Now imagination can be studied for the role it plays in relating one thing to another.

Imagination at the Center of Relationship

Imagination is truly at the heart of all acts of relating. It enables the individual to perceive or conceive the connection between the various aspects of experience discussed, at least in part, above. This approach can be illustrated as a look at imaginative activity with an inward view, toward the person's interior world where images of experience are developed and linked. Imagination also has an outward dimension, such that it brings people together to inform, sustain, and share the workings of each other's imaginations. In the following pages, imagination will be studied as it takes a central position in reference to each of these relational settings. Additionally, two special cases of relationship will be looked at for their bearing on a deeper understanding of Francis' imaginative activity. These are: imaginative cross-identification with another, and fear-invoked fantasy.

Inner Relationship:
A Look Toward the Interior Dimension of
Relation-Formation

The capacity of the imagination to take hold of experience and bring it into a relational matrix has already been mentioned, but few theorists attempt to explain, in greater detail, how the imagination operates when it is actually forming relationships. In this respect, Object Relations Theory is a step ahead, but even it is a theory and not a proven formula. ORT, like any of the theories and views to be considered, relies on comparative language to suggest that the imagination works similar to some familiar operation when it is engaged. Most theorists not involved with ORT are content to dwell more on the overall importance of establishing relationships for the process of meaning-making.

Ray Hart offers an example of the tendency to talk around the operation of the imagination when he calls it the "seat of connection between perception and thinking."[48] The notion of a "seat of connection" is vague enough to shroud an exact conception of relation-formation while depicting the process in locational terms. David Bryant links the act of imaginative *relating* with the linguistic technique of metaphor. As in metaphor, "the uncovering of hitherto unrecognized relationships is what generates new insights."[49] Object Relations Theory will show that in many instances the relatable object images reside within the mind in an unrelated state. Bryant goes on to suggest that relationship is dependent, in some sense, on contrast when he writes, "For metaphor is first of all a clash of meanings embedded in language, through which a new meaning emerges."[50] Similar to metaphor, the meaning born from the connection of mental imagery can arise in unexpected forms.

Andrew Greeley shares the view that some conflict of experience is involved in the process of relating images, in this case, of things divine. Greeley speaks of the encounter with "otherness" as "the origin first of the image and then of the concept of God."[51] Greeley describes the relating of images as a communal activity. He observes that many folklore traditions pieced together a limited repertoire of images and pictures and then reorganized them as needed to make certain points about human experience.[52] Bringing this idea from the level of the community to the level of the individual, he offers the possibility of a *preconscious*, to be found between the unconscious and the conscious. This *preconscious* is seen by philosophers as the locus of creativity, and it is here, he contends, that the reshuffling of images occurs.[53] Michael Riposa describes imaginative activity as "the ability to rearrange and reconfigure old bits of information, to manipulate them playfully, creating or discovering new relationships, new insights."[54] *Playful manipulation* also fails to fully clarify how relations are formed in the imagination, but it points to the activity of play that ORT theorists as well as others have identified as essential to the work of the creative imagination. Before specifying the part of play as one of the links between people and imagining, a few things can be said about the outcome of relating sense impressions, images, and mental constructs.

Sometimes what lies within is revealed by the outward expression. The kind of externally directed perception that an individual is able to achieve as a product of the inner workings of the imagination reveals a little more of what happens during the imaginative process which is otherwise difficult to observe. A number of scholars point toward a holistic vision of the world as the resultant perspective. Kathleen Fischer insists that imagination enables people to perceive a harmony of difference which yields a unity.[55] This view certainly supports Bryant and Greeley's implication that the relational imagination mediates conflicts between images. Fischer adds that "the indirect language of the imagination can also hold together paradoxes which we are unable completely to understand, for example, that God is both merciful and just, terrible and gentle, transcendent and immanent."[56] Similar examples are found in the experience of Francis who was able to find riches in poverty and joy in his suffering, while viewing the world in a broader context.

Also using the notion of harmony, Richard Knowles remarks, "We might say that imagination is a particular way of moving in the world.... a way of moving in harmony with the rhythm of the world and others."[57] Tracy clearly designates the perception of wholeness as the ultimate outcome of the imaginative process. He declares, "In the final moments of all interpretation, beyond but through explanation into some appropriated understanding, we discover ourselves as a finite part, as participatory in, belonging to yet distanced from some essential aspect of the whole."[58] Another scholar, who points out the importance of a unified outlook on life, deserves equal credit with some ORT theorists for connecting play with meaning-making. Hans Georg Gadamer confirms that a person who understands reality as play is "someone who is able to see the whole of reality as a circle of meaning, in which everything is fulfilled."[59] He adds that others can share this perspective, or specifically the content of play-inspired imagining, when they also experience it as a unity.[60] It should be clear at this point that the imagination is widely regarded for its hidden capacity to form distinction, and even chaos, into a unified whole.

An External Benefit of Imagination:
Its Capacity to Bring People into Relationship

It was stipulated earlier that Francis' imagination brought him into an interactive contact with all of created reality and beyond. This is not simply an imaginative conception of relational unity; it is a progression of the person beyond the narrow confines of an isolated selfhood into the set of possible relationships. Knowles recognizes this function when he claims that the imaginative mode "invites one ... into participation and contact with the world and other people."[61] He argues that, "Imagination includes a certain form of perceiving, but it is more than that; it also includes willing and, more centrally, a movement toward action," a "willingness to become engaged."[62] Through *willingness*, he suggests, one is motivated "to encounter things and people as they are and move into risk and uncertainty."[63]

Greeley has another take on the formation of relationships through imaginative interaction. He mentions that, "Religion as story leaps from imagination to imagination, and only then, if at all, from intellect to intellect."[64] He contends that interpersonal relationships not only develop out of this imaginative interaction, they also have a powerful effect on the shaping of the imagination, particularly when the influence is a family relationship.[65] This all happens when the story telling, which he labels "religious discourse," works "to stir up in the other person resonances of experiences similar to that which the storyteller himself or herself has had."[66] Such an act of bringing two individuals' experiences into harmony is the basis of interpersonal solidarity, an interest of other theorists.

Tracy makes the point: "each of us understands each other through analogies to our own experience or not at all."[67] Using a communications approach, he calls the relationship of understanding between people "real conversation." "Real conversation occurs only when the participants allow the question, the subject matter, to assume primacy. It occurs only when our usual fears about our own self-image die."[68] He also writes, "For understanding *happens*; it occurs not as a result of personal achievement but in the back-and-forth movement of the conversation itself."[69] A significant term that Tracy uses in this last sentence is "back-and-forth movement." It ties him to the notions of play given such a prominent role in the process of interpretation and understanding by Gadamer.

While Tracy associates a relationship of understanding with conversation, Gadamer has inspired another scholar to insist that, "understanding takes the form of a fusion of horizons."[70] Beneath this image of fused horizons is a concept very similar to Tracy's. Bryant proposes that, "The event of understanding... calls for the willingness to lose oneself in pursuit of the subject matter, to be absorbed in the back and forth movement of play in the dialogue."[71] He finds that this interchange, or the fusing of horizons, is best achieved by the imaginative technique of construal, "taking-as," which he prefers to Warnock's limiting ocular term "seeing as."[72] In any case, Bryant realizes the potential applications of Gadamer's play ideas to a study of the imagination. He determines that play shapes consciousness, and that it can just as easily involve two or more people as it can involve one person and some encountered experience in the generalized fashion employed by Gadamer.[73]

Given the connections Bryant makes between play and the imagination, and the significance of play from an ORT perspective of imagination that will be drawn out in the next chapter, a more careful look at Gadamer's views is warranted. When he speaks of play, Gadamer gives it a conceptual status with a fair amount of autonomy from the person or persons engaged in it. In fact, he describes the player as one who "takes up the attitude of play."[74] While it is common to think of playing with someone, a simple observation of a child deeply involved in play by his or her self is a quick reminder that *play* also characterizes the interaction between child and world. Gadamer does conclude that play must be open to spectators to be complete, but fundamentally, he describes it as the activity of one person, directed toward something vaguely near the periphery of his or her reach.[75] Play is a "to and fro movement which is not tied to any goal which would bring it to an end"; it "represents an order in which the to-and-fro motion of play follows of itself."[76]

Hart advances a term that can be used to clarify what Gadamer is saying. Hart proposes that human beings possess an "ontological instability" which leaves them open to transformation through a "modifying relation."[77] Gadamer's notions on play credibly demonstrate how ontological instability can be tapped in order to participate in a modifying relation. He claims that, "Play fulfills its purpose only if the player loses himself in his play."[78] To make this happen, "The structure of play absorbs the player into itself, and thus takes from him the burden of initiative, which constitutes the actual strain of existence."[79] It is as if play brings an individual's ontological instability to the point at which it opens up to change. In many ways, play begins to sound like a parallel to the process of intensification described as part of the initial experience imparted to the imagination. Gadamer uses the familiar example of the work of art that "has its true being in the fact that it becomes an experience changing the person experiencing it."[80]

It is primarily as a ground for the fusing of imaginative horizons that play can be seen as central to imaginative activity thus far, but play as a prelude to establishing internal mental relationships is an important conceptual area for ORT. Gadamer supports this understanding when he explains a movement very much like the act of entering the transitional sphere. He remarks: "The player experiences the game as a reality that surpasses him."[81] He goes on to speak of play in terms of entering into a transforming structure in which play finds "its measure in itself and measures itself by nothing outside it."[82] As the following chapter will reveal in detail, the transitional sphere is a place where the claims of reality are suspended. Similarly, Gadamer argues that play "no longer permits of any comparison with reality as the secret measure of all copied similarity."[83] He is implying that play allows the lifting of reality's rigid grasp of perception to make possible the activity which yields new insights, new understanding. Could it be the attitude of play, then, that permits a less constraining environment for the relating of images while also providing for engagement with others to share and sustain this imaginative activity? Object Relations Theory carefully fleshes out the connection between play, the formation of images, and human interaction.

Special Cases of Relationship in and through the Imagination

The working of the imagination has been related to the back and forth motion of play. This is a valuable analogy when it is applied to the interaction between a concept and the imagination such that both an external relationship and the imagination are reciprocally influenced. An example of this is seen in the two special cases for the imagination, the first of which can be used to probe Francis' relationship with women and how this affected his imagination. He personified the value and virtue of poverty, a concept, in the guise of a woman, and he, like Bernard, expressed distinctly male-to-male relationships in maternal terms.

Ann and Barry Ulanov observe that the imagination crosses over gaps in a person's life to achieve a kind of wholeness that other theorists have also mentioned. The integration of disparate elements in one's life and imagination are integrated in an effort to make sense of the world and one's place in it.[84] In this light, imaginative cross-identification along gender lines represents a healthy rather than a pathological stance. The Ulanovs find that this kind of imaginative act reveals an understanding that none of us are complete in ourselves.[85] They determine that, "A man... can cross identify with a woman's maternal instincts and capacities. That will bring much to his life and to others, as he becomes a good male-mother who can tend children or nurture the growth of those who work with him or for him."[86] Francis very clearly adopts this position when he writes to Brother Leo. He states, "As a mother to her child, I speak to you, my son."[87] In addition to the outward aspect of cross-identification on interpersonal relationships, the Ulanovs consider the return effect on the imagination. They write that cross-identification "enriches the imagination by extending our capacities for sympathy and empathy, and it makes it possible for us to put ourselves in the other persons' shoes, to go to deeper places. We imagine ourselves in other persons' bodies."[88] Beyond the many references to following in the footsteps of Jesus, Francis also extends the idea of identifying with the least of his brothers. He exclaims, "They [Friars] should be glad to live among social outcasts, among the poor and helpless, the sick and the lepers, and those who beg by the wayside."[89] While this last example is not directly tied to a cross-gender identification, it highlights the resultant empathetic experience Francis seems to have had and sought to pass on to his brothers.

The second special case of relationships lays bare a limitation to the potential richness of the imagination and a hindrance to the relationships that could otherwise be established through imaginative activity. Arguably, Francis was able to steer clear of this problem area for the imagination, which is fantasy. Knowles maintains that fantasy includes "daydreaming, dreaming, wishful thinking," and extremes of "delusions and hallucinations."[90] Fantasy, or *phantasy*, was rightly looked upon with suspicion by classical and medieval scholars since it represents a movement toward gross and unhealthy individualism. Knowles points out that "forgetting or absenting oneself from the life context seems to be an essential constituent of fantasy."[91] As he describes it, fantasy stands against everything that has previously been said positively about imagination; it is a source of alienation. Knowles compares fantasy to "a private mono-logue, an autistic meandering which bypasses the need to shape the experience or to communicate it to others."[92] He goes on to say that fantasy includes an "autistic interpretation of reality, the absence of intersubjective contact and di-alogue."[93] Francis did spend a fair amount of time in seclusion, but if he had been lost in fantasy, the workings of his imagination would not have been com-municated to others if they were communicable at all. Nonetheless, there is an aspect of fantasy that, when overcome, may have led him to an even greater im-aginative capacity.

Knowles asserts that fantasy originates out of fear. He finds that fantasy ex-ists to control or contain fear and is therefore shaped by fear.[94] One source of fear that Francis admits to is the leper, the sight of whom he found bitter, ac-cording to *The Testament of St. Francis*. Of course, it might be suggested that his real fear was of death as epitomized by the leper.[95] If Francis' encounter with the lepers was as central an event as it is claimed here, then he may have, at one time, faced the danger that Knowles warns of: "Often in life one comes to iden-tify the self completely with the narrow personality that is formed in response to fear."[96] But this cannot be the final conclusion for Francis. Knowles determines that, "Fear and fantasy stand in contrast to [hope, imagination, and love]... and comprise a mode of experience which excludes them. One cannot, at the same time, be fearful and also hopeful, imaginative, or loving."[97] As his writings at-test, Francis bore each of these latter three attributes in abundance. If he first imagined in fear, he clearly transformed and transcended that fear.

William Lynch relates one of Francis' attributes, hope, to imaginative activ-ity in an insightful way that counters the alienating consequence of fantasy. He observes that, "Hope not only imagines; it *imagines with*. We are so habituated to conceiving of the imagination as a private act of the human spirit that we find it almost impossible to conceive of a common act of *imagining with*."[98] Hope, like a well-working imagination, is directed outward to the world of possible relationships; it supports *imagining with*, which is why Lynch sets it over against the imaginative component that he calls the "absolutizing instinct."[99] This concept, he says, "is not really an action of the imagination. Rather, it is a creator of fantasy, distortion, and magnification."[100] Thanks to the instinct's magnifying function, "Everything assumes a greater weight than it has."[101] Small issues and incidents grow large to the extent that one is not able to inter-nally integrate one's concerns and needs into a manageable whole. Hope, on the other hand, "is an interior sense that there is help on the outside of us."[102]

As Lynch sees it, imagination works at the service of hope to counter the absolutizing instinct. Instead of allowing an issue to grow out of proportion, imagination enlarges reality in such a way as to minimize the impact of the issue of concern.[103] Lynch adds that it is the imagination's task to pierce through fan-tasy and misconception to reach reality, and its follow-on task is to find isolated facts and place them into "a perspective and landscape" where they will not be left about to be absolutized as a total reality in themselves.[104] The corrective that Lynch suggests to counter the absolutizing moment, and maintain the broadest possible perspective, is a posture of mutuality.[105] This adoption of another's views as part of one's own also supports the socially interactive remediation that Knowles offers for fantasy when he explains that the fantasy mode can be challenged when others do not accept or conform to it.[106] This is all very much in line with the relating of experiences, images, and mental constructs that has been discussed thus far.

Following up on Knowles' connection between fantasy and fear, Lynch mentions death as a source of fear. He claims that one is only afraid of dying when it is understood in isolation.[107] As Chapter Six will lay out more completely, much of Francis' imaginative activity was directed toward relating death to a broader context. Emerging from a fear of death, the saint comes to understand and express it as a welcome step to eternal life, as a return to origins, and, anthropomorphically, as his sister. From Lynch's perspective, Francis' open response to death would be a clear sign that he has not absolutized death, since the absolutized object cannot be transcended.[108] Death, like Francis' other relationships to the world, is integrated into a more holistic context.

Lynch makes a final point of interest related to Object Relations Theory. He asserts that each image of an infant is an absolute.[109] ORT would agree with his analysis since it considers the infant's interior world to begin with part-objects that initially represent the absolute whole of reality which is the mother-infant bond. Gradually, a well adjusting child forms enough object representations that no one object dominates or becomes an absolute.

Imagination has been associated with relating and relationships on several planes. Just about anything the imagination is capable of doing is, in turn, reducible to some form of relation. One of these is the link between the individual and time.

Imagination at the Crossroads of the Past and the Possible:
Its Ability to Mediate Time, Potential, and Transcendence

So far, the imagination has been studied for its involvement in two aspects of the human encounter with existence: experience and relationship. The next dimension to be considered, *time*, is one that touches upon the previous two. Time could be described as a succession of ordered instances--instances of experience. Time is also the dimension that holds those instances in a distinctive order, in relationship.[110] In actuality, time is so closely bound to the imagination that it would be impossible to conceive of any instant but the present without the use of imagination. This section will review some of the ideas theorists have shared regarding the association of time and the imagination, not because Francis' writings reveal a heightened interest in time, but because they show attentiveness to possibility and transcendence. Time is simply a natural building block to the understanding of potentiality and transcendence, a change in one's view of the world. Imagination will, therefore, be presented as a link between the past, the present, and the unrealized potential that dwells in the future.

Imagination Looking Back

As Tracy points out, "Every present moment is, in fact, formed by both the memories of the tradition and the hopes, desires, critical demands for transformation for the future."[111] The previous chapter made clear the emphasis that early theories of imagination placed on the past and the role of memory in holding the individual in a state of continuity with all that the past has to offer as meaning. The majority of modern scholars, whose views are exhibited here, are more intrigued by the imagination's ability to look forward and inspire forward thinking action.

When the past does come under consideration, recent theories largely view it as an imaginative foundation and a limited source of validation for current imagining.[112] Nonetheless, it would be difficult to think deeply into the future without at least some reference to the past. Edward Oakes finds that there are two distinctive influences on an individual's perception which can, nonetheless, cooperate in the formation of images. He explains that one's imaginative activity can be "provoked by the possible," and "disciplined by the past."[113] Jo Ellen Parker contends that it is a typological imagination that brings the past to bear on one's imaginative perception. She confirms that the typological imagination "perceives all things as existing simultaneously in two realms, the material and the spiritual."[114] This kind of dual existence affords the past its impact. Basing her explanation on the typologies identified between the Old Testament and the New Testament, she asserts that, "typological interpretation subverts the common-sense perception of the linear nature of time, for it perceives two or more widely separate historical moments as bound into one timeless instant of prophecy and fulfillment in the mind of God."[115] One supposes that this activity should have the same effect on the human mind. Francis' writings give evidence that this is so.

Edward Robinson has an idea that might be viewed as contradicting Parker's theory. Instead of seeing a direct relationship between one moment in time and another, he proposes a reversal of the cause and effect flow within time as the means to engaging a creative imagination. He calls this the capacity to dwell in "a state of suspended expectation," by which intention follows after the effect of imagining, and past does not definitively condition one's imagining of the future.[116] In another alternative approach to the past, Fischer suggests that the nature of time is not perceptually altered, rather, "the imagination loosens and dissolves past images in order to recombine them in new forms for the future."[117]

Green links the imagination to the past through paradigms. Just like a scientist thinks according to a specific scientific paradigm, Green determines that religious people also imagine according to a religiously inspired paradigm. As a connection to the past or a pre-existent way of understanding, Green defines a paradigm as "a pattern after which something can be modeled or by which something can be recognized."[118] He advances from this definition to another: "A paradigm, therefore, is best defined as a normative model for a human endeavor or object of knowledge, the exemplar or privileged analogy that shows us what the object is like."[119] When a current paradigm, that encompasses past and present, ceases to adequately model the structure within which a person imagines, a new paradigm is adopted through a paradigm shift. The new paradigm can still be considered a link with a tradition of thought or imagination, but it will shortly be shown as just as much a bridge to the future.

At the waypoint between past and future is the language that holds them on a continuum. Since it is as symbol that memory can most easily be loosened and dissolved, as well as carried forward, Fischer can claim that, "the language of imagination" is "symbolic disclosure."[120] Her remark that, "All forms of symbolic disclosure suggest more than they can clearly state," correlates with Tracy's idea that an original event, from the past, is an "event of disclosure-concealment."[121] According to either of the last two views, the past has its influence on the imagination, but it clearly does not have the level of authority implied by a typological imagination.

Riposa proposes that, "the religious imagination has been portrayed as functioning most perfectly when it takes the form of an infinitely determinable 'nought,' detached and responsive to whatever appears."[122] Like so many other views, Riposa depicts the imagination as standing between images, thoughts, and experiences coming from the past, and images of what is possible at some unrevealed point in the future. In a similar way, Bryant claims that it is "seeing as... that enables the past and future to impinge on the present."[123] Francis is able to imaginatively make the most of the past because he never considers the possibility, now widely believed, that sacred and secular history are not interrelated. Keeping this interface open enables Francis, and others from his era, to envision Jesus' direct impact on their lives and time.

Imagination Looking Forward

There are several theories of imagination that reject the idea that the future has not happened and therefore, on the basis of time, it lacks existence. Furthermore, they do not accept the notion that *possibility* is unrealized and therefore unreal. These theories work with the future as if it is more than just a consequence of the continuity of successive instances, and they give possibility almost an air of tangibility. Two theorists describe these related concepts in terms of a *more* that is indirectly present to the imagination. Fischer maintains that, "The paradox of the imagination is that, although it speaks in terms of individual and unique things, it always suggests more than it actually perceives and describes directly."[124] Likewise, Riposa claims, "The ability to perceive this 'more,' to recognize in any given situation of experience the potential for discovering new information, is a function of the imagination."[125]

Oakes indicates that human beings are driven by their very nature to be oriented toward future possibility, and this capacity is enabled by the imagination. He explains, imagination "tells us that man is a being who is innately and fundamentally open to possibility. Imagination's presence in the mind tells us that the human mode of being is not limited to the here-and-now but is always being projected forward, spurred on by the encounter with (imagined) possibility."[126] Fischer makes the association between imagination, the future, and possibility even more explicit. She explains that imagination connects one to the future which is possibility not yet realized.[127]

The unique ability of the imagination to look ahead into the *more* has been portrayed in differing ways by theorists. Robinson describes his notion of creative imagination as "vertical imagination," which takes a horizon expanding vantage point.[128] Just as the familiar landscape steadily changes when a pilot pulls back the stick to increase altitude, someone endowed with creative imagination visualizes the world according to a new order of proximity, boundaries, and landmarks. Robinson contrasts the vertical imagination with "lateral imagination," which is the aspect of imaginative activity that can become manifest in some form and be shared across a community.[129] Another depiction of forward-looking imagination links "a sense of the possible" with hope.[130] Lynch exclaims, "Hope is indeed an arduous search for a future good of some kind that is realistically possible but not yet visible."[131] Rather than rendering his picture of imagination as simply some source of great vision, he also reveals it as a potentially deep well of patience. He contends that imagination can be utilized to "wait for the emergence of a larger moment and a larger time."[132] Much like the vertical imagination, hope is carried on by the ability to visualize a living scenario from a better point of view.

Based on the amount of hope Francis stakes in the future, he must perceive it to be very real and very meaningful. He gives up so many of the satisfactions most people associate with the present moment in order to assure his participation in the possibility that awaits him.

Imagining, Change, Transformation, and Transcendence

There is a step beyond seeing what the future has to offer. The individual can allow the future to take shape within his or her own life. For Francis this involves embracing change for the better, allowing and supporting transformation in one's relationships, and transcending what was, for the best of what could be. Robinson identifies the imagination's role in this process as it could apply to anyone. He asserts, "The creative imagination in fact is the open imagination, the imagination that prompts us to think the unthinkable, to conceive the inconceivable, to imagine the unimaginable. It is thus our natural, inborn faculty for transcendence, for rising above the limits of what previously seemed possible."[133]

What is transcendence? A more complete look at the link between imagination and transcendence necessitates a clearer understanding of the latter term. Robinson has already identified a *limit* as that which must be moved above. He clearly thinks of transcendence in vertical terms. *The American Heritage Dictionary* reveals that the Latin origin of the word refers to climbing over, which involves a vertical and a lateral transition. Among the word's current definitions the dictionary also takes account of both axes.[134] For this work, *transcendence* will convey the very general idea of any change, up or over, that leads an individual past some limitation to an improved or preferable perspective of situation. Fischer frames this change as a participation in a new level of symbolic truth. She remarks, "Only by fully participating in the details of the symbol can we experience the wholeness of the truth it conveys." And conversely, "the truth of the imagination calls for participation.... Such participation in the truth of imagination is able to transform us."[135] Bryant describes a change in one's openness to the world when images mediate a transcendence of self. He observes that these images "do not take the place of objects of perception, of a world transcending our subjectivity, but mediate between the world and the self in a way that opens the self to the world."[136]

Thus far it becomes apparent that the change involved in transcendence does not give the individual sudden access to a hidden world. Rather it is a change of or within the individual that allows him or her to perceive differently. Paul Crowley finds this to be true of Ignatian spirituality. He commends this spiritual path for "its utterly concrete referentiality to the time and space within which human existence takes place and within which God becomes incarnate," and also "its simultaneous transcendence of ordinary sensory experience such that the meaning of such experience is found in God and the fulfillment of human existence in cooperation with God's desires."[137] Crowley could just as well be speaking of Francis' spirituality.

Green's theory of paradigmatic imagination also evinces a form of transcendence. Based on Thomas Kuhn's scientific conception of a paradigm shift, from which his theory is adapted, Green finds that the old paradigm is exchanged for a new one with a methodology, set of questions, and data sources that more adequately contend with the essential data and answer the pertinent questions and issues.[138] When the move to a new paradigm occurs, it is "not gradual and cumulative but logically (and psychologically) discontinuous, like a visual gestalt shift in which the elements of perception suddenly come together in a new and unanticipated configuration."[139]

Green's notion of changed perception is very much in line with the idea of transcendence explicated earlier. Relying on Gestalt Theory he reiterates the point that the same set of data can be seen to represent different entities dependent on what aspect the data is seen in by different individuals.[140] A paradigm shift is first and foremost a perception shift. Green clarifies that it is not a matter of one additional fact bringing about the new way of seeing; rather, it is a matter of seeing all the facts within a new perception-shaping pattern. Once the new pattern is in place, and the world begins to make sense according to it, there is really no return to a previous pattern or paradigm. Green calls this characteristic: irreversibility, which, nonetheless, does not preclude vestigial elements of an earlier pattern surviving in the new pattern.[141] He also mentions the characteristic of incommensurability, stating, "They involve different schemes of organization that allow no common standard of measurement according to which both could be reduced to the same terms."[142] Francis' supposedly graphic renunciation of his parentage is symbolic of the transcending entry into a new paradigm. It is sudden. There is a clear break with the past, and he releases all that could bring him back to his prior way of living and seeing. Additionally, he forsakes his paternal identity which is the basis of the existent social structure. It is difficult to say how factual Thomas of Celano's rendition of Francis' conversion is, but Thomas certainly includes elements that hint at the kind of transcending experience of which Green speaks.

Diverting slightly from the course several other theorists have taken, Scarry describes an imaginatively based change in the world that includes a physical feature. She speaks of the productivity that results from the interplay of pain and the imagination. Scarry maintains that, "Work and its 'work' (or work and its object, its artifact) are the names that are given to the phenomenon of pain and the imagination as they begin to move from being a self-contained loop within the body to becoming the equivalent loop now projected into the external world."[143] This process of externalization does not only move pain outward where it has a better chance of encountering a healing presence; it also produces "an object that was not previously in the world."[144] For Scarry, transcendence, of pain in her theory, is more than a perceptual change. She notes that imagining is often directed toward "a total reinvention of the world," but in many instances, it is realized as a "fragment of world alteration," as an artifact which is able to be experienced collectively.[145] For Francis, perhaps it could be said that his image is his artifact, the one thing that remains from his imaginative struggle with life and the God who authored it. His is an image of change, transformation, and transcendence.

The Imagination and God: How We Relate to the Divine and Express that Relationship

Many of the theorists whose writings are surveyed in this chapter are chosen for their interest in both the imagination and its religious applications. Not all of the scholars view this association positively. Nonetheless, their varying approaches can be shaped into three focal areas. (A) The imagination facilitates the ability to believe in things that require faith for verification. (B) The imagination supplies a matrix for belief in which it is not the images but the endeavor to work with religious imagery that primarily supports the process of belief. (C) The imagination is central to understanding God's efforts to reach and move people.

The Imagination between Believer and Believed

Faith in God by necessity cannot have a clear and present object. There must be a void between the person of faith and the thing in which belief is placed. Yet, the void cannot be absolute. There must be some way to establish and maintain an awareness of the object; there must be some representation within the human subject toward which the thoughts, emotions, and desires proper to faith can be directed. Some might want to argue that there should be nothing standing between the believer and his or her God, but this line of reasoning ultimately runs against the entire tide of revelation. In the Judaeo-Christian tradition, God meets humanity, yes, through unseen acts of grace, but also through deed and word, which are carried on in the contents of the imagination. And thus it is the imagination that gives the believer some lingering aspect of the encounter with the divine so that he or she may ponder, love, and seek God. It is the imagination that stretches out across the void of sub-ultimate reality reaching to ultimate reality like a delicate umbilical thread holding creature and creator in a tenuous communion.[146]

Green seeks to preserve a view of the religious imagination similar to that related above. He states, "More formally: imagination is the anthropological point of contact for divine revelation. It is not the 'foundation,' the 'ground,' the 'preunderstanding,' or the 'ontological basis' for revelation; it is simply the place where it happens—better, the way in which it happens."[147] Green sees this view surviving a slowly developing philosophical challenge to the authenticity of Christian Faith as understood in light of the human imagination. Kant and Georg Wilhelm Friedrich Hegel (1770-1831) were some of the earlier philosophers to refer to religion as a product of the imagination. Green observes, "They agree that religion is imaginary, and they both mean by this term that religious truth is inextricably linked with images dependent on sense experience. Furthermore, they agree that religion nevertheless really does express truth."[148] It is not hard to see how ideas like this were greeted with some apprehension in their time. They allowed another philosopher, Ludwig Feuerbach (1804-1872) to go a step further and clearly relate and reduce imagination to the illusory, in the sense of "not real" or "counter to Reality." This is a reduction of religion to an imaginative act that conceals the truth.[149] Green notes that it was a simple matter for Karl Marx (1818-1883) to unleash the social and political implications of Feuerbach's ideas.[150] Green concludes that it took the decline of positivistic religious thought and the scientific conceptions it upheld for the imagination to be once again considered of value to religion.

Crowley is among many thinkers who realize the renewed possibilities for exploring religion in terms of imagination. Since God is experienced within time and space, Crowley calls imagination "a natural instrument of religion."[151] Scarry conveys that the imagination must continually fulfill an active role in supporting belief. She explains that a material culture is easily sustainable while a culture of belief requires an ongoing effort of reinvention.[152] Scarry says of believing: it "is close to being a synonym for what has been called here 'imagining.'"[153] Specifically, "'belief' is the capacity to sustain the imagined (or apprehended) object in one's own psyche, even when there is no sensorially available confirmation that that object has any existence independent of one's own interior mental activity."[154]

In summary, it would be difficult to maintain belief in something without a reminder of what it is that one has placed one's belief in. This might not be the case if God persists in the form of an idea that recurs free of any imagery, but Scripture is quick to remind the believer that the Creator is revealed in the midst of creation, and the Word took its most complete shape on the lips and in the actions of a corporal being who participated in the bounty and trials of the natural world. And what of the Spirit? The third part of the Trinity is most often recalled from memory as a subtle impression on the senses and by the action it inspires. Without the imagination, how would the actions of the Holy Spirit be expressed to believer and unbeliever alike? Without the imagination, how could Francis, or anyone else for that matter, believe in anything that was not immediately and distinctly present to the senses? Without the imagination, there would be no belief.

Imagination Providing the Field of Images Involved in Faith

It seems that an isolated image of God independent of any other imaginary associations is not a sufficient ground to support the process of belief as far as the imagination is involved. Although it can be asserted that the Creator has an existence distinct from creation, the God of Belief, the God who is believed-in, is inextricably linked to the believer by a matrix of belief that includes images, ideas, emotions, desires and the presence of grace.

The Ulanovs refer more freely to the contents of an individual's imagination than most theorists. They note the importance of personal God-images that reside in the imagination, but they also make the point that such images must be seen in relationship to the shared God-image of a tradition.[155] This association allows the personal image to become meaningful in its own way, which is not to say that it undermines the traditional imagery that gives it context. In fact, the individual's relationship to the God who is *all* would be less complete than it otherwise could be without a reasonable number of images contributing to a current, comprehensive image. Think of the stunted faith that would form solely around an image of the angry God in the apse of the National Basilica of the Immaculate Conception in Washington, D.C. (the depiction is of Jesus), or the marvelous hand in the cloud, or the kindly bearded grandfather of some medieval and renaissance religious artwork (a depiction not easily rectified with orthodox iconographic guidelines). Clearly there are so many more individual images that could come together to comprise the unified image of God that a person holds at any one time. Key among these are the feminine images that are seldom able to participate overtly in the communally adapted Christian image of God.

The imagination's ability to work with such a variety of images validates Tracy's analogical approach to talking about the divine. Analogy, as similarity-in-difference, comprises both affirmation and negation.[156] Analogy allows one to say that God is like an angry man, but God is not reducible to an angry man. It also allows one to say that God is like a kindly grandparent, but God is not simply a kindly grandparent. The dialectical aspect of negation does not shut down the ability to imagine God; rather, in the care of a creative imagination, it keeps the image of God dynamic, vibrant, and alive as new images are drawn upon, and untenable images are set aside or modified throughout the life of faith. Ronald Hepburn expresses the value of this unusual imaginative activity that seems not to want to finally clarify its object. He maintains that, in its efforts to image the divine, imagination, "if it strenuously endeavors, then confesses its failure, it may be nearer to success, though it cannot itself tell us if this is really so."[157]

Were it common practice to somehow avoid the imaginative compilation of images described above in favor of holding tenaciously to a single God-image then the fears of iconoclasts from ages past would be justified. Idolatry begins when an image becomes an endpoint and further movement toward the one imaged is inhibited. Fischer recalls an insight that sits well with a theory of multiple images guiding the focus of faith. She claims, "we do not believe in the images themselves; we see through them."[158] While a single image might claim belief to itself, a dynamic of multiple images, each presenting an aspect of God without making a claim that it has captured the fullness of divine nature, more closely reveals the role of the imagination in forming a perception of God.

Some of the most common images of God are personified images such as the kindly grandparent, but Fischer observes the utilization of impersonal images that allow one to approach God apart from the usual subject/object duality.[159] She uses examples such as God as a ray of light or God as an "experience of the ultimate coming through finite reality, to the depth at the heart of matter."[160] Images along these lines suggest interaction more than emotional attachment, and therefore keep the combining of images more vigorous and lively when linked with personified images.

Some spiritual paths call for eschewing images altogether. Many contemplative spiritualities endeavor to encounter God free from the limitation of imagery, but the Ulanovs suggest that this is never quite possible. They insist that, "Even when we go beyond images we use an image, the one of imagelessness."[161] Stanley Hopper describes a movement to an imageless experience that nonetheless ends with the kind of image referred to by the Ulanovs. He explains that non-knowing is a transcendence of knowledge from sensory experience through "analytical conceptual 'knowledge' down to the symbolic level, through that to the level of archetypal recognitions (with its source in what we wondrously call the 'unconscious') and through that to what we term in the West the 'ground of Being.'"[162] When terms like *the ultimate*, and *the ground of Being* receive regular use they begin to accrue their own series of representational images. The mind will use imagery to apply meaning to abstractions such as these.

In general, there are many images that are available or become available for the undertaking of belief in God. At times one image will prevail over the others, or seem more pertinent, but any individual's complete perception of God will be formed by a structure of numerous images, as well as the feelings, intentions, and thoughts that hold the structure in place. It is in the imagination that the pieces are gathered and the edifice is erected.

Imagination and the Work of God

"In the beginning was the Word, and the Word was with God, and the Word was God.... And the Word became flesh and dwelt among us, full of grace and truth... And from his fullness have we all received, grace upon grace" (Jn 1: 1, 14, 16). This is a central Christian teaching on the mission and role of Jesus, but it only begins to reveal what Jesus does and seeks to do in this world. He teaches people to direct their way of experiencing the world to the highest good. He expresses new ways for people to relate to one another, their cultures, and the world at large. Jesus opens eternity to the multitudes who are willing to embrace it fully, and he also gives humanity a lesson in transcending a narrow-sighted way of perceiving and being a part of reality. In short, Jesus taps into the imagination's ability to interact with experience, relationships, time, and transcendence. What Francis does for the narrower sector of individuals who come to know of him directly or indirectly, Jesus does on a larger scale. They both become living icons of God's solicitude for human existence.[163] Confirming the importance of this divine application of imagination, Cheryl Forbes identifies Jesus as "imagination incarnate."[164] As such, it is not surprising that Jesus touched imaginations as much as hearts. In fact, one might wonder whether it is possible to touch the proverbial heart without the prior assistance of the imagination.

Forbes links the imagination with the *imago Dei* or image of God within a person.[165] John Bowker specifies how this is possible. He makes the provocative assertion that Jesus "first located the effect of God in his own person and shared it with others, and [is the one] who was constrained by this into the novel outcome, the figure who evoked allegiance as the locus of theistic effect in the world."[166] And how best to spread this effect outward but through a web of imaginations!

From the way the imagination has been associated with Jesus so far, it becomes increasingly obvious that several scholars envision the imagination factoring heavily into the course of the revelation of God to humanity. This revelation can never be understood only in the contracted sense of propositional truths; it must be recognized as the fundamental and enduring encounter between Creator and creature. Hart suggests that revelation is "God's solicitation to be," which he calls "a solicitation effected concretely not in an ontological language tradition but by courtesy of the historico-deiform imagination."[167] While the present study relies on Green's work to exemplify a particular theory of imagining (paradigmatically), the thesis of his book is that the imagination is the *anknüpfungspunkt*, or the anthropological point of contact for revelation sought after by Karl Barth and Emil Brunner in their 1934 running debate.[168] Green cautions that the imagination is not the cause, foundation, or basis of belief in God. It is, as stated earlier, simply where revelation happens.[169] He observes that for Brunner, whatever the natural point of contact for revelation may be, it "consists in man's ability to be addressed."[170] Green goes on to describe the origin of revelation. His view is that God made an impression on the imaginations of the original witnesses which is, in turn, more or less expressed to subsequent believers when they enter into the patterns that this impression-expression makes available.[171]

Catholic Christians have long believed that the so-called patterns of faith that convey God's revelation are found in both the Church's tradition and its Scripture. While, in one sense, this entire study highlights sainthood, which is an aspect of the Catholic tradition that calls for living imaginatively according to certain models of holiness, Luke Timothy Johnson indicates the manner in which Scripture is tied in with the imagination. He claims that, "Scripture itself imagines a world. By imagining a world, scripture brings it into being."[172] Johnson is in no way implying that Scripture is based in imaginative fantasy. Instead, he notes that, "Like all imaginative creations, the scriptural world is rooted in the physical realm where humans live."[173] The parallels between living in Johnson's scriptural worldview and the ORT approach to forming an outlook on the world, also a way of being in it, are unmistakable. Johnson maintains that, "People act on the basis of the imagined world in which they dwell, and by acting on what they imagine, they help establish their world as real."[174]

What is the nature of this world encountered in Scripture? Johnson mentions that it is smaller than the worldview most people hold today but "more richly furnished."[175] He adds that it is "a world in which every creature is at every moment summoned into being by a Power and Presence that is at once distant and close, ageless and instant."[176] Johnson goes on to say that reality experienced as "always and everywhere related to God...reveals the world and at the same time reveals God."[177] It will become apparent that Francis has adopted a similar way of seeing God's ongoing participation in creation, but his view allows for a broader perspective than Johnson suggests. Furthermore, it will become clear that Francis has formed his imagination around deeply embossed images of who and what Christ is.

Imagination and the Generation of Meaning

Throughout the forgoing look at views of imagination concurrent with those of Object Relations Theory the matter of meaning-making has been brought up repeatedly. Beginning with the acceptance of raw experience and the weaving of relationships, through the consideration of time, change, and God, the end objective has been to imaginatively work out meaning. This could include applying, discovering, gathering, or even fabricating meaning. In some sense, ORT deals with meaning in all these variations. As a final prelude to exploring the ORT perspective of imagination, the topic of meaning will be addressed in a threefold manner. The imagination will be understood as playing a part in seeking a specific interpretation as meaning, which could be expressed as contracting meaning. The imagination will also be studied as it expands meaning to a less defined or broader dimension. Finally, meaning will be observed as it occurs in patterns and processes.

Contracting Meaning

When two people stand in the same place, at the same time, with the same basic capacity of observation, it might be expected that their account of an experience would be identical, but this seldom turns out to be true. The reality of individual imaginations ensures that experience will not be given meaning in exactly the same way by two individuals. Since experience is polyvalent, it has the potential of generating numerous possible meanings. It is typical for the experiencer to reduce the possible meanings down to one. This is a tightening down of meaning that is often associated with interpretation. The imagination reaches an interpretation by noting likenesses between existent images and the emerging image being formed by the experience. The imagination also interprets by synthesizing multiple images to form a single image. It is even suggested that the imagination uses the volatile meanings embedded in emotions to help form an interpretation.

Finding Meaning Through Likeness

Warnock conveys the idea that imagination does not just re-call images. Through images and relationships it allows a person to interpret what is present in the immediate perceptual world.[178] To operate in a world understood as *perceptual* requires what she describes as a heightened interpretive capacity, since distinct meaning is not a given in such an environment.[179] When the topic of imagination is brought up in general conversation, Green maintains that "interpretive imagination" is the most commonly intended definition.[180] He explains that this type of imaginative activity uses more accessible images in comparison with an experience or its less well-formed and hence less accessible image.[181] This heuristic activity enables one to assign meaning as a recognition of likeness. Green also uses a related term, "perceptual imagination," which involves seeing-as.[182] This is not re-presentation as in a duplication of an original; rather, it is re-presentation of an image in a new light, in a new relationship. Green attempts to drive home the point that imagination does not just rely on something being picturable-as, but experienced-as, in a way that could include hearing-as, and maybe even feeling-as. This view expands the possibilities for designating meaning based on likeness.

Hopper is interested in interpretation through likeness on the linguistic level, but he reveals a serious challenge to this endeavor. He recognizes that a continuous chain of association between a concept and its "root metaphor" sustains meaning.[183] The difficulty occurs not when the connection is lost to this base metaphor, or what Tracy would call similarly a "prime analogue," but when the metaphor itself is no longer grounded.[184] This is a problem on the level of the structure of interpretation which reveals the potential weakness of this avenue to meaning, the path most commonly followed.

Finding Meaning Through Synthesis

Earlier the imagination was highlighted for its ability to perceive unrealized potential. The designation of meaning to a collection of otherwise unstructured sense data opens what is merely potential to what is realized as actual through an interpretive process. Two builders can look upon a pile of lumber, and one can visualize a beautiful ship while the other sees a grand home. Each has reduced a jumble of wood to a distinctive final product, a creation. Riposa remarks that, "interpretation necessarily involves the constructive power of imagination."[185] What the builders can achieve externally with their physical skills, they achieve, first, interiorly with their imaginations. Hepburn describes this ability to form parts into a meaningful whole on another level. He observes the imagination's "epistemological role in converting undifferentiated sensation into a world over-against myself as a subject."[186]

Maria Harris explains the constructive or synthesizing formation of meaning as a result of compositive imagination. This is a third category that she adds to Wheelwright's confrontative and distancing imaginations mentioned in a previous section. She declares that this is the type of imagination that "leads us to discover meaning."[187] Based on her belief that "in everything that exists there is a bit of everything else," she finds that compositive imagination enables one to make connections and at the same time envision the related elements in a harmony that has never been envisioned before.[188]

Harris derives her concept of the compositive imagination from Wheelwright's category of the metaphoric imagination. Wheelwright uses the idea of metaphor in a different sense from Hopper. Rather than an association formed in likeness, Wheelwright expresses a forced synthesis of images. He specifies that metaphoric imagining "involves a fusion between two or more concrete images, each perhaps carrying certain emotive and ideational associations."[189] Imagining in this fashion entails "a readiness to see this and that in a single perspective and thus forming a single individuality."[190] He goes on to downplay a likeness among images when he observes that, "The essence of metaphor consists in the nature of the tension which is maintained among the heterogeneous elements brought together in one commanding image."[191] While some theorists see the imagination deriving meaning from the apparent compatibility of images (likeness), Wheelwright's view demands, instead, the creation of the recognition of a relationship that instills meaning in an experience. He asserts that, in its most evocative sense the metaphoric tension stands "as a living paradox, a vibrant, highly charged tension between more or less incompatible meanings."[192] Francis' ability to discover the meaning of joy in poverty and suffering is a clear reflection of this type of imaginative activity and his personal capacity to fashion a meaningful world from the experiences available to him.

Feeling One's Way Through Meaning

Just as the imaginative processing, discussed throughout this chapter, is a response to an experience, emotion can also be considered a response. It is difficult to say whether emotion acts as a parallel to imaginative activity or if it is a follow-on response to the image derived from the activity. Scholars who focus on the emotions will vary in their stands on this point, but two scholars of the imagination indicate that emotion has been associated in the past with meaning-making. Warnock notes a close connection between an image of an object and the emotion one is able to attach to it, explaining that emotion has even been described as a kind of impression.[193] This would equate emotion with image in its rudimentary stage. On the other hand, Warnock learns from Coleridge that the imagination has three purposes: to bring about an image, to recognize its universal significance, and to "induce in us deep feelings in the presence of the image."[194] Accordingly, emotion follows after the primary imaginative activity, affecting the process of meaning-making in a manner that could clarify meaning through intensification of perception or cloud it through the distortion of unproportional or misapplied emotion.

Feminist theory challenges the theoretical influence of emotion on the derivation of meaning from experience. Paula Cooey notes that scholars of feminist theory have granted experience a degree of irreducibility due to its basis in emotion, but she questions the rationality of this position since emotion can easily reinforce some negative aspects of women's experience.[195] She cites a growing consensus among psychologists that feeling or emotion "is interpretive, rather than 'raw' data from which interpretation is subsequently constructed."[196] Earlier she remarked that experience gains its authority from its claim to *noesis*: "from the subject's perspective experience becomes authoritative because it yields insight, illumination, or revelation."[197] In other words, experience has authority when it is realized as meaningful. Emotion, when associated with the imagery relevant to an experience, bolsters the authority of the experience, the impact of its meaning, by intensifying and heightening the conviction surrounding it. Cooey's cautionary note deserves attention. The persuasiveness that emotion can lend to a particular meaning does not guarantee the reality or truth of that meaning, only that it will be held to be so, more tightly. Francis, who comes across as a very empathetic person, did bring emotion into his imaginative development of a religiously meaningful world, but from what is known of emotion, it did not drive the meaning he reveals in his writings, it simply supports the profound level of it all, and his ability to act upon it.

Expanding Meaning

Imagination has been shown to play a central part in the formation of particular, contracted meaning. It takes multiple points of experience and shapes them into a single point of perception. But, imagination is a wonderfully versatile capacity; it can also move meaning in the opposite direction, from the particular to the general. It seems that many people are willing to travel through their temporal existence comfortably afloat in a quiet sea of concrete, empirically based understanding. From time to time, a tempest brews up to shatter the tranquility of each person's still waters. The result is a confrontation with a major life event for which a contracted interpretation is no life-preserver. Events of this scale cause one to ask the big, abstract questions about the meaning of life. The loss of a loved-one, an incurable medical condition, or senseless cruelty are common examples of this phenomenon. For Francis, the horrors of war, imprisonment, and serious illness may have brought on this level of search for meaning. Many of these tragedies push people into an encounter with Tracy's "limit-of-experience."[198] These encounters thus call for an expansion of meaning that does not seek a discrete answer but, more to the point, a satisfactory understanding of one's participation in something larger than a personal life project. Several scholars reveal the imagination's ability to engage in this widening search for meaning through the use of symbol and archetype.

Symbolic Meaning

One of the most effective tools that have been bestowed upon the human being to safely navigate the turbulent waters of existence is the capacity to symbolize and respond to the symbolic as a way to carve out meaning from experience. It is unfortunate, then, that Hopper can speak of a tendency in traditional theology "to contain the symbolic in a science and to reduce mysteries to knowledge."[199] Clearly there are some aspects of human experience that deserve a more meaningful expression than this reduction allows. Ernst Cassirer suggests that life presents the individual with too much to be dealt with on a purely empirical level. He states, "For all mental processes fail to grasp reality itself, and in order to represent it, to hold it at all, they are driven to the use of symbols."[200] He goes on to claim that thought itself cannot occur without symbols. "Symbolic forms are not imitations, but *organs* of reality, since it is solely by their agency that anything real becomes an object for intellectual apprehension, and as such is made visible to us."[201]

Cassirer gives symbols, including myth, art, language, and science, great scope when he defines a symbol as an entity "which produces and posits a world of its own."[202] As such, the symbol would be almost a self-contained world of meaning instead of an image that captures the imagination's attention and directs it toward a deeper level of meaning. It seems that a more open-ended concept of symbol better expresses its ability to participate in meaning-making or - taking. Riposa's description of "semiotic capacity" falls a little closer to an understanding of the *symbolic* that includes the flexibility to expand meaning. He calls it "the ability to perceive ordinary sense objects as signs, potentially rich in meaning."[203] Francis' *Canticle of the Creatures* is a notable demonstration of this semiotic capacity.

The ability of a person to work comfortably with symbols is the foundation of highly creative imaginative activity. This is a real dividing point in the way people envision life. When children are observed engaged with a coloring book and crayons, it appears that they follow two different tendencies. There are those who insist on coloring within the lines and those who do so more-or-less, and often less. In later years, some of these children, grown-to-adulthood, might still take great care to maintain distinctive boundaries. They will not just follow external guidelines; they will exist by them. For such people, the fact that the imagination can discover more than one type or level of meaning in a symbol can prove to be a source of great frustration or anxiety. The other group of children learned to believe that a green cow could be just as beautiful as the green grass she was eating in their picture. They have already begun to play with a world of possibilities, and the versatility of the *symbolic* will enable them to grow in a meaningful world and expand this meaning to meet the problems and opportunities brought in on every new tide.

The latter scenario is permeated with hope because of the ability of signs and symbols to be altered, added to, or replaced with respect to the meaning and understanding that one is trying to work with or achieve. Riposa exhibits the indeterminateness of the imagination as he declares that, "everything that enters into experience is potentially a sign, and every sign is multivalent."[204] He reveals the dynamic nature of symbolism when he confirms that, "Human beings are engaged in a continuous process of interpreting signs, discovering their meaning, creating new signs."[205] Warnock expresses this dynamism similarly: "Imagination is the power of seeing things as they are, namely as symbolic, and of creating new symbols (and to a lesser extent new images) to express the ultimate nature of the world."[206] It is for this reason that Cooey urges the development of spiritualities that are not disengaged from temporal reality. Those that rely solely on an otherworldly perspective tend to limit the individual's ability to challenge existing orders of symbol systems.[207] By nature a symbol system is volatile. Without this feature it ceases to function as an active conveyor of meaning.

Archetypal and Semiotic Meaning

A sign or symbol can be seen as an external parallel to the image that remains internal to the imagination. While the present work does not depend on a strict distinction between sign and symbol, and thus uses the terms interchangeably, other studies accentuate the difference. Carl Jung (1875-1961) contends that signs do little more "than denote the objects to which they are attached," adding little descriptive value and carrying no meaning in themselves.[208] A symbol, on the other hand, "possesses specific connotations in addition to its conventional and obvious meaning."[209] It "implies something more than its obvious meaning."[210] Much of the accessible knowledge about imaginative activity comes from observing its manifestation in external symbolic acts. The recognition, rearrangement, and production of images, already described, has a counterpart in symbolism. An image could easily be described as an internal symbol; each refers to something else. Even though bringing an image to mind on a specific occasion or moving images into new relationships are sources of imaginative originality, the most definitive source would be the formation of a new image. Several scholars elucidate this occurrence in terms of signs and symbols.

Where do new signs and symbols come from? Riposa contends with this question using the theory of semiosis. He writes, "Human experience, from the simplest sensations and emotions to the most complex judgments about states of affairs, takes the form of semiosis."[211] "Semiosis is an interpretive process that involves the continuous production of new signs, each itself subject to further interpretation."[212] When interpretation involves or requires the use of new signs, it is clearly not directed toward the contracted form of meaning mentioned earlier, but Riposa does not go far enough in explaining how the new signs and the expanded meaning are brought about.

A number of other theorists use an archetypal approach to look at the formation of signs or symbols. The word *archetype* gained great attention in Jung's work. He defines it as "a tendency to form... representations of a motif."[213] The motif is not exactly the symbol. It is more a pattern according to which one forms symbols. Jung acknowledges the significant criticism he has endured for his contention that archetypes have a kind of preexistent presence in the mental landscape.[214] According to his view the archetype stands as an *a priori* of the symbolic imagination.

Hopper uses Jung's concept to lay bare the transitive nature of symbols in the act of making meaning. He notes that, "When language fails to function at the metaphorical or symbolic levels, the imagination goes deeper, soliciting the carrying power of archetype, translating the archetype from the spent symbolic system into fresh embodiments."[215]

Wheelwright lists an archetypal imagination in his four-part schema for the imagination. He identifies archetypes as "preconsciously rooted symbols inherited 'from the past,' equipping our thought and imagination with an ancestral dimension without which true reverence, and therefore the very substance of our conscious life, would go dry and dead."[216] His definition is not a significant departure from Jung's terminology if a motif is understood as a grand symbol from which specific symbols are derived for specific needs. Wheelwright explains that the archetypal imagination, which he also designates "Emblematic Imagination," operates "by grasping the particular idea and the transient image in relation to something more universal and perduring."[217] It is as if the imagination is looking at a common or sense-perceived object, a small piece of existence, and setting it onto a much larger canvas, filling in the background with the broad swaths of life that would not be apparent in its usual surroundings. When Harris takes up Wheelwright's schema, she assigns the archetypal imagination as "the capacity to see the particular as embodying in some way a more universal significance, perhaps a higher or deeper meaning than it carries in itself alone."[218] From what has been said of the imagination's use of relationship, Wheelwright's notions appear to give a closer approximation of the workings of the imagination when it is involved in expanding meaning. Francis' supposed interest in the simple elements of nature must be seen in this light. A bird giving Francis her attention would not be just an animal instinctively aware; it would be a sign or symbol that all of creation takes interest in the word and works of God.

Meaning Found in Order

In this chapter, the review of contemporary writings on the imagination indicates that meaning can be formed imaginatively through a narrowing down of possible images to a single or limited image that is affirmable for its likeness to the object that one seeks to understand. This contraction of meaning is often labeled *interpretation*, but it could go by other titles as well.[219] The search for meaning also profits from the workings of the imagination when the imagination links objects of direct experience with a less distinct but grander landscape to broaden the pool of meaning that can be derived from any experience. In addition to the contraction and expansion of meaning, it is possible to come into contact with meaning by attending to the everyday processes and patterns of life.

Meaning in Process

The challenge to using an imagination connected with processes or patterns is to become aware of the very patterns and processes where they are found. Riposa recalls the medieval term *acedia*, which is often seen as "an inability to perceive the religious significance of things."[220] *Acedia* is also recognized as: "spiritual sluggishness, dullness in prayer, boredom with the rituals of devotion."[221] Yet, it is the repetitious nature of some aspects of life that Riposa considers a necessary precursor to spiritual insight. He argues that enduring a habitual lifestyle has the benefit of "enhancing attention, reducing distraction, and facilitating the flow of information."[222] It appears that opening oneself to the ebb and flow of existence may be the best option when imaginative deduction or induction fails to divulge understanding. For some scholars, meaning is gained by allowing traditional or natural processes to run their course and also by re-cognizing the patterns that bind activities and relationships into a whole.

Bowker uses an information process and systems analysis approach to reli-gious imagination. He finds that religions possess a deep pocket of resources that can be drawn from to formulate new, "life-giving" realizations.[223] He main-tains that, "the continuity of a religious tradition depends on the appropriation of what has up to that point been fundamentally resourceful, and on the translation of these resources into the construction of utterance in life."[224] If *utterance* stands for the expression of meaning, then meaning is actually found in the open channel of information between the resource and the realization. Using Chris-tianity and Francis to exemplify this, it could be said that Francis stood before the open floodgates of Scripture and oral/pictorial Christian tradition, soaking in understanding as he turned to manifest his experience of Christ for a world standing dry on the banks. While acting upon his experience may have helped to clarify his understanding, Francis must have been wet with meaning to even begin his conversion.

In his article, Bowker details how one aspect of habit can partake in the im-aginative process. He notes that religious information networks or systems "re-sult in individuals whose brain-behavior is informed with particular cues of in-formation and pictures of reality which are retrieved for the construction of life."[225] Stull actually uses the term "process-oriented imagination."[226] He im-plies that this imagining is a continuous activity that has the ability to replenish meaning. Imagination can be regarded as both object-oriented and process-oriented. One becomes aware of both the product of the imagination, the object, and the process by which it is achieved while one actively attends to the work-ings of the imagination. When the process is observed as primary, Stull explains that it "constantly disrupts its own products."[227] By returning the imaginative focus to an earlier-formed image, the image undergoes a reappraisal that yields a new image with the likelihood of an attendant new level of meaning.

Meaning in Pattern

Beyond the order and meaning discovered in a regular process there is another order to be found in the organizing arrangements of elements and inte-ractions. Warnock determines that, the creative imagination sees and expresses ideas that are perceived "as the pattern, design or essence of things."[228] Cassirer also speaks of conceptualized meaning, but he locates it in a form versus a pat-tern. He exclaims, "But what are concepts save formulations and creations of thought, which, instead of giving us the true forms of objects show us rather the forms of thought itself."[229] In a notion developed from Kant, he is able to con-firm that meaning is not found in the product of the form, the thought. Instead, Cassirer insists that, "we must find in these forms themselves the measure and criterion for their truth and intrinsic meaning."[230]

If meaning is present in the pattern or form, then it is Green who is best able to lay out the imaginative effort that will produce either one. He regards imagin-ing as "the taking of paradigms to explore the patterns of the larger world."[231] His placement of pattern at the base of all knowledge, understanding, and meaning is a direct challenge to Kant's view that the whole is known as a synthesis of its parts, a synthesized whole.[232] Green claims that, "the whole can be neither more nor less than the sum of its parts since it is not a sum at all."[233] He advances that it is on the level of pattern that the parts are perceived, and more specifically, recognized as a specific whole.[234] The whole is not envisioned by gathering together all the constituent factors; it only becomes apparent when the factors are experienced within the perception-shaping pattern. In Green's view, the paradigm becomes all-important. It serves to "reveal the larger patterns in broad areas of experience that might otherwise remain inaccessible because they appear incoherent or bewildering in their complexity."[235] A similar conviction leads Tracy to assert, "In some matters, only the paradigmatic is the real."[236] Francis may not have known of paradigms, but it should not be shocking to suggest that he discovered meaning according to a distinct perception-shaping pattern, that he imparted something of it to others, and that he developed his outlook as a shift from a degenerating pattern. In this light, a look at Francis' imaginative activity from an Object Relations Theory perspective will prove insightful. After all, when object representations are arranged in a notable relationship, are they not forming a pattern that influences the way new representations are perceived?

Summary

In this chapter, the works of numerous contemporary scholars were reviewed for insights into the workings of the imagination from viewpoints other than the Object Relations Theory perspective to be taken up in the next two chapters. The ideas exhibited in this chapter, which indicate just what the imagination can and cannot do, share much in common with ORT. Imagination was shown as a place where experiences are brought out of the chaotic morass that human beings are born into. It is then, in the imagination, that order is given to the experiences. Order is granted particularly by the arrangement of relationships between the image inspired by an experience and an ever-wider selection of images that it can be linked with. Imagination, in turn, was identified for its ability to play a part in the human being's external relationships in and with the physical world. Another possibility that the imagination makes available is the individual's capacity to make the most of time as a function of transformation and transcendence, and a study of the religious imagination would be remiss without reference to imagination's role in supporting belief. The final section broke down three ways of imaginatively deriving meaning. Imagination was shown to contract meaning to an interpretation, expand it to a symbolic level, and discover it in the patterns and processes that make up everyday life. It is the latter two areas that are of greatest interest for a look into the workings of Francis' imagination.

It must be obvious that this chapter presents a very expansive vision of the imagination and what it can do. Some aspects of mental apprehension, contained herein, could have been placed in a different topographical category, but it is believed that the human encounter with a world of experience is best expressed through a model of the imagination. Throughout this chapter, the findings of the selected theorists were arranged around certain focal points that correspond, sometimes loosely and sometimes closely, with key tenets of Object Relations Theory regarding the imaginative creation of a meaning-filled world. Where it was possible, connections were made with Francis' imaginative activity. Of specific interest to a study of Francis' writings will be the relational topics that lead to a discernment of wholeness and harmony, as well as topics in transcendence, belief, and perception-shaping in general.

Notes

1. It should be noted that *imagination* is being used as a singular term in this chapter. In spite of the earlier critique of the term "Medieval Imagination," the present usage is justified. *Imagination*, herein, refers to the operations of this human capacity, which is, more-or-less, a constant. The earlier employment of the term "Medieval Imagination" was directed to the consideration of the content of imaginations, which may have been a more homogeneous body in its time, but it still stands as a reduction of the wealth of imaginative content that was existent.

2. These categories are suggested by the focuses selected by the authors themselves. Other categories may exist, but the selected literature highlights these groupings. In some cases authors support more than one category.

3. While ORT offers, perhaps, the most comprehensive approach to studying the workings of an individual's imagination, other theories and views can bring further understanding to the imaginative activities of a figure like Francis.

4. Mary Warnock, *Imagination*, (Berkeley: University of California Press, 1976), 152

5. Philip Wheelwright, *The Burning Fountain: A Study in the Language of Symbolism* (Bloomington: Indiana University Press, 1954), 80-93.

6. Ibid., 80.

7. Ibid., 82.

8. Maria Harris, *Teaching and Religious Imagination: An Essay in the Theology of Teaching* (San Francisco: Harper, 1987), 17.

9. Wheelwright, 83.

10. Harris, 17.

11. Wheelwright, 86.

12. David Tracy, *The Analogical Imagination: Christian Theology and the Culture of Pluralism* (New York: Crossroad, 1981), 108.

13. Ibid., 409.

14. Ibid., 125.

15. Ibid., 111.

16. Ibid., 114.

17. Ibid., 118, 235. Tracy applies the concept of preunderstanding to both experiencing and interpreting.

18. Ibid., 174, 178.

19. Ibid., 408.

20. Ibid.

21. Ibid., 408, 412. Tracy puts forward the Christ event as a primary analogue.

22. Warnock, 196.

23. Ibid., 198.

24. Ibid., 10.

25. Ibid., 133.

26. Ibid., 21.

27. Tracy, 129, 409.

28. Warnock and other contemporary theorists rely heavily on Kant's views found particularly in the following work. Immanuel Kant, *Critique of Pure Reason*, trans. Norman Kemp Smith (New York: St. Martin's Press, 1965), A118; A124; B151-152, et passim.

29. Warnock, 30.

30. Ibid., 46.

31. Ibid., 50.

32. Ibid., 62.

33. Garrett Green, *Imagining God: Theology and the Religious Imagination* (Grand Rapids: Eerdmans, 1989), 62.

34. Ibid., 63.

35. Ibid., 63-65.

36. Ibid., 63.

37. Elaine Scarry, *The Body in Pain: The Making and Unmaking of the World* (New York: Oxford University Press, 1985), 166.

38. Ibid., 5.

39. Ibid., 16.

40. Ibid., 5-6.

41. Bradford T. Stull, *Religious Dialectics of Pain and Imagination* (Albany: State University of New York Press, 1994), 2.

42. Ibid., 20.

43. Scarry, 162.

44. Ibid., 164.

45. Ibid.

46. Ibid., 162.

47. Ibid. Much of spiritual experience falls under this concept of providing an object when none is perceivable. This occurs particularly when the experience is of an ineffable nature. Moses' meeting with God is an early example. The God who is beyond object meets the man, at the level of his condition, in the form of a common object, the bush, in turn, made uncommon by the presence of non-consuming fire (Ex 3.2-3).

48. Ray Hart, *Unfinished Man and the Imagination: Toward and Ontology and Rhetoric of Revelation* (New York: Herder and Herder, 1968), 114.

49. David Bryant, *Faith and the Play of Imagination* (Macon GA: Mercer University Press, 1989), 100.

50. Ibid. I contend that the relationship of embedded meanings in language is used to mirror internal imaginative activity.

51. Andrew M. Greeley, *The Religious Imagination* (Los Angeles: Sadlier, 1981), 8.

52. Ibid., 10.

53. Ibid., 15-16. Note that he also uses location terminology.

54. Michael L. Riposa, *Boredom and the Religious Imagination* (Charlottesville: University of Virginia Press, 1999), 133.

55. Kathleen R. Fischer, *The Inner Rainbow: The Imagination in Christian Life* (Ramsey NJ: Paulist Press, 1983), 67.

56. Ibid., 121.

57. Richard T. Knowles, "Fantasy and Imagination," *Studies in Formative Spirituality* 4 (1985): 61.

58. Tracy, 130.

59. Hans Georg Gadamer, *Truth and Method* (New York: Seabury Press, 1975), 101.

60. Ibid., 102.

61. Knowles, 61

62. Ibid.

63. Ibid.

64. Greeley, 17.

65. Ibid., 18, 61. Greeley notes that boys seem to develop religious imaginations most effectively under the influence of good relationships with both the mother and the father (See also page 49). As stated in Chapter One, there is no reason to believe that Francis' early relationship with his father could not support the formation of a good, working imagination.

66. Ibid.

67. Tracy, 451.

68. Ibid., 101.

69. Ibid.

70. Bryant, 6.

71. Ibid., 110.

72. Ibid., 115, 105, 103.

73. Ibid., 106, 126.

74. Gadamer, 96.

75. Ibid., 98.

76. Ibid., 93, 94.

77. Hart, 122.

78. Gadamer, 92.

79. Ibid., 94.

80. Ibid., 92.

81. Ibid., 98.

82. Ibid., 101.

83. Ibid.

84. Ann Ulanov and Barry Ulanov, *The Healing Imagination: The Meeting of Psyche and Soul* (Daimon, 1999), 15-16, 33.

85. Ibid., 81.

86. Ibid. While the Ulanovs appear to be influenced by Jung's archetypal theories, there is also an indication that they are fully aware of ORT.

87. Francis of Assisi, *A Letter to Brother Leo*, in Marion Habig, ed. *St. Francis of Assisi: Writings and Early Biographies: English Omnibus of Sources for the Life of St. Francis.* (Quincy, IL: Franciscan University Press, 1991), 118.

88. Ulanov, 82.

89. Francis of Assisi, *The Earlier Rule*, in Regis J. Armstrong, J.A. Wayne Hellmann, and William J. Short, eds. *Francis of Assisi: Early Documents.* Vol. 1, *The Saint* (New York: New City Press, 1999), 39.

90. Knowles, 53.

91. Ibid.

92. Ibid., 54. Note that *autistic* as used in this sense does not refer directly to the condition of a person diagnosed with autism or Progressive Developmental Disorder. Nonetheless, the situation in which an experience is not taken hold of or reacted to in any fashion, such that it seems to pass right by the individual's sensing, imagining, and understanding capacity, reflects the counter-experiential notion being discussed in the text.

93. Ibid., 58.

94. Ibid., 54.

95. See Arnoldo Fortini, *Francis of Assisi*, trans. Helen Moak (New York: Crossroads, 1981), 208-210. Fortini describes a medieval ritual of last rights and burial that was performed for lepers long before their inevitable death. By this ritual they became in essence, walking dead.

96. Knowles, 56.

97. Ibid., 55.

98. William F. Lynch, *Images of Hope: Imagination as Healer of the Hopeless* (Baltimore: Helicon, 1965), 23.

99. Ibid., 106.

100. Ibid.

101. Ibid.

102. Ibid., 40.

103. Ibid., 36.

104. Ibid., 244.

105. Ibid., 249.

106. Knowles, 57.

107. Ibid., 246.

108. Ibid., 247.

109. Ibid.

110. The notion of time being used in this work is necessarily simplistic and not vary-ing far from the rudimentary concepts of past, present, and future. Extensive studies have been made on the subject of time, and these come from various academic disciplines. Antje Jackelén has written a book that reveals the complexity of the subject in several disciplines while at the same time making a root connection at the level of relationships. See Antje Jackelén, *Time and Eternity: The Question of Time in Church, Science, and Theology* (Philadelphia: Templeton Foundation Press, 2005).

111. Tracy, 119.

112. The confirmation or corrective for one's imaginative activity is not just found in the archived tradition, it is most importantly taken from the active, living tradition. After all, it is within the living tradition that one's images are either accepted or rejected.

113. Edward T. Oakes, "A Life of Allegory: Type and Pattern in Historical Narratives," in *Through a Glass Darkly: Essays in the Religious Imagination*, ed. John C. Hawley (New York: Fordham University Press, 1996), 135.

114. Jo Ellen Parker, "A Lesson in Reading: George Elliot and the Typological Imagi-nation," in *Through a Glass Darkly*, 105.

115. Ibid.

116. Edward Robinson, *The Language of Mystery* (Philadelphia: Trinity Press Interna-tional, 1987), 17-18.

117. Fischer, 23.

118. Green, 50.

119. Ibid., 54.

120. Fischer, 31.

121. Ibid.; Tracy, 409.

122. Riposa, 134.

123. Bryant, 88.

124. Fischer, 12.

125. Riposa, 132.

126. Oakes, 134.

127. Fischer, 7.

128. Robinson, 12.

129. Ibid.

130. Lynch, 32.

131. Ibid., 23.

132. Ibid., 35, 37.

133. Robinson, 12.

134. *The American Heritage Dictionary of the English Language* (1982), s.v. "Tran-scend."

135. Fischer, 18-19.

136. Bryant, 90.

137. Paul G. Crowley, "Ignatian Imagination and the Aesthetics of Liberation," in *Through a Glass Darkly*, 62.

138. Green, 46. For Kuhn's original conception see: Thomas S. Kuhns, The Structure of Scientific Revolutions (Chicago: University of Chicago Press, 1970).

139. Green, 47.

140. Ibid., 50. Green uses Wittgenstein's "duck-rabbit" as an example.

141. Ibid., 55.

142. Ibid., 57.

143. Scarry, 170.

144. Ibid.

145. Ibid., 171.

146. This is not to imply that the imagination replaces grace in a *nouveau anthropologie*. It might be said that grace, like revelation in Green's theory, impinges upon the human being through the soul, but also, somehow, through the imagination so that it might be given some further expression in the world.

147. Green, 40.

148. Ibid., 17. Green adds that Kant and Hegel both suspected that one must transcend the sensible, that which applies to the senses, in one's search for the truth, Samuel Taylor Coleridge (1772-1834) retained an appreciation for the essential role of sensible symbols throughout such a pursuit. See: Green, 20.

149. Ibid., 23.

150. Ibid.

151. Crowley, 62.

152. Scarry, 172.

153. Ibid., 180.

154. Ibid.

155. Ann and Barry Ulanov, 32

156. Tracy, 415, 418.

157. Ronald W. Hepburn, "Religious Imagination," in *Philosophy, Religion and the Spiritual Life*, ed. Michael McGhee (Cambridge: Cambridge University Press, 1992), 131.

158. Fischer, 121. John of Damascus framed much of his defense of icons on this idea.

159. Ibid., 117.

160. Ibid., 117, 8.

161. Ann and Barry Ulanov, 38.

162. Stanley Romaine Hopper, *The Way of Transfiguration: Religious Imagination as Theopoiesis*, ed. R. Melvin Keiser and Tony Stoneburner (Louisville: Westminster/John Knox Press, 1992), 222-223.

163. It goes without saying that Francis became an image of Jesus the image.

164. Cheryl Forbes, *Imagination: Embracing a Theology of Wonder* (Portland OR: Multonomah Press, 1986), 49.

165. Ibid., 22.

166. John Bowker, *The Religious Imagination and the Sense of God* (Oxford: Clarendon Press, 1978), 126.

167. Hart, 122.

168. Green, 29, 31.

169. Ibid., 40, 42, 43.

170. Ibid., 33.

171. Ibid., 106.

172. Luke Timothy Johnson, "Imagining the World Scripture Imagines," in *Theology and Scriptural Imagination*, ed. L. Gregory Jones and James L. Buckley (Oxford: Blackwell Publishers LTD, 1998), 3

173. Ibid.
174. Ibid., 4.
175. Ibid., 3.
176. Ibid., 4.
177. Ibid.
178. Warnock, 102.
179. Ibid., 103.
180. Green, 66.
181. Ibid.
182. Ibid.
183. Hopper, 106.
184. Ibid., 210; Tracy, 408.
185. Riposa, 125.
186. Hepburn, 128.
187. Harris, 18.
188. Ibid.
189. Wheelwright, 93.
190. Ibid., 99.
191. Ibid., 101.
192. Ibid., 122.
193. Warnock, 37.
194. Ibid., 82.
195. Paula M. Cooey, *Religious Imagination and the Body: A Feminist Analysis* (New York: Oxford University Press, 1994), 46.
196. Ibid., 48.
197. Ibid., 45.
198. Tracy, 174.
199. Hopper, 208.
200. Ernst Cassirer, *Language and Myth* (New York: Harper Brothers, 1946), 7.
201. Ibid., 8.
202. Ibid.,
203. Riposa, 133.
204. Ibid., 149.
205. Ibid., 6.
206. Warnock, 70.
207. Cooey, 14-15.
208. Carl Jung, *Man and His Symbols* (New York: Doubleday and Co., 1964), 20.
209. Ibid.
210. Ibid. While other theorists will vary on the meaning and signifying range associated with each term, Jung's description of symbol gets at the idea conveyed in these pages.
211. Riposa, 143.
212. Ibid.
213. Jung, 67.
214. Ibid.
215. Hopper, 220.
216. Wheelwright, 92.
217. Ibid.
218. Harris, 19.

219. Other possibilities include: explanation, construal, and definition as the process of defining.

220. Riposa, 3.

221. Ibid., 2.

222. Ibid., 116.

223. Bowker, 311.

224. Ibid., 315.

225. Ibid., 8.

226. Stull, 22.

227. Ibid., 21.

228. Warnock, 70.

229. Cassirer, 7.

230. Ibid., 8.

231. Green, 69.

232. Ibid., 53.

233. Ibid., 51.

234. Ibid.,52.

235. Ibid., 67.

236. Tracy, 130.

CHAPTER FOUR
D.W. WINNICOTT AND THE OBJECT
RELATIONS THEORY

Prologue to a Theory

This chapter and the following chapter will argue, among other things, that a person's imagination begins in the arms of his or her mother. The combined insights of these two chapters, dedicated to a thorough explication of Object Relations Theory, will be used to analyze the religious creativity, the genius, of Francis of Assisi, which is the subject of the final chapters. The earlier review of the imaginative activity of Aelred of Rievaulx and Bernard of Clairvaux gave some historical indication of the importance of the maternal-infant relationship in early childhood. Several contemporary scholars share Winnicott's interest in this area, the topic of the present chapter, and its related application in adulthood. The expansion of ORT as it is used to make sense of other human experiences according to the thoughts of Paul Pruyser, John McDargh, and Ana-Maria Rizzuto will be taken up in the next and closely related chapter. Each of these theorists contributes to an Object Relations Theory perspective on the imagination. Amidst the developments of the theory provided by the above mentioned scholars, themes brought up in the previous chapters will be studied in the light of ORT. These include: experience, relationship, change, the image of God and faith in God, and meaning. To make the connection between ORT and Francis' imaginative activity more direct, the themes of trust, play, and the ability to be alone will also be considered.

It is strange, then, that such a theory, which ties maternal influence to an account of imagination that is generally open to a positive integration with religious experience, should find its seeds in Sigmund Freud's (1856-1939) linking of religion and illusion. D.W. Winnicott, like most students of the human mind in the early twentieth century, began his observations of childhood behavior under the shroud of Freud's theories. In an odd twist, it is where Freud saw a limitation to living fully in the grip of reality that Winnicott identifies the quintessential requirement for a person to be able to grip reality in its fullness. The focal area is illusion. It is what Freud unsympathetically considered religious ideas.[1] He called the religious illusion a neurosis associated with "infantilism," as he went on to insist, "Men cannot remain children forever; they must in the end go out into 'hostile life'. We call this 'education to reality'. Need I confess to you that the sole purpose of my book is to point out the necessity of this forward step."[2]

All that Freud had to say of illusion was not finally unsupportive of the direction in which Winnicott takes the concept. Freud conceded that, "An illusion is not the same thing as an error; nor is it necessarily an error."[3] He went on to say, "Illusion need not necessarily be false-that is to say, unrealizable or in contradiction to reality."[4] Perhaps this was the chink in the armor of Freud's theory that enables Winnicott to recognize the fundamental role of illusion in a child's creative movement toward a meaningful relationship with reality. Illusion at the service of creativity is seen as the dividing line between Freud and Winnicott by at least one observer of the latter thinker. Rosemary Dinnage compares the two theorists in respect to artistic creativity. She finds that Winnicott's theory allows for it and Freud's theory does not.[5]

One of Winnicott's most significant contributions to the advancement of psychology, involving illusion, is the idea of transitional phenomena. He explains that these "represent the early stages of the use of illusion, without which there is no meaning for the human being in the idea of a relationship with an object that is perceived by others as external to that being."[6] Elsewhere, Winnicott observes that illusion is a necessary pre-cursor to the formation of an object representation in an infant's mind. He notes that the infant begins life with the illusion that the mother's breast is a part of itself. Gradually, as the infant experiences the fact that the breast is not an ever-present element of its microcosmic world/self/body, disillusionment sets in and forces the mental processing that ultimately yields the consideration of the existence of a separate object.

Criticism of a Theory

This chapter begins a look at the imagination from the perspective of Object Relations Theory using the term *illusion*. In addition to this word several others will be employed to represent imaginative activity, including: creativity, play, and cultural experience. Regardless of the positive approach to the imagination suggested by each of these terms, the use of Object Relations Theory to work with religious concepts has not escaped criticism. One of the most scathing critiques of this endeavor comes from Roy Herndon Steinhoff Smith. He claims that ORT is anti-religious because it seeks to uncover the mystery of the religious development of the human person. However, his reading of the theory seems to be broad but perchance not deep enough to catch its hypothetical and analogical nuances. He lacks precision in his use of the fundamental term *reality*, which he allows to stand without the crucial distinctions of internal and external. In another instance, he interprets more substance into the notion of edenic experiences than would a psychological theorist inclined to the use of symbolism for the purpose of explanation.[7] Smith's critique of the use of adultomorphisms may be somewhat more justified, but ORT is, overall, striking for its recognition of a clear pattern of development that sets infant and adult at distinctly opposite ends of the psychological development spectrum.[8]

ORT has also come under scrutiny from feminist theorists. Diane Jonte-Pace observes that some feminists see mothering, interdependency, and relationality, all central features of ORT, as part of an enforced social structure.[9] For the most part, however, Jonte-Pace finds more hope for ORT to be applied with sensitivity to these aspects of women's experience.[10] She recognizes the theory's "maternal-infant matrix as a psychological source of religious experience and religious ritual."[11] She explains that unification, nourishment, and renewal, all emphasized by ORT, are ritual themes found in Christian liturgies but first encountered by the individual within the infant-mother relationship.[12] She also points out that Freud's theories of human motivation rely on instinctual drives while ORT situates "interpersonal relatedness" as the basis of motivation.[13] Jonte-Pace claims, furthermore, that, "Winnicott's rich understanding of transitional objects leads to a psychological view of religion as illusion, wherein, one might say, God is both created and found."[14]

The Theory

In general, it can be said that Object Relations Theory provides a way of examining the infant human act of creating a world to live in and fill with meaningful features. This observation looks ahead to the same effort carried on throughout life in the form of humanistic endeavors to participate in cultural and religious activity. Having taken up the origins of the theory, and accepting that ORT is not without its critics, the current chapter will present the fundamental bases of Winnicott's theory (in his words and those of some of the many scholars influenced by him) and reveal specific points that advance an understanding of the highly creative/imaginative personality as a footing for the study of the workings of Francis of Assisi's imagination.[15]

Winnicott and the Infant's First Few Months

Adaptation is the key descriptor of the earliest period in a newborn infant's life. It is not so much a matter of the child adapting to the world but of the mother adapting the world to the needs of the child. Winnicott makes clear the crucial necessity of supporting the infant at this time. He comments, "At the start adaptation needs to be almost exact, and unless this is so it is not possible for the infant to begin to develop a capacity to experience a relationship to external reality, or even to form a conception of external reality."[16] In a strange turn of events, it is failure that leads to success in the infant's imaginative development. Winnicott writes, "The good-enough mother, as I have stated before, starts off with an almost complete adaptation to her infant's needs, and as time proceeds she adapts less and less completely, gradually, according to the infant's growing ability to deal with her failure."[17] This slowly reduced support causes the infant to experience distress for which he or she seeks relief. As Susan Deri describes it, good mothering places satisfaction at the point where tension leads to a wish for such satisfaction.[18]

The primary observable tension a new infant seeks to alleviate is hunger. The mother's capacity to meet this necessity by offering her breast or a bottle, before the tension rises too high, essentially fools the infant into believing that he or she produced the relieving object through a wishful desire. The result is a feeling of omnipotence on the part of the child who desires and instantly possesses what is desired. Madeleine Davis and David Walbridge regard this omnipotence as an initial illusional experience.[19] Winnicott explains that the infant forms a subjective phenomenon, the mother's breast, right where the infant repeatedly encounters it. The mother's positioning of the objectively actual breast in that particular place is what links the infant's creative act with reality.[20] Although the infant, in this early stage, does not recognize otherness, Jonte-Pace is not off the mark in calling Winnicott's account "a dual process of creation of the other from within and discovery of the other from without."[21] She adds that it is difficult to separate the two aspects since, "in illusion, creation (from within) and discovery (from without) interpenetrate."[22] It must be noted that imaginative creation of an object has not occurred at this point per se. Winnicott contends that object relations begin, in the early stages, with part objects, such as a breast, until roughly the age of one, when whole object relating takes place.[23]

Arnold Modell observes that the mother's advancing failure to meet an infant's needs is the cause of separation anxiety that "provides the motive for the child's first creative play, and, in turn, separation anxiety (to which the fear of death is added) may be the motive for the institution of a magically created environment."[24] The separation anxiety, or any other name that could be applied to this experience, should be mediated in a balanced fashion. Winnicott finds that the mother's adaptation must decrease in proportion to the infant's "growing ability to account for failure of adaptation and to tolerate the results of frustration."[25] On the other hand, "exact adaptation resembles magic and the object that behaves perfectly becomes no better than a hallucination."[26] It is the tolerable tension or anxiety of incomplete adaptation that "makes objects real, that is to say hated as well as loved."[27] What the infant experiences when adaptation falters is termed "the insult of reality" by Davis and Walbridge who maintain that it is mitigated by the infant's activity of omnipotently creating what it simultaneously encounters in reality.[28]

It quickly becomes clear that imaginative creativity begins with illusion. Winnicott conveys the notion that early in life the infant operates under the illusion that there is something truly there which exists in conjunction with the infant's ability to create.[29] Using the term *fantasy* to refer to the autistic dimension of illusion, he remarks that *fantasy* "may be thought of as the imaginative elaboration of physical function."[30] The infant begins with the illusion that the breast is a part of itself, but as adaptation wanes, disillusionment sets in to alert the infant that its creation has a separate existence.[31] At this time the infant begins to confront the "Reality Principle," which is "the fact of the existence of the world whether the baby creates it or not."[32]

Winnicott is right to locate the foundation of imaginative creativity in early infancy. He says, "Given the chance, the baby begins to live creatively, and to use actual objects to be creative into and with."[33] Dinnage moves the focal point of early creativity away from adaptation and onto an intersection of worlds. She insists, "The key to the making of things, then, is concurrence: when what the child expects and what the world offers intersect, the object is both found and created at the same moment."[34] Central to the notion of an intersection between illusion and reality is Winnicott's concept of transitional phenomena occurring in transitional space. Transitional phenomena are primarily object representations that facilitate the interrelationship of internal and external reality that takes place in a psychologically neutral ground, called the transitional area, transitional space, potential space, illusional sphere, or intermediate area, alternatively. Michael Eigen finds, that upon entering the transitional space, "The infant here lives in an atmosphere of creativity, participates, as it were, in a creativity bath."[35]

Eigen's *creativity*, taking place in the transitional space, shows forth in so much more than an aesthetically appreciable product. For Winnicott, creativity refers to the establishment and sustenance of a relationship with reality. He writes, "The transitional phenomena represent the early stages of the use of illusion, without which there is no meaning for the human being in the idea of a relationship with an object that is perceived as external to that being."[36] He also calls the space where this relationship is brought about a third part of life "to which inner reality and external life both contribute."[37] At another point, Winnicott gives an example of how inner and outer worlds can share influence on one's illusion processing. He explains that in the transitional space there reside "objects that are not part of the infant's body yet are not fully recognized as belonging to external reality."[38]

The most significant object found in the transitional space is the transitional object which the infant uses to control the tension or anxiety of maternal absence. Eigen uses the transitional object to reveal an incomplete connection between the individual's internal reality and external reality, which is similar to the connection described by Winnicott. He remarks, "The transitional object carries the meaning of that which is, yet is not mother and that which is, and is not self."[39] These statements reveal a unique situation taking place within the transitional space. Because the person is not working strictly with reality or with fantasy/illusion, Winnicott demands that the question is never asked: "'Did you conceive of this or was it presented to you from without?'"[40] At this point in its development the child is involved in what Eigen calls object relating, a stage he locates between transitional experiencing and object usage. In object relating, Eigen claims, "The object is meaningful but not yet experienced as wholly other."[41] The reason for this, he explains, is that, in the transitional area, at this time "self and other are neither one, nor two, but somehow together make up an interpenetrating field."[42] *Interpenetration* is one more term that can be added to *concurrence*, *crossover*, and *intersection* when describing what happens in the creative imagination. This is ORT's effort at structuring the relational matrix that was shown in the last chapter to be a feature of imaginative activity. The transitional space is seen, here, as a mental middle ground, a neutral zone, where differing, but not always opposing forces can enter into associations, or at least temporary alliances.

Winnicott and the Rest of Early Childhood

It is difficult to say exactly where one aspect of early creative imagining begins and where another ends. Children develop at varying speeds, and phases of imaginative creativity often overlap. Nonetheless, the movement from earliest infancy into the rest of the maturational process can be marked with some accuracy. It occurs as soon as the mother begins to decrease her meticulous adaptation to the child's needs. Winnicott asserts that creativity follows a typical path beyond this point. He writes, "There is a natural progression to the individual infant's creation of a whole world of external reality and to the continuous creating which at first needs an audience and which then eventually creates even the audience."[43] Freud devised a framework that led to the division of early childhood between the oedipal period and the pre-oedipal period such that maturation came to be seen as dependent on surviving the so-called oedipal conflict. When Winnicott mentions this early life crisis, he identifies it more positively as "a relationship between three whole objects."[44] Since this phase involves whole objects, it could begin anywhere between object relating and object usage. Davis and Walbridge use another term that loosely denotes the time at which the present look at early childhood comes to an end. They propose the idea of *personalisation* as the point when the psyche of the infant will dwell completely within the body. This is a delicate connection to the body that is not permanent in the infant and can be seen to be lost at times for some adults.[45]

It cannot be emphasized enough that the formation of a creative imagination parallels the course of an infant's development from simply existing to existing in relationship. The critical discovery that enables this distinction is the encounter with otherness. It is an encounter that begins in the safety of the transitional space, using the transitional object. The transitional object has its precursor in the infant's imaginatively omnipotent creation of the tension-alleviating maternal breast. It then becomes the wished-for part-object breast of the transitional experiencing period, and it slowly transforms into the whole object that is the mother as the infant moves through object relating and into object usage. Winnicott uses the term *transitional* since the infant is moving from experiencing actual objects as a continuous part of him or herself to experiencing objects as something other than his or her self. He designates the transitional object as the "first not-me possession."[46] Since the transitional object began as a source of distress relief, it comes as no surprise when Winnicott comments, "I should mention that sometimes there is no transitional object except the mother herself."[47] In fact, he concludes that later-in-life transitional objects persist as symbols of the mother-child union.[48] Henry Copolillo, who studies the continued existence of transitional objects among more mature subjects, adds "nursery rhymes, cartoons, fairy stories, and movies" to the list of possible transitional objects.[49]

As the infant moves into the object usage phase the ability to regard otherness becomes particularly important. At this point, both the infant and the person interacting with the infant must recognize an object as not belonging exclusively to the inner world of the infant. Winnicott finds that an object, "if it is to be used, must necessarily be real in the sense of being a part of shared reality."[50] When the infant moves out of object relating and into object usage, there is a shift from subjective activity to a perspective from which it is understood that the object is truly there.[51]

When the infant is able to perceive that an object exists as other than a part of itself, and this reality is bolstered by others, a final important feature of early imaginative development begins to take shape. Through experiencing the loss and rediscovery of a highly desired object, such as the mother, the infant comes to realize that the object is able to continue to exist even when it is not part of the infant's immediate experience of the external world. This is called object constancy. Winnicott directly attributes the establishment of object constancy to the mother who returns regularly to alleviate the child's distress.[52] Eventually, the transitional object, which represents the alleviating factor of the maternal return in the child's mind, becomes more important to the child than the actual mother.[53] In a statement that indicates the continuity between early imaginative activity and a lifetime of creativity, Winnicott maintains that the infant reduces this stress of separation "by filling in of the potential space with creative playing, with the use of symbols, and with all that eventually adds up to a cultural life."[54] Martin Welch directs his attention to one facet of cultural life that he claims is central to the calming of separation anxiety. He argues that the use of language as a transitional object is "the earliest creative use of language."[55] For the infant, this begins with echolalia, the soothing repetition of another person's sounds and words.[56]

Another feature of object constancy ensures that objects are fully comprehended as having a separate existence from the infant. This early creative activity involves a destructive conflict with an object that causes the reality of otherness to impinge upon the infant's tiny world. Winnicott explains that between relating to an object and using it comes the act of "placing the object outside the area of the subject's omnipotent control."[57] As long as the object remains within the grasp of the infant's omnipotent control it cannot be experienced as other. To break the object free of this perceptual association the subject destroys the object as something that is part of her subjectivity. If she is successful, the object survives the destruction and assumes its place as a part of reality that persists external to the child.[58] Through this act, the infant not only fills her external world; she also develops a source of objects to relate to and be influenced by in return. Winnicott remarks that the destruction-surviving object "develops its own autonomy and life, and (if it survives) contributes-in to the subject, according to its own properties."[59] Making a point that is essential to the religious and spiritual implications of ORT, Winnicott contends, "The object is always being destroyed. The destruction becomes the unconscious backcloth for love of a real object; that is, an object outside the area of the subject's omnipotent control."[60] What he is implying here, is that an object image, such as that of God (my example), cannot both remain a denizen of one's fantasy world, where omnipotent control can be applied, and also be truly a focus of one's love.[61] The loved object must be experienced as other, yet still in relationship to oneself. When Eigen comments on this paradoxical "I love you" and "I destroy you" connection, he concedes, "Together they constitute a sustained reaching out, a joyous gambit."[62] In Francis' situation, his love for God was arguably made possible by his profound humility which sustained the sense of otherness even while he so desperately sought to unite with God.

Coinciding with the early use of transitional space are several other important features of childhood that are critical to the formation of a creative imagination. These aspects include the development of a sense of self, the ability to play, and the ability to be alone. A fairly distinct sense of self is a prerequisite to the recognition of otherness that has been touted above for its importance. Self understanding also fulfills an important role in play and the meaningful encounter with isolation. Jonte-Pace learns from Winnicott that the sense of self and other and the capacity to be in relationship develop from the mother-infant matrix.[63] Eigen uses an unfolding relationship with *otherness* to express the formation of a conception of self. He notes that in transitional experiencing "there is the freedom prior to a clear cut sense of sameness of difference, and in the latter [object usage] the freedom brought about by news of difference."[64] Speaking further about the entrance into object usage, he adds, "It opens the way for a new kind of freedom, one because there is radical otherness, a new realness of self-feeling exactly because the other is now felt as real as well. The core sense of creativeness that permeates transitional experiencing is reborn on a new level.... The subject can use otherness for true growth purposes, and, through the use of difference as such, gains access to the genuinely new."[65] Such a connection between the growth of a sense of selfhood and creativity is made explicit in Winnicott's writings when he asserts that creativity is "that which (and nothing else) proves to the child that he or she is alive."[66] In other words, the experience of something as a new feature of reality affirms the existence of one's distinct selfhood.

Winnicott ties imaginative creativity and the formation of a sense of self in with the second theme-aspect of play. He observes, "It is in playing... that the individual child or adult is able to be creative and to use the whole personality, and it is only in being creative that the individual discovers the self."[67] At the same time, he insists on the uninhibited development of a selfhood. He seems to indicate that a falsely imposed integration or composition of self is a detriment to the playful environment out of which creativity emerges and a more natural sense of self evolves.[68] In actuality, creativity arises from, and is therefore reliant upon the presence of, the un-integrated state of the personality, according to Winnicott.[69]

Although play is normally associated with childhood, play, as a feature of maturing adult experience, will receive more attention in the following section. Nonetheless, it is well known that play begins in infancy. Winnicott finds that it commences between mother and child when the child experiences the omnipotence associated with the magical control of an object at the same time the child begins to have some actual experience of the object.[70] As the feeling of omnipotence begins to fade and the awareness of otherness increases, the child moves into a stage where its play overlaps with the mother's play, such that they form a relationship based on play.[71] In describing the internal mechanisms of play, Winnicott recalls, "Into this play area the child gathers objects or phenomena from external reality and uses these in the service of some sample derived from inner or personal reality. Without hallucinating the child puts out a sample of dream potential and lives with this sample in a chosen setting of fragments from external reality."[72] Again tying creativity to play, Winnicott calls playing "a creative experience taking up space and time, and intensely real for the patient."[73] Since play can be so intensive, it is difficult to bring it to an end. Winnicott recognizes that the onset of basic human instinct is one thing able to do this. The activation of instinct challenges the autonomy of the child which is a key component of the capacity to play. Winnicott writes, "Bodily excitement in erotogenic zones constantly threatens playing."[74] A bowel movement can be observed to bring about the immediate cessation of the most active toddler's play, but the pertinence of these observations does not end with the child. A life of strict self-discipline, such as Francis of Assisi, Aelred of Rievaulx, and Bernard of Clairvaux adopted, appears, in this light, to sustain rather than restrain playfulness and creativity, for what is the purpose of such a lifestyle if not to control or redirect the intrusion of unruly instincts?

In the previous chapter play was characterized by its back and forth nature. What is striking about the present account of childhood play is that its deepest imaginative state often occurs without an actual or physically existent partner. A seven-year old girl arranges her dolls and stuffed animals in a classroom setting and teaches them for over an hour, or a four-year old boy fights off the dreaded stuffed sea-dinosaur with his ship full of plastic pirates. It is the ability to be alone, but not exactly alone, that facilitates the active use of the imagination in the following circular pattern. The ability to be alone provides an atmosphere in which to be imaginative, and the ability to be imaginative sustains the ability to be alone by filling in the emptiness or sense of loss. Winnicott proposes, paradoxically, that the ability to be alone develops while a small child and specifically in the presence of the mother.[75] Deri points out the importance of providing an independent play area to bring about this capacity. This would be a place where the child learns to play and discover and create while alone but securely in the presence of the mother. Deri suggests that there is more to this development than the non-intrusive presence of the parent. The nurturing adult must also outlive the "symbolic-destruction" of the child's periods of rage.[76] This supports object constancy, but most significantly for Winnicott, it supports the continuous presence of a "good" object in the psychic reality of the child.[77] The presence of "good" objects underlies the growing element of trustfulness in the child's life. The important connections between object constancy, "good" objects, trust, and the use of a creative imagination become more clear as a person matures, but like the other bases of a creative imagination, playfulness and the capacity to be alone, trust has its seminal origins in infancy. From Anni Bergman's viewpoint, the ability to be alone occurs through a series of excursions into "the outside world" which is the distance a child comfortably travels beyond the mother-child space.[78] She notes that by the age of two to three the child has internalized the mother as an object such that the child "can imagine and accept her being elsewhere."[79] This ability to be alone, along with the ability to play and the capacity to distinguish self and other, forms the basis of the creatively imaginative life. In the following section their importance will be seen in connection with other aspects of the maturing imaginative personality.

Winnicott and the Maturing Individual

The available evidence for Francis' imaginative activity survives only from his adult years. For this reason the mature aspects of the creative imagination, as expressed by Object Relations Theory, will offer the best ground for analyzing the workings of his imagination. To maintain continuity with the general review of imagination previously presented, Winnicott's thoughts on the development of adult creativity will be arranged in terms of experience, relationship, change, faith or belief, and the making of meaning. Throughout this effort the underlying themes of play, alone-ness, and trust will be regarded for their support of imagination. Although the subject has turned to a phase of maturity there will be frequent references back to periods of early development, but this is only consistent with the nature of Object Relations Theory which finds that a good-enough childhood is fundamental to the formation and use of a creative adult imagination.[80]

The Experiencing Subject

Winnicott's writings display the connection between imagination and experience as clearly as any theorist of imagination mentioned earlier. Similar to the other theories and views, Winnicott discusses the imagination's role as an initial point of contact with experience in addition to serving as a relational matrix. His primary contributions in these areas are an understanding of the effect of play on experiencing and the use of transitional phenomena to form the relational matrix.

Eigen is particularly focused on the element of experience in Winnicott's writings since the former theorizes that Winnicott was attempting "to develop something of a phenomenology of creative experiencing."[81] Eigen goes on to add: "the primary object of creative experiencing is not mother or father but the unknowable ground of creativeness as such."[82] Although he offers an apt philosophical expression for what is occurring at some point in the process of experiencing, to call *creativeness* the object of the individual's efforts is stopping a little short of the final aim of this activity, which I believe is to experience oneself as a distinct self or person existing in meaningful relationship with others. In line with his view, Eigen contends that Winnicott's chief theoretical advancement lies in the importance he places on the creation of a symbol "of symbolizing experiencing itself."[83] Although talk of *symbolizing experiencing* pertains more to the far end of the imaginative activity spectrum, at meaning-making, it does point toward what Eigen observes as the primary quality of experiencing according to Winnicott's theory--that is "its intangibility or immateriality."[84]

In ORT, the focal point of experiencing is not on the object causing sensations but rather on the activity which receives, processes, and gives meaning to these sensations. From this perspective, the interest is not in the existence of an object that can be experienced (and imagined), it is on the existence of a human capacity to experience (and consequently imagine). This capacity requires, in the first place, a mental place of reception for the experience, which has been called the initial point of contact. Other theorists have remarked that such contact intensifies the experience, or the experiencer's experiencing, in a way that represents or sets the experience apart in addition to reducing the inhibition or heightening the attentiveness of the experiencer. Winnicott has his own approach to intensification. He begins with play, calling the adult transitional space an "intermediate area of experience" that is "in direct continuity with the play area of the small child who is 'lost' in play."[85] The very idea of being lost in play includes two aspects of the afore-mentioned intensification. Children who are playing at this level have given themselves completely to the project at hand. They are not concerned with the daily needs of life during these moments or the peripheral goings-on of others in the same space. Their attention is captured by the play, so much so that the presence of an observer does not inhibit the child's activity. Rather, it is simply dismissed. The object of the play activity is so important during this time that it could also be said to be set apart from mundane distractions. It is Winnicott's invaluable insight that the workings of the imagination take in experience in a manner reflective of a child's play, and also that this form of playing occurs in connection with the persistence of the transitional area or space in the adult. He further conjectures that this "intermediate area of experience," in the transitional space, "constitutes the greater part of the infant's experience and throughout life is retained in the intense experiencing that belongs to the arts, and to religion, and to imaginative living, and to creative scientific work."[86] The implication is obvious enough that some dimension of youthful playfulness, particularly as it supports open attentiveness, must carry on into adulthood if one is to live an imaginative life. Conversely, anything that hinders the ability to be deeply aware will constrict imaginative activity. A highly complex or demanding lifestyle or some impediment to attentiveness would cause this. Celano's presentation of Francis' youth makes a point of highlighting the saint's playfulness.

In other works, Winnicott links the focusing aspect of child's play to the kind of deep concentration from which adults are not easily moved.[87] While the term *concentration* suggests a highly active yet controlled mental state, there is still the contention that imaginative experiencing must occur under un-inhibiting circumstances, circumstances which also include a minimization of interpersonal distractions associated with being alone. Winnicott gives a sense of this when describing the sequence of creativity. "Relaxation in conditions of trust based on experience" is given as the precursor to "creative, physical, and mental activity manifested in play."[88] As Eigen describes it, "In the transitional dimension creative experiencing is open and fluid, if also profoundly heightened."[89] Another remark that Winnicott makes, could be considered a form of intensification. It is the suggestion that the individual constructs a "personal or inner world, with a sense of responsibility for what exists or what goes on there."[90] It is not too much of an extension to label responsibility as an intensifier of attentiveness.

One might ask why so much interest is directed toward experience when the topic is imaginative creativity. Unlike the expression of creation given in the Scriptural account, the human being does not create out of nothing. (Gen 1. 1-

31) The formation of an inner world is dependent on the presence of something, an ongoing series of encounters with otherness that demand of the infant, and later the adult, an explanation that provides both structure and meaning to these experiences. When Scripture mentions the formlessness and abysmal nature of original creation there is a more affirmable parallel with the individual's imaginative development.(Gen 1.2) This is the initiation of experience as chaos. Just as form was applied to give order to original creation, and meaning was appended to the unfathomable abyss, imaginative creativity gives order and relationship to experience. It would be ridiculously reductionistic to claim that ORT offers an alternative explanation for the origins of all creation, but the reverse is a more valid assertion. The Biblical explanation does, by coincidence, reflect the same movement from disorder to order found in imaginative activity. When the infant is living as a part of the mother-child monad it is fair to say that the world is formless and beyond meaning.

The effort to derive order from the chaos of a suddenly impinging world of infant experience begins with the establishment of a dividing line between internal and external experience. This is a division that must stand throughout life, but loosely. Winnicott remarks about "the perpetual human task of keeping inner and outer reality separate yet interrelated."[91] It is his identification of the transitional space that makes this separation conceptually feasible in the first place. As "an area that is not challenged," it is possible for experiences to be held and considered and worked with here without the need to categorize them immediately as actual or conceived.[92] It is where the chaos of raw experience can be tolerated while the individual tests possible relationships and ultimately establishes some form of meaning.

Winnicott's description of the developing perception of otherness adds to the understanding of how order is set to disordered experiences.[93] When the infant exists as if the mother is a continuation of his or her self there is no order. Everything is of the same order or rather of no order at all. There is no upper or lower, no greater or lesser, no this or that; there is only the mother-infant monad. Initially, the world of experience does not extend beyond this entity from the infant's perspective. Since it would be impossible to relate one thing to another when all is the same thing, the infant must begin to recognize otherness if it is ever going to recognize relationships that dispel chaos. There is no relating when there is nothing sustaining a separate existence with which to relate. Eigen exemplifies the significance of this capacity as he comments, "Self-other awareness is itself the core of symbolizing experiencing and perhaps remains humankind's most creative activity at various levels of developmental complexity."[94] Eigen also clarifies the manner in which disorder and the recognition of otherness come together throughout life in the transitional sphere. He writes, "The subject lives through and towards creative immersion [in the transitional area] (including phases of chaos, unintegration, waiting). What he symbolizes and seeks more and more of is the absorption of creative experiencing and the way this makes use of objects through successive waves of self-other awareness."[95]

Eigen is not the only observer of Winnicott's theory to note examples of the imaginatively creative encounter with chaos, disorder, and meaninglessness in mature individuals. Dinnage uses ORT to work with the "inexplicable" in profound aesthetic experiences.[96] Similarly, Gilbert Rose conceives "of the creativity of everyday life as residing in the power of the ego to de-differentiate, abstract, and reintegrate in the service of mastery."[97] His use of the term *de-differentiate* hints at a removal of distinctions in an effort to return to a conception of an experience prior to the application of order. As such, his idea denotes the search for a new way of seeing order. Elsewhere Rose again employs the notion of abstraction to draw some sense out of the throng of chaotic experience. He proposes that the transitional process continues beyond the transitional object "as creative imagination…. It samples the pluralism of reality, withdraws and readvances, attempting to abstract coherent configurations composed of both self and nonself elements."[98] He also points out that it is the creative imagination that is central to this process of moving experience from disorder to coherency. Ultimately, if order is to supplant disorder, it will occur through the establishment of internal relationships in a relational matrix.

The previous chapter verifies a widely held appreciation among many imagination theorists that imagining involves bringing together images, other mental constructs, and external experiences to form relationships that are manifested in new images. Nonetheless, these thinkers leave cause for frustration when one asks: How, where, and why does this occur? Winnicott's theory more completely answers these questions about a relational matrix. The last two questions are explained away, simply, by stating that relations take place in the transitional sphere at the service of forming a perception of the world including self and other. To answer how the relating is able to happen, it must be recalled that the transitional space is an area where the elements of inner reality (raw, illusionary imagery and mental constructions) can coexist with aspects of outer reality (sense experience and communally sharable ideas). From this interaction some thoughts and images return to the inner world of the individual where they might be used in future cognitive and imaginative activity. Other thoughts and images are manifested externally in imaginative products that fellow imaginers might come across and put to use.

In language typical of the way he describes relating, Winnicott writes, "We experience life in the area of transitional phenomena, in the exciting interweave of subjectivity and objective observation, and in an area that is intermediate between the inner reality of the individual and the shared reality of the world that is external to individuals."[99] He uses the word *interweave* to describe how images relate in imaginative activity. With undertones of symmetry and precision, this term is far less jarring than the one Clare Winnicott uses in reference to her husband's insight. She calls the transitional sphere: "the limitless intermediate area where external and internal reality are compounded into the experience of living."[100] Another analogy is the bridge between the internal and external world mentioned by Davis and Walbridge, as well as Rose.[101] Eigen specifies the early version of the internal-external connection as an "inherent fit between the infant's creativeness and the world."[102] A close fit may be necessary during the early formation of a child's imagination, but the mature original or creative imagination does not require an exacting degree of similarity to some vague communal imagination. As Paul Pruyser observes, it is most important that it strikes "a responsive chord" with other imaginations.[103] In any instance, attempting to depict how the relationships are formed in the transitional sphere may be asking too much at this point in time. Winnicott's environmental description of an un-challenged resting place is the real insight since it goes the furthest in revealing the required internal conditions for bringing experience, thought and image to-gether. In other words, he is able to clarify how the relating occurs at an interac-tive level, not a mechanical level.

External Manifestation of Relational Aspect of Imagination. As the previous chapter demonstrated, there is a connection between the internal relational oper-ation of the imagination and a person's capacity for observing or engaging in relationships in the external world. These external relationships, which hold the potential to be expressed in some imaginatively public or sharable way, can be thought of according to dimensions of intimacy. The nature of such relationships will be considered from an ORT perspective as they range from a recognition of otherness to interpersonal communication, group formation, concern for another, and finally love. To further frame the formation of good or positively oriented relationships there will also be a brief look at the failure to develop or maintain the ability to relate.

The very act of forming an image of something other than the self, as well as one's day-to-day functioning as-if there are other objects and other subjects to relate to, both begin with the infant's growing awareness of otherness. Winni-cott's transitional object, that signifies the appearance of something that is "not-me" in the infant's world, fulfills an immensely important role in early relating. He observes that, in the first place the transitional object, "stands for the breast, or the object of the first relationship."[104] He also identifies transitional objects as symbols of the mother-child union.[105] Davis and Wallbridge set recognition of otherness as a precondition for maturity which "involves an acceptance of a 'not-me' world and a relationship to it."[106] Eigen senses the natural development observable in Winnicott's theory as the child "passes through phases in which the distance between self and other is taken for granted (transitional experienc-ing) and is acutely experienced (object usage)."[107] Much of the emphasis on a relationship to otherness is directed toward other human beings. Davis and Wallbridge write, "The term 'object'... needs to be taken in its particular mean-ing as opposite of 'subject.' In fact, it more often refers to a person or a part of a person than to a thing. So 'object relationship' really conveys the idea of a per-sonal relationship."[108] Interpersonal relating will continue to be a primary focus of this section, but the theory would be much less rich as a whole if it neglected to account for and even encourage meaningful relationships with the world of impersonal objects. Deri verifies the presence of this latter element in Winni-cott's theory. She recalls that he sees inner and outer world as able to "harmon-ize, intermingled within the same act, the same perception, or the same physical object."[109] The difference between relating to a person and relating to any other object is that the person also has subjectivity, which makes personal relation-ships considerably more complex.

The clearest indication that a person has imaginatively formed an object representation of anything else with which to share the world is that he or she shows some regard for the object. If the object is inanimate, such as a large stone, for example, this person might step around or over it. If the object is another person, and thus also a subject, the appropriate form of regard is to communicate. Like so many aspects of adult experience or interaction, Winnicott ties communication back to early childhood. He finds that adult verbal communication is a continuation of youthful play.[110] Once Winnicott points out this comparison, it is difficult to ignore the back and forth characteristic both share in common, but the insightfulness of this linkage goes even deeper. He adds two important pieces of information. First, play occurs in the potential space.[111] If communication is a form of play, it too uses the potential space. Secondly, he writes, "it is play that is universal."[112] If the action/interaction of play sustains the transfer of understanding and experience than it appears that this is made possible by mutual exposure and sharing of elements from individual transitional space. This means that playing, communicating, and ultimately relating, involve entering into the transitional space of others, or more to the point, entering into the imaginative world of another in search of recognizable and shareable elements.

Another of Winnicott's observations is that play can take the form of somatic communication, expression through bodily action or gesture.[113] This will be important when considering Francis' views on communication, but it is also supportive of an observation Davis and Wallbridge make about this topic. They claim, "In order for there to be a relationship between separate individuals, therefore, it is necessary for communication to be to some extent indirect, explicit and deliberate."[114] Body language can be either of the first two if not always deliberate. The principal point these observers of ORT make is that "it is the potential space that allows the individual to communicate at once directly and indirectly."[115] Since transitional space relates external reality and internal reality, it is the one place where explicit language and imagination-dependent indirect language can be formulated and received. For a study of Francis' imagination, it is some of his indirect messaging that will reflect the workings of his imagination most distinctly. Davis and Wallbridge might agree since they suggest, "if communication were totally explicit it would also be totally meaningless."[116] Communication, relying on the imagination at the transmission and the reception point, carries the most complete meaning.

Communication is not limited to two people, just as the workings of imaginations can be shared between several people. The bond of commonality found through communication can easily spread to a multitude of individuals as they come to form a group. Winnicott conjectures that imaginative activity is also fundamental to this level of relationship. He notes that we can "form a group on the basis of our illusory experience."[117] He goes on to say, "This is a natural root of grouping among human beings."[118] Unfortunately, unreal and destructive illusion can sustain the similar imaginations of a group as easily as constructive illusion can. Winnicott is more interested in the positively purposeful alignment of imaginations that occurs through cultural endeavors. He explains that the shared experience of adults is not so much one person's sharing the objectivity of another's subjective phenomena; rather it is a matter of enjoying one's "personal intermediate area" without demanding that others accept its produce, then others are able to acknowledge their "own corresponding intermediate area, and are pleased to find a degree of overlapping, that is to say common experience between members of a group in art or religion or philosophy."[119]

The perception of otherness engenders a series of mutual relationships. "If you exist than I exist. If I can express myself to you then you can express yourself to me. If I can find common ground with you than you can find common ground with me." Each of these relationships implies an expansion of one's imaginative world, and an increase in the depth to which one is immersed in it. The next level of relationship, *concern*, indicates a deeper plunge into the intimacy of one's involvement with others. At one level of analysis, *concern* is more outwardly directed toward another than the previous levels entail. An individual is concerned for another without an immediate consideration that the other person feels concern in return. Winnicott affirms the benefit of this dimension of relating when he asserts, "a capacity for concern is at the back of all constructive play and work."[120] He contends that *concern* is the "enrichment and refinement" of the ambivalent love-hate relationship with the mother as a whole-object.[121] More directly he explains that *concern* is the positive approach to the otherwise negative condition of guilt.[122] He finds that guilt exists where there is no object toward which a reparation gesture can be offered after the vicissitudes of the ambivalent relationship. When there does exist such an object the response is one of concern.[123] In its earliest development, as depicted here, *concern* still retains an orientation back in toward the self. Concern eases the stress experienced as a result of the simultaneous desire for and destruction of another. Beyond this, at the height of relational life there is a predominance of motion outward toward another in the form of love.

Object Relations Theory, with its consideration of early childhood states of mother-child unity, might be expected to give a picture of love that comprises a deeply unified condition in which borders of self or subjectivity fade. On the contrary, ORT emphasizes the necessity of a clear perception of self and other if love is to be possible at all. Modell expresses the idea thus: "Mature love requires an acceptance of the non-self."[124] In an odd but well-discerned approach, Winnicott links love with object destruction. When an object survives the onslaught of infant rage or an adult equivalent, such as disavowal, the destruction allows the object to emerge from the person's omnipotent control as real and as lovable because it has its own existence.[125] There are some significant implications here for religion, especially religion in the Middle Ages. Much popular religious practice in this period was directed toward manipulating the intentions of the divine milieu under the guise of gaining God's favor. What Francis revealed by his lifestyle, and Winnicott indirectly substantiates, is that the God who does not alleviate the pain of the afflicted, bestow wealth on the less fortunate, warm the cold, or feed the famished at the slightest demand of the religious supplicant, is the God who has a separate existence and can be loved. This is the God who becomes, for the person, real as God rather than illusory as a phantasm of the autistic imagination. But love, as expressed here, is not restricted to God. Healthy, uplifting, productive love in general calls for a clear awareness of otherness for the sake of reaching out to and for the other. Davis and Wallbridge point out another conceptual benefit of Winnicott's take on love. They find that transitional space provides the environment that is conducive to this level of relationship, calling potential space "the common ground in affectionate relationships where instinct tension is not a main feature."[126] Love, then, requires the imaginative creation of object representations that stand apart as objects upon which intimate feelings and abundant externalized value can be bestowed, but this begins in that intermediate place where self-preservation does not set the object at too great a distance while allowing for its distinct existence.

Winnicott has indicated that to love is to love another, and most thinkers set this as the apex of relationship. At the same time, a study of imaginative creativity must recognize that the imagination gone awry is responsible for the inability to love or in any sense relate effectively near the dysfunctional end of the relational spectrum. Modell equates creativity that is not communicable with a failure to recognize and respect otherness. He argues for the necessity of a tradition that links the creative expressions of members of a community.[127] In ORT terms, loss of other-awareness is the regressive side of transitional phenomena wherein the individual does not seek a relationship to external reality.[128] Winnicott explains this self-isolation as the distinction between fantasying and dreaming. He writes, "dreaming and living have been seen to be of the same order, daydreaming being of another order."[129] When fantasying occurs in disassociated states, the person moves into the daydream or fantasy considering him or herself to be completing a concrete activity while to an outside observer nothing has occurred; there is no contribution to life.[130] It is very important not to confuse this autistic regression with the ability to be alone that supports imaginative activity. Judith Kestenberg and Joan Weinstein observe, "The essential loneliness of the creative experience is derived from the experience of the infant, who has lost touch with his mother."[131] The kind of aloneness that sparks creativity does not turn in on itself, and it is not a state of self-reliance. The imaginatively creative person uses the time apart to envisage relationships with others, relationships that have a basis in reality. In a call for the kind of interdependence that can make good use of periods spent alone while embracing the importance of interacting with others, Winnicott points out that, "Independence is never absolute."[132] Similarly, Jonte-Pace finds that there is an appropriate degree of dependence that is to be sought in a balance with autonomy, and while Freud valued independence as an indication of maturity, ORT urges interdependence.[133] The creation of a world begins with a relationship to otherness and in turn makes possible such relationships.

To Change, Transform, and Transcend. The earlier survey of non-ORT views of imagination used the concept of time to structure a discussion of change, potentiality, and transcendence. Among Object Relations theorists, it is the individual's personal environment that is the field of change, even though past, present, and future constitute a portion of this multi-dimensional space. In reflecting on Winnicott's ideas, Davis and Wallbridge contend, "The inherited potential which is at the core of the person cannot be realized without an adequate environment."[134] The notable feature of this environment, which originates as the mother-infant interface, is its variability. It changes, and it must change as the imaginative formation of the infant's world unfolds. Modell uses the term *transformation* to describe this ongoing occurrence. He writes: "What is created is not an entirely new environment but a transformation of that which already exists."[135] Another way to think about this change is that it involves the matching of two fields of potentiality, the infant's created world and the larger or actual world. A matching of worlds is consonant with the emerging awareness of otherness that Winnicott associates with the mother's failure to sustain the illusion of initial mother-infant unity.[136] Using a temporal reference to describe the experience of this changing environment, he suggests that the infant confronts maternal failure by "remembering, reliving, fantasying, dreaming; the integrating of past, present, and future."[137] Kestenberg and Weinstein mention the use of Winnicott's transitional objects as a response to the anxiety attendant with an altered environment. Tying the objects to recollected and expected points in time, they write, "Transitional objects are created in loneliness. They are based on feeling alone, yearning for past intimacy, and the recreation of past togetherness, while weaving into it current wishes and hopes for the future."[138] Bergman identifies the transformation in spatial terms. She observes that at first there is no space between the mother and child, but, then, as the world beyond the mother entices the child, the space is expanded.[139] Whether environmental transformation occurs as a function of time or space, Winnicott points out the common activity that places the individual relative to both of these axes; it is play, which, he remarks, takes "up time and space."[140]

The changing environment is the place where the individual exists, and it is the place from which he or she has experiences. ORT theorists comprehend that it is not just the individual who changes the environment. The environment, as the locus of otherness, in turn changes the individual in the way he or she experiences him or her self and also in the way he or she will go on to experience life. Such change in the individual is a form of transcendence. The person moves from one level of who he or she is and how he or she experiences reality to an even more imaginatively creative level. Again, the response to otherness is crucial. Modell recalls that "an essential element of creativity is an acceptance of that which is outside the self."[141] Rose confirms that there is a necessary interrelationship between relating to others and forming one's own sense of self.[142] Who a person is at any point in development depends to a great degree on who and what that person perceives, or even imagines, him or herself not to be. Eigen expresses transcendence as "a continuous process where-in self and other are freshly recreated through one another."[143] The more extensive an individual's imaginative perspective of otherness becomes, the greater will be the transcending movement of self. Eigen explains that otherness and difference can be used for personal growth. He proposes that discovering another to be real yields "a new realness of self-feeling."[144] The kind of liberation that he proposes here is not far off from the freedom of creativity that Winnicott associates with play.[145] The ability to engage in the intense back and forth interaction with an imaginatively mediated world of otherness amplifies the experience of self in context while softening the ego's defensive posture against challenge and change.

"But what if self-object boundaries, like perception, thought, and forms of art, breathe and grow and change in the transitional process of everyday creativity?"[146] Rose asks this question to point out that there is vast potential for transcendence in the way one experiences oneself and the way one experiences the broader world. He indicates that creative activity can "bring us into a new relationship with reality or actually reconstitute it in some way.[147] Using the phrase "a new relationship with reality," confirms that he is not suggesting a transposition into a new reality, but rather a transition from one way of seeing the same dynamic reality to another, not unlike a paradigm shift. Arguing for originality in this commonly available ability to imaginatively visualize the world more meaningfully, Winnicott insists that no matter how similar the environmental or even genetic circumstances, each child finds itself "equipped with some capacity to see everything in a fresh way, to be creative in every detail of living."[148] Eigen accentuates the point that, for Winnicott, creativity is directed toward "the emergence of new experiential dimensions."[149] This is not a level that is achieved and then sustained. It is not a stale or enforced view that is taken on and never updated. Winnicott's graphic words reveal the seriousness of his efforts to urge transcending such static outlooks. He writes, "By creative living I mean not getting killed or annihilated all the time by compliance or by reacting to the world that impinges; I mean seeing everything afresh all the time."[150] The argument for Francis' originality in imaginative expression depends heavily on Winnicott's notion of actively seeing-afresh. Francis' imagination is not completely unlike Bernard's, for instance, but neither is it the same, since Francis' background, training, and, in particular, his collection of experiences all differ from Bernard's.

Trusting to Believe. After a cursory look, ORT, from Winnicott's founding perspective, would seem to say very little about belief or faith in God, even though he presents the necessary psychological basis for loving an object beyond one's subjective sphere. Where he gives support to a Christian sense of belief or faith is in the area of trust. The capacity to trust is not only a precondition for believing in a deity who is for the most part encountered in image and thought; the presence of trust in an individual personality is also a strong indicator of a highly creative imagination. As a caveat, to suggest that faith finds its seed in the child's earliest relationship in no way supplants the Christian concept of a movement of grace prior to faith. On the contrary, it allows for the consideration that God reaches out to humanity utilizing the reality that from our earliest historical origins we are physical and emotional nurturers of our offspring. It is no coincidence that the creature created to be most needy at its birth is the creature that is most fully able to reveal the existence of the Creator, as Francis does.

Trust is not an instinctual characteristic of infants. Unless it develops by a fairly early age, the infant will not be able to sustain an imaginatively created world filled with others. Trust emerges with object constancy when an infant uses it to accept that an object continues to exist without being present to the infant's senses. Winnicott ties this even further back into infancy when the object is separated from the child's omnipotent control through the process of object destruction.[151] The recognition of the first "not-me" object is, at the same time, the first act of trust. In his effort to compare Winnicott's ideas in the area of faith to those of other theorists, Eigen corroborates the notion that faith seems to be based on the experience of a real object surviving destruction.[152] He maintains that, "In transitional experiencing the infant lives through a faith that is prior to clear realization of self and other differences; in object usage [which follows object destruction] the infant's faith takes this difference into account, in some sense is based on it."[153]

The actions of the mother, as she disrupts the infant's illusion of omnipotent self-sufficiency, simultaneously build up the idea of reliability in the infant. She no longer meets all needs exactly, but she returns after a bearable time away to substantiate the transitional object representation that holds the infant's anxiety at bay. This reliability, which under girds trust, depends on the positive development of empathy in the mother.[154] Winnicott also speaks of another aspect of trust, confidence in the present moment and the future. He notes that this occurs when good internal objects are stable, a condition that simultaneously supports the capacity to be alone.[155] Deri identifies the parent's tender embrace of the infant, a sign of empathy, as the source of good objects. She relates parental holding to the development of the so-called "skin boundary" between inside and outside. Such a boundary, when effectively established, permits the inside to be a good place, and if it is a good place, "then it is worthwhile to fill it with good things."[156]

One might ask why trust is so important for adult imaginative activity. An act of trust was certainly necessary for the infant to accept that something or someone actually existed where he or she imagined that object or person to be. But, this is a passing incident of trust that is almost instantly taken for granted by people who will be able to function in a communal world. Winnicott signifies the importance of an ongoing stance of trust to counter fear. He observes that peoples' imaginative lives depend on a feeling of freedom from fear "of both themselves and others."[157] One possible source of self directed fear that Winnicott discusses is uninhibited impulse. If left to distinctly internal mechanisms, he states that the impulse will be inhibited absolutely. This is clearly less preferable than allowing the impulse to be brought under gradual and gentle control by the mother, which makes fair allowance for something Winnicott juxtaposes with creativity, spontaneity.[158] He further clarifies that trust or confidence, which counter creativity-stunting fear, develop from the sense that the infant will not be "let down" in its needs.[159] Werner Muensterberger connects trust directly to Winnicott's potential space by describing this area as "primarily a metaphor of the ambience between the mother and child... it is meant to be a resonant expanse associated with emotional substance, a 'sense of trust matched with reliability."[160] Other theorists of the imagination, not associated with ORT, identify an overwhelming concern with the *absolute* as a block to meaningful imaginative activity. Muensterberger points out that the potential space "is the suspense of the absolute."[161] As such it is the one place where the imagination can stir in confidence.

Winnicott contends that there is evidence for a continued relationship between transitional phenomena and trust in adulthood. He finds that, "A need for a specific object or a behavior pattern that started at a very early date may reappear at a later age when deprivation threatens."[162] Simon Grolnick studies Etruscan funerary art as transitional objects that bridge "the interface between life and death."[163] In this role they not only allay anxiety, they offer confidence at an advanced stage of life that one's existence has some form of meaningful continuity. On a related note, Dinnage declares that all artistry requires "trustfulness... that what he is doing is worthwhile."[164] Winnicott adds, "Artists... remind us that the struggle between our impulses and the sense of security (both of which are vital to us) is an eternal struggle and one that goes on inside each one of us as long as our life lasts."[165] Trust, then, enables the individual to uphold an optimistic vision of the world. It frees one from the inclination to live instinctually by purely defensive images and measures. Trust is an essential feature of an imagination wherein the transitional space contains constructive or positive images, the basis of an imaginative spirituality that embraces rather than flees from the potential offered by reality.

Meaning: The Apex of Imaginative Activity. The application of meaning to some experience or feature of life is implied every time Winnicott uses the term creativity. He writes, "Creativity, then, is the retention throughout life of something that belongs properly to infant experience: the ability to create the world."[166] It should be clear by now that he is not referring to the formation of any physical substance that makes up what is commonly known as the world. He is referring to the imaginative development of an inner landscape that is a fair representation of what exists or occurs in the world that is shared, in many of its facets, with others. In the end, creativity boils down to the ability to relate aspects of inner and outer world in combinations or patterns that add to or support an unfolding structure of meaning that began with, and can never be explained apart from, the infant's first relationships with nurturing figures. Accordingly, all creativity is a continuation of the infant's endeavor to imaginatively make sense of the broader world and his or her relationship to it. For this reason, imaginative creativity is an unceasing activity. A similar insight leads Modell, to claim, "The psychology of creativity, which is the psychology of the created environment, can therefore be modeled on the psychology of object relations."[167] Consequently, a spirituality that envisions the world through the lens of divine creativity, as Francis' does, can reveal the "creative impulse" that may just be the creature's nearest reflection of the creator.[168]

Meaning is formulated. It is communicated with others, and it is built upon to sustain a meaning-filled communal life. The construction of meaning is an imaginative activity because it involves the joining of internal images and concepts that yield new and original images as a product, in addition to associated thoughts. Winnicott describes this interaction as occurring through object representations that stand for the thing they represent just as an image does. Similar to the other areas of human existence that have been studied through the lens of imagination, the formulation of meaning takes place in the transitional sphere. It is here that illusion and disillusionment lead the child to first perceive otherness and relate this early encounter to experiences such as hunger and its satisfaction.[169] Winnicott determines that, "From birth, therefore, the human being is concerned with the problem of the relationship between what is objectively perceived and what is subjectively conceived of."[170] For all practical purposes, it is an intended accident that allows the mother's ministrations and the baby's needs to come together under the precise conditions that facilitate the useful joining of illusion with actuality.[171]

The first attempt to apply meaning is the transitional object. It is able to sooth separation-anxiety for the simple reason that the object now has meaning. Winnicott observes, "The transitional object may therefore stand for the 'external' breast, but indirectly, through standing for an 'internal' breast."[172] His use of *standing for* phraseology reflects the meeting of inner and outer worlds at waypoints of meaning. The transitional sphere is where the meetings occur, where the connections are made, but it is not always a place of hard and fast connections. When the infant or the adult is permitted to form, fill, and use the transitional space without the imposition of inhibiting constraints, new combinations of images are possible, and the resultant image can stand for something in an original way with fresh meaning.[173] Imaginative creativity expressed in this way, as meaning, enables Dinnage to propose that, "the artist fuses his inner world with the one outside."[174]

Communicating Meaning. The back and forth motion of play is a good description for what must happen for any significant meaning to be communicated. There is little or no direct transfer of meaning between individuals. As Davis and Wallbridge indicate, meaningful communication cannot be completely explicit.[175] It is in the nature of profound meaning, such as the meaning of the origin, purpose, and end of life, to be somewhat multivalent. The interpretation of such meaning is never exact since individuals do not share the identical images to back up meaning. Instead, Winnicott points out that there can be a degree of commonality, overlapping, or correspondence between individuals' intermediate areas, which is where images are gathered, and meaning is shaped.[176] When experience is fashioned into meaning, the images one person brings together to stand for an experience do not equate to those of another person having a simultaneous version of that experience, but there can be a similarity or resonance between the representational images. Modell indicates that a tradition can be used as an arena for discovering the similarities.[177] Communication of meaning, then, is not a matter of reproducing the same meaning in two or more individuals. It is a matter of allowing pertinent images to be expressed to reflect perspectives of an experience that each person can take into his or her transitional area to supplement, re-organize, or even establish imagery for the experience. There is a parallel between creativity and meaning when Winnicott says: "to draw like Picasso one has to be Picasso—else it is uncreative."[178] If meaning is a product of imaginative creativity it can never be the same for two people even when an experience is described as equally meaningful.

ORT shares the idea, with the general theories of imagination, that symbolism is the primary language of imagination based meaning. Eigen observes, "For Winnicott the symbolic begins at the level of lived experience, prior to language."[179] Symbolism allows for a deeper level of communication, which prompts Davis and Wallbridge to point out that the use of symbols "is a way of being in touch with the inner psychic reality."[180] Winnicott explains how symbolism originates with the first sparks of creativity. The infant begins to develop "creative signs" that relate to the creation of desired objects in his or her mind. The too-good mother empties these signs of meaning by negating their function. The good-enough mother responds to them in appropriate time, rendering the sign (cry) efficacious and meaningful.[181] The next level of symbolism occurs with the transitional object. The eventual back and forth play of symbolic communication depends on the prior ability to form transitional objects. Since the symbol suggests what it is referring to without actually being that object, there is a direct connection with transitional objects which are the first efforts to recognize at once both similarity and difference.[182] Along the same lines, Deri describes "symbol-formation" as the function of connecting and uniting opposites.[183] The ease with which an infant forms and uses transitional objects will indicate future success at working with the symbolic communication of meaning which inevitably relies upon object representations, the imagery of the mind. At the same time, confusion in an infant's growing capacity to operate with similarity and difference has long-term ramifications when it comes to communicating symbolically. Winnicott finds that symbolism entails the capacity to distinguish between fantasy and fact.[184] Elsewhere he offers the comparison between dreaming and fantasying. In dreaming, elements of the dream have symbolic value, and therefore carry potential meaning. In fantasy, the elements of the fantasy stand for what they are.[185] They take on the full aspect of reality without any externally observable connection to it. Fortunately, most people are able to engage some level of meaning-transmitting symbolic interaction, which includes symbolic expression and what Deri calls "symbolic perception," the ability to observe the symbolic expressions of life "that lends rich coloring to seemingly ordinary objects."[186]

Building meaning into life. Transformative spirituality looks for a way to affect the world for good. ORT reveals how this can take place through meaning-based activities on two levels. For the individual and for the community, meaning is not a fixed resource. Something is discovered to be meaningful, and then, over time, that meaning diminishes. It is like a child at play. One moment her attention is captivated by a toy. In the next moment she has moved on to seek something else around which to radiate her activities. But it is possible to keep life full of meaning and not just in a series of sound-bites or brief flashes of meaning that titillate the soul and then wilt, leaving one pining for the next momentary satisfaction like so many of today's media programs. First there has to be a willful effort, a struggle even, to see the world, or take the world, as meaningful. This may have been Francis' greatest faculty, but it is not for him alone. In the second place, there must be a common font of meaning, a place where the meaningful products of imaginative creativity come together to challenge, inspire, and sustain the life of meaning. Winnicott identifies this activity as culture.

"Creative living" is what Winnicott labels a life constructed around meaning. He insists that a sense of meaningfulness is at the heart of creative living, and a lack of it is uncreative living.[187] Comparable to Deri's "symbolic perception," he first uses the term "apperception," claiming that creative living is a matter of apperception.[188] The *American Heritage Dictionary* defines this term as "conscious perception with full awareness," and "the process of understanding by which newly observed qualities of an object are related to past experiences."[189] These definitions hearken back to the attentiveness that the imagination directs towards experience in addition to the linking of existing images to achieve meaning, as highlighted by ORT. Winnicott also ties *apperception* to a sense of worth derived from life.[190] Another phrase he uses is "creative impulse."[191] This should not be confused with creative apperception. Instead, it is the impetus to creative living that drives the will to seek meaning in life supported by the faith Deri has already described as "an optimistic, trusting attitude to the surround and a motivated connectedness toward its objects."[192]

Culture, the meaning-building activity of a society, could not exist without the individual search for meaning in the same way that the personal search for meaning reciprocally demands the continuity provided by a cultural system. Rose finds that this is a natural relationship for human beings since he sees the work of the ego as "creating and rediscovering personal and collective meanings which bridge the two fluidities of inner and outer reality."[193] The collective meanings, which refer to cultural life, encompass all forms of meaning, but it clearly includes religion as one possible source.[194] Although Paul Pruyser's contributions to ORT go into much more detail in the area of culture, the initial insight is credited to Winnicott who prefers the term "cultural experience." He makes it clear that, "Cultural experience is located in the potential space between the individual and the environment."[195] Elsewhere he mentions that transitional object phenomena "appear to form the basis of the whole cultural life of the adult human being."[196] Ruth Miller studies one example of this in which the poems of Emily Dickinson are presented as the transitional objects of the author.[197] At the same time, they have certainly added to the cultural formation of the community of readers who have come into contact with them. Beyond locating cultural experience in the potential space, Winnicott also designates cultural interaction as the mature form of the transitional space, indicating that it is the third area between inner and outer reality. It is an area he also regards as play.[198] Emilie Sobel observes that culture, as a prolongation of the transitional area into adult play, can be found in poetry, particularly that of Gerard Manley Hopkins.[199] Leonard Barking sums up well the connection Winnicott makes between culture and the work of the creative imagination. He writes, "Works of art themselves are not the issue, but rather the relationship between playing and the formation of transitional objects and phenomena, which leads to shared and symbolic play and to cultural experience."[200]

This overview of imaginative development through the lens of Winnicott's theory provides a footing for understanding the ways in which human beings are able to form a spiritual view of the world by means of the creative imagination. Winnicott reveals the significance of openness to environmental experience, awareness of otherness, and the establishment of a web of internal and external relationships. He lays bare the human capacity to perceive meaning in reality through the psychodynamic integration of experience, openness to transcendence, and symbolic representation. One aspect of transcendence has become particularly notable—the achievement of more constructive and outreaching ways of experiencing self and other in relationship which will also be seen as a property of Francis' spirituality. While Winnicott did not set out to exhibit innate personality characteristics that exclusively support the structures of religious faith, he has determined that one pillar of belief, trust, is an internal disposition reflecting the presence of a collection of good internal objects. In the following chapter there is a consideration of the work of other theorists who probe the applications of ORT to specifically religious topics, including religion as a cultural good, religious faith, and personal images of God.

Notes

1. Sigmund Freud, *The Future of an Illusion*, (New York: W.W. Norton and Co., 1961), 38.

2. Ibid., 63.

3. Ibid., 39.

4. Ibid.

5. Rosemary Dinnage, "A Bit of Light," in *Between Reality and Fantasy: Winnicott's Concepts of Transitional Objects and Phenomena,* ed. Simon A. Grolnick and Leonard Barkin (Northvale, NJ: Jason Aronson Inc., 1995), 366.

6. D.W. Winnicott, "Transitional Objects and Transitional Phenomenon: A Study of the First Not-me Possession," *The International Journal of Psycho-Analysis* 34 (1953): 95.

7. Roy Herndon Steinhoff Smith, "The Denial of Mystery: Object Relations Theory and Religion," *Horizons* 16, no. 2 (1989): 247, 254.

8. Ibid., 249.

9. Diane Jonte-Pace, "Object Relations Theory, Mothering, and Religion: Towards a Feminist Psychology of Religion," *Horizons* 14, no. 2 (1987): 314.

10. Ibid., 311.

11. Ibid.

12. Ibid., 323.

13. Ibid., 312.

14. Ibid., 323.

15. Winnicott prefers the term creativity. For the purposes of this study, creativity, which involves the use of internal imagery in the form of object representations, should be seen to equate to imaginative activity.

16. D.W. Winnicott, "Transitional Objects and Transitional Phenomenon," 94.

17. D.W. Winnicott, *Playing and Reality* (London: Tavistock, 1971), 10.

18. Susan Deri, "Transitional Phenomena: Vicissitudes of Symbolization and Creativity," in *Between Reality and Fantasy,* 50.

19. Madeleine Davis and David Wallbridge, *Boundary and Space: An Introduction to the Work of D.W. Winnicott* (New York: Brunner and Mazel, 1981), 98.

20. Winnicott, "Transitional Objects and Transitional Phenomenon," *International Journal of Psycho-analysis 34 (1953)*: 95.

21. Jonte-Pace, 322.

22. Ibid., 323.

23. D.W. Winnicott, *The Family and Individual Development* (New York: Basic Books, Inc., 1965), 10. Although an age identifier has been given in this case, it must be realized that ORT theorists shy away from locking in a specific age for any of the stages of development described herein, since children clearly develop at differing paces.

24. Arnold H. Modell, "The Transitional Object and the Creative Act," *Psychoanalytic Quarterly* 39. (1970): 248.

25. D.W. Winnicott, *Playing and Reality,* 10.

26. Ibid., 11.

27. Ibid.

28. Davis and Wallbridge, 58.

29. Winnicott, *Playing and Reality,* 12.

30. D.W. Winnicott, *The Family and Individual Development,* 7.

31. Winnicott, *Playing and Reality,* 11.

32. Winnicott, "Living Creatively," in *Home Is Where We Start From: Essays by a Psychoanalyst* (New York: W.W. Norton, 1986), 36.

33. Winnicott, *Playing and Reality,* 101.

34. Dinnage, 370.

35. Michael Eigen, "The Area of Faith in Winnicott, Lacan and Bion," *International Journal of Psycho-analysis* 63 (1981): 414. The term transitional space is used almost interchangeably with transitional sphere, potential space, and transitional phenomena throughout the literature on ORT. It should be noted, however, that the last term, transitional phenomena, also refers to the mental/imaginative processing, or illusion processing, that occurs in this space.

36. Winnicott, "Transitional Objects and Transitional Phenomenon," 95.

37. Ibid., 90.

38. Winnicott, *Playing and Reality,* 2.

39. Eigen, 414.

40. Winnicott, "Transitional Objects and Transitional Phenomenon," 95.

41. Eigen, 414.

42. Ibid.

43. Winnicott, *The Family and Individual Development,* 12.

44. Winnicott, *The Maturational Process and the Facilitating Environment: Studies in the Theory of Emotional Development,* (Madison CT: International Universities Press, 1965), 82.

45. Davis and Wallbridge, 41.

46. Winnicott, *Playing and Reality,* 4.

47. Ibid., 5.

48. Ibid., 101.

49. Henry P. Copolillo, "Maturational Aspects of the Transitional Phenomenon," *International Journal of Psycho-Analysis,* no. 48 (1967): 243.

50. Winnicott, *Playing and Reality,* 88.

51. Ibid.

52. Ibid., 97.

53. Ibid., 7.

54. Ibid., 109.

55. Martin J. Welch, "Transitional Language," in *Between Reality and Fantasy,* 416.

56. Ibid.

57. Winnicott, *Playing and Reality,* 89.

58. Ibid., 90.

59. Ibid.

60. Ibid., 94.

61. One significant implication of this notion is that religion as an exclusively personal project cannot sustain a real love of a real God.

62. Eigen, 418.

63. Jonte-Pace, 314.

64. Eigen, 415.

65. Ibid. Eigen's description reflects the paradox of the difference-in-tension brought up in the previous chapter.

66. Winnicott, *The Family and Individual Development,* 12.

67. Winnicott, *Playing and Reality,* 54.

68. Ibid., 64.

69. Ibid.

70. Ibid., 47.

71. Ibid., 48.

72. Ibid., 51.

73. Ibid., 50.

74. Ibid., 52.

75. Winnicott, *The Maturational Process and the Facilitating Environment*, 30.

76. Deri, 55-56.

77. Winnicott, *The Maturational Process and the Facilitating Environment*, 31-32.

78. Anni Bergman, "From Mother to the World Outside: The Use of Space During the Separation-Individuation Phase," in *Between Reality and Fantasy*, 156.o

79. Ibid., 160.

80. ORT does not completely ignore the period of adolescent development, but much more attention is given to the association between adult experience and its originating influence in infancy. This tendency may in part be responsible for Smith's critique of the theory's so-called adultomorphisms.

81. Eigen, 430.

82. Ibid., 431.

83. Ibid.

84. Ibid., 431.

85. Winnicott, "Transitional Objects and Transitional Phenomenon," 96.

86. Ibid., 97.

87. Winnicott, *Playing and Reality*, 51.

88. Ibid., 56.

89. Eigen, 414.

90. Winnicott, *The Family and Individual Development*, 8.

91. Winnicott, *Playing and Reality*, 2.

92. Ibid., 2.

93. Ibid., 89-90.

94. Eigen, 420.

95. Ibid., 431.

96. Dinnage, 368.

97. Gilbert J. Rose, "The Creativity of Everyday Life," in *Between Reality and Fantasy*, 355.

98. Ibid., 354.

99. Winnicott, *Playing and Reality*, 64.

100. Clare Winnicott, "DWW: A Reflection," in *Between Reality and Fantasy*, 18. Emphasis mine.

101. Davis and Wallbridge, 57; Rose, 357.

102. Eigen, 414.

103. Paul Pruyser, *The Play of the Imagination: Toward a Psycho-analysis of Culture* (New York: International University Press, 1983), 161.

104. Winnicott, *Playing and Reality*, 9.

105. Ibid., 101.

106. Davis and Wallbridge, 57.

107. Eigen, 429.

108. Davis and Wallbridge, 43.

109. Deri, 46.

110. Winnicott, *Playing and Reality*, 40.

111. Ibid., 41.

112. Ibid.

113. Ibid., 43.

114. Davis and Wallbridge, 118.

115. Ibid., 125.

116. Ibid., 119.

117. Winnicott, *Playing and Reality*, 3.

118. Ibid.

119. Ibid., 14.

120. Winnicott, *The Maturational Process and the Facilitating Environment*, 73.

121. Ibid., 75.

122. Ibid., 73.

123. Ibid., 82.

124. Modell, 245.

125. Winnicott, *Playing and Reality*, 94.

126. Davis and Wallbridge, 65.

127. Modell, 246.

128. Ibid.

129. Winnicott, *Playing and Reality*, 26.

130. Ibid., 27.

131. Judith S. Kestenberg and Joan Weinstein, "Transitional Objects and Body Image Formation," in *Between Reality and Fantasy*, 90.

132. Winnicott, *Playing and Reality*, 84.

133. Jonte-Pace, 313, 312.

134. Davis and Wallbridge, 34.

135. Modell, 244.

136. Winnicott, *Playing and Reality*, 10.

137. Ibid.

138. Kestenberg and Weinstein, 90.

139. Bergman, 152-153.

140. Winnicott, *Playing and Reality*, 50.

141. Modell, 244.

142. Rose, 358.

143. Eigen, 416.

144. Ibid., 415.

145. Winnicott, *Playing and reality*, 53.

146. Rose, 358.

147. Ibid., 355.

148. Winnicott, "Living Creatively," 37.

149. Eigen, 428.

150. Winnicott, "Living Creatively," 37.

151. Winnicott, *Playing and Reality*, 94.

152. Eigen, 416.

153. Ibid., 413.

154. Winnicott, *The Maturational Process and the Facilitating Environment*, 48.

155. Ibid., 32, 31.

156. Deri, 48.

157. Winnicott, The *Family and Individual Development*, 30.

158. Ibid., 11.

159. Ibid., 32.

160. Werner Muensterberger, "Between Reality and Fantasy," in *Between Reality and Fantasy,* 10.

161. Ibid.

162. Winnicott, "Transitional Objects and Transitional Phenomenon," 91. See also: Merton J. Kahne, "On the Persistence of Transitional Phenomena into Adult Life," *Inter-*

national Journal of Psycho-Analysis 48 (1967): 250-256. He cites three case studies exemplifying transitional objects in maturity.

163. Simon Grolnick, "Etruscan Burial Symbols and the Transitional Process," in *Between Reality and Fantasy,*381.

164. Dinnage, 366.

165. Winnicott, *The Family and Individual Development,* 33.

166. Winnicott, "Living Creatively, " 36.

167. Modell, 244.

168. Winnicott, *Playing and Reality,* 69.

169. Ibid.,10-12.

170. Ibid., 11.

171. Ibid.

172. Ibid., 10.

173. See Coppolillo, 242, 244. He cites case study evidence of a mother who inhibited the natural use of transitional objects by forcing her own chosen objects upon the child. The result was "a violent identity crisis."

174. Dinnage, 375.

175. Davis and Wallbridge, 119.

176. Winnicott, *Playing and Reality,* 14.

177. Modell, 246.

178. Winnicott, "Living Creatively, " 48.

179. Eigen, 420.

180. Davis and Wallbridge, 89.

181. Winnicott, *The Maturational Process and the Facilitating Environment,* 51.

182. Winnicott, "Transitional Objects and Transitional Phenomenon," 92.

183. Deri, 50.

184. Winnicott, *Playing and Reality,* 6.

185. Ibid., 33.

186. Deri, 50.

187. Winnicott, "Living Creatively," 46.

188. Ibid., 39.

189. *The American Heritage Dictionary* (1982), s.v. "apperception."

190. Winnicott, *Playing and Reality,* 65.

191. Ibid., 69.

192. Deri, 50.

193. Rose, 358.

194. Winnicott, *Playing and Reality*, 3.

195. Ibid., 100.

196. Winnicott, *The Family and Individual Development,* 13.

197. Ruth Miller, "Poetry as Transitional Object," in *Between Reality and Fantasy,* 449-468.

198. Winnicott, *Playing and Reality,* 102.

199. Emilie Sobel, "Rhythm, Sound and Imagery in the Poetry of Gerard Manley Hopkins," in *Between Reality and Fantasy,* 427-445.

200. Leonard Barking, "The Concept of the Transitional Object," in *Between Reality and Fantasy,* 529-530.

CHAPTER FIVE
OBJECT RELATIONS THEORY AFTER WINNICOTT

Thanks to Winnicott's willingness to challenge Freud's drive theory with a theory based on the formative and motivational effects of the numerous inter-relationships of internally constructed object representations, it is possible not only to conceive of early human development in a new light, but also to reach an understanding of how this series of image-connected relationships can influence mature thought, feeling, and the search for meaning in the face of significant experiences that were previously neglected or negated by many members of the psychological field. Three theorists, in particular, have dedicated much consid-eration to the possible gains to be made by looking at religion from an ORT perspective and looking at ORT from a religious standpoint. To that end Paul Pruyser focuses on the maturing aspect of illusion processing and the imagina-tive attainment of cultural experience. John McDargh applies ORT to the matter of self-development and faith, and Ana-Maria Rizzuto explains the psychologi-cal formation of God-images as they play a role in personality formation.

Paul Pruyser

Paul Pruyser lists religion amongst other goods of culture including: art, li-terature, science, and music.[1] Although religion is not his singular interest he goes far in expressing the workings of the maturing imagination for religious purposes when he expands Freud's two-world schema to a three world model based on Winnicott's transitional space. In Pruyser's writings the transitional space constitutes the illusionistic world (or sphere) which is situated between Freud's autistic and realistic worlds.[2] Pruyser's most pertinent contributions to an understanding of imaginative activity will be shown to lay in his explication of religion as a cultural activity and the illusion processing that makes cultural activity possible. His views will be probed through a study of perceptual reality, the nature of the illusionistic sphere, culture as a product of illusionistic activity, the imagination tutored by and for culture, and various approaches to describing the formation of images.

Reality and Culture

A description of the less tangible dimensions of reality will set the basis for Pruyser's explication of the influence of culture on the religious imagination engaged in illusion processing. He acknowledges that all encounters with reality are not direct. In many cases it is the indirect, incomplete, or inaccessible nature of some types of experience that stand at the core of meaningful experiencing. Mentioning Tracy's "limits-of-experience" situations, Pruyser observes that these "can lead to acknowledgement of a gap in being between the human subject and the divine object."[3] He adds that, "The limit encountered in certain existential situations... becomes variably defined as coming up against one's own limited power or authority, or knowledge, restricted radius of action, narrow perception, failure of reasoning, inadequate in expression, failure of nerve, and captivity."[4] Similar types of experiences, not formed primarily out of sense data, are mentioned by James Jones and Christopher Bollas. Jones relates such experience to Rudolph Otto's concept of "the holy," but he argues that "'the holy' is not itself an object I experience, rather it is a special way of experiencing various objects or states of consciousness."[5] Bollas advances the notion of an "unthought known." He claims that one can imagine an idea in a way that is not directly connected to "knowing exactly what it is that I think."[6] Where sense data is not available or sufficient for giving shape to the meaning of an experience, as these other thinkers indicate through their examples, Pruyser puts forward the application of "transcendence and mystery" as "tools for coming to terms with limit or 'borderline' situations."[7] He writes: transcendence "implies a space-time frame of large dimensions that can manage distinct loci of 'here' and 'yonder' (in whatever direction and at whatever distance) and of 'before' and 'after.'"[8] Accordingly, Pruyser specifies transcendence in terms of a difference, movement, or change in space and time. I suggest that transcendence can also refer to a change of state, such as a movement from complacent to concerned, unaware to aware, sad to joyous, unborn to born, and damned to saved. Of mystery he writes that it implies "a language frame... that can manage such variables as: speaking and listening, thundering and hearing the thunder, a still small voice, the spoken and unspoken, and especially the borderline experience of the ineffable – all caught up in a relation between parties felt to be of unequal power and authority."[9] Pruyser goes on to insist that borderline experiences of the sort described above "push linear reasoning over the brink and greatly tax denominative language. Hence they promote a switch to symbols which, like those of the poet, do a better job of evoking and rendering the felt meanings of these experiences than do conceptual thought, thing-language, and purely rational discourse."[10] Winnicott has made it clear, and Pruyser corroborates, that symbolic activity is a form of imaginative activity that begins to reveal the nature of perceptual reality pertinent to this study.

Reality, as ORT portrays it, is clearly never a distinct entity that is wholly available to examine and experience through the senses. Reality for human beings exceeds a narrow definition because of the imagination, which is less to say that the imagination constructs something deemed to be real than to say that reality can be encompassed in a fuller measure as a result of the imagination.

Pruyser finds that this is so because "the capacity and function of the imagination transcends sense data."[11] He is certain that there is an "objective context" to most imaginative activity, but he notes that perception is also based on the individual's "mental set or intention."[12] He points out elsewhere that reality has many aspects because of variability in the sense capacity for confronting the external environment in addition to the fact that each person develops with a unique internal environment.[13] Such variables aside, Pruyser also recognizes the existence of a common dimension of imaginative activity that reveals what he calls "reality-as-a-whole" or "total reality."[14] This is a communally available, roughly general perception of reality that anyone holds the possibility of adding to, taking from, or otherwise altering. He exemplifies the connection between the wider reality and a personal view of reality when he considers that image can refer to both an artist's internal vision and the artifact that it yields for others to observe.[15]

Identifying the earliest imaginative efforts to link an individual reality with a collective reality, Studzinski explains that the transitional object is the infant's "beginning attempt to establish a relationship to a world beyond the mother."[16] In Pruyser's terms, the effort to tie personal imaginative activity to the broader world occurs in the illusionistic sphere. He creates a comparison table that delineates the activities that are proper to each of the three worlds. From this table he explains that, "Between autistic dreaming and realistic working lies the opportunity to play and to engage in symbolic transactions, shared with and supported by other civilized people."[17] It is the significance of this intermediate area that it enables individuals to develop unique perceptions of reality while simultaneously weaving these varying perspectives into a more or less common way of visualizing many facets of reality. Ritual events or some form of physical acting out of imaginative content exemplify the effort to use play and symbolic transacting to link these personal and communal visions of what is real.[18] In fact, it would be difficult to accept an aspect of common reality as personally real and meaningful were it not for the imaginative process in the illusionistic sphere that also seeks to advance personal views of reality into the realistic sphere. The illusionistic sphere, which promotes play and other forms of relating, is also where religious imaginative activity is born. Studzinski contends that, "The illusionistic world is of vital importance to religion because it is the space where one encounters transcendence. The objects found there are more than fabrications of the individual mind and more than perceptual images of the real world impinging on the senses."[19] A thorough explication of Pruyser's understanding of the illusionistic area will advance the insight ORT has into religious imaginations and their outlook on reality.

World of Illusion

In the illusionistic world, Pruyser finds that there is an "engagement in illusionistic activities, abounding in imaginative processes and entities that not only prove shareable, but are in fact institutionalized in the social order."[20] While there must be bridges between the three worlds, he spends much time contrasting the illusionistic world with the real world, finding that the first sets tutored fantasy against the sense perception source of the second. He furthermore indicates that the illusionistic world is based on inspired and logical connections in addition to symbols while the real world can be understood in terms of signs and indices. Possibly his most distinguishing contrast is that of the play that evolves from the illusionistic sphere as opposed to the work that is central to the realistic sphere.[21] For each of these worlds there is also an associated type of object. The autistic world has its internal objects, and the real or factual world has external objects, the things known primarily to sense data. For the illusionistic world Pruyser proposes the existence of a "transcendent object," which goes "beyond the subjectivity and hiddeness of internal objects as well as beyond the objective and patently public nature of external objects."[22] He considers Winnicott's transitional object to be the first or initiatory transcendent object.[23]

The contrasts between the realistic and illusionistic worlds, listed above, add to the evidence which counters historic views that associate an image with imitation.[24] Pruyser bears out the originality of objects emerging from the illusionistic world when he insists that the transitional space, and "the actions engendered within it, are *sui generis*."[25] He remarks, "Images, then, are not necessarily copies of anything, but original products of the human mind when it is engaged in imagining."[26] However, originality does not prohibit a sharing of images. Studzinski confirms that one is able to gain access to "an image of someone else's imagining."[27] These could be used either for imitation purposes or at the service of producing new images. Excessive reliance on their use in the former case, for imitation, could be a sign of a limited imagination. In the opposite direction, it is doubtful that any image could be created were it not for the encounter with one or more pre-existing images.[28]

There is no certainty that each person will form a workable or fully functional illusionistic sphere. Pruyser suggests that too much activity in the inner reality or the outer reality may render the transitional sphere undeveloped.[29] Even a well-formed imaginative use of the illusionistic sphere has its dangers. He warns that, "The imagination is constantly threatened from two sides: from the side of autism by hallucinatory entities and events, and from the side of realism by actual entities or events."[30] While Pruyser, following Winnicott's lead, describes the illusionistic world as an intermediate place, he often expresses a strong dichotomy between each of the spheres. Nonetheless, some intrusion across the vague boundaries of each world is to be expected and is also necessary. Pruyser points toward the obvious value of such crossovers when he asks, "Could we know anything about the outer world or the inner world unless we bring the two together, in play—in culture?"[31] Having expressed the illusionistic sphere as the continuation or mature version of the transitional space, his explanation of the influence of culture in this area and the illusion processing that takes place here adds to ORT's capacity to describe the inner workings of the imagination.

Illusion Processing at the Service of Culture

To grasp Pruyser's understanding of the encounter between the religious imagination and reality in all its dimensions requires a better appreciation for the dynamic features of illusion processing in support of an individual's cultural participation. Since he views religion as an aspect of culture, it will be probed as such, comparing religion to a work of art. This will set the groundwork for an explanation of what goes into training or tutoring the imagination to work with object representations and their images as illusion processing takes place.

Pruyser broadens the possibilities for the study of religion by considering it through a psychological lens as a cultural activity. He comments, "Prompted by Winnicott's ideas, I have constantly sought to reconstruct the childhood antecedents of the thought processes and skills that go into dealing with art, literature, science, religion, and music," which he also calls the "goods of culture."[32] Pruyser remarks that religion is studied with other cultural entities because it is widely manifested in a cultural context.[33] It is hard to miss the fact that Francis creates his own religious culture, or at least sub-culture, when he formed his orders. Perceiving the nurturing influence that culture sometimes has, Pruyser reveals the self-perpetuating effect of religion being a cultural activity when he writes, "Religion is religion; it comes from religion and will give rise to religion."[34] He makes a more direct connection between religious-cultural activity and an individual's imaginative activity when he asserts that "religious development hinges on a set of developments that could be called illusion processing."[35] Throughout his writing Pruyser puts on view the close connections between illusion processing, the imagination, and culture. Elsewhere he employs the term "illusion to designate cultural phenomena."[36]

Maybe the clearest connection to be made between culture and illusion is the back and forth, interactive motion of play, so central to ORT. More than once Pruyser emphasizes the origin of the word illusion as play, pointing out that the word comes from the Latin verb *ludere* and the noun *lusus*, which refer to "intense or serious play."[37] Play is clearly a critical undertaking when it is seen for its role in cultural endeavors to make sense of reality. Pruyser notes that "coming to terms with reality (in its inner and outer aspects) requires coming to terms with playing."[38] Other theorists are similarly inspired to see the connection between imaginative activity, play, and culturally related efforts to formulate meaning. Jones looks to Winnicott as an early propagator of the view that the to and fro interaction of play reflects the way individuals discover meaning instead of having it forced on them in a one-way fashion. He observes in Winnicott's theories that culture doesn't stand over the person, pre-determining him or her, "Rather the individual and the social world exist in a mutual, reciprocal relationship to each other."[39] While Studzinski notes that, "Creative imagination, the source of illusion, leads people to see the profound meaning of their experience," he is quick to offer a template to test for the communal validity and benefit of an individual's religious illusionistic activity.[40] He asks whether an illusion preserves "the surplus shared meaning to which the religious community's tradition points," or does it reduce that meaning?[41] According to Pruyser's thoughts, a negative answer signifies that illusion is too close to the autistic sphere, and there is no culturally enhancing or shareable outcome and no benefit to personal growth.[42] On the other hand, a positive answer is received when the product of religious imaginative activity is broadly accepted as an uplifting and meaning- filled segment of the structure of the religion's cultural edifice. To highlight the meaning-building potential of religion-as-a-cultural activity, religion can be compared to another image-forming cultural phenomenon--art.

In many ways the work of an artist who gives new form and order to objects and substances taken from nature is one of the most effective analogies for the workings of a creative imagination which can manifest itself in products that include art but also musical pieces, literary works, and religious expressions, to name a few. Pruyser notes this connection and what is involved when the two mediums of art and religion come together. He explains that natural objects which take on religious significance often do so in a way that involves mystery and transcendence.[43] For the elements of mystery and transcendence to have any meaningful effect they must be engaged in the illusionistic sphere, but for them to have such an effect requires a delicate balance of interior and exterior influence. Pruyser warns of the consequences when either of the two worlds contributing to the illusionistic world has an overwhelming influence on religious creativity. He writes, "If too natural, too realistic, art vanishes into mere representation and religion into mere rationality.... If too subjective, too autistic, art and religion will fail to get a hearing since they come too close to delusion and hallucination."[44]

Several thinkers pick up on the role of the intermediate area to sustain the precarious balance from which a meaningful artwork or religious expression can be created. For religious expression, Jones recalls Winnicott's seminal influence, pointing out a growing trend among some theorizers to hold "that religious beliefs and practices can be understood as 'transitional phenomena' in Winnicott's sense: neither purely subjective nor completely objective."[45] For artistic creativity, Studzinski determines that great art, the great imaginative creation, "has tremendous power to pull us into our potential space to share the illusion."[46] Similarly he finds that the religious classic pulls observers into their potential spaces "where they can confront what is most immediate and personal in their lives, their meaning, purpose, and destiny."[47] Bollas uses Murray Krieger's theory of the aesthetic moment to describe the subject/object interface that takes place in the illusionistic sphere and moves the individual to new heights of meaning. Bollas suggests that, "The aesthetic space," like the transitional space, "allows for a creative enactment of the search for this transforming object relationship."[48] He adds that, "The aesthetic experience is an existential recollection of the time when communicating took place primarily through this illusion of deep rapport of subject and object."[49] Bollas presents the kind of early interior relationship that might be needed for Pruyser's transcendent object to have its effect, which is, in turn, reflected in the latter thinker's description of an object image that sustains the capacity for isolation at the service of creativity. Pruyser contends that, "Most theorists today would probably agree that the capacity to be alone means having within oneself a dynamic, trustworthy, reliant image of the benevolent mother."[50] An image of this nature, derived from the real world experience of a nurturing and caring maternal figure, as well as the autistic world counter-influences of instability, fear, and desire, points toward the delicate work of illusion processing to formulate an object-image that has meaning, purpose, and effect. Evidence of Pruyser's underlying maternal object representation will be sought in Francis' writings to corroborate his artistic creation of a religious culture. It can be suggested that this image is just what supported his creation of a spiritual way of life.

Forming and Tutoring the Imagination

Pruyser's theory of illusion processing comes across even more clearly when it is understood as an imaginative activity that varies in its development and application from person to person. In fact the primary differences can often be attributed to external, cultural influences that come to bear on the imaginative formation of each individual. These effects are the result of directed effort on the part of another person, or simply from incidental, day-to-day contact in a particular social-cultural setting. Pruyser notes that "most pedagogies do not take image formation and imagination for granted, but rather seek to shape and tutor them in specific directions."[51] Speaking of endeavors to inform the activities of the nascent illusionistic sphere, he designates the transitional sphere as "that peculiar benign conspiracy in the child's social ambience that introduces the child to modes of cognition, feeling, and action of a unique kind."[52] He also mentions a significant direct influence on the religious imagination. He maintains that "the essential transmission of religion to children takes place through story- telling and engagement in ritual. Without stories, no religion."[53]

In addition to shaping and tutoring, Pruyser uses the concept of *cultivating* to denote what is occurring when a person is engaged in both a culture's passive and active attempts to configure the inner imaginative environment, for better or worse.[54] He explains that civilization has developed a world of shared illusion into which one must be trained or tutored for illusion processing to be productive.[55] What is more, he labels this shared illusion as the "collective imagination" when he claims, "Illusionistic objects... evolve from a tutored fantasy rooted in the collective imagination of the human mind and its history."[56] Pruyser specifies exactly how the social environment is able to reach so deeply into the inner workings of the imagination when he writes, "Thus the imagination, especially the culturally tutored fantasy, fashions the symbols, stylizes the modes of dealing with symbols, and sets the rewards for engaging in symbolic activity."[57] Pruyser is not suggesting, however, that the imagination is a puppet or mirror of the social world. Much of a person's ability to operate effectively in the illusionistic sphere comes from his or her own efforts. In addition, he finds that people can have more or less practice operating within the intermediate sphere.[58] Those who are most adept at using the transitional space to work with reality use what Meissner calls "interpretive judgment" when he proposes that, "Knowledge of reality always involves interpretive judgment, but when the matter of judgment becomes more distanced from the level of simple physical perception, reality becomes increasingly a function of judgment rather than perception."[59] Meissner expands the idea when he conveys that, "Reality is grasped and acknowledged in reference to meanings, which are at once resident in the structure of reality but which are constituted subjectively by interpretive and symbolic processes of the mind."[60]

Observing the dynamics involved in the interface of the autistic and realistic worlds in part reveals why illusion processing requires some form of tutoring to yield any sense of sharable meaning. While taking into consideration Winnicott's view that the transitional sphere separates inner and outer worlds, Pruyser argues that civilization, as a construction from both worlds, exists as that fragile balance of forces coming from either. He calls civilization a "precarious achievement that needs constant nurture and a great deal of vigilance against intrusions from either the autistic or the realistic side."[61] In this instance, guarding against intrusions does not infer shunning the influence of the very private interior world or the very public exterior world in the formation of a cultural worldview. It means ensuring that illusion processing has occurred and unprocessed input from either side does not unduly affect or control the outcome, the product of imaginative activity. Pruyser again expresses the danger of "autistic encroachments," more so, upon religion than science and art, and, at the other end of the spectrum, the problem of identifying imaginative or illusionistic activity directly with the realistic sphere.[62] One example of autistic encroachment arises when a ritual act becomes "a compulsion grimly performed in fear of failure or imperfection."[63] It is clear enough that this and similar examples are a hindrance to healthy illusion processing, which is why Pruyser instead goes into greater detail displaying the hazards stemming from the often times taken-for-granted realistic world. He suggests that realistic intrusions on religion cause it to become "institutional and what was once the more spontaneous manifestation of imagination becomes the rigid chore of those with a stunted imagination."[64] He speaks further of a "single-minded dedication to the realistic world" which impedes an individual's "playfulness," "novelty-producing, potentially creative imagination," and ability to "engage in as-if thinking."[65] All such concerns prompt Pruyser to recommend a sensible form of reality testing in order to avoid madness.[66] By reality testing he seems to mean that play and symbolic transacting must be "shared and supported by other civilized people," which in itself becomes an opportunity for tutoring.[67] Speaking autobiographically, he comments, "I received much approval and help from adults in keeping traffic with the imaginable—as long as my thoughts, words, and acts proved shareable with other people, or better, touched a responsive chord in them."[68]

Pruyser's "responsive chord" image may be the most apropos descriptor of the effort to inform the imagination. It suggests that tutoring the imagination can yield meaning that extends from one person to others yet is not systematically duplicated or echoed. The connections that occur when an imagination undergoes tutoring reflect some of the same relational themes that persist throughout an ORT understanding of imagination. Pruyser also credits much of the tutoring to parents who support imaginative development with essential prerequisites like human interaction and a trustworthy environment. "In a word, the transitional object is a product of active imagining on the part of the child, reinforced by the family's participatory creation of a transitional sphere which has all the features of play."[69] It is also the maternal object representation that sustains a sense of relatedness at the heart of the capacity to be alone when object constancy has been sufficiently supported. Pruyser writes that this capacity is based on a trustworthy image of "the benevolent mother."[70] At another point he insists that childhood must involve trust in order to "elaborate the transitional sphere."[71] And similarly, it is a "trusting relationship to the outside world" that he associates with the ability to form good internal objects.[72] Once tutored, the imagination, participating in culturally mediated meaning, sustains the individual's relational capacity. Pruyser confirms that, "Much of the 'relatedness' between people occurs through this collective imagination."[73]

Formation of Images

In one sense it can be said that imaginative activity, illusion processing, involves the formation or combination of images. This much is carried over from Winnicott, but Pruyser reveals that imagination is much more complex when he points out that images, as object representations, include cultural objects, words, pictures, and melodies in addition to person's and things.[74] Pruyser describes image formation as: a result of waiting and wishing, distinguishing between good and bad, symbolic transacting, an innate tendency toward transformation and transcendence, and as a process of internalization. The presence of so many methods to describe image formation and illusion processing may reflect, in part, the mystery in which imaginative activity is still enshrouded, but, more so, these various means point to Pruyser's understanding of the intricacy of working with and creating new and potentially meaningful images. At the same time, most of the following attempts to describe the constructive side of illusion processing are interconnected in one way or another.

The passage of time, which has already been associated with change and transformation, is a rudimentary instigator of image formation. Pruyser uses the term "successivity," which refers to one experience succeeding another, to explain the infant's expanding world of space and time.[75] Foretelling the uninhibited concentration needed for adult creativity, the infant makes the most of successivity by waiting. During this period of waiting, images of space and time collapse into each other.[76] Pruyser explains that, "Waiting is the simplest state: the infant waits for his hallucinatory image to become an actually present mother."[77] The openness to experience suggested by waiting can be shattered by strong affect which, Pruyser points out, can "annul" space and time as expanding potentiality and can also bring the formation of imagery to an end.[78] Slightly more advanced are two states that presage later stages of religious desire and faith. These are pining for the anticipated satisfaction and hoping, which involves a belief that the satisfaction will come.[79] The connection Pruyser draws between objects and desires is that objects are formed to satisfy desires, and, as a corollary, the lack of a meaningful object (image) can indicate a frustrated or unsatisfied desire.[80] He links the most common object representation, that of the mother, with "wish-fulfilling thoughts," and in a further association he determines that wishes yield ideals: an ideal object and an ideal self.[81]

Ideal is an appropriate starting point for discussing *good* and *bad* since *ideal* refers not just to good over bad but to that which is conceived as best. Pruyser infers that *ideal* signifies potentiality, the way something could be, when he claims that it implies "directionality."[82] With this in mind, applying

Pruyser's view to conceptualizations of object representations of self and God may provide a more worthy sense of the creature-creator relationship than simplistically relying on a bad versus good association. Pruyser's directionality expresses the notion of lesser to greater and how one *is* to how one could or should *be*. Jones holds closer to a bad versus good notion for idealization in religion. He proposes that idealization of something is key to experiencing it as sacred, and "to be religious is, among other things, to idealize something or someone."[83] The problem with religious idealization, as Jones presents it, lays in the dichotomous object relationship of bad self versus good God.[84] The difficulty here is not in the fact that God is good, but in accepting the insinuation that God's creation is bad rather than limited, affected, or disadvantaged in some way. Pruyser's concept of idealization displays human potentiality over human conditionality. Where Jones is clearly more helpful in building on the description of meaningful object formation he describes idealization as an "intensification of experience beyond typical human experience," which revisits earlier discussions of experiential intensification.[85] Nonetheless, the formation of images as good or bad seems to be a basis for much unsophisticated imaginative activity.

Pruyser conveys that applying a designation to an object, in this case as good or bad, gives it greater substance or permanency. He comments that, "the nameability of anything vouchsafes its existence in one form or another. Naming, therefore, is bound to have a bearing on the production and form of mental images."[86] One effect that naming has is in the establishment of order amidst chaos. Pruyser maintains that as a result of pleasure and pain experiences, "Good and bad function from birth on—if not prenatally also—as the most basic subjective ordering principle."[87] He goes into more detail explaining the processing of illusion as good or bad from an early age, declaring that as a mother decreases her adaptation to an infant's needs and frustration builds up "the child becomes forcefully aware of the outer world as a mixed pattern of positive and negative stimuli which he must come to terms with."[88] Coupled with this, on the positive side, Pruyser asserts that all that evolves from the transitional sphere elicits feelings of pleasure, "the pleasure of play, inventiveness, creativity, and novelty of perspective."[89] The experience of pleasure and pain as a precursor for perceiving good and bad has a lifelong influence on the process of relating and categorizing images. Pruyser confirms that these poles "stand in dialectical relationship to each other. One cannot experience or know one without the other; each is the other's antithesis."[90] In many ways, illusion processing relies on the effort to either actualize or overcome this way of relating object representations in order to establish new, more complex object relationships that yield new images.

In addition to showing the mediation between positive and negative experiences of reality, Pruyser also specifies the working of another feature of illusion processing. While comparing a symbol to a sign he presents a means by which the world of sensible data is able to reveal a world that, by nature, defies such data. He finds that a symbol is far more dynamic and valuable than a sign, just so long as a symbolic indication is not taken as a realistic proposition in the sense of something that always is and does as it appears.[91] As an aspect of illusion processing, he explains that what takes place in the transitional sphere is "the practice of attachments to symbols."[92] In other words, experiences are linked with, hopefully relevant, symbols in an effort to assign the experiences to a deeper degree of meaning than a commonplace encounter with stimulation. Symbolism is particularly important for religious illusion processing. Pruyser comments that unlike mathematics with its signs, religion relies on symbols which "ambiguously conceal and reveal—they mediate between the seen and unseen. Not precisely definable, they stand with one leg in the concrete world and are there existentially apprehended as pointers to and potential disclosers of, a truth not yet fully grasped."[93] In many ways, Francis' life could be depicted as a series of symbolic transactions of this sort.

Pruyser is, in part, responsible for a further unfolding of the transitional object concept that Winnicott first latched onto in order to explore and express the mysterious inner workings of human imaginations. Pruyser argues that "transitional objects are illusionistic objects and the transitional sphere is typified by illusionistic thought and illusionistic transactions."[94] Studzinski, who views transitional objects as the forerunners of transitional phenomena throughout life, finds that these phenomena support an ongoing adaptation to the external world for the adult.[95] Similar to Pruyser's illusionistic transactions, Studzinski speaks of a creative process whereby "surplus meaning" is applied to some aspect of physical reality.[96] Pruyser hints at some of the other features of illusion processing when he puts various functions of the transitional object on view. It pulls together the inner world and the outer world, a sense of maternal presence, and a view of self in relation to the physical world. The transitional object, as a first possession, also involves the formation of boundaries, and, as a drive object, it withstands the crushing and collapsing of some of these same boundaries when it is the subject of love and hate attacks. The transitional object can be missed or longed for, and it accepts the child's projections upon itself.[97] Additionally, Pruyser suggests that the ambivalence with which a transitional object is approached, allows for the possibility of disbelief, upon which possibility belief depends.[98] By tracing the implications of Winnicott's theory into adult life, Pruyser advances not only the explanatory potential of ORT for the workings of mature imaginations; he also expands the way in which transitional objects can be understood to participate in illusion processing for religious purposes when he describes a transitional phenomenon as a transformational object and later as a transcendent object.

Jones comments that, "In religious experience what is transformed is both our way of knowing and what it is we know."[99] His recognition of the central role of transformation in religion confirms Pruyser's insights and related work by Bollas. Pruyser observes that there is a change in both the subject and the way an object is perceived that causes a transformation. He explains that an object is assimilated such that it "is modified to fit [the] organism's capacity for and manner of absorption," and through accommodation, "the organism, having some degree of functional plasticity, fits itself in some way to its object and thus undergoes some change."[100] This enables Pruyser to say that, "the object becomes a function of the subject," and, alternately, "the subject becomes a function of the object."[101] He uses a comparison of art and religion to further depict the kind of change that illusion processing can produce. He writes, "Just as art is not a representation of reality, but a thoroughgoing transformation of stimuli from inner and outer worlds into a unique illusionistic novelty, so religion transforms human experience into an imaginative, illusionistic conception that is *sui generis*."[102] The most likely source for the transformation is revealed by Pruyser's comment that, "Psychological experience starts with fragments that are gradually built into wholes."[103] Combining images in this manner is a kind of synthesis occurring in the transitional sphere. "Synthesis does not merely combine—it transforms the elements brought to it."[104] A related term he uses to refer to image-combination is evocation, which "presumes a view of self and world, and a kind of perception" in which "subject and object are not radically different but overlap and interpenetrate as if they shared essential qualities."[105]

Bollas takes the idea of the transformative properties of illusion processing to a more technical level. He makes the assertion that the transformational object precedes the transitional object since the maternal figure is first encountered as a source of transformation through her ministrations.[106] This takes place because the infant's early experience of the maternal figure is less "as a discrete object with particular qualities than as a process linked to the infant's being and the alteration of his being."[107] Bollas adds, "It is undeniable, I think, that as the infant's 'other' self, the mother transforms the baby's internal and external environment."[108] As the infant matures there is a shift from an actual process in which the mother eases the environment for the infant to one in which the object is symbolic of the process. This shift is from transformational object experiencing to transitional object experiencing.[109] Bollas theorizes that, "A transformational object is experientially identified by the infant with processes that alter self experience. It is an identification that emerges from symbiotic relating, where the first object is 'known' not so much by putting it into an object representation, but as a recurrent experience of being—a more existential as opposed to representational knowing."[110] He points out that there is an adult search for a similar transformation in which the "object is sought for its function as a signifier of transformation. Thus, in adult life, the quest is not to possess the object, rather the object is pursued in order to surrender to it as a medium that alters the self, where the subject-as-supplicant now feels himself to be the recipient of enviro-somatic caring, identified with metamorphosis of the self."[111] The similarity between this pursuit and religious conversion must be stressed.

Both Pruyser and, in turn, Bollas indicate that object relating can occur through an encounter with experiences that cause transformation in the way an object is perceived and in the perceiver. Change at this level brings the person having the experience to a new experiential plateau reminiscent of Green's paradigm shift. Pruyser might regard it more as contact with transcendence or as a transcendent moment, which could require one to "go beyond" a current state of being.[112] The illusion processing that brings about this change yields a transcendent object, the first of which is the infant's transitional object.[113] Pruyser determines that transcendent objects "have a touch of the sacred and tend to be charged with symbolic surplus values."[114] If he is correct, the formation and reaction to such an object would require a strong imaginative capacity to incorporate symbolic perception into one's way of life, which is corroborated by his notion that, "Dealing with transcendent objects is highly ritualized, and behavioral responses to these objects require delicacy and finesse."[115] At times, Bollas' expression of a transformational object seems to resemble a transcendent object. He claims that in adult life there is a search for an object that yields a profound change in the self.[116] He writes, "to seek the transformational object is to recollect an early object experience, to remember not cognitively but existentially—through intense affective experience—a relationship which was identified with cumulative transformational experiences of the self."[117] He also calls the transcendent type of encounter "the experience of an object that transforms the subject's internal and external world."[118] Viewing object representations as transitional, transformational, and transcendent objects is one way to present Pruyser's theory of illusion processing. Another, even more technical approach involves the notion of internalization.

Object Relations Theory is based around the idea of imaginatively encountering an experience, taking it in, and making it one's own as a possession. Pruyser is among other theorists who label this, in its most basic manifestation, as internalization. A brief discussion of the three forms of internalization, incorporation, introjection, and identification, reveals more about the inner activity of illusion processing. Pruyser describes incorporation as the earliest or most rudimentary form of internalization. It is suggestive of the notion of taking within one's body.[119] Certainly, it is not difficult to see that this is the infant's first, primary means of exploring the larger world when any object brought to him or her is moved quickly, if also uncoordinatedly, to the mouth for inspection and acceptance or rejection. Pruyser gives a common outcome of this kind of internalization that also relates to an altered experience of self. He notes that moments of displeasure cause the initiation of a "bad part object," which is incorporated to form "a bad part self."[120] A more positive religious concept that points to the internalization of experience is the Eucharist. With a slight twist, Bollas offers an analogous example of incorporation. He claims that during an aesthetic moment there is a "surprise, complemented by an experience of fusion with the object... of feeling held by the object's spirit."[121] Meissner simultaneously points out the difference between an introject and incorporation, and the reason why incorporation as a psychological activity may not have any imaginative value for others. He exclaims that, "With incorporation an object loses any status as an external object, with introjection there is a simultaneous preservation of an object's external status while a representational internal object is formed."[122] It is quickly apparent that introjection reflects a more accurate picture of meaningful imaginative activity.

Pruyser presents introjection as an advanced form of internalization over incorporation.[123] He notes that introjections form during the period of an infant's language development and, therefore, often involve hearing an inner voice.[124] Eigen insists that introjection, and its related activity of projection, support the infant's early myth that nobody has existence apart from him or herself. When introjection and projection fail to sustain the myth object usage commences.[125]

The idea behind introjection and projection is that fantasy attributes can be assigned, at first indiscriminately, to object representations of self and other since such a distinction is not immediately firm. Once otherness is confirmed in the experience of the infant, traits of the *other* are taken, through introjection, for the object-image of the self, or, through projection, traits of self-experience are split off and designated for the object-image representing otherness. Meissner provides one of the most clear-cut descriptions of this process. He explains that, "introjection involves a reciprocal attribution of parts of object representations to the self-representation," and "projection involves an attribution of parts of the self-representation to an object representation."[126] He is able to compare introjection/projection with a transitional object since both represent a "combination of derivatives from the inner and outer worlds which are assimilated to the inner world."[127] Meissner reveals how the transitional object is able to support significant personal meaning when he observes that projection applies subjectively derived qualities to an object.[128] On the other hand, introjection of attributes from a transitional object can cause it to be completely internalized and thus cease to function as a transitional object even though it exists in the inner world as an object representation that can still be related to transitionally as needed.[129] While much attention is paid to the projection of negative impulses, Meissner finds that positive impulses can also be projected.[130] One might imagine the effect of projecting Christ-like qualities onto the object-representation of another person as Francis conceivably did.

Meissner declares that identification and introjection provide "the basic roots by which object relations are internalized."[131] Of these, Pruyser concedes that identification is the most advanced form.[132] Perhaps it might be better to call identification the most complete form, since, as Pruyser puts it, "traces of incorporation and introjection may well cooperate in the making of these later relationships."[133] This kind of object relationship moves beyond *as-if* perception and into the realm of perceiving, thinking, and acting—*as*. Pruyser lists Ignatius of Loyola's *Spiritual Exercises* and Thomas a Kempis' *Imitation of Christ* as "classical pedagogies" for internalization by identification.[134] Whether it is identification or introjection, the formation of religious images through some form of internalization plays a part in the way Francis expected himself and his followers to relate to and view others.

This survey of some of Paul Pruyser's views of and contributions to an Object Relations Theory perspective on imagination adds to the validation of the theory's use to probe adult religious imaginative activity. Pruyser shows that there is a broad range to what and how one can experience as real. Much attention has been paid to expressing the importance of connecting personal experiences of reality with a communal perspective, all the while affirming the unique and original creativity that is possible in the cultural realm. Many of the themes common to other theories of imagination were touched upon, including the building of meaningful experience from disordered experience, the formation of relationships, transformation and transcendence, trust, and the capacity to be playful in order to interact with a world bountiful in experiences.

John McDargh

John McDargh concentrates on the human ability to have faith in something. He aligns this development with the ongoing formation of a sense of self emerging out of an inborn seeking for what can be accepted as real. His contribution to an Object Relations Theory perspective on imagination will be touched upon in terms of a relationship to reality. In this fashion, the following topics will reveal not just the emergence of a life of faith, but, looking more broadly, of a life formed out of an imaginative, spiritual pursuit of reality. The topics include the individual's inclination toward what is real, the development of a sense of self in connection with reality, and the search for God, which is an appropriate segue into Ana-Maria Rizzuto's views.

McDargh recognizes a powerful drive in human beings that cannot be easily relegated to explanation by an instinctual drive theory. He insists that, "It is a significant discovery... that there is a human grasping to know, i.e., to be in a relationship to the real which is as fundamental as the need for breath or bread."[135] He goes on to say, "psychoanalysis has attempted to understand how the growing human person is gifted with that 'primordial grasp of the real' which makes the adult sense of reality an achievement most persons are fortunate enough to take for granted."[136] McDargh also mentions a "conatus" or "intention towards Reality Itself."[137] However, other than being birthed into the world that is measured by sense data and often mistakenly only associated with the full and final extant of reality, the child does not possess an immediate access to reality, as suggested by a "'primordial grasp,'" or "conatus." The child is introduced to reality by a careful nurturing of his or her capacity to form and link images. But McDargh understands that the child does not begin life with a complete perception of reality in any sense. This is evident by his comment that infants first relate to part objects. He proposes that, "It is precisely as these 'part objects' become identified and consolidated in the child's experience that a relationship with the full reality of a whole object (person) begins to become possible."[138] What is particularly noteworthy in this idea is that reality is initially encountered in conjunction with the formation of an object representation of otherness in the form of a person. This person, who is the initial experience of reality, in turn, is the one who helps the infant to formulate the images that continue to expand the depth and breadth of his or her perception of reality.

The further expansion of reality does not go on unsupported after its initial discovery. McDargh sees a "fundamental faith" at work sustaining "the will to make that inquiry and hence capacity for a creative and imaginative engagement with 'reality.'"[139] Rather than looking at a drive to seek reality, such a concept of faith hints at the notion of instead being drawn out into a fuller experience of reality while simultaneously being coaxed and assured, through faith, that relational participation in a grander, more glorious world is a necessary and well-taken chance. Such a faith, as a component of the spiritual life, might help the individual to ignore the specter of ir-reality, a nihilistic tendency, emerging from the autistic sphere that embraces hopelessness in the form of a nagging doubt that reality as the individual perceives it, is a sham, a hallucination utterly disconnected from any substance or ideal that could render it real and, at last, meaningful. This ghost of the unreal is, conceivably, why ORT theorists, such as McDargh, affirm the need "to take for granted" so many operations of the imagination.[140] When this essential delusion is achieved, it is reinforced by, but also carries the benefit of, "the capacity for feeling real, creative, and spontaneous," as a result of "the careful modulation of the process by which the child is brought to realize the existence of an external world."[141] McDargh also points out that a "sense of being real" and a "sense of being in relationship to a real and meaningful world" are essential elements in the initiation of the recognition of selfhood, which is the ensuing topic.

It is reasonably determined that it would be impossible for a person to experience anything as real beyond his or her microcosmic world if there was no clearly defined notion of being an individual self from which to perceive. There is a mutual relationship between the awareness of otherness and the awareness of individuality, but McDargh finds that, in human development, this relationship is never firmly fixed. He explains that a child undergoes separation and individuation from the mother in the first three years, but the ongoing formation and maintenance of a sense of self comes and goes, creating a tension between a perception of radical individuality and then of unity with a greater whole.[142] The in and out shift of awareness allows some people to discern what is experienced in profound spiritual events of union and, at the same time, fashion a spiritual way of life that embraces the hope and meaning of union with something transcendent, something more. McDargh credits the transitional object with regulating these moments of "undifferentiated merger" and the more typical times of distinct individuality as a continuous activity throughout life.[143] It might even be said that these incursions of unified awareness are amongst the "dangerous opportunities and opportune dangers," that he insists are necessary to advance the sense of self.[144]

The sense of individual selfhood is described by McDargh as a psychological dynamic that relies on imaginative activity to foster internal and external relationships. He determines that the self emerges through "the ceaseless interaction of the inner world of the individual and an ever expanding arena of interpersonal interactions."[145] Similarly, McDargh speaks of an affective relationship which an individual carries on throughout life with the complex of memories, images, and mental representations which arise from the earliest experiences of human relationships.[146] He explains that in ORT "the person is not constituted by the isolated play of impersonal instinctual energies, but by the inter-play of human persons—both as those relationships actually occur in the world and as they are carried on in conscious and unconscious fantasy or, we might say, as they are internalized."[147] For these relationships to pay off in an imaginative perception of reality that is able to have an impact on the collective reality an element of central importance to faith and the productive workings of the imagination must take root as part of a sense of self. This element is trust.

McDargh remarks that trust is based, in the first place, on availability of the parent, which necessarily shifts from absolute to partial as the child matures.[148] He adds that it is the parent's availability for "loving self-donation and their capacity to tolerate ambivalence" which enables the child to develop the trust that is at the center of faith.[149] At the same time the infant is developing his or her own toleration of ambivalence as the splitting off and projection of negative qualities diminishes, and the parental caregivers begin to exist as whole objects in the infant's world.[150] Seeing the world, including oneself, in terms of ambivalence, of good and bad, allows for the possibility of trust connected with idealization. Jones shows that idealization is part of the movement into transitional experiencing, which, he states, requires trust.[151] He notes that an idealized object, a person, place, or thing, is able to evoke trust.[152] He goes on to assert that, "A trusting relationship with an idealized other seems to be an important facilitator of surrendering one's hold on objectifying reason. Such loosening of the constraints of normal, rational existence is necessary for entering into the transitional realm or reconnecting with the primary process—those psychological movements through which transformation takes place."[153] This "loosening of constraints" can be associated with three offshoots of trust, the ability: to be alone, to be dependent, and to play, which then foster an imaginative relationship with created reality.

Trust, in the form of faith, is integral to the capacity to be alone. McDargh relates this to Winnicott's concept of object constancy, and also to "a process of internalization… whereby the child is able to maintain the sense of well-being and relatedness even in the absence of the parent."[154] The value of this capacity for the workings of imaginations has been firmly established by other theorists, but McDargh extols the importance of what seems to be an opposing feature of trust, the ability to be dependent. This is an important point for the study of religious imaginative activity since many religious characters express a sense of reliance on divine providence and mercy. Briefly, McDargh connects the ability to be dependent with the admission of an "ultimate need, one that exceeds the resources of any finite source of love and strength."[155] This raises the idea that one is drawn by a feeling of need, possibly spurred on by a limit situation, which cannot finally be satisfied or soothed by a meaningful but limited maternal object representation. On the other hand, it is quite reasonable to maintain that an image of a maternal figure is a component of a more profound and unfaltering "source of love and strength," worthy of the more significant dependency that McDargh points to. He affirms that mature dependency is sustained by object representations emerging from past relationships.[156] The ramifications of these points for the human search for God are somewhat apparent, but McDargh also brings up a concern about the failure of trust that is an obstacle to such a quest and to the foundation of selfhood from which that pursuit begins. He observes that, "Without a fundamental sense of trust in the reliability and the availability of love and care, without the processes of faith that renew and sustain that sense, one can be left with an intolerable sense of weakness and vulnerability in which the self is constantly at risk."[157] The implication can be drawn that a strong sense of self depends on a deep trust in a sustaining relationship with a God-like internal object. Before looking more fully into the imaginative quest for God there is still the topic of play to be visited once more.

McDargh recalls that "the good-enough mother" guarantees and preserves the "background of safety which makes possible play."[158] Play, from which a recognition of self and otherness is imaginatively worked out throughout life, is seen to rely on the same early source of trust that upholds the ability to be alone and also dependent. McDargh determines that parental presence enables the transitional object phenomena to occur as a space for play, which involves "manipulating the external world for the satisfaction of an inner vision. More generally it means relaxing one's need to respond and react and instead acting out of a spontaneous, creative core of self."[159] The trust that yields the various capacities just discussed clearly supports an imaginative engagement with all that can be experienced as real in the created world as well as the search for a spiritual relationship with the creator of that world.

Through ORT, "we are finally enabled to understand why it is so inescapably human to seek for the face of the divine, the face that makes faith possible," proposes McDargh.[160] His description of this search for God is, at base, a continuation of the imaginative effort to grasp reality. It is part of an internal dynamic, and it is a relationship that can be characterized as vital to one's sense of self and one's ability to participate more deeply in the reality that is the created world. McDargh calls faith, which correlates with the search for God, an "organization of psychic energies."[161] On a similar note he says there is a conscious and unconscious configuration "of affect, imagery and memory formed around the complex symbol 'God.'"[162] This kind of activity reflects the nature of the internal dynamic that binds human beings up in a relationship with God. McDargh concludes that, "we carry on a lively relationship with our own very private, very personal images of God."[163] Yet, there is still more that can be discovered about the search for divine reality when considering how and why people relate to their God images.

With ORT it is possible to see the relationship between God representations, self representations, and the feelings that there-in arise.[164] McDargh points out the psychological interest in "the affects and feelings that are given shape and direction in the ongoing process of constructing, cathecting and decathecting object representations of a reality regarded as transcendent."[165] The process, that he mentions, gives some insight into the nature of the God-images that a person might be dealing with. He reveals that a specific image may wax and wane in its influence over an individuals' immediate perception of God. In fact, as McDargh points out, people seldom attend to the totality that is God. He explains that typically interest is focused on penultimate centers of meaning and value rather than engaging directly and intentionally in a relationship with God in God's ultimacy.[166] The meaning or value may shift from experiences of God's concern to experiences of wrath, or judgment, or forgiveness. In each case, the guiding image of God, formed out of various sub-images, will participate in the individual's assessment of the present situation.

The focal image of God at any point in time also plays a predominant role in reflexive meaning, the meaning one discovers of oneself. This is one way that God enters into human subjectivity. McDargh explains that individuals always form object representations of significant others, including God, in conjunction with self-representations.[167] In other words, self-perception is never free from the personal judgments issued by the object representations of other people or entities, but not directly by those figures themselves. It is how the individual perceives him or herself being perceived that affects the sense of self. Obviously, the way one considers oneself to appear in the divine gaze will have a weighty authority over self-perception. McDargh also indicates two reasons why God images play such a significant part in one's relationship to reality. In the first place, he conveys that, "The need of every emerging human self is to be seen and valued as one is."[168] He adds that God tends to eventually replace the parents in this regard.[169] In the second place, he finds that object representations evolve toward the transcendent in order to sustain people in the face of human finitude and to satisfy their orientation "toward a deeper and richer sense of the real."[170] Seeking for what is real in one's experience of the world and of oneself is, then, inextricably linked with an imaginative search for a relationship with God.

Ana-Maria Rizzuto

Ana-Maria Rizzuto observes that "men cannot be men without illusions."[171] She goes on to claim that, "The type of illusion we select—science, religion, or something else—reveals our personal history and the transitional space each of us has created between his objects and himself to find 'a resting place' to live in."[172] Rizzuto gives careful attention to the natural offshoot of Object Relations Theory from its origins in Freudian thought.[173] An area where this divergence is particularly clear, and of interest to the present study, is the formation of God-images. A brief mention of the distinction between her view and Freud's theory will lead into a discussion of God-image formation as a process, as a function of the transitional object, as a factor in human transformation, and as a new way of relating. Rizzuto's work will further display the nature of God-images by specifying how these images are variously used in life.

While maintaining a close theoretical tie to the Freudian origins of psychoanalysis, Rizzuto spends a fair amount of time probing Freud's struggle with religion. In fact, she has written a separate work entitled *Why did Freud Reject God,* in which she examines the evidence that Freud may have been unable to form a suitable God-image.[174] In her more general work on images of God, *The Birth of the Living God,* she notes that Freud places full emphasis on the father-son relationship amidst the oedipal conflict as the source of the God-image.[175] In addition to the downplayed maternal influence on a child's psychic development, Rizzuto challenges various other features of Freud's understanding. First, she points to research which indicates that God-images originate in both the pre-oedipal and oedipal periods of a child's development. She also finds that there is little data to corroborate his notion of a memory trace of a primeval father that awakens an infant's orientation to a potent male figure.[176] In her studies, no patient formed a God-image from only one source as found in Freud's exalted father figure.[177] Additionally, Rizzuto counters Freud's conviction that people believe in God as an idea rather than as a result of object representation.[178] Image formation in terms of object representation is a more fitting expression of the dynamic process that Rizzuto reveals to underlie the human effort to relate to God.

While Rizzuto finds a majority of psychoanalytic literature treating object representations as "discrete entities," she describes them as more intricate processes.[179] She insists that, "It is the many complex sexual and nonsexual, as well as representational, ideational components, present in the child which contribute to the genuine creation of an imaginary being."[180] Elsewhere she proposes that object representations "originate in creative processes involving memory, and the entirety of psychic life."[181] She clarifies the involvement of memory which, it should be recalled, played a prominent role in some early theories of imagination. Rizzuto explains that the process forms a representation at the moment of relating, after which the imaginative activity becomes a memorial process.[182] In any instance, the process is not completely a private issue. She speaks of communal participation, first as the infant-parent community, and then the wider community, which substantiates the superior nature of a being greater even than the parents.[183] In either version of community there must be room for the emerging individual to play. In her description of a "space to play" there is a kind of freedom with one's objects, to relate to them as one wishes, or even spontaneously.[184] Developmentally one of the most important objects to be engaged with in the freedom of play is the transitional object. Rizzuto contends that, "God, psychologically speaking, is an illusory transitional object."[185] Like other transitional objects, the God object includes at least a half composition from the other primary objects in life, especially the parents.[186] However, unlike the other transitional objects, the God representation does not diffuse into cultural phenomena in the sense that Pruyser presents.[187]

Beyond describing the formation of a God-image as a process in general and as a transitional object, it can also be scrutinized in connection with a specific process of transformation of self and also as a new way of relating within an old relationship. Rizzuto precedes her discussion of God-images by associating ORT with an understanding of the development of self.[188] An early influence on the sense of the self is the maternal caregiver's capacity to hold the child deeply in her gaze so the child can see him or herself through the expressions of the caregiver. Rizzuto contends that two important events occur through this crucial activity. The child begins the life-long endeavor to hold a meaningful self understanding. At the same time, the child derives that understanding from the way he or she views the parent's conception of him or herself.[189] From a religious standpoint, the fundamental importance of this latter input into a sense of self is that through the subtle message of a glance children come to discern themselves as God-given, or not, in the eyes of another.[190] When the more favorable early relationship to God is offered, and possibly also when the less favorable association is accepted, the child is launched into life with a God-image that stands at the ready for future use. Rizzuto notes that, amongst other things, this representation remains available "for the continuous process of psychic integration."[191] She gives two examples where the image of God undergoes a transformation in conjunction with a transformation in the individual. She determines that, "The God representation changes along with us and our primary objects in the lifelong metamorphosis of becoming ourselves in a context of other relevant beings."[192] A more acute change takes place through conversion.

She declares, "I understand conversion to be the ego-syntonic release from repression in a given individual of an earlier (or even present) parental representation linked to a God representation."[193] In either case, the ongoing development of self coincides with a change in the way God is imagined or perceived by a person in a process that reflects what Bollas would eventually associate with transformational objects.

Rizzuto also finds that images of God participate in a transformation that occurs when new relating takes place in an old relationship. She remarks that there is a second birth of God when the "God of the child-hero encounters the 'God of Religion.'"[194] This run-in does not replace a personal image with an official image; instead it causes them to interact. Rizzuto determines that the influence of official religion on God-image formation is only felt after the God-image has formed. The official influence is added, but a new image is not put in the original image's place.[195] Much of this type of relating occurs as the individual matures. She explains that there is significant change at the time of puberty, with the onset of the capacity for "abstract logicomathematical conceptualization. For the first time the child is able to grasp a concept of God beyond the limits of his God representation."[196] While this expanding perception is initially used for personal philosophical purposes, Rizzuto observes that the new way of relating to one's God-image never breaks away from the earliest relations.[197] She notes that "the mature person reencounters the God of his childhood in later years at every corner of life."[198] This is similar, she says, to a mature relationship with one's parents.[199] Another example is from the mystics who, she claims, have a libidinal relation with God which is not so much seeking parent love as seeking "mature, object-related love."[200] Amidst a detailed portrayal of the formation of God-images, Rizzuto also dedicates some discussion to the imaginative use of God-images for religious/humanistic purposes.

Being human and being religiously oriented come together at many points for Rizzuto. She conjectures that in one sense, religion is not an illusion. "It is an integral part of being human, truly human in our capacity to create nonvisible but meaningful realities capable of containing our potential for imaginative expansion beyond the boundaries of the senses."[201] She adds that, without this capacity, "the entire domain of culture becomes a flat, irrelevant world of sensory appearance."[202] She equates one of these non-visible realities to an image of God as distinct from a mere concept of God. The latter is the God of the theologians and is primarily a product of secondary process thinking which causes her to remark: "But this God leaves us cold."[203] On the other hand, Rizzuto finds that the image of God, for some, coalesces into an emotionally graspable representation of God.[204] This representation retains its usefulness throughout life since God, as a transitional object, "is always potentially available" and can serve as the backboard of the vicissitudes of life.[205] At the same time, such availability does not reflect a constant state of God-image awareness in most people. Rizzuto notes that, more often, the God representation is picked up and utilized at significant or transformative moments in life only to be set down again until the next event.[206] Rizzuto suggests that one exception to this rule is death, as she indicates that the image of God binds one to the things that make it possible to proceed without absolute terror to the grave.[207] Tales of Francis' death imply the existence of a very powerful and meaningful God-image for the saint.

Considering Rizzuto's connection between image and memory more fully, it is possible to see how an object representation of God can be used in her memorial process. She mentions that any encounter with an aspect of reality is object related, and object representation is a synthesis of "compounded memories."[208] While the image of God plays a meaning-giving role in these encounters, it surely also has a significant part in the development and maintenance of one's psychological apparatus. Rizzuto argues that each person has a storehouse of available memories of objects which can be brought together in various combinations to work through psychic challenges.[209] She contends that these object memories, which are "retrieved as a representation" and often will include aspects of the God-image, come together to sustain self understanding and self expectation.[210] The representations then participate in a process of moving from "present object and self representations to past object and self representations," which may be a means of linking current experience with the past in an imaginary way.[211] At times the most powerful of these representations elicit a visceral memory, a felt sensation, or a physiological response.[212] Is it possible that Francis' attention to the humanity and suffering of Jesus entailed this factor in any way?

******

Winnicott's development of the Object Relations Theory, along with the contributions of Paul Pruyser, John McDargh, and Ana-Maria Rizzuto in this chapter, reveals a coherent concept of imagination that is coincident with their views on human development. Many of the notions and themes that hold an ORT perspective on imagination together can now be associated with passages and images found in the writings of Francis of Assisi in order to reveal the imaginative way he perceives, shapes, and shares his world.

Notes

1. Paul W. Pruyser, *The Play of the Imagination*, ix.

2. Note that Pruyser uses the term *illusionistic sphere* to refer to Winnicott's transitional space as it persists in a mature individual. Illusion processing is nearly synonymous with imaginative activity and has a close connection with the relating of object representations mentioned previously. The terms will be used more or less interchangeably with transitional sphere/space, and imaginative activity/creativity, respectively.

3. Paul W. Pruyser, "Forms and Functions of the Imagination in Religion," *Bulletin of the Menninger Clinic* 49, no. 4 (1985): 354.

4. Ibid.

5. James W. Jones, *Terror and Transformation: The Ambiguity of Religion in Psychoanalytic Perspective* (New York: Taylor and Francis, 2002), 53. See also Rudolph Otto, *The Idea of the Holy: An Inquiry into the Non-rational Factor in the Idea of the Divine and its Relation to the Rational*, trans. John W. Harvey (London: Oxford University Press, 1958).

6. Christopher Bollas, *The Shadow of the Object: Psychoanalysis of the Unthought Known* (New York: Columbia University Press, 1987), 10.

7. Pruyser, "Forms and Functions of the Imagination in Religion," 354.

8. Pruyser, *The Play of the Imagination*, 155.

9. Ibid., 156.

10. Ibid.

11. Ibid., 6.

12. Ibid.

13. Paul Pruyser, *Between Belief and Unbelief* (New York: Harper and Row, 1974), 222.

14. Ibid., 223.

15. Pruyser, *The Play of the Imagination*, 1.

16. Studzinski, *Tutoring the Religious Imagination*, 27. Keep in mind that the mother-infant world begins as a single entity from the infant's nascent perception.

17. Pruyser, "Forms and Functions of the Imagination in Religion," 360.

18. Pruyser, *The Play of the Imagination*, 11.

19. Studzinski, 29.

20. Ibid., 63.

21. Pruyser, "Forms and Functions of the Imagination in Religion," 360. See Table 1. Note also that Pruyser distinguishes between symbols and signs, giving the former prominence in imaginative activity.

22. Pruyser, *The Play of the Imagination*, 67.

23. Ibid.

24. Ibid., 4.

25. Pruyser, *Between Belief and Unbelief*, 112.

26. Pruyser, *The Play of the Imagination*, 6.

27. Studzinski, 30.

28. A pre-existing image would be an image that exists prior to a specific act of imagining. This is not a claim for Jung's archetypal image, since, in some cases, the image is externally supplied, often by the mother during infancy.

29. Ibid., 114.

30. Pruyser, "Forms and Functions of the Imagination in Religion," 365,

31. Pruyser, *Between Belief and Unbelief*, 241.

32. Pruyser, *The Play of the Imagination*, ix.

33. Ibid., 152.

34. Ibid., 4.

35. Pruyser, "Forms and Functions of the Imagination in Religion," 361.

36. Pruyser, *The Play of the Imagination*, 165.

37. Ibid. 68. See also 165.

38. Pruyser, *Between Belief and Unbelief*, 241.

39. Jones, 46.

40. Studzinski, 25.

41. Ibid., 30.

42. Pruyser, *Between Belief and Unbelief*, 203.

43. Pruyser, "Forms and Functions of the Imagination in Religion," 353.

44. Ibid., 359.

45. Jones, 101.

46. Studzinski, 30.

47. Ibid., 31. He also points out that prayer is a means to enter the potential space. See 36-37.

48. Bollas, 29. See also: Murray Krieger, *Theory of Criticism: A Tradition and its System* (Baltimore: John Hopkins University Press, 1976).

49. Ibid., 32. Krieger points out (p. 13) that the aesthetic experience could not happen without the stimulating object, but it is caused primarily by the one stimulated. In other words, objectivity and subjectivity both participate.

50. Pruyser, "Forms and Functions of the Imagination in Religion," 366. Religious implications for Marian devotion and spirituality directed toward God-as-parent are suggested in this comment.

51. Pruyser, *The Play of the Imagination*, 2.

52. Ibid., 77.

53. Ibid., 159.

54. Ibid., 9.

55. Ibid., 70.

56. Pruyser, "Forms and Functions of the Imagination in Religion," 360.

57. Ibid., 362.

58. Pruyser, *Between Belief and Unbelief*, 113.

59. W.W. Meissner, *The Paranoid Process* (New York: Jason Aronson, 1978), 115. Note that he is describing perception as a sense data experience and not in the sense of *perceiving-as* which can be understood as a form of judgment itself.

60. Ibid.

61. Pruyser, *The Play of the Imagination*, 71.

62. Ibid., 172.

63. Ibid.

64. Ibid.

65. Pruyser, "Forms and Functions of the Imagination in Religion," 367.

66. Pruyser, *The Play of the Imagination*, 166.

67. Pruyser, "Forms and Functions of the Imagination in Religion," 360.

68. Pruyser, *The Play of the Imagination*, 161.

69. Ibid., 60.

70. Ibid., 174.

71. Pruyser, *Between Belief and Unbelief*, 203.

72. Pruyser, "Forms and Functions of the Imagination in Religion," 367.

73. Ibid., 360. "Once tutored" is not meant to suggest that the imagination does not continue to undergo formation throughout life, but it seems that there is a point at which an imagination can be said to have reached a level of autonomy from the childhood

sources of its imagination without losing a connectedness with these sources. The point must also be made that Pruyser is not offering a strict notion of collective imagination in which there is no significant deviation among images and imaginative activity between people. His notion is more of an imaginative field from which people select some aspects of their imagery and pay into it in turn with their own imaginative contributions.

74. Pruyser, *The Play of the Imagination*, 56.

75. Ibid., 15.

76. Ibid., 19.

77. Ibid.

78. Ibid., 16, 19.

79. Ibid., 19.

80. Ibid., 50.

81. Pruyser, *Between Belief and Unbelief,* 109, 199.

82. Ibid., 201.

83. Jones, 5.

84. Ibid., 55.

85. Ibid., 60-61.

86. Pruyser, *The Play of the Imagination*, 31.

87. Ibid., 44.

88. Pruyser, "Forms and Functions of the Imagination in Religion," 358.

89. Pruyser, *Between Belief and Unbelief,* 219.

90. Pruyser, *The Play of the Imagination*, 55.

91. Pruyser, "Forms and Functions of the Imagination in Religion," 367, 361.

92. Ibid., 362.

93. Pruyser, *The Play of the Imagination*, 154.

94. Ibid., 58.

95. Studzinski, 29.

96. Ibid.

97. Pruyser, *The Play of the Imagination*, 59-60.

98. Pruyser, "Forms and Functions of the Imagination in Religion," 362.

99. Jones, 102.

100. Pruyser, *The Play of the Imagination*, 38.

101. Ibid.

102. Ibid., 165.

103. Ibid., 50.

104. Pruyser, *Between Belief and Unbelief,* 240.

105. Pruyser, *The Play of the Imagination*, 6.

106. Bollas, 15.

107. Ibid., 4.

108. Ibid., 13.

109. Ibid., 15.

110. Ibid., 14.

111. Ibid.

112. Pruyser, *The Play of the Imagination*, 67.

113. Ibid.

114. Ibid.

115. Ibid.

116. Bollas, 15. Note that Bollas does not use the term transcendent, but his description of transformational objects includes many similarities, in nature, to Pruyser's transcen-

dent object. The two concepts do not conflict. They are different approaches to expressing the nature of change in an individual's imaginative perception of the world.

117. Ibid., 17.
118. Ibid., 28.
119. Pruyser, *The Play of the Imagination*, 52-53.
120. Ibid., 49.
121. Bollas, 31.
122. Meissner, *The Paranoid Process*, 537.
123. Pruyser, *The Play of the Imagination*, 52-53.
124. Ibid.
125. Eigen, 415.
126. Meissner, *The Paranoid Process*, 100.
127. Ibid., 100.
128. Ibid., 537-538.
129. Ibid., 538.
130. Ibid., 568.
131. Ibid., 536.
132. Pruyser, *The Play of the Imagination*, 54.
133. Ibid.
134. Ibid., 174.
135. John McDargh, *Psychoanalytic Object Relations Theory and the Study of Religion: On Faith and the Imaging of God* (Lanham, MD: University Press of America, 1983), 49.
136. Ibid.
137. Ibid., 50.
138. Ibid., 18.
139. Ibid., 79.
140. Ibid., 49.
141. Ibid., 219.
142. Ibid., 73. For a more detailed discussion of separation and individuation see: Margaret S. Mahler, Fred Pine, and Anni Bergman. *The Psychological Birth of the Human Infant: Symbiosis and Individuation* (--: Basic Books, 1975).
143. Ibid., 226.
144. Ibid., 88.
145. Ibid., 88.
146. Ibid., 18.
147. Ibid., 17.
148. Ibid., 216.
149. Ibid.
150. Ibid., 94-95.
151. Jones, 103.
152. Ibid.
153. Ibid., 104.
154. McDargh, 81-82, 86.
155. Ibid., 87.
156. Ibid., 84.
157. Ibid., 86.
158. Ibid., 229.
159. Ibid., 226.
160. Ibid., xvi.

161. Ibid., 88.

162. Ibid., 124.

163. Ibid., 5.

164. Ibid., 144.

165. Ibid., 143.

166. Ibid., 74.

167. Ibid., 121, 129.

168. Ibid., 230.

169. Ibid.

170. Ibid., 113.

171. Ana-Maria Rizzuto, The *Birth of the Living God: A Psychoanalytic Study* (Chicago: University of Chicago Press, 1979), 209. One supposes that she intends a gender neutral interpretation of "men."

172. Ibid.

173. For a detailed outline and analysis of Freud's seminal contribution to Object Relations Theory see Chapters Two and Three of *The Birth of the Living God*.

174. Ana-Maria Rizzuto, *Why Did Freud Reject God?: A Psychodynamic Interpretation* (New Haven: Yale University Press, 1998).

175. Rizzuto, *The Birth of the Living God*, 16.

176. Ibid., 25-27.

177. Ibid., 44.

178. Ibid., 28.

179. Ibid., 74-75.

180. Ibid., 46.

181. Ibid., 44.

182. Ibid., 75.

183. Ibid., 50. This point of Rizzuto's contradicts Smith's assertion that she in particular neglects the .social and cultural dimension of the formation of a God representation. See Smith, 261.

184. Ibid., 81-82.

185. Ibid., 177.

186. Ibid., 179.

187. Ibid., 178.

188. For example: Ibid., 43.

189. Ibid., 186.

190. Ibid., 183.

191. Ibid., 180.

192. Ibid., 52.

193. Ibid., 51.

194. Ibid., 8.

195. Ibid., 10.

196. Ibid., 200.

197. Ibid.

198. Ibid., 7.

199. Ibid., 46.

200. Ibid., 47.

201. Ibid., 47.

202. Ibid.

203. Ibid., 48.

204. Ibid.

205. Ibid., 179.
206. Ibid., 203.
207. Ibid., 179.
208. Ibid., 76, 77.
209. Ibid., 55.
210. Ibid., 56, 55.
211. Ibid., 57.
212. Ibid., 57.

CHAPTER SIX
EXPERIENCE AND RELATIONSHIP:
THE IMAGINATIVE ACTIVITY OF
FRANCIS OF ASSISI

An earlier introduction to Francis of Assisi from the viewpoint of people who had a close-at-hand vantage point of his life presented him as a young man emerging from a strained family life and struggling against a social vortex that would predetermine the life he should lead. After some periods of adventure and suffering he publicly confronted and disavowed his father, opening the path to a new way of life that would include a combination of his previous habits of spending time away from the distractions of daily life, punctuated by events of exhilarated response to reality as he was now beginning to encounter it. While such stories and the later-in-life legends that are connected with Francis seem to capture popular attention, it is Francis' own writings that offer the most reliable insights. These writings indicate the workings of his imagination and reveal the means by which he was able to draw others to the spiritual way of life he crafted and sustain them as they followed "the footprints of our Lord Jesus Christ."[1] While his writings are not quite as dramatic as those about him, they often hint at elements found in the more popular accounts. Nonetheless, an approach to Francis from a psychological point of view cannot hope to unearth evidence to support all the stories, nor can it expect to present a full personality profile. The current effort hopes to show, merely, that an Object Relations Theory perspective on imagination can be used as one possible lens through which to analyze Francis' writings with the intention of showing that the saint's highly creative imagination is at work during the formulation of many of his expressions of religiously spiritual life, and that it is a very central feature of this life.

Since there is no direct access to Francis' imagination the most that this work can offer is a plausible attempt to link an ORT perspective on imagination, as detailed in the previous chapters, with concepts, expressions, and images found in Francis' writings that can be identified or associated with imaginative activity. In some cases these items are traceable to other sources, particularly Scripture, but it is how, why, and in what combinations these passages are used that point toward Francis' original imaginative activity. To maintain continuity with previous chapters, Francis' imaginative activity will be probed in terms of experience, relationship, change, faith and images of God, and meaning. The first two foundational topics of experience and relationship will be used to focus Francis' works in this chapter with the latter three topics being covered in the following chapters. Each of his writings that clearly show signs of the engagement of the imagination will be explored under these focal topics. These works will be considered, as far as possible, in the order given by the applicable volume of *Francis of Assisi: Early Documents,* however, in order to structure certain key themes, it will be necessary to work outside the given order at times.[2] Perhaps what will stand out as most significant in Francis' writings is that he is less the dreamer, caught up in the imaginative world of many of his early biographers, and more a master of the imagination, guiding others to open the possibilities of their own imaginations and the imaginations of those under their influence, in pursuit of a meaningful world and a relationship to it and the author thereof.

Experience

From the ORT theorists and other students of the imagination it is apparent that the imagination is the first point of contact with experience, accepting it out of chaos or some less meaningful context, intensifying the manner in which the experience is attended to, establishing it in a relational matrix (that has been termed, among other things, the transitional area), and finally presenting it in the form of something that can be *experienced-as*, or more precisely: *perceived-as*. Although perceiving an experience in a new order of relationship pertains predominantly to the topic of meaning, the use of *perceiving-as* language is also a gauge of experiencing that requires an imaginative attempt to re-order or re-contextualize an experience.

Initial Encounter

ORT makes it clear that the ability to recognize something as real and, therefore, subject to human experience commences with the first awareness of otherness. For this reason the initial encounter with experience will be described first in terms of other-awareness, then as contending with disorder, and finally as limit-of or borderline experiences which challenge the extent of human awareness, reawaken a sense of disorder, and throw us into the imaginative pursuit of meaning.

In ORT the ability of an infant to imaginatively create a world, to link an interior, illusionistic landscape with exterior reality, is doomed to failure if the child does not begin to see and accept that he or she is not the sole participant in reality. Throughout Francis' writings he regularly directs attention beyond the individual toward brother, neighbor, inanimate creation, and God in an effort that accentuates other-awareness even though this effort is meant, first of all, to heighten a sense of humility. While Francis' biographers described his youthful vanity, and he implies the same when conceding the self-centeredness of sin in his early formative years, he clearly redirects this orientation for himself and others.[3] In the *Letter to All the Faithful* he commands, "We must be charitable, too, and humble, and give alms, because they wash the stains of sin from our souls."[4] Each of these activities is a way of reaching out toward another with a corresponding movement away from self-absorption. He encourages his readers to intentionally adopt an attitude that not only sets others apart but raises them up in esteem so that *otherness* may never be taken for granted. Francis writes, "We should not want to be in charge of others; we are to be servants, and should be subject to *every human creature for God's sake*."[5] He explains how to maintain this attitude even when in a senior position: "The man who is in authority and is regarded as the superior should become the least of all and serve his brothers, and he should be sympathetic with each of them as he would wish others to be with him if he were in a similar position."[6] A comparable reversal of roles for the sake of sharing another's viewpoint and thus sustaining the perspective on otherness is found in *Religious Life in Hermitages*. In reference to switching imaginatively conceived roles the participants are urged to "exchange places with the mothers, according to whatever arrangement seems best suited for the moment."[7]

In some cases Francis attempts to inculcate a sense of otherness without setting any one person apart. In *The Rule of 1221* he writes, "No one is to be called 'Prior.' They are all to be known as 'Friars Minor' without distinction, and they should be prepared to wash one another's feet."[8] Francis suggests a similar honor when the brothers come together. He insists that they should "diligently show reverence and honour to one another without murmuring."[9] In a follow-on passage he greatly plays up the situation of otherness with Jesus' *turn the other cheek* ideal. "They should not offer resistance to injury; if a man strikes them on the right cheek, they should turn the other cheek also towards him. If a man would take away their cloak, they should not grudge him their coat along with it. They should give to every man who asks, and if a man takes what is theirs, they should not ask him to restore it."[10] This valuation of the other at the expense of one's personal selfhood comes across as rather severe in the modern-day world that is influenced by humanistic thought, but it gives Scriptural support to Francis' vision of the Gospel lifestyle, and it places a sense of otherness as a constant backdrop for his spiritual, imaginative construction of the world.

Elsewhere in *The Rule of 1221* Francis again encourages his followers to "be subject *to every human creature for God's sake*," and this requires that they "not boast or be self-satisfied."[11] The concept of creature and creator arises regularly in his texts, and it sets up a tension of otherness. He observes of God, "You created all things spiritual and physical, made us in your own image and likeness, and gave us a place in paradise."[12] While noting this most distinctive Biblical basis for human relatedness to the divine, Francis quickly follows with, "Through our own fault we fell."[13] In almost every case where the saint observes the height of the fundamental human-divine relationship he mitigates it with mention of the fall from unity into otherness. No longer does the creature associate him or herself within the single image of divinity; now the otherness of God represents the source of his or her otherness. A few lines that make this particularly clear read: "our Lord and God who has given and gives us everything, body and soul, and all our life; it was he who created and redeemed us and of his mercy alone he will save us; wretched and pitiable as we are, ungrateful and evil, rotten through and through."[14] It is these latter elements that point to individuality within a Christian anthropology, and they also give way to a profound sense of otherness.

There are a number of situations in Francis' writings where God can be seen to exhibit characteristics that ORT associates with maternal caregivers. One depiction should be considered under the category of otherness. Recalling that a child discovers his or her individuality by being viewed as such through the eyes of another, the spiritual recognition of God as other is brought up in *The Blessing for Brother Leo*. The full translation goes: "God Bless you and keep you. May God smile on you, and be merciful to you; May God turn his regard towards you and give you peace. May God bless you, Brother Leo."[15] This image brings to mind a popular modern statuette of a mother and infant that has the mother's head turned toward the infant at her breast. The statuette seems to capture a universal pose for a mother and child. It is striking how natural this position is for the new mother and infant. As far as the text is concerned, it is not that Francis originally envisions this kind of encounter between God and humanity; the passage comes from the book of Numbers (Nm 6:24-27). The point is that Francis envisions it as the circumstances in which Leo should see himself. It is the very attitude that Francis would have his close friend take in reference to God who is both distinctly close and definitively other.

A final writing where otherness and relatedness are held in tension is *The Canticle of the Creatures*. The topic of disorder and order will follow shortly, but the Canticle is notable for establishing an order among the elements of creation. Each is assigned a function or attribute or both, and it is on the basis of these functions and attributes that features of creation can be seen in terms of their otherness. For instance, Brother Sun provides light and is "beautiful" and "radiant in all his splendour."[16] Brother Wind sustains creatures and he is both "fair and stormy."[17] Sister Water is, "So useful, lowly, precious and pure." while Brother Fire provides light and is: "Full of power and strength."[18] Where imaginative activity requires the ability to perceive a difference in tension, otherness in this passage is the difference-factor among the elements which yearn to praise God in Francis' world-vision. Francis' effort to direct his followers' attention beyond themselves into a reality that is populated and upheld by otherness is the first step in his endeavor to fashion a spiritual outlook on reality that outlives him still.

Chaos

To say that experience begins in chaos may sound a bit harsh even though it is an accurate description of initial infant experiencing as posed by ORT. The idea of experience as disordered or emerging from a less or no longer meaningful context is a more appropriate beginning for an analysis of the kind of experiencing offered by Francis. In early childhood, the in and out awareness of otherness and the achievement and loss of meaningfulness connected with the struggle for object constancy might have been accurately described as chaotic.

In healthy maturity there is little likelihood that object constancy will falter. Instead, there is the problem of living in a world where the complexity of life expands faster than the individual's capacity to sustain or apply meaning to the rising tide of experience. Today this is often called stress. Francis very aptly uses a term that has a modern equivalent, *anxiety*.[19] Where English speakers might use the words *don't worry,* in current-day Italy the nearly equivalent phrase is often heard: *Non te preoccupare!* Francis may have used the latter notion in his time. Where, according to one translation, he writes, "I therefore beg of you… do not forget God or swerve from his commandments because of the cares and anxieties of this world…," another translation uses "preoccupations."[20] While the English *worry* refers more than anything else to an inner state, *preoccupation* suggests a failure to see the whole of life and its grandeur and significance because one is *occupied* with a few, or a single, less significant details. Francis' attempt to fashion a life according to good order reveals his awareness of the disorder that stands as a barrier to such an achievement.

Francis' early biographers recount his serious and progressive vision malady and the torturous treatments he endured to halt the eventual loss of sight.[21] Because so much imagery develops out of life experience it is conceivable that Francis' approach to disorder was primarily formulated in terms of vision and suffering. Although it is difficult to determine exactly when the issue of his sight would have influenced his imaginative activity, physical suffering was part of his experience prior to the more deeply religious period of his life.[22] Regardless of any uncertainty that surrounds the influence of his imagination in youth, Francis' references to a limited perception of reality, seen and unseen, and suffering, his and that of others, stand as indicators of the initial disorder of experience.

Francis' *vitae* develop an impression of a young man in mid-conversion who was confused by God's calling and often acted out in spontaneous if not excessive displays of devotion. As the editors of *Francis of Assisi: Early Documents* point out, there is a claim that Francis expresses his uncertainty in a prayer before the Crucifix of San Damiano, the very place where he is said to have received his initial mission.[23] The *vitae* material, if nothing else, reflects the confusion, incomplete understanding, or lack of order with which he was viewing the world. From the writings of the saint comes a comparable expression: "enlighten the darkness of my heart and give me true faith, certain hope, and perfect charity, sense and knowledge."[24] It is clear from the unfolding of this prayer that the darkness of which the saint speaks is not melancholy or gloom but rather an inability to perceive rightly in pursuit of something "true" or real.

Francis shares the suspicion of the human body and a steady consciousness of the devil held by many other medieval religious figures. In Francis' case these tendencies also serve to highlight his outlook on disorder. In the *Letter to All the Faithful* he presents the image of a body wrongly ordered to the things of the world. Using an oft repeated phrase, he admonishes, "In body they are slaves of the world and of the desires of their lower nature, with all the cares and anxieties of this life."[25] As a one-time captive himself, if the stories are tenable, Francis would have known the suffering and the offensiveness of medieval imprisonment. He ties the concept of captivity with the ultimate religious expression of disorder where he mentions of some people: "in spirit they are slaves of the devil. They have been led astray by him and have made themselves his children, dedicated to doing his work."[26] He uses poor vision imagery to explain how this malevolent ordering comes about. He declares that, "They lack spiritual insight because the son of God does not dwell in them, and it is he who is the true wisdom of the Father.... They can see clearly and are well aware what they are doing; they are fully conscious of the fact that they are doing evil, and knowingly lose their souls."[27]

In the very next paragraph Francis links bad vision with deception, a disorder of perception. "See, then, you who are blind, deceived by your enemies, the world, the flesh, and the devil, our fallen nature loves to commit sin and hates to serve God."[28] Added to the disordered condition of deception, in which what seems to be is not so, in the Armstrong et al translation, Francis uses another oppositional pair of concepts, sweetness and bitterness.[29] Perhaps it is no mistake that sweetness and bitterness are first mentioned in juxtaposition with deception. Initially, in this passage, bitterness is aligned with a relationship to God. Then, in the *Letter to All the Faithful*, Francis refers to "All those who refuse to taste and see how good the Lord is and who love darkness rather than light."[30] These are some of Francis' few indirect images of food, and in another translation the taste was sweet rather than good.[31] In general, sweetness can be seen as a harmony of scent and, in particular, taste. The unharmonious opposite of this sensation is the bitterness of something that must be rejected or avoided. While both examples draw attention to disorder, Francis may have intentionally aligned deception with bitterness and following God's order in the first case. In the second instance, where the term *deception* does not play a role in the contrast between a God-oriented order and a darkened perception of reality, sweetness is now connected with God.

The latter distinction between sweetness and disordered darkness foretells the foundational, positive ordering principle against which all other forms of disorder can be compared and reduced in essence. It is not simply to God that reality must be rightly ordered; for Francis it is to God-as-good that all forms of order must aspire. In one of several such passages Francis explains that God "has borne so much for us and has done and will do so much to us; he is our power and our strength, and he alone is good."[32] Francis often refers to other attributes of God, but God's goodness stands out most forcefully in his writings. From the perspective of ORT, the eventual effort to reorder imaginative perception of the world according to an intangible ideal, goodness, stands against the less imaginative attempt to order the world according to things of the body. If the things of the body can be conceived as representing the world of sense data and the instinctual, impulsive response to it, it becomes more apparent why Francis challenges the world and the body as sources of order. Such a basis of experience does not allow for a rich imaginative envisioning of reality in all its potential.

A passage that further evidences the point that Francis has a natural understanding of the workings of the imagination and knows how to inspire others to an imaginatively creative vision of reality is found in the *Letter to All the Clerics*. Where he writes, "the sensual man does not perceive the things that are of the Spirit of God," it is apparent that a spiritual life requires a unique outlook.[33] If Francis bases these lines off the Scriptural passage identified by the editor of *The Omnibus of Sources* (1 Cor 2:14), he is again concerned with a misconception of some aspect of the wider reality. The complete passage in the Scriptures includes the idea of spiritual discernment and seeing things as "folly" in its absence.[34] Another example of Francis' writings where there is a discussion of things seen in an order that is somehow skewed is found in The *Letter to all Superiors of the Friars Minor.* Francis points out that there are "portents in heaven and on earth, which are very significant in the eyes of God, but are disregarded by the majority of people, including religious."[35]

Some of the recently considered examples of disorder represent confusion in the way order is conceived. Disorder can also be understood as an inability to concentrate on any significant matters at hand or for there to be no central focus to one's attention and activity. Perhaps this condition even includes an autistic-like failure to grasp the importance of potentially meaningful experiences as they pass by. The closest term that Francis uses for this state is "idleness," which he regards as "an enemy of the soul," adding that "those who serve God should be always busy praying or doing good."[36] Because *idleness* can link a lack of attention with a lack of intention, Francis, here, identifies another form of confusion that necessitates imaginative intervention. While work may move the individual too far away from Pruyser's hallucinatory world to engage illusionistic activity, Studzinski's idea that prayer is access to the transitional sphere, is supportive of Francis' guidance to combat idleness.

Money is another area of disorder for Francis. As a one-time participant in the nascent but expanding capitalist market based economic system, Francis may have observed how the traditional order of life and commerce was changing before his eyes.[37] Although there is much debate about the connection between voluntary poverty and the Franciscan way of life, one thing is clear; Francis sees that money and finances hold the possibility of distracting people from a spiritual life directed toward God. In an attempt to exemplify the false valuation many people were beginning to apply to money he declares, "We should have no more use or regard for money in any of its forms than for dust;" to point out the confusion he adds that "those who think it is worth more... expose themselves to the danger of being deceived by the devil."[38] These lines, of course, do not clear up the poverty question in Franciscan Studies. It must be recalled that one of Francis' early responses to God's call was to gather stones (an alternately used translation for dust) to rebuild San Damiano.[39] In this light, money, like stones, could feasibly be considered valuable as a tool to serve God when put back into the right order of relationship.

In the *Fragments,* which are incomplete exhortations or draft versions of a rule of life, Francis brings attention back to the devil as the primary source of confusion. The saint warns, "As he prowls about he wants to ensnare a person's heart..., to choke out the word and precept of the Lord from our memory, and, desiring a person's heart, to blind it through worldly affairs and concerns."[40]

Francis envisions the heart as the core of one's spiritual perception. In this passage, the image of some beast spearing the defenseless heart could easily overshadow the real message about disorder overwhelming a sense of order. He mentions the idea of misperceiving something as beneficial, the "reward or assistance," and from this the perception of right order is prevented when memory, as past-oriented imagination, is choked, and the heart, as future, potential-oriented imagination is blinded.

Another aspect of disorder comes in the form of suffering. Francis claims, "they must endure persecution and death from their enemies, both visible and invisible."[41] Not only is suffering contrary to the good order of health and well-being, as Francis observes, it is also not always obvious where the cause of suffering originates since some enemies are not easily perceived. Another literary medium where Francis ties confusion together with suffering is *The Office of the Passion*. A selection of these prayers would have been read in specific sequences throughout the day according to the liturgical season. Such regular repetition enhances the influence of the ideas and images contained therein.[42] The primary Scriptural source for *The Office of the Passion* is the Psalms. While the psalmists mention confusion more than once, in the scriptural prayer for the *Holy Virgin Mary*, to be said at *Sext*, the writer laments, "for your sake I bear insult, and shame covers my face."[43] An interesting feature of Francis' use of the concept of shame is that another translation of this same Psalm (Ps 69:8) chooses, instead, the word *confusion*.[44] Whether Francis simply had a different translation is a question better answered by Scripture sources, but it is not too much to suggest the possibility that he intentionally identifies shame with a confused perception of the order of reality. While further examples of suffering will be considered as limits-of-experience and as preparatory to change, it seems that, among all the sources of disorder, experiences of suffering may be most clearly described as chaos.

The Edge of Experience

Tracy's limit-of-experience and Pruyser's borderline situation represent special cases in the discussion of the order and disorder of experience.[45] It is not that these experiences lack for order, it is that they surpass the range of order that a person is able to be familiar with. As such, they challenge individuals to look beyond the rational norms that most people in a given time-period utilize in ordering the relationships of their experiences. For this reason they spur some of the most dynamic and meaning-seeking imaginative activity. Francis takes great advantage of limit situations in stimulating the imaginations of his followers, but he also goes a step further. In a sense, he creatively induces limit conditions to move the imaginative process forward and establish a new way of seeing.

The most clear-cut limit-of-experience is the one that ends all sense-data experience; this is death. It is also one of the two most prominent limit situations Francis attends to in his writing. Suffering is the other. Francis' attention to death might be considered exceedingly morose, even for his times, were it not for his Christian belief in an eternal life and a two-world perception of reality in which the spiritually charged life is the first stage of eternity being lived out in the here-and-now of daily physical reality. But, the point of the matter is that eternal life bears no imaginative substance if there is no juncture point calling the believer to peer beyond the joys and challenges of everyday life to grasp at the hope and the potential sought in the eternity of God. Another point to consider regarding death is that entry into a religious order involved, in a sense, a person's death to the secular world.

A connection of passages that distinctly reveals the manner in which Francis presents death to his readers is found in the *Letter to All the Faithful*:

> You imagine that you will enjoy the worthless pleasures of this life indefinitely, but you are wrong. The day and the hour will come, the day and the hour for which you have no thought and of which you have no knowledge whatever. First sickness, then death, draws near.... We should all realize that no matter where or how a man dies, if he is in a state of mortal sin and does not repent, when he could have done so and did not, the devil tears his soul from his body with such anguish and distress that only a person who has experienced it can appreciate it.[46]

Francis explains that the time of death, and thus the scope of earthly life, is beyond the order of one's knowledge and experience. He also brings his followers right up to the conceptual moment of death and expresses that the final instant is unknowable. After death he mentions the tortures of hell, a bountiful font for medieval imaginations, but more time is spent discussing the dissolution of the person's estate and body, both of which no longer really pertain to the deceased individual's experience.[47] By this technique, Francis signifies the disjuncture in experiencing that will be part of each person's experience no matter how much effort is put into disregarding this reality. It is his way of forcing a confrontation with death so that the individual can begin to imaginatively visualize a fuller reality of life according to new dimensions of relationship and meaning.

The *Letter to All the Faithful* includes a reference to Francis' physical suffering. He writes, "because of my sickness and ill-health I cannot personally visit each one individually."[48] Although Francis does not use this opportunity to instigate the workings of any of his follower's imaginations, it does substantiate his imaginative activity in two ways. First, pain and suffering, whether observed or experienced, can initiate the disorder of a limit condition. Other than pointing to some form of injury, pain does not explain itself. It disorders all other forms of experiencing by usurping the prioritization of the things one can or would attend to. In the second place, pain and suffering spur imaginative activity by initiating the creation of their own object, as Scarry pointed out previously. The editors of *Francis of Assisi: Early Documents* use Francis' admission of his personal suffering in their translation of this text to list various times in his life where his physical health would have endured severe hardship. These include imprisonment and illness.[49]

The *Letter to All the Faithful* also includes an interesting expression of the limit set by death. Francis states, "Then his speech begins to fail and so the unfortunate man dies an unhappy death."[50] Death, in this case, is encapsulated by the dying person's inability to verbally share the experience of it. Shortly following this comment Francis adds a very unique expression of death. He asserts, "All the talent and ability, all the learning and wisdom which he thought his own, are taken away from him."[51] The editors of *Francis of Assisi: The Early Documents* describe this as a "threefold formula" and a symbol "highlighting the total loss of all things."[52] If loss of this magnitude is not a limit situation it would be difficult to identify a better example, and Francis regularly seeks to push people to a confrontation with this form of limit using statements such as: "Consider and realize that the day of death is approaching."[53]

A less graphic type of limit situation is found in Francis' frequent references to Eucharistic theology in which sense data is unable to confirm the presence of Christ in the sacrificial elements on the altar. The saint observes that, "We know his body is not present unless the bread is first consecrated by these words. Indeed, in this world there is nothing of the Most High himself that we can possess and contemplate with our eyes, except his Body and Blood, his name and his words, by which we were created and by which we have been brought back from death to life."[54] He is very clear here that the totality of what can be experienced is not restricted to tactile, visual, or other sense-based categories, yet the capacity to move beyond these categories is a real challenge. In the *Letter to a General Chapter*, Francis revisits this issue. Speaking of the one Eucharist upon a multitude of altars, he explains that, "We see that he is present in numerous different places, yet he remains indivisible."[55] Francis' numerous uses of Eucharistic theology conceivably exercise the imaginative capacity, his and others', to grapple with concepts that defy easy categorization and explanation.

The experience of God presents a further limit situation in Francis' vision of the world. Using conceptions of God, Francis creates a purposeful tension between his effort to experientially mirror the life of the Son of God while depicting God as a being inaccessible to human experiencing. In *The Rule of 1221*, Francis describes God as "without beginning and without end, he is unchangeable, invisible, indescribable, and ineffable, incomprehensible, unfathomable."[56] It is plausible that such words point toward Francis' endeavors to contemplate and encounter God beyond these limitations. He refers to God in this way again in *The Admonitions*. In this case he claims that, "the Father dwells in light inaccessible and that God is spirit, and St John adds, No one at any time has seen God. Because God is a spirit he can be seen, only in spirit; it is the spirit that gives life; the flesh profits nothing."[57]

The *Fragments* contain a reference to suffering that is more likely to catch the imaginative attention of readers than the last reference to this limit. Francis speaks of the "injury, sorrow and punishment, martyrdom and death" that must be loved.[58] Death also receives special mention in *The Canticle of the Creatures*. While the editors of *Francis of Assisi: The Early Documents* suggest that the statement on death is distinct among all Francis' allusions to the topic because it exemplifies God's immanence, it is also similar to the others as it is able to prompt a limit situation. [59] Francis writes, "All praise be yours, my Lord, through Sister Death, from whose embrace no mortal can escape. Woe to those who die in mortal sin! Happy those She finds doing your will! The second death can do no harm to them."[60] The inescapability of death is, however, tempered by shrouding death in a praiseworthy female image.

Francis' *vitae* tell the story of a profound religious conversion. Francis' own words in his *Testament* compress that story into a few short but meaningful lines. What is still present is a limit experience that draws Francis' attention in and opens the way to a new capacity to relate to and thus visualize all of creation. He recalls, "When I was in sin, the sight of lepers nauseated me beyond measure; but then God himself led me into their company, and I had pity on them."[61] It seems that Francis sought to deny the existence of suffering and death made all-to-clear by leprosy. It was pointed out earlier that lepers were given a final blessing in a liturgical ceremony that resembles a funeral. The powerful apprehension directed towards lepers, found in this passage, stands as one of Francis' own most pivotal limit encounters, an encounter about which he felt strongly enough to include it as one of the few autobiographical items in his writing. The sense of this experience is raised again in a scriptural prayer. Francis may have seen the parallels between his experience and that of the psalmist who inspired the words: "I am numbered with those who go down into the pit; I am a man without strength. My couch is among the dead."[62] Here it is the helplessness of the situation that appears to bring on the limit-of-experience. Another translation of this Psalm (Ps 88: 5-6) more clearly establishes the idea of living like the lepers, as-if dead: "like one forsaken among the dead, like the slain that lie in the grave, like those whom thou dost remember no more..."[63] While Francis does not speak directly about the loss of memory, the more complete text does point to this type of limit-of-experience.

The essence of Object Relations Theory is the giving of order to experiences that require an initial ordering or a reordering. If all experience carries its own explicit meaning this would not be necessary, but such is not the case, and Francis clearly recognizes the fact. Various passages from his writings attest to his awareness of the need to see things anew, in a fresh, yet original, order. What is more, his writings indicate a perception of certain experiences that shake individual confidence in the given order of day-to-day life and necessitate a search for new meaning. Limit experiences are central to this activity, but they also serve to bring a tremendous amount of imaginative attention to bear on certain vital experiences. In this manner they intensify experiencing.

Intensification

This term has been described as bringing an experience to the forefront, highlighting it, or placing it at a point of central attention. ORT theorists use terms like play, mystery, and transcendence to reflect what is happening when an experience is being imaginatively processed. *Illusion* in its root meaning has been associated with intense play which pulls the imaginer into the illusionistic sphere or the transitional space. Mystery and transcendence burst open the dimensions within which an experience can be conceptualized. Collective aspects of imagination present certain experiences as primarily worthy of imaginative consideration, and communal faith is a principal drive of this feature. The various limits-of-experience described above are just a few examples where Francis utilizes mystery and transcendence, in Pruyser's sense of the words. Francis' reference to back-and-forth interactions, perception of fundamental Catholic beliefs, and the expansive reality of God also serve to point out the intensification of awareness that he directs toward some experiences. Above all, Francis is adept at guiding his readers to focus their attention and avoid distractions that will inhibit the intensity of experiencing.

In the *Letter to All the Faithful* he starts a statement with: "See, then, you who are blind," and earlier he proposes: "We should praise him and pray to him day and night, saying, Our Father, who art in heaven, because we must always pray and not lose heart."[64] These passages call on people to gather in their attention and to give that attention fully to God and, therein, the image of God. The experience of God in the Eucharist is one in particular where Francis seeks to incite and concentrate the imagination. Employing a play on words he writes, "Surely we cannot be left unmoved by loving sorrow for all this; in his love, God gives himself into our hands; we touch him and receive him daily into our mouths. Have we forgotten that we must fall into his hands?"[65] The image of the hands is clarified by the reversal or back and forth interaction of who is in whose hands. It signifies the play taking place within the transitional sphere. In *Letter to all Superiors of the Friars Minor* the experience of the Eucharist is again highlighted when Francis associates the corporeal presence of Christ with a gesture. "When the priest is offering sacrifice at the altar or the Blessed Sacrament is being carried about, everyone should kneel down and give praise, glory, and honour to our Lord and God, living and true."[66]

After the introduction to *Letter to the Rulers of the People*, Francis intensifies attention to the image of death by writing: "Consider and realize that the day of death is approaching."[67] A paragraph later he advises the rulers: "put away all worry and anxiety and receive the holy Body and Blood of our Lord Jesus Christ fervently in memory of him."[68] Here he indicates that imaginative memory is sustained by clearing away distractions. Unfettered attentiveness is such a bedrock of his ideal for his religious order that he makes it one of the first tenets of *The Rule of 1221*. The first chapter is entitled: "The Friars are to Live in Obedience, without Property, and in Chastity."[69] Later in the same document Francis gives this distraction-free lifestyle the authority of a divine command. He asks his followers, "put away every attachment, all cares and solicitude, and serve, love, honour, and adore our Lord and God with a pure heart and mind; this is what he seeks above all else."[70]

When Francis remarks, "Almighty, most high and supreme God, Father, holy and just Lord, King of heaven and earth, we give you thanks for yourself," he is proclaiming God's transcendence. God does not seem ultimately distant in this statement due to the designation of fatherhood, but there is enough space to form an experiential gap.[71] When experience is, instead, intensified by mystery, Francis uses the yearning for that which cannot be completely experienced as his intensification technique. He says, "We should wish for nothing else and have no other desire; we should find no pleasure or delight in anything except in our Creator, Redeemer, and Saviour; he alone is true God."[72] In *The Rule of 1223*, *desire* is matched with *attention* as too much interest in education is equated with distraction. The saint insists, "Those who are illiterate should not be anxious to study. They should realize instead that the only thing they should desire is to have the spirit of God at work within them, while they pray to him with a heart free from self-interest."[73]

Intensification of the present moment of experience is also achieved by the simple command to listen. Francis begins *The Canticle of Exhortation for the Ladies of San Damiano*, with "Listen."[74] Similarly, in the *Letter to the Entire Order*, he writes, "Listen, then, sons of God and my friars, and give ear to my words. Give hearing with all your hearts and obey the voice of the Son of God."[75] In this case, attending to the experience at hand is given further support by the *ear of the heart* image that Francis uses repeatedly.[76] Visual attention to the experience of God is aligned with the desire of the angels to see God. Francis refers to God "upon whom the angels desire to look."[77] He adds to this a contrasting, unacceptable perception: "Surely this is a great pity, a pitiable weakness, to have him present with you like this and be distracted by anything else in the whole world."[78] The same text uses both transcendence and mystery to further grasp and initiate the imaginative activity of the reader. For transcendence Francis exclaims, "Our whole being should be seized with fear, the whole world should tremble and heaven rejoice, when Christ the Son of the living God is present on the altar in the hands of a priest"[79] More simply, for mystery, Francis observes that, "the Lord of the whole universe,... [would] hide under the form of a little bread, for our salvation"[80] *A Letter to the Entire Order* is ended with another reference to mystery. Referring to one of the most beautiful and elusive Christian mysteries, Francis addresses the triune God "who live and reign in perfect Trinity and simple Unity...."[81]

The Testament of St. Francis raises the importance Francis gives to the Eucharistic mystery where he writes, "I want this most holy Sacrament to be honoured and venerated"[82] In *The Admonitions* Francis goes so far as to teach people how to initiate imaginative perception through mystery. Learning from the apostles he advances: "With their own eyes they saw only his flesh, but they believed that he was God, because they contemplated him with the eyes of the spirit. We, too, with our own eyes, see only bread and wine, but we must see further and firmly believe that this is his most holy Body and Blood, living and true."[83]

A further example of a distraction-free condition, used frequently, is the notion of a pure heart. Francis writes, "A man is really clean of heart when he has no time for the things of this world but is always searching for the things of heaven, never failing to keep God before his eyes and always adoring him with a pure heart and soul."[84] The effort to see God through mystery is not an endless task. Indicating that mystery will at some point no longer shroud the sight of God, Francis offers praise to the Lord as he understands that in the heavenly kingdom "we shall see you clearly."[85] Until that time, however, the need to imaginatively perceive God and the things of God persists. From the evidence given, it is clear that Francis recognizes the significance of intensifying the experience of the present moment in order to spark imaginative interaction with creation and the creator.

This section has identified items of Francis' writings that uphold the contention that the saint's imaginative activity begins in a confrontation with experience as elucidated by an ORT perspective on imagination. The primary texts display a profound other-awareness, and they reveal Francis' search for a higher degree of order in the disorder of many human experiences. Francis was shown to utilize limit-of-experience conditions to both expose the existence of disorder and focus attention on a variety of critical experiences. Other techniques, used by the saint, add to the intensification of an experience that moves the imaginative process forward. According to most theories of imagination the next step in the process involves setting the experience into a relational matrix. ORT identifies this matrix as the transitional area or transitional space. The following section will look at passages that indicate the presence of both internal and external relationships that point toward the imaginative engagement of the transitional space.

Relationship

Object Relations Theory explains that the creative act of perceiving reality depends on a process of relating internal images to structure and sustain this sense of reality and give meaning to it. We could never hope to touch directly upon any of Francis' internal images, but his use of images and the series of image-based relationships that he draws out in his writing certainly point toward the interior workings of his imagination. Three categories of images will be considered in this section and a fourth will be analyzed in another chapter. The first category will be loosely titled: *Family Relationships* since it will include images of the maternal figure, a re-envisioning of how the family can be imaged, some less positive views of family, and perceptions of women in general. The second category involves the way Francis sees the relationships among his brothers in the order and, to a lesser extent, people outside this group. The third, and surprisingly smaller, grouping of relationships will include those referring to creation in its entirety and in particular. Perhaps the most prevalent set of images are those portraying relationships to and of God. These will be held back for further consideration in the section covering faith and the image of God in the next chapter.

Family Relationships

As ORT has made clear, the human being first begins to sense the existence of a reality beyond him or herself in the eyes of the maternal caregiver. The mother provides a stable environment and then, slowly, begins to destabilize that environment. It is the mother's ability to return at the critical moment, present her object image where the child creatively seeks that image, and assuage the child's distress, which facilitates the burgeoning imaginative capacity. In time the child learns to retain the image of the maternal figure even in her absence. Winnicott and Pruyser have both noted the importance of this event as its effect carries on across a lifespan. This maternal image proliferates throughout Francis' writings, and, in marked contrast with the writings of Aelred of Rievaulx, it is a wholly affirming image. In close connection with his positive outlook on the maternal figure, Francis aligns a number of good and bad images of family. He uses the upbeat images to reveal a new way to perceive the possibility of human relatedness as a family in contrast to the negative images which could be construed to represent his dealings with his father.[86]

One of Francis' first identifiable writings, the *Letter to All the Faithful*, includes a very optimistic image of the maternal role embedded within a description of family. This image has distinct poignancy since it includes an imaginative gender cross-identification. Speaking of people who truly love God, Francis explains that the Holy Spirit will make "his dwelling in them and there he will stay, and they will be children of your Father in heaven whose work they do. It is they who are the brides, the brothers and mothers of our Lord Jesus Christ."[87] The various family roles found in this passage hint at the very dynamic image of family that Francis works with throughout his other writings.[88] Each role has its function, all are important, and none but the good father seems to be permanently connected with one being, God the father. The lines following this passage explain how every role is fulfilled. Francis proposes that, "A person is his bride when his faithful soul is united with Jesus Christ by the Holy Spirit; we are his brothers when we do the will of his Father who is in heaven, and we are mothers to him when we enthrone him in our hearts and souls by love with a pure and sincere conscience, and give birth by doing good." [89] Union, obedience, love, fecundity, and work are the operative features of this family. It should be noted that task-for-task the mother is relied upon the most.

Francis goes on to point out the many blessings of the family that has just been described: "How glorious, how holy and wonderful it is to have a Father in heaven. How holy it is, how beautiful and lovable to have in heaven a Bridegroom. How holy and beloved, how pleasing and lowly, how peaceful, delightful, lovable and desirable above all things it is to have a Brother like this, who laid down his life for his sheep..."[90] Take notice of the descriptors of the relationships in this passage. Francis uses concepts like holiness, glory, consolation, beauty, wonder, love, gratification, humility, peace, sweetness, and, what might be the end result of these, desire. Several of these expressions give a sense of the back-and-forth interrelationship that is mature play. In contrast, is the bondage that constrains the relationship of people who refuse to undertake the hardships of this family way. Referring to individuals "who refuse to do penance," Francis writes, "They have been led astray by him [the devil] and have made themselves his children, dedicated to doing his work."[91]

Many, but not all, of Francis' maternal images involve Mary. The *Letter to All the Faithful* has one of these in which the object constancy of the maternal image makes a stressful choice of life tenable. Francis associates Jesus with Mary "in whose womb he took on our weak human nature. He was rich beyond measure and yet he and his holy Mother chose poverty."[92] The point to be made is that Francis sought to imagine Mary as a participant in his life of poverty, a life filled with stress. Could it be that her presence indicates the object constancy of the maternal image which in turn makes this lifestyle bearable?

In *Religious Life in Hermitages* Francis employs an image of the maternal figure to show that a deeply religious lifestyle is born out of the solicitude of a mother. He begins the rule with the words: "Not more than three or at most four friars should go together to a hermitage to lead a religious life there. Two of these should act as mothers, with the other two, or the other one, as their children."[93] The mothers are expected to follow the role of Jesus' friend Martha, looking after the day-to-day details while the sons give their undivided attention to Jesus, much like Martha's sister Mary. As Francis does not seem to be a proponent of image-free contemplation it would appear that he expects the sons to be engaged in imagining the image of Christ during their solitude. If this is so, he also indicates the importance of using one's ability to be alone when engaged in imaginative activity. He writes, "after Terce the silence ends and they can speak and go to their mothers"[94] The implication that the nearness, yet absence, of the maternal figure provides a degree of security for the imaginative process is further born out by the statement that the mothers should "keep their sons away from them [outsiders], so that no one can speak to them. The friars who are sons are not to speak to anyone except their mother or their *custos* [custodian]."[95] Within this rule

Francis lays out the perfect conditions for imaginative play. Also recall Pruyser's point that an image of the mother sustains the capacity to be alone. The image of a mother protecting a son from unwanted or distracting words may additionally be autobiographical if Lady Pica often shielded the young Francis from his father's verbal tirades or work-related demands. Further signifying the dynamic nature of the family image that Francis is working with, he adds, "Now and then, the sons should exchange places with the mothers, according to whatever arrangement seems best suited for the moment."[96]

Many of Francis' images can be traced to a Scriptural source, but this does not negate the unique meaning and purpose his images hold. A diligent study of certain books of the Bible leaves the reader with an abundance of images, easily far more than Francis chooses to include in his writings. Some background knowledge of the saint's life, coupled with a careful look at the context in which a Scriptural image is used, can reveal something more about his intention. As a source of some-what archetypal images the Bible is a textbook for the tutoring of Francis' imagination. A comparison of one of Francis' biblical passages with the legend of his paternal renunciation displays the way a personal experience is enmeshed with internal object images. In *The Rule of 1221* he uses passages describing family disavowal from the Gospels of Matthew, Mark and Luke: "And everyone who has left house, or brothers, or sisters, or father, or mother, or wife, or children, or lands, for my name's sake, shall receive a hundredfold, and shall possess life everlasting. " (Lk 14:26, Mt 19:29, Mk 10:29, Lk 18:30).[97] Along the same lines, a selection from Psalms could be used to narrate Celano's depiction of the final moments of the spectacle in which Francis gives up his filial rights including the clothes furnished by his father.[98] A scriptural reading to be said at *None* laments: "Indeed, many dogs surround me, a pack of evildoers closes in on me. They look on and gloat over me; they divide my garments among them, and for my vesture they cast lots."[99] This passage conveniently relates images of Francis and others in the context of giving up one's clothing and all that this could stand for.[100]

As part of his re-envisioning of the family relationship, Francis points out the need to let go of preexisting conceptions of the bonds that hold a family together. Later in *The Rule of 1221* he rearranges some of the severed relationships. He admonishes his readers that, "All you are brothers. And call no one on earth father; for one is your Father, who is in heaven."[101] At times Francis even mixes the sentiment proper to different types of relationships. In the same text he writes, "They are bound to love and care for one another as brothers, according to the means God gives them, just as a mother loves and cares for her son."[102] A similar notion is expressed in *The Rule of 1223:* "Wherever the friars meet one another, they should show that they are members of the same family. And they should have no hesitation in making known their needs to one another. For if a mother loves and cares for her child in the flesh, a friar should certainly love and care for his spiritual brother all the more tenderly."[103]

Participation in a maternal role is further evidenced by images of Jesus being born to the brothers, where they stand as midwives. In *The Admonitions* Francis proclaims: "Every day he humbles himself just as he did when he came down from his heavenly throne into the Virgin's womb; every day he comes to us and lets us see him in abjection, when he descends from the bosom of the father into the hands of the priest at the altar."[104] By bringing together an experience of Christ on the altar with images of Christ's birth Francis creates a new image of the central Catholic ritual. He is not denying the significance of the Eucharist as a sacrifice; instead he is linking the gift of Christ's death with the gift of his birth. Another passage corroborates the importance of receiving Christ at his birth. In the midst of a series of scriptural prayers for the *Vespers of the Lord's Birth* Francis includes: "this most holy and well loved son is given, for our sakes a child is born on the wayside and laid in a manger because there was no room for him in the inn."[105] The authenticity of Francis' reenactment of the crèche scene at Greccio is given support by his mention of these birthing images.[106]

From many of the foregoing passages Francis apparently does not hold maternal affection in poor regard, and consequently, the same could be said of his overall view of the maternal imagery. In this sense, his writings are much more in line with the works of Bernard of Clairvaux, who was known for a good relationship with his mother. This can also be seen in Francis' elated references to the Mother of God. He dubs her "the glorious and ever blessed Virgin Mary," and the "mother, blessed Mary, ever Virgin."[107] The purity of Mary's virginal status is so important to Francis that he seems to want to disassociate her conception of Jesus from a gender-based image of God. In a scriptural prayer he describes her as the "daughter and handmaid of the most high King and Father of heaven; you are the mother of our most holy Lord Jesus Christ; you are the spouse of the Holy Spirit."[108] There is nothing technically unorthodox about this arrangement, but distinguishing between the Father's paternal role and the Holy

Spirit's participation in the holy conception might say something about Francis' re-envisioning of the family bond and his perception of his conception in the first place. There may be a brief parallel here with Aelred's parental image.

The maternal image applied to his followers and the related image of Mary both signify a positive perception of women, but these are only two special case examples. Francis' view of other women is not so clearly spelled out in his writings. My own view of Francis as a great liberator has been challenged by his willingness to accept the cloistered life for Claire of Assisi and the other women in the Order.[109] However, one sign that he has a somewhat more progressive view of women is that he does not indulge in the age-old and troubling assumption that women were a primal source of temptation for men. In *The Rule of 1223,* he uses no disparaging references to women when setting down the rule against entering a monastery of nuns.[110] Also, in *The Rule of 1221*, sins associated with sexual behavior come well after sins related to common responsibility, the treatment of other brothers, obedience, and greed. Where the sins that could involve women are finally mentioned, the term for *evil* is tied to the way one looks at or personally behaves with a woman, not with her directly.[111] Under the rule for fornication this act is specifically said to be at the temptation of the devil.[112] Another indication that Francis has a wholesome vision of women in general is that he designates each of the virtues as a woman in *The Praises of the Virtues.*[113]

In Francis' writings the maternal image is also delicately linked with God. The saint does not specifically entitle God: mother, but he appends many maternal attributes to God. After recounting the transcendence of the deity he adds descriptors like: "kind, lovable, delightful and utterly desirable beyond all else, for ever and ever."[114] In the *Letter to a General Chapter,* Francis reminds his readers that, "God deals with you as with sons."[115] He also selects some Psalms (Ps 22:10-11) to be read *At Matins* that can be interpreted to suggest a role for God as foster mother: "You have been my guide since I was first formed, my security at my mother's breast. To you I was committed at birth, from my mother's womb you are my God. Be not far from me."[116] The final clause insinuates separation anxiety. A later scriptural prayer for *None* says, similarly, "Hide not your face from your servant."[117] These passages offer no final proof that Francis envisioned God singularly as a mother, but they do substantiate Rizzuto's conclusion that no object-representation of God has a single source.

Numerous images of the maternal figure, Mary, and other women have been drawn out of Francis' writings. These images suggest the powerful effect of the infant's earliest mother-child relationship on the process of imagination throughout life. The image of this union, it seems, has so deeply penetrated Francis' imaginative fabric, his transitional or potential space, that vestiges of it show up in so many of his other images. The following section will turn to relationships among Francis' brothers and all people.

Relating to Another

Francis may not have intended to start a religious order.[118] His first priority was to follow in the path of Jesus, but he quickly accepted responsibility for the spiritual life of people who chose to follow him. A majority of his writings about the interactions of people dwell on the specific relationships between the men who took up Francis' way of life.[119] References to these latter relationships, where they indicate imaginative activity, will be covered first, considering the afore-mentioned elements of communication, group formation, concern, and love. A brief consideration of general relationships will follow. Throughout this section the passages will be ordered according to the elements just listed, beginning with communication.

The Basis of a Brotherhood

Communication. The discussion of family images in Francis' writings gives a strong indication of the way he intends his brothers to live, work, and move people closer to God. It is to be done as a new family, and this family will need to communicate among its members, to live as a group in most cases, to share concern for each other, and to embrace each other in a brotherly love worthy of the God who brings them together and is the ultimate point of reference in their search for meaning. From the perspective of ORT, communication is not simply a matter of transmitting data back-and-forth between participants. At its best, communication enables the transfer of meaning between two individuals. It involves engaging comfortably enough in a back-and-forth interaction with another person that one is able to enter into their transitional space while allowing the other to do the same in return. Since communication is more than the exchange of raw data, ORT points out that it can be explicit in its message, but it must also be implicit if significant meaning is to be shared.

A passage that reveals Francis' imaginative orientation to communication applies equally to the relationship between brothers and other people. After declaring, in *The Rule of 1221,* that friars may not preach without permission, he makes an exemption. He declares, "All the friars, however, should preach by their example."[120] While preaching is an art-form of communication meant to capture the mind, heart, and imagination of people in an audience, in comparison with preaching by example, no verbal expression requires the same level of an imaginative back-and-forth effort to link observed action with intended message.[121] The implicit nature of this type of communication can have great impact when the transmitter and recipient share a similar context. For this reason, gestural communication may be more effective among the brothers. *The Rule of 1223* eliminates the exemption to preach by deeds. In a move that may have been pressed upon Francis to avoid leaving the faithful in confusion, the exemption was replaced by the command: "Moreover, I advise and admonish the friars that in their preaching, their words should be examined and chaste. They should aim only at the advantage and spiritual good of their listeners, telling them briefly about vice and virtue, punishment and glory, because our Lord himself kept his words short on earth."[122] Nonetheless, the subjects that could be announced still owe themselves to imaginative expression, and the writer certainly has an image of Jesus capturing attention with the straightforward influence of his word.

Some features of the exemption to preach by deeds are retained earlier in *The Rule of 1223* under the chapter heading "How the Friars are to Travel about in the World." Here Francis writes, "And this is my advice, my counsel, and my earnest plea to my friars in our Lord Jesus Christ that, when they travel about the world, they should not be quarrelsome or take part in disputes with words or criticize others; but they should be gentle, peaceful, and unassuming, courteous and humble, speaking respectfully to everyone, as is expected of them."[123] This passage indicates which deeds deliver a poor message, but it also exhibits the importance of reducing the barrier to communication which is too easily erected between individuals. One is less likely to engage in defensive communication with someone perceived as meek, peaceful, *et cetera.* The same accessibility of communications applies between senior and subordinate within the order. Francis writes, "The ministers, for their part, are bound to receive them kindly and charitably, and be so sympathetic towards them that the friars can speak and deal with them as employers with their servants. That is the way it ought to be; the ministers should be the servants of all the friars."[124] Such communication requires a re-imagining of relationships. In a footnote to this passage the editors of *Francis of Assisi: Early Documents* point out that the term *familiarity,* from *familiaritas,* can mean "that of a family, of a servant, of familiarity or intimacy, or of solidarity."[125] Most of these meanings support the openness of communication.

The Group. Francis makes it abundantly clear who is not a member of the group he considers his brothers when he writes about those "who refuse to do penance and ... indulge their vices and sins and follow their evil longings and desires."[126] He also shares some of his insight on what it takes to be part of the group that is his brotherhood. It is possible to form a group around what is held in common. Unfortunately, greed, jealousy, and mistrust can easily infiltrate this bond and leave the group members permanently at odds with each other. Francis' answer to this dilemma is to offer a new vision of what any one individual can ever hope to truly claim as a possession. In *The Rule of 1221* he writes: "We must be firmly convinced that we have nothing of our own, except our vices and sins."[127] By a stroke of genius Francis has landed on the one entity that can hold a group together, a personal, yet collectively acknowledged, sense of limitation and thus need, which, conversely, is the one thing that any one person would not selfishly seek to claim more of than his or her own share. Francis also emphasizes this point when he writes: "they must give no thought even to the slightest faults of others, but rather count over their own in the bitterness of their soul."[128]

In a well-ordered group with a recognized hierarchical structure, obedience becomes an important factor. Francis connects the image of his personal humility and obedience to that of the obedient brother to make this role and image easier for other brothers to embrace. The saint insists: "I am determined to obey the Minister General of the Order and the guardian whom he sees fit to give me. I want to be a captive in his hands so that I cannot travel about or do anything against his command or desire, because he is my superior."[129] Written after Francis has turned over the leadership of the order, this passage is obviously not a call to recognize his power; it is a step toward the possibly unachievable ideal of a group operating with a single will. Francis uses the image of a flock of sheep to further shape a common vision around suffering. *The Admonitions* contain a passage about the Lord's sheep based on the *Imitation of Christ* that reads: "They followed him in trials and persecutions, in ignominy, hunger, and thirst, in humiliations and temptations, and so on. And for this God rewarded them with eternal life."[130] There is even a reward, eternal life, set out for those who persevere in living out this image of fraternity.

Concern. The more tight-knit a group is, the more intimate will be the bonds holding it together. Moving beyond shared information and a common interest, the members can begin to develop a sense of concern. ORT suggests that this response develops out of the infant's ambivalent relationship with the mother who is so deeply desired yet must be imaginatively destroyed in order for her to exist as a distinct *other* in the infant's world. Poorly handled, this interaction leads to guilt when there is no distinct object toward which to direct these feelings. When an object-image is available, the resultant feeling is one of concern. One important feature of this response is that it always seems to retain a reflexive aspect. The situation or needs of another cause me to gauge my own situation vis-à-vis the condition of the other.

A concern for the moral-spiritual well-being of another is prominent in Francis' writings. In *The Rule of 1221* Francis writes: "It is a fearful thing to fall into the hands of the living God, and so the ministers must keep close watch over their own souls and those of their friars."[131] Note that this instance of concern is appended with a threat. In the same passage, Francis states that, "If a friar is clearly determined to live according to the flesh and not according to the spirit, no matter where he is, the others are bound to warn, instruct and correct him with humble charity."[132] This gentle approach to the failings of another also comes with a firm warning. Francis adds that one must "be careful not to be upset or angry when anyone falls into sin or gives bad example; the devil would be only too glad to ensnare many others through one man's sin."[133] The sin of a brother is also a cause for concern in A *Letter to a Minister*. In this work, Francis proposes: "The other friars who know that he has sinned should not embarrass him by speaking about it. They should have the greatest sympathy for him and keep their brother's fall a secret."[134] Both of the latter passages on sin recognize and seek to imaginatively overcome the component of concern that turns the person in upon their own response and against others in a group.

There is no boundary to concern. Francis shows this when he commands: "Everyone who comes to them, friend or foe, rogue or robber, must be made welcome."[135] Behind this approach may be Francis' image of the poor Christ coming in the clothes of someone viewed with contempt. When the encounter is with other brothers Francis offers a practical expression of attempted concern: "And all the friars, no matter where they are or in whatever situation they find themselves, should, like spiritually minded men, diligently show reverence and honor to one another without murmuring."[136] Shortly after specifying that the brothers should look after each other with the care of a mother Francis writes that, "If a friar falls ill, no matter where he is, the others may not leave him, unless someone has been appointed to look after him as they should like to be looked after themselves."[137] After another reference to motherly concern in the *Letter to Brother Leo*, Francis advises his friend: "And if you find it necessary for your peace of soul or your consolation and you want to come to me, Leo, then come."[138] The combination of a maternal and a personal expression of concern are noteworthy.

To Love. The most significant insight ORT has on love is that it must be directed toward and for a distinct other if it is to be in any sense real, vital, or meaningful. Although Francis' expression--"In that love which is God"--might seem to confuse a feeling with a definitive object, other passages clarify God's distinct existence in Francis' world.[139] *The Rule of 1221* connects brotherly love with the image of God loving each of the brothers. Francis explains: "Let them love one another, as the Lord says: *This is my commandment: love one another as I have loved you.* Let them express the love they have for one another by their deeds, as the Apostle says: Let us not love in word or speech, but in deed and truth."[140] Later Francis adds an expression of the absolute bond that is love. Where he appears to be talking about the brothers he writes, "Nothing, then, must keep us back, nothing separate us from him, nothing come between us and him."[141] This ideal conception of utter union, by its negation of what stands between the brothers who should love each other, reveals Francis' awareness that love begins where two or more individuals become aware of each other from their individuality. Of added interest is the point that this bond reflects the mother-infant monad, the once was and still sought after form of union. Francis specifies the purpose of love in a *Letter to a Minister*. Since love is an outpouring of oneself for another, Francis writes, regarding a sinner, "And should he appear before you again a thousand times, you should love him more than you love me, so that you may draw him to God; you should always have pity on such friars."[142]

Expanding the relationship

There are a few interesting examples of an imaginative approach to relationships with people outside the order. These are worth analyzing inasmuch as they show a paradoxical outlook or one contrary to the norm of the time. Some texts also display Francis' ability to perceive the world with an expansive view, one which takes in increasingly more of the totality of reality. Francis and his followers to this day have a close relationship with the poor. They embrace voluntary poverty for the sake of solidarity with Christ's poor, the truly impoverished.[143] In a statement from *The Rule of 1221* Francis verifies the common perception of the poor and other outcasts while seeking to re-image that perception. Referring to the brothers he writes that, "They should be glad to live among social outcasts, among the poor and helpless, the sick and the lepers, and those who beg by the wayside."[144] While other people saw the poor as the coincidental recipients of the charity that would ensure their salvation, Francis saw a God-given obligation. He writes, "Alms are an inheritance and a right which is due to the poor because our Lord Jesus Christ acquired this inheritance for us."[145] By tying the concepts of legacy and justice together with alms Francis re-conceives the patronage system that was facing its own challenge from the rising merchant class. Normally a patron is due a certain percentage of the productivity of the members of the next lower tier in the structure, as well as their honor and willingness to stand by the patron in conflict. In return the patron offers a certain level of security. Since everyone from the tailor to the king has a charitable obligation, Francis' image sets the poor at an unprecedented height in the scale of patronage. In the *Fragments* Francis reaffirms the solidarity with the poor by declaring: "Let them express the delight for the poor that they have for one another."[146]

At a time when many priests were suspect for their training, morality, and general fitness for duty, Francis sought to bolster the sacredness of their office by giving people a new way to envision and respond to them. In *The Testament of St. Francis* he remarks that, "God inspired me, too, and still inspires me with such great faith in priests who live according to the laws of the holy Church of Rome, because of their dignity, that if they persecuted me, I should still be ready to turn to them for aid.... I am determined to reverence, love and honour priests and all others as my superiors. I refuse to consider their sins, because I can see the Son of God in them and they are better than I."[147]

In a passage from the *Letter to All the Faithful* that further signifies Francis's penchant for visualizing an ever-expanding web of relationships, he writes: "To all Christians, religious, clerics and layfolk, men and women; to everyone in the whole world, Brother Francis, their servant and subject, sends his humble respects, imploring for them true peace from heaven and sincere love in God."[148] A more detailed rendition of this expanded relationship vision is found in *The Rule of 1221* where the following groupings of people are encouraged "to persevere in true faith and in penance:"

> Priests, deacons, subdeacons, acolytes, exorcists, lectors, porters, and all clerics and religious, male or female; we beg all children big and small, the poor and the needy, kings and princes, labourers and farmers, servants and masters; we beg all virgins and all other women, married or unmarried; we beg all lay folk, men and women, infants and adolescents, young and old, the healthy and the sick, the little and the great, all peoples, tribes, families and languages, all nations and all men everywhere, present and to come.[149]

One can almost picture Francis stretching his imagination to include as many people and in as diverse an order as possible. Note that he calls upon the poor prior to the "kings and princes." Men and women are both listed in several categories, and he thinks in terms of people outside the normal organizational categories of his locality, mentioning people of different "races, tribes, and tongues."

What is more telling of Francis' vision of a world, in which two realities expand inter-related, is the fact that he precedes the above mentioned grouping of people "on earth" with a similar list detailing all those beings who are likely to be denizens of heaven. Beginning with Mary, the list also includes all forms of angels, "Innocents, Apostles, Evangelists, Disciples, Martyrs, Confessors, Virgins... and the other saints, living and dead or still to come."[150] One distinction between these two lists is the timeframe. The inventory of those on earth covers the present and future only, while the catalog of the heavenly hosts also encompasses the dimension of the past. He is identifying a point of conjunction where those who persevered in faith in the past are no longer part of the earthly coalition; they fill the ranks of souls who were and are saints in the spiritual field of Francis' vision. His view of relationships reaches to the farthest conceivable extent.

A View of Creation

As one of the most popular bird feeders or yard ornaments in the world, Francis of Assisi is often associated with God's creation as it is found in nature. Legendary stories about him preaching to the birds and taming a wild wolf surely add to this view of the saint.[151] His writings do not dispel this perception, although much of his imaginative activity surrounding created reality is associated with one work, *The Canticle of Brother Sun*, otherwise titled *The Canticle of the Creatures*.[152] Prior to considering the imaginative effort involved in this abundantly meaningful piece of literature, more general references to creation will indicate Francis' unceasing awareness of the fundamental divine creative activity. Next, passages will be presented that link creation with the desire to possess things, and, then, the human body as a creation will be discussed.

Creation in general

One Biblical passage from the book of Revelation (5:13) seems to have a significant influence on Francis' imagination. He repeats all or part of it more than once, or uses closely related passages. The central idea is that God is rightfully praised by, through, or in the many and varied results of divine creativity. In the *Letter to All the Faithful* Francis insists, "Every creature in heaven and on earth and in the depths of the sea should give God praise and glory and honour and blessing; he has borne so much for us and has done and will do so much good to us."[153] Francis finds the same concept in smaller segments of Scripture put together in the *Exhortation to the Praise of God*. He moves from "Heaven and earth, praise Him," to "All you rivers, *praise* the Lord. All you children of God, praise the Lord" (Ps 69:35; Dn 3:78; Dn 3:82). While it seems that Francis is working with ever more localized images of praise, he may be doing something else too, or instead. A few lines later he adds: "All you creatures, bless the Lord. All you birds of heaven, praise the Lord. All you children, praise the Lord" (Ps 103:22; Dn 3:80; Ps 113:1).[154] In this passage, after talking about two situations of non-human elements of creation he then turns to the term *children*, potentially making the connection between human generative activity, with its level of care, concern, and love, and the generative nature of God as creator.

It is difficult to discern whether the socially transacted image of baptismal water is one that plays into much of Francis' image processing or whether water, as a vital element of nature, fills this role for some other reason. One thing that is clear, however, is that Francis appears to be predisposed to selecting scriptural images that include water; the two previously cited texts do for instance. In a scriptural prayer for *Sext* he selects a text that declares: "Let the heavens be glad and the earth rejoice, let the sea and what fills it resound; let the plains be joyful and all that is in them. "[155] Water is mentioned again, but the one item that he did not include from the full Biblical text is trees (Ps 96:11-12). A final reference to water is found in *The Praises Before the Office*. Here Francis repeats a passage from Revelation (Rv 5:13). Early in the text he writes: "Bless the Lord, all you works of the Lord," and a few lines later he inserts: "Praise him in his glory, heaven and earth, 'and every creature that is in heaven and on the earth and under the earth, and such as are on the sea, and all that are in them."[156] With this rendition of the passage from Revelation he is more true to the Biblical version by including the subterranean creatures who were left out in his earlier version, but, more significantly, again water plays a part.[157]

Owning Creation

After discussing, in *The Testament of St. Francis*, the very basic items of clothing each brother is to use, Francis utters some very powerful words: "We refused to have anything more."[158] This is not a conclusive statement on the Franciscan relationship with voluntary poverty, but it does point toward the distinction Francis visualizes between created reality and what I mean by material reality. Created reality stands in solidarity with humanity in praise of God. Material reality is a subset of created reality that can be controlled or possessed. It is thus able to impede all other human relationships when its value and utility are misperceived. In the *Letter to the Rulers of the Peoples* Francis shows how one's relationship with possessions can inhibit the more important relationship with God. He writes, "Consider and realize that the day of death is approaching. I therefore beg of you with all the respect I am capable of that you do not forget God or swerve from his commandments because of the cares and anxieties of this world which you have to shoulder." He then adds: "When the day of death comes, all that they thought their own will be taken away from them."[159] In effect, he is saying that the notion of a permanent relationship with one's possessions is a delusion, a delusion that prevents people from envisioning the hoped-for permanence of a relationship with God.

Francis further expresses the likelihood that possessions will hinder a relationship in *The Rule of 1221* where he points out the contention that arises in connection with possessions: "No matter where they are, in hermitages or elsewhere, the friars must be careful not to claim the ownership of any place, or try to hold it against someone."[160] Francis offers two images that return material possessions, in the form of money, back to their status as created reality. He says that, "we should have no more use or regard for money in any of its forms than for dust."[161] He also writes that, "If ever we find money somewhere, we should think no more of it than of the dust we trample under our feet."[162] This change of perception does not completely devalue money; it simply resets where individuals will see money on a scale of utility. If you must walk a great distance in the service of God a trail of dust is much easier on the feet than a trail of money. Francis' exception to the money prohibition for the care of the sick indicates that he can see a specific and limited use for this possession.[163] He presents another image to display what takes place when money unsettles a good relationship.

Referring to the image of Judas Iscariot, he writes, "If any of the friars collects or keeps money, except for the needs of the sick, the others must regard him as a fraud and a thief and a robber and a traitor, who keeps a purse."[164] Francis is recalling how Judas set his relationship to a material possession higher than the intimate relationship he would otherwise have had with Jesus.

Body Images

The human body plays a very interesting role in Francis' imaginative activity. Actually, the body is portrayed in three inter-related images. One body is driven by instinctual desires. It is not the body that is physically weak; rather, it is the body that lacks the strength achieved through an alignment with a God-centered will. Where this latter situation of proper alignment does exist it yields a glorious body that serves God through an imaginatively inspired engagement with the works of God. Francis observes some of this positive aspect of the body at the same time that he sees a lesser bodily image involved in drawing away from God. In the back-and-forth game of imagining the body, the view of a second type of body image that is capable of carrying and serving Christ plays the antithesis to the version Francis describes as shunning God. In time, like most people who have contemplated the meaning of their bodies across a good number of years, Francis seems to have altered his perception to a third image. No longer is the body depicted as the dominator of the spirit, seeking to lead it down unhealthy pathways, nor is it an ever-glorious God-bearer. Francis' view of the body shifts to one in which the body acts as a restraint to the spirit, holding it in check, slowing it down. Eventually, his use of body images dwindles. He mentions it much less frequently in his later writings, and the many occurrences of the theme in *The Rule of 1221* are dropped in *The Rule of 1223*.[165]

When Francis speaks against the body, in the form of "our lower nature," he resorts to the language of hatred, but this is always a conditional dislike. While referring to people in a well-ordered relationship with God he explains that "Our lower nature, the source of so much vice and sin, should be hateful to us."[166] This is not a direct loathing of the body; rather, this is a disdain for the body that is involved in vice and sin. In the same work he condemns people who neglect to do penance and thus "indulge their vices and sins and follow their evil longings and desires... In body they are slaves of the world and of the desires of their lower nature."[167] When Francis uses the phrase "evil longings and desires," it is not easy to determine whether he means something akin to unfettered instinct, or narcissistic behavior, or a combination of the two, but his use of physical imagery like "indulge" and "follow" is indicative of another challenge to making an interpretation across many centuries. Francis and his contemporaries very much lived in a two world universe. The body, with its ability to act in the physical world is seen as the human agent in that world, while the spirit or soul fulfils similar duties in the spiritual world. Part of Francis' imaginative genius entails his vision of the spirit becoming the primary agent in the physical world. The result was an inevitable conflict with the body. Added to this confrontation is the suggestion that a disordered relationship between the soul and the physical world can render the soul as an outcast of the spiritual world, the world of heaven, and leave it at the mercy of the physical world. Francis graphically implies this with his warning that, "And worms feast on his body. So he loses both body and soul in this short life and goes to hell, where he will be tormented without end."[168]

The Letter to All the Faithful contributes more to the body-related imagery. Francis explains that, "we must renounce self and bring our lower nature into subjection under the yoke of obedience; this is what we have all promised God."[169] This portrayal of the body, as a draft animal, seeks to turn imagery from the physical world back against itself, since the kind of servitude and obedience involved are anchored in the spiritual world. Francis goes on to say: "It is not for us to be wise and calculating in the world's fashion; we should be guileless, lowly, and pure. We should hold our lower nature in contempt, as a source of shame to us, because through our own fault we are wretched and utterly corrupt, nothing more than worms ..."[170] Note that the body is not inherently worthy of scorn and contempt, but it happens to be so due to willful action triggering personal fault. Observe also that the result of this fault does not apply to the body alone but to "we," perhaps representing the total person, body and soul. Corporeal disintegration thus applies to both.

The Rule of 1221 has more of the same kind of negative body imagery. In successive paragraphs Francis refers to "leading a worldly life," and living "according to the flesh."[171] In the latter case the statement is immediately accented by the phrase: "And not according to the Spirit."[172] This expression might be related to the saint's dictate to "conduct themselves spiritually."[173] Francis also declares: "We must keep a close watch over ourselves and let nothing tarnish the purity of our senses," possibly indicating that the body can be a wholesome thing when it is spiritually cared for.[174] This statement implies a kind of stewardship that is advanced by Francis' belief that, "We must be firmly convinced that we have nothing of our own, except our vices and sins."[175] In this light, the body is not a possession or at least not a permanent one. Further exemplifying the clash between the physical and spiritual world, Francis writes: "The Spirit of God, on the other hand, inspires us to mortify and despise our lower nature and regard it as a source of shame, worthless and of no value."[176] In *The Admonitions*, Francis uses battle terminology. He observes that, "Many people blame the devil or their neighbor when they fall into sin or are offended. But that is not right. Everyone has his own enemy in his power and this enemy is his lower nature which leads him into sin."[177] Francis then adds that if one holds the lower nature "under his control... no other enemy, visible or invisible, can harm him."[178] The image he uses here implies that the body is not so much a threat as a window of opportunity through which the real threat can gain access when left to its own devices, these being perhaps the instincts.

In spite of the darkened image Francis presents of the body, he is not a strict anti-materialist. The body is not an absolute impediment to living spiritually such that it must be gotten rid of. Regardless of the poor treatment he seems to have provided for his body, he is conscious of the fact that the body does have some basic requirements, and these deserve respect. He concedes, "But if they are in want, the friars could accept other material goods for their needs, just like the rest of the poor, but not money."[179] He uses Gratian as an authority to justify this stance, writing that, "In times of urgent need, the friars may provide for themselves as God gives them the opportunity, because necessity knows no law."[180]

While it is commonplace today to speak of a proverbial heart that is the source of certain kinds of thoughts and feelings that may be spiritual in nature, Francis, at times, associates the heart with the evil body. He determines that, "vice and sin come from the heart of man."[181] A few paragraphs earlier he offers an alternative view of the heart and body connection. While placing himself and his brothers in a maternal image he notes that all are "mothers to him when we enthrone him in our hearts and souls by love with a pure and sincere conscience, and give birth to him by doing good."[182] This re-envisioning of the body is not carried out as fully as his new family image, but it is present in his writings.

The notion of a body placed at the service of God is also found in *The Rule of 1221*. He proposes that "the friars must always remember that they have given themselves up completely and handed over their whole selves to our Lord Jesus Christ."[183] The complete giving reflects back to the maternal carrying and birthing image in which the mother gives over her body for the needs of the child. Further hinting that the body is meant to be, and can be, well-ordered, Francis proclaims: "Of your own holy will you created all things spiritual and physical, made us in your own image and likeness, and gave us a place in paradise."[184] In Francis' imagination it is conceivable that paradise represents the once and hoped for time and place when both spirit and body are in a harmony of obedience to the will of God. The issue of God's likeness is made clearer in *The Admonitions* where Francis exclaims: "Try to realize the dignity God has conferred on you. He created and formed your body in the image of his beloved Son, and your soul in his own likeness."[185]

Francis again mentions the body and soul connection with God's creativity when he asks people to "love our Lord and God who has given and gives us everything, body and soul, and all our life."[186] The description of giving as a continuous activity of God adds to the idea that there is no possession of the body, only a period during which the person is a caretaker until and while God has need of the body. Another expression of this relationship occurs in *The Admonitions*. Francis writes: "A man takes leave of all that he possesses and loses both his body and his life when he gives himself up completely to obedience in the hands of his superior."[187] In *The Paraphrase of the Our Father*, Francis describes how both the body and soul can be expended together for God. This occurs by "seeking your glory in everything; and with all our strength by spending all our energies and affections of soul and body in the service of you alone."[188] In *The Praises of the Virtues*, Francis offers a final image of a body that is so enmeshed with the soul under obedience to the will of God "that it subjects a man to everyone on earth, and not only to men, but to all the beasts as well and to the wild animals so that they can do what they like with him, as far as God allows them."[189]

The Canticle of the Creatures

There may be no other piece of literature written by Francis that so clearly reveals the inner workings of his imagination than *The Canticle of the Creatures*. This is particularly so from an ORT perspective. The canticle includes a series of relationships between God images, images of humanity, female and maternal images, environmental influences, an image of a vital personal experience, and a reflection of a then current social event that bears meaning for Francis. In fact, the canticle touches on nearly every form of relationship that has been or will be discussed in this work. Poetic in form, its implicit nature leaves it open to various searches for meaning, none of which are likely to fully unveil its mysterious depths.

The editors of *Francis of Assisi: Early Documents* point out one mystery right away. Although it may seem to be a technicality, Francis' use of the word *per* cannot be singularly identified with a certain meaning. Where the saint's writing is translated as: "All praise be yours, my Lord, through Sister Moon and stars," the editors of *Francis of Assisi: Early Documents* point out that other possible translations, in the place of *through,* could have included: *for* or *by.*[190] The problematic issue is that each translation makes some sense, and Francis may have intended the looser understanding fashioned by a concurrent consideration of each variant. Not only is creation an agency of God's praise (by) but also a reason for God's praiseworthiness (for) and a participant in the subsequent praise (through). Such a mixture of three images within one imagistic statement is not inconceivable from an ORT perspective.

The editors make another point that is worthy of reconsideration. They suggest that the canticle is "a song of God's creation, in which human beings, because of sin, had no part."[191] The utter exclusion of humanity from this song is a little too extreme. The basis of the editors' position is Francis' exclamation that humanity is no longer worthy to speak the divine name."[192] These words are then associated with a declaration that "All praise is yours, all glory, all honour and all blessing," are reserved strictly for God.[193] The restriction on the use of God's name, in light of the Old Testament injunction against such use, may indicate the establishment of an appropriate distance from which the transcendent God could safely be worshipped. It may be a stance for prayer rather than an exclusion from prayer.[194]

If the restriction on the use of God's name is not a stance for prayer, then, recollecting the discussion of the various body images, Francis may, at first, be imagining human beings who are not in an acceptable relationship with their creator, those not acting according to God's will. This makes sense since the various other creatures that do participate in the song are shown to be following the natural order of creation. When Francis speaks of the sun he writes: "Who brings the day; and light you give to us through him."[195] Surely this is following the will of the God of Genesis who proclaims: "Let there be lights in the firmament of the heavens to separate the day from the night"(Gn 1:14). Other creatures also fulfill the divine intention. The air and weather sustain fellow creatures; fire gives light, beauty, and comfort, and the earth sets an order to all creaturely existence.[196] An alternative image of the human being is eventually able to join in the song of praise. This is the person who conforms to the will of God by doing what Jesus did, pardoning, suffering, and remaining faithful. Supporting the conjecture that this is an additional, preferable, image of the human person is the belief that this stanza was added later in Francis' life: "All praise be yours, my Lord, through those who grant pardon for love of you; through those who endure sickness and trial. Happy those who endure in peace, by you, most high, they will be crowned."[197]

Beyond the image of a God who must be related to in a specific fashion or not at all, Francis presents God as a being who acts through creation to reveal concern for creation. God gives the light of the sun for "us," and the sustenance provided through the air and weather is given all that God made. Furthermore, water is intended to be "useful," and the earth is productive in order to feed us."[198] In the few lines that contain these expressions of divine solicitude Francis associates the delicate beauty of nature with the efficient practicality of a divine order to things. He envisions the God who gives abundantly and with good reason.

Considering the two world schema that Francis works with, a description of reality relying on the first nine lines of the canticle would be insufficient, but then he adds death as an essential feature of his vision of life. For Francis, God's providence is involved in this too. He writes: "All praise be yours, my Lord, through Sister Death, from whose embrace no mortal can escape."[199] The editors of *Francis of Assisi: Early Documents* identify this view of death as more optimistic in comparison with earlier versions in Francis' writings.[200] Actually, this account includes the more fearful descriptions when he exclaims: "Woe to those who die in mortal sin!" but there is also hope in his subsequent comment: "Happy those She finds doing your will! The second death can do no harm to them."[201] Like the two primary images of a relationship with God, either for or against, there are two particular image-types of corporeal death, each of which has an eternal consequence, and each of which participates in Francis' imaginative reflection on death. This is why death is such a vital feature of life for the saint; it is not an end just as Francis' imaginative entry into death with the lepers was not a final experience. It was, instead, a life-shaping, forward-looking encounter that initiates a new life of seeing and being with Christ.

As further evidence of God's care for humans in *The Canticle of Brother Sun*, death is shown as a woman. She is not just any woman, though; she is Francis' sister, a part of his expanded vision of family and reality. She shares in the generally positive outlook on female images that Francis also displays when he describes Sister Moon and stars as "bright and precious and fair," or Sister Water as "lowly, precious and pure."[202] The repetition of the concept of "precious" regarding both women is a distinctive indicator of value in Francis' eyes, a worthiness that is inherited from the sister who bears offspring (fruit), provides nourishment, and offers guidance and discipline, "our Sister Mother Earth."[203] If Aelred of Rievaulx was describing death in connection with a sister-mother image, the sororal aspect would somewhat temper his poor maternal image, but this is not the case for Francis whose vague history and more clear personal literary evidence indicates a greater appreciation of female imagery.

It is generally accepted that Francis' previously mentioned lines about granting pardon and enduring trial refer to an event in civil society that captures Francis' attention.[204] Francis is seeking to heal the discord between two local leaders, but he is doing it by offering them an image of Jesus. He sees a chance to infuse meaning into the situation to bring about change, and he does this with an image of the suffering Christ who is still able to forgive. Francis links a God image with an image of the human person at his or her best to formulate this meaning.

Many types of image-based relationships have been discussed in the foregoing sections. This is just a partial indication of the numerous images that must occupy Francis' transitional space as he seeks to embrace a world fertile in experiences waiting for someone with a creative imagination to give meaning to it. Ample evidence has also been presented that Francis understands how to initiate the imaginative activity of others. This is a talent that he most likely cultivated by attending to his highly productive imaginative capacity where his openness and attentiveness to experience allowed such to meld into images which gained a clarity of meaning by their association with other, now related, images in his transitional sphere. The following chapters will turn toward a consideration of how Francis uses his imagination to bring about change, relate to God, and formulate meaning within his perception of reality.

Notes

1. Francis of Assisi, *The Rule of 1221*, in Marion Habig, ed. *St. Francis of Assisi: Writings and Early Biographies: English Omnibus of Sources for the Life of St. Francis.* (Quincy, IL: Franciscan University Press, 1991), 31. References to Jesus' footprints are numerous in his writings, suggesting that he wanted his brothers and sisters to visualize themselves following the path down which God was leading them.

2. Due to the richness and occasional bountiful ambiguity of certain passages from Francis' writings some will be used more than once and in differing contexts. For example, a text that is used to discuss disorder may also have something to say about change, which bears a certain relationship to disorder.

3. See for instance: Francis of Assisi, *The Testament of St. Francis*, 67.

4. Francis of Assisi, *Letter to All the Faithful*, in Marion Habig, ed. *St. Francis of Assisi: Writings and Early Biographies: English Omnibus of Sources for the Life of St. Francis.* (Quincy, IL: Franciscan University Press, 1991), 95.

5. Ibid., 96.

6. Ibid., 95-96.

7. Francis of Assisi, *Religious Life in Hermitages*, in Marion Habig, ed. *St. Francis of Assisi: Writings and Early Biographies: English Omnibus of Sources for the Life of St. Francis.* (Quincy, IL: Franciscan University Press, 1991), 73.

8. Francis of Assisi, *The Rule of 1221*, 37.

9. Ibid., 38.

10. Ibid., 42. The image of giving a cloak, albeit scriptural in origin, stands out in Francis' legend as well as the source legend for much of his vita, the vita of St. Martin of Tours. Francis does use clothing as an image at various points in his writings. His earlier avocation as a clothe merchant may be as much of an inspiration to his use of such imagery as the Scriptural passages which resonate with his experience. Francis' attention to clothing imagery has a parallel in Aelred of Rievaulx's use of banqueting imagery.

11. Ibid., 43, 44.

12. Ibid., 50.

13. Ibid.

14. Ibid., 52.

15. Francis of Assisi, *The Blessing for Brother Leo*, in Marion Habig, ed. *St. Francis of Assisi: Writings and Early Biographies: English Omnibus of Sources for the Life of St. Francis.* (Quincy, IL: Franciscan University Press, 1991), 126.

16. Francis of Assisi, *The Canticle of Brother Sun*, in Marion Habig, ed. *St. Francis of Assisi: Writings and Early Biographies: English Omnibus of Sources for the Life of St. Francis.* (Quincy, IL: Franciscan University Press, 1991),130

17. Ibid.

18. Ibid.

19. Francis of Assisi, *Letter to All the Faithful*, 97; Francis of Assisi, *The Rule of 1221*, 38

20. Francis of Assisi, *Letter to the Rulers of the People*, 116; Francis of Assisi, *A Letter to the Rulers of the People (1220)*, in Regis J. Armstrong, J.A. Wayne Hellman, and William J. Short, eds. *Francis of Assisi: The Early Documents.* Vol. 1, *The Saint* (New York: New City Press, 1999), 58.

21. Thomas of Celano, *First Life*, in Marion Habig, ed. *St. Francis of Assisi: Writings and Early Biographies: English Omnibus of Sources for the Life of St. Francis.* (Quincy, IL: Franciscan University Press, 1991), 316.

22. See for instance Thomas of Celano, *First Life*, 231-233.

23. Armstrong et al, *Francis of Assisi: The Early Documents: The Saint*, 40.

24. Francis of Assisi, *The Prayer before the Crucifix (1205/06)*, in Regis J. Armstrong, J.A. Wayne Hellman, and William J. Short, eds. *Francis of Assisi: The Early Documents*. Vol. 1, *The Saint* (New York: New City Press, 1999), 40.

25. Francis of Assisi, *Letter to All the Faithful*, in Marion Habig, ed. *St. Francis of Assisi: Writings and Early Biographies: English Omnibus of Sources for the Life of St. Francis*. (Quincy, IL: Franciscan University Press, 1991), 97; The Armstrong et al translation places a similar notion, using servitude instead of slavery, in the *Earlier Exhortation*, which they separate from the *Letter to All the Faithful*. See Francis of Assisi, *Earlier Exhortation To the Brothers and Sisters of Penance (1209-1215)*, in Regis J. Armstrong, J.A. Wayne Hellman, and William J. Short, eds. *Francis of Assisi: The Early Documents*. Vol. 1, *The Saint* (New York: New City Press, 1999), 43.

26. Francis of Assisi, *Letter to All the Faithful* , 97.

27. Ibid. Note the contrast between spiritual blindness and visual perception of their own wrong-doings. Armstrong et al use the actual term "blind" in place of lacking spiritual insight.

28. Ibid. When deception is mentioned again in the *Later Admonition and Exhortation*, it is associated with people who "are blind because they do not see the true light, our Lord Jesus Christ." See Francis of Assisi, *Later Admonition and Exhortation*, in Regis J. Armstrong, J.A. Wayne Hellman, and William J. Short, eds. *Francis of Assisi: The Early Documents*. Vol. 1, *The Saint* (New York: New City Press, 1999), 50. The Latin text uses the three relevant words in a row to accentuate the point: *Videte Caeci decepti....* The Latin basis of deceive is *de* and *capio* which suggests that something is taken from the "deceived." In this case, it is the ability to see rightly. See Jean-Francois Godet and Georges Mailleux, *Corpus des Sources Franciscaines*, vol. 5, *Opuscula sancti Francisi, Scripta sanctae Clarae* (Louvain: Cetedoc, 1976), 85.

29. Francis of Assisi, *Earlier Exhortation, Francis of Assisi: Early Documents: The Saint*, 43.

30. Francis of Assisi, *Letter to All the Faithful*,94.

31. Recall that food and banqueting images were a primary tool of Aelred of Rievaulx.

32. Francis of Assisi, *Letter to All the Faithful*, 97.

33. Francis of Assisi, *Letter to All Clerics*, in Marion Habig, ed. *St. Francis of Assisi: Writings and Early Biographies: English Omnibus of Sources for the Life of St. Francis*. (Quincy, IL: Franciscan University Press, 1991), 101.

34. The New Oxford Annotated Bible (RSV) uses the term *folly* which suggests seeing something as foolish or at least somewhat out of context.

35. Francis of Assisi, *Letter to all Superiors of the Friars Minor*, in Marion Habig, ed. *St. Francis of Assisi: Writings and Early Biographies: English Omnibus of Sources for the Life of St. Francis*. (Quincy, IL: Franciscan University Press, 1991), 113.

36. Francis of Assisi, *The Rule of 1221*, 38.

37. For a description of the commercial changes taking place during Francis' timeframe see: Lester K. Little, *Religious Poverty and the Profit Economy in Medieval Europe* (Ithaca: Cornell University Press, 1978), 20-25.

38.Francis of Assisi, *The Rule of 1221*, 38.

39. Francis of Assisi, *The Earlier Rule, Francis of Assisi: Early Documents: The Saint*, 70.

40. Francis of Assisi, *Fragments (1209-1223)*, in Regis J. Armstrong, J.A. Wayne Hellman, and William J. Short, eds. *Francis of Assisi: The Early Documents*. Vol. 1, *The Saint* (New York: New City Press, 1999), 88.

41. Ibid., 89.

42. Armstrong et al, *Francis of Assisi: The Early Documents: The Saint*, 139.

43. Francis of Assisi, *The Office of the Passion,* in Marion Habig, ed. *St. Francis of Assisi: Writings and Early Biographies: English Omnibus of Sources for the Life of St. Francis.* (Quincy, IL: Franciscan University Press, 1991), 145.

44. Francis of Assisi, *The Office of the Passion,* in Regis J. Armstrong, J.A. Wayne Hellman, and William J. Short, eds. *Francis of Assisi: The Early Documents.* Vol. 1, *The Saint* (New York: New City Press, 1999), 145.

45. The terms *limit situation* or *limit conditions* will be used throughout the remainder of the text to refer loosely to both *limit-of experience* and *borderline situation.*

46. Francis of Assisi, *Letter to All the Faithful,* 97-98.

47. Ibid., 98.

48. Francis of Assisi, *Letter to All the Faithful,* 93.

49. Regis J. Armstrong, J.A. Wayne Hellman, and William J. Short, eds. *Francis of Assisi: The Early Documents.* Vol. 1, *The Saint,* 45, note D.

50. Francis of Assisi, *Letter to All the Faithful,* 98.

51. Ibid.

52. Armstrong et al, *Francis of Assisi: The Early Documents: The Saint,* 51, Note B. This translation includes only the elements of power, knowledge, and thought.

53. Francis of Assisi, *A Letter to the Rulers of the Peoples,* 116.

54. Francis of Assisi, *Letter to all Clerics,* 101.

55. Francis of Assisi, *Letter to a General Chapter,* in Regis J. Armstrong, J.A. Wayne Hellman, and William J. Short, eds. *Francis of Assisi: The Early Documents.* Vol. 1, *The Saint* (New York: New City Press, 1999), 119.

56. Francis of Assisi, *The Rule of 1221,* 52.

57. Francis of Assisi, *The Admonitions,* in Marion Habig, ed. *St. Francis of Assisi: Writings and Early Biographies: English Omnibus of Sources for the Life of St. Francis.* (Quincy, IL: Franciscan University Press, 1991), 78.

58. Francis of Assisi, *Fragments, Francis of Assisi: Early Documents: The Saint* 87.

59. Francis of Assisi, *The Canticle of the Creatures,* in Regis J. Armstrong, J.A. Wayne Hellman, and William J. Short, eds. *Francis of Assisi: The Early Documents.* Vol. 1, *The Saint* (New York: New City Press, 1999),114, note C.

60. Francis of Assisi, *The Canticle of Brother Suns,* in Marion Habig, ed. *St. Francis of Assisi: Writings and Early Biographies: English Omnibus of Sources for the Life of St. Francis.* (Quincy, IL: Franciscan University Press, 1991), 131.

61. Francis of Assisi, *The Testament of St. Francis,* in Marion Habig, ed. *St. Francis of Assisi: Writings and Early Biographies: English Omnibus of Sources for the Life of St. Francis.* (Quincy, IL: Franciscan University Press, 1991), 67.

62. Francis of Assisi, *The Office of the Passion,* 143.

63. The New Oxford Annotated Bible (RSV).

64. Francis of Assisi, *Letter to All the Faithful, 97, 94.*

65. Francis of Assisi, *Letter to all Clerics,* 101.

66. Francis of Assisi, *Letter to all Superiors of the Friars Minor, 113.*

67. Francis of Assisi, *Letter to the Rulers of the Peoples,* 116.

68. Ibid.

69. Francis of Assisi, *The Rule of 1221,* 31.

70. Ibid., 48-49.

71. Ibid., 50.

72. Ibid., 85.

73. Francis of Assisi, *The Rule of 1223,* in Marion Habig, ed. *St. Francis of Assisi: Writings and Early Biographies: English Omnibus of Sources for the Life of St. Francis.* (Quincy, IL: Franciscan University Press, 1991),64.

74. Francis of Assisi, *Canticle of Exhortation for the Ladies of San Damiano (1225),* in Regis J. Armstrong, J.A. Wayne Hellman, and William J. Short, eds. *Francis of Assisi: The Early Documents.* Vol. 1, *The Saint* (New York: New City Press, 1999), 115.

75. Francis of Assisi, *Letter to a General Chapter, 104.*

76. See for instance the Armstrong et al translation: Franics of Assisi, *A Letter to the Entire Order, Francis of Assisi: Early Documents: The Saint,* 116.

77. Francis of Assisi, *Letter to a General Chapter,* 105.

78. Ibid.

79. Ibid.

80. Ibid., 105-106.

81. Ibid., 108.

82. Francis of Assisi, *The Testament of St. Francis,* 125.

83. Francis of Assisi, *The Admonitions,* 79.

84. Ibid., 183-84.

85. Francis of Assisi, *The Paraphrase of the Our Father,* in Marion Habig, ed. *St. Francis of Assisi: Writings and Early Biographies: English Omnibus of Sources for the Life of St. Francis.* (Quincy, IL: Franciscan University Press, 1991), 159.

86. Michael Goodich has written an interesting article connecting medieval holiness with an unhealthy upbringing. He observes three patterns: "childhood neglect or deprivation, resentment against an absent or allegedly cruel father, and a period of emotional distress in late adolescence which is resolved through religious commitment." His findings, however, are suspect since he relies heavily on saints' vitae for anecdotal evidence for his patterns. These are the same vitae which are thoroughly patterned themselves, and since he is looking at mendicant models, most of these are derived from the tumultuous legends of Francis and Clare. See: Michael Goodich, "Childhood and Adolescence Among Thirteenth-Century Saints," *History of Childhood Quarterly* 1 (1973): 285-309.

87. Francis of Assisi, *Letter to All the Faithful,* 96. The Latin term used to specify spouse in this line is "Sponsi," which is the male spouse, rendering the role of the brothers that of the female spouse. Francis arranged this image with the maternal image but separated the two female images with the male image of brother, which upholds the idea that he sought to inculcate a very dynamic set of images for his brothers. For the Latin text see Godet and Mailleux, *Corpus des Sources Franciscaines,* 215.

88. Francis also identifies himself specifically with the maternal role in: Francis of Assisi, *Letter to Brother Leo,* 118. He says: "As a mother to her child, I speak to you, my son."

89. Francis of Assisi, *Letter to All the Faithful,* 96.

90. Ibid.

91. Ibid., 43. The image of the Devil's children is used several times throughout Francis writings, including: Francis of Assisi, *The Rule of 1221,* 47

92. Francis of Assisi, *Letter to All the Faithful,* 93.

93. Francis of Assisi, *Religious Life in Hermitages,* in Marion Habig, ed. *St. Francis of Assisi: Writings and Early Biographies: English Omnibus of Sources for the Life of St. Francis.* (Quincy, IL: Franciscan University Press, 1991), 72.

94. Ibid.

95. Ibid., 61-62. The inclusion of the minister and custodian seems to be a precautionary afterthought.

96. Ibid., 62

97. Francis of Assisi, *The Rule of 1221,* 31-32.

98. See Thomas of Celano, *The First Life of Saint Francis by Thomas of Celano,* 241.

99. Francis of Assisi, *The Office of the Passion,* 146.

100. Donald Spoto suggests that the renunciation was an act of *ars concionandi*, a technique used in secular or public dispute to make a point outside the range of rational proof. Nonetheless, the specific act chosen would require imagination. See Donald Spoto, *Reluctant Saint, The Life of Francis of Assisi,* 54. For an earlier reference to the *ars concionandi* see: Raoul Manselli, "Gesture as Sermon in St. Francis of Assisi," *Greyfriars Review* 6, no. 1 (1992): 39.

101. Francis of Assisi, *The Rule of 1221*, 49.

102. Ibid., 40.

103. Francis of Assisi, *The Rule of 1223*, 61-62.

104. Francis of Assisi, *The Admonition*, 78.

105. Francis of Assisi, *The Office of the Passion, 155.* Norbert Nguyên-Van-Khanh points out that "beloved son" is Francis' most significant title for Christ. See Norbert Nguyên-Van-Khanh, *The Teacher of his Heart: Jesus in the Thought and Writings of St. Francis*, trans. Ed Hagman (St. Bonaventure, New York: Franciscan Pathways, 1994), 133.

106. See Thomas of Celano, *The First Life of Saint Francis by Thomas of Celano*, 299-300.

107. Francis of Assisi, *The Rule of 1223*, 50-51.

108. Francis of Assisi, *The Office of the Passion,* 141.

109. Although there were some examples of women religious leading holy lives outside the enclosure Francis' esteem for and sense of honor regarding women may have provoked him into this course of action, all ecclesiastical pressure aside.

110. Francis of Assisi, *The Rule of 1223*, 64.

111. Francis of Assisi, *The Rule of 1221*, 42.

112. Ibid.; In the Armstrong et al translation the connection with devilish temptation is even more definitive. See Francis of Assisi, *The Earlier Rule, Francis of Assisi: Early Documents: The Saint,* 73.

113. Francis of Assisi, *The Praises of the Virtues,* in Marion Habig, ed. *St. Francis of Assisi: Writings and Early Biographies: English Omnibus of Sources for the Life of St. Francis.* (Quincy, IL: Franciscan University Press, 1991), 132-134. It could be argued that the virtues stand as a type for Mary in Francis' mind, but the fact that each virtue is sister to another virtue suggests that Francis is working with more than one female image for this text.

114. Francis of Assisi, *The Rule of 1221*, 52. It is the combination of these descriptors that gives the sense of a maternal image.

115. Francis of Assisi, *Letter to a General Chapter*, 104. The reference to children could reflect either a maternal or a paternal image. It is the notion of giving of oneself to children that suggests a more maternal distinction, as found in the Armstrong et al translation. See Francis of Assisi, *A Letter to the Entire Order,* in Regis J. Armstrong, J.A. Wayne Hellman, and William J. Short, eds. *Francis of Assisi: The Early Documents.* Vol. 1, *The Saint* (New York: New City Press, 1999), 117.

116. Francis of Assisi, *The Office of the Passion,* 143.

117. *Ibid.,* 152.

118. Spoto, 73.

119. This preponderance of writings for men is not a definitive indication of his greater interest in the men of the order versus the women. It is conceivable that he was involved in many aspects of the spiritual guidance of Clare's sisters. Clare's frequent references to Francis support this. At the same time, the sisters' had a very adept leader in Clare, who would have been more familiar with the specific trials and needs of those living the cloistered life.

120. Francis of Assisi, *The Rule of 1221*, 44.

121. Manselli suggests that gesture, as sermon, "operates on two levels, one intuitive and immediate, the other symbolic, evocative, didactic." See Manselli, 47.

122. Francis of Assisi, *The Rule of 1223*, 63.

123. Ibid., 60.

124. Ibid., 63.

125. Francis of Assisi, *The Later Rule*, in Regis J. Armstrong, J.A. Wayne Hellman, and William J. Short, eds. *Francis of Assisi: The Early Documents*. Vol. 1, *The Saint* (New York: New City Press, 1999),105, Note A.

126. Francis of Assisi, *Letter to All the Faithful, 97.*

127. Francis of Assisi, *The Rule of 1221*, 45.

128. Ibid., 41.

129. Francis of Assisi, *The Testament of St Francis*, 69.

130. Francis of Assisi, *The Admonitions*, 81.

131. Francis of Assisi, *The Rule of 1221*, 35.

132. Ibid., 35-36.

133. Ibid., 35.

134. Francis of Assisi, *Letter to a Minister,* in Marion Habig, ed. *St. Francis of Assisi: Writings and Early Biographies: English Omnibus of Sources for the Life of St. Francis.* (Quincy, IL: Franciscan University Press, 1991), 110.

135. Francis of Assisi, *The Rule of 1221, 38.*

136 .Ibid.

137. Ibid., 40. According to the editors of *Francis of Assisi: The Saint*, Francis takes this specific phrasing from Augustine, *Epistola* Cl. II, 40, iv, 4. He uses this reflexive orientation of concern in various places throughout his writing. See Armstrong et al, *Francis of Assisi: Early Documents: The Saint*, 71, note C.

138. Francis of Assisi, *Letter to Brother Leo*, 122.

139. Francis of Assisi, *Letter to All the Faithful*, 98.

140. Francis of Assisi, *The Rule of 1221*, 72.

141. Ibid., 52. The translation in Armstrong et al, *The Earlier Rule, Francis of Assisi: Early Documents: The Saint,* 85, indicates that nothing should stand between the brothers. The reference to nothing standing between us and God is less apparent.

142. Francis of Assisi, *Letter to a Minister*, 110.

143. In Francis' time it was not unusual for monks to be identified as "Christ's poor" or the "poor one's of Christ." Francis was among several other reformers who directed concern for the poor back onto those who tragically suffered from it.

144. Francis of Assisi, *The Rule of 1221*, 39.

145. Ibid., 39. In the very next line Francis acknowledges the value the poor have to the rich.

146. Francis of Assisi, *Fragments, Francis of Assisi: Early Documents: The Saint*, 89.

147. Francis of Assisi, *The Testament of St. Francis*, 67.

148. Francis of Assisi, *Letter to All the Faithful*, 93. In Armstrong et al a footnote to this reference points out that Kajetan Esser considers the sentence unclear due to punctuation problems. The fact that it contains a reference to all people living in the world and groups different categories of people is significant to the current analysis. See Armstrong et al, *Francis of Assisi: The Saint*, 45.

149. Francis of Assisi, *The Rule of 1221*, 51.

150. Ibid.

151. See Thomas of Celano, *The Life of Saint Francis of Assisi by Thomas of Celano: The Second Book, Francis of Assisi: Early Documents: The Saint*, 234. Also see Thomas

of Celano, *The Life of Saint Francis of Assisi by Thomas of Celano: The First Book, Francis of Assisi: Early Documents: The Saint,* 192.

152. For a thorough look at the canticle in which it is interwoven with so many other features of Francis' life and story see: Eloi LeClerc, *The Canticle of Creatures: Symbols of Union,* trans. Matthew J. O'Connell (Chicago: Franciscan Herald Press, 1977).

153. Francis of Assisi, *Letter to All the Faithful,* 97.

154. Francis of Assisi, *Exhortation to the Praise of God,* in Regis J. Armstrong, J.A. Wayne Hellman, and William J. Short, eds. *Francis of Assisi: The Early Documents.* Vol. 1, *The Saint* (New York: New City Press, 1999), 138.

155. Francis of Assisi, *The Office of the Passion, 155.*

156. Francis of Assisi, *The Praises Before the Office,* in Marion Habig, ed. *St. Francis of Assisi: Writings and Early Biographies: English Omnibus of Sources for the Life of St. Francis.* (Quincy, IL: Franciscan University Press, 1991), 138.

157. My emphasis on water may be coincidental since these are all passages from another source, but the presence of water is a common element to each passage that Francis chose in order to express his desire to show and bring about praise to God. It may have been the element that he used as a search criterion while working through the Scriptures. There is no shortage of theorists diagnosing Francis' ailments; perhaps he was suffering from a condition that included a great sense of thirst.

158. Francis of Assisi, *The Testament of St. Francis,* 68. There are six words in this English translation, and four in Armstrong et al, *Francis of Assisi: Early Documents: The Saint,* 125. The Latin requires only three, although the original phrase began with *et,* yielding a fourth word that is not used in the English translation. For the Latin text see Godet and Mailleux, *Corpus des Sources Franciscaines,* 163.

159. Francis of Assisi, *Letter to the Rulers of the Peoples,* 116.

160. Francis of Assisi, *The Rule of 1221,* 38.

161. Ibid.

162. Ibid.

163. Ibid., 38-39.

164. Ibid.

165. It is entirely possible that Francis was neither responsible for nor interested in dropping the body imagery in *The Rule of 1223,* but the tone of his reference to the body still changes in other later writings.

166. Francis of Assisi, *Letter to All the Faithful,* 95. Armstrong et al use a more direct reference to body. See Francis of Assisi, *Earlier Exhortation, Francis of Assisi: Early Documents: The Saint,* 43.

167. Ibid., 97.

168. Ibid., 98.

169. Ibid., 95.

170. Ibid., 96.

171. Francis of Assisi, *The Rule of 1221,* 35.

172. Ibid., 36.

173. Ibid., 43.

174. Ibid., 42.

175. Ibid., 45.

176. Ibid.

177. Francis of Assisi, *The Admonitions,* 82.

178. Ibid.

179. Francis of Assisi, *The Rule of 1221,* 32.

180. Ibid., 40. Armstrong et al identify the connection with Gratian. See Armstrong et al, *The Earlier Rule, Francis of Assisi: Early Documents: The Saint,* 71, from *Decretum Gratiani* P. II, C.q. 1 glossa ante c. 40.

181. Francis of Assisi, *Letter to All the Faithful,* 97.

182. Ibid., 96.

183. Francis of Assisi, *The Rule of 1221,* 44.

184. Ibid., 50.

185. Francis of Assisi, *The Admonitions,* 80.

186. Francis of Assisi, *The Rule of 1221,* 52.

187. Francis of Assisi, *The Admonitions,* 78.

188. Francis of Assisi, *The Paraphrase of the Our Father,* 160.

189. Francis of Assisi, *The Praises of the Virtues,* 134. In point of fact, there are other bodily related images in Francis' writings. In particular, there are several images related to how the body is clad, however, these images will be held back until the final chapter where they will be considered under the topic of *meaning.*

190. Francis of Assisi, *The Canticle of Brother Sun,* in Marion Habig, ed. *St. Francis of Assisi: Writings and Early Biographies: English Omnibus of Sources for the Life of St. Francis.* (Quincy, IL: Franciscan University Press, 1991), 130; Armstrong et al, *Francis of Assisi: The Early Documents: The Saint,* 114, Note A.

191. Armstrong et al, *Francis of Assisi: The Early Documents: The Saint,* 113, Note D.

192. See Francis of Assisi, *The Canticle of Brother Sun,* 130.

193. Ibid.

194. Another possible interpretation of this line is more etymological. The room for interpretation is due to the use of an early Italian dialect for the original version. Francis wrote: *"et nullu Homo ene Dignu Te mentovare." Mentovare* has been popularly translated as *mention* based on the Latin root *mentio.* An alternative approach would be to consider a derivative of *mentis* or *mente* for mind and *vario* or *varus* for altering or deviating. This would yield: to change the mind or change the idea. The resulting translation might be closer to: and no human being is worthy to think differently of or about you. Of course this only holds if Francis used *Te* loosely. For the early Italian text see Godet and Mailleux, *Corpus des Sources Franciscaines,* 154.

195. Francis of Assisi, *The Canticle of Brother Sun, 130.*

196. Ibid., 130-131. See also the Armstrong et al translation: Francis of Assisi, *The Canticle of the Creatures, Francis of Assisi: Early Documents: The Saint,* 114.

197. Francis of Assisi, *The Canticle of Brother Sun,* 131. See also Armstrong et al, *Francis of Assisi: Early Documents: The Saint,* 114, note B, and the introduction to *The Canticle of the Creatures,* page 113. My emphasis on conformity to the will of God allows a sense of continuity between the ideas expressed in Note D on page 113 and Note B on page 114.

198. Francis of Assisi, *The Canticle of Brother Sun,* 130-131.

199. Ibid., 131.

200. Armstrong et al, *Francis of Assisi: The Early Documents: The Saint,* 113, Note C.

201. Francis of Assisi, *The Canticle of Brother Sun, 131.*

202. Ibid., 130. Although lowly might not seem to be a positive descriptor, when taken as humble it seems less derogatory.

203. Ibid., 131. The guidance and discipline is suggested through her sovereignty.

204. Armstrong et al, *Francis of Assisi, Early Documents: The Saint,* 113. See the introductory paragraph.

CHAPTER SEVEN
CHANGE, FAITH, AND THE IMAGE OF GOD: THE IMAGINATION OF FRANCIS OF ASSISI

This chapter will analyze Francis' use of imagery in his writings where these images touch on two broad areas that are central to the fashioning of a spiritual view of life. The kind of spirituality expressed in Francis' writings is not a retreat from the experiences of reality. As this entire work attempts to show, his spirituality sought to embrace experience and imaginatively fashion a sense of meaning that places reality into a new, expansive perspective. As this is the case, various degrees of change will be considered in order to reflect the movement into a more meaning-driven relationship with reality in its created, interpreted, and God-given spiritual dimensions. Once this is accomplished, there will be a turn to the ultimate object of Francis' imaginative activity, faith and the image of God. Faith will be discussed as a development of the earliest trusting relationship, and various images of God will be sown together from the saint's writings to substantiate the Object Relations Theory claim that numerous object representations interact in the transitional space to form an ever-evolving vision of significant objects, such as God.

Change, Transformation, and Transcendence

A study of Francis inevitably touches on his ability to bring about change. After all, he is a religious reformer. The present study is less about the actual changes he is able to cause and more about the workings of his imagination that enable him to fashion images of a world that calls people to transform their way of seeing and pushes them to transcend their way of *being*. Initially, Francis' recognition of the presence of change as a feature of the spiritual life will be considered. Following this, his writings will be culled for examples of the kind of transformative life he envisions, and finally there will be a review of expressions of the individual's ability to transcend his or her perception of a personal state of being in the world.

ORT, with its ability to explain artistic creativity, has been shown to say much about the various forms of change, and play is at the origin of change. Winnicott indicates that play allows a person to modify the environment since it involves action in time and place, but while the individual is changing his or her personal environment the environment is, in turn, having a similar effect on the person. At the same moment that Francis is imaginatively altering the way he and others envision the world as both physical and spiritual, he is also revealing the way in which a changed perception can influence who and what we come to see ourselves as. Pruyser has demonstrated the importance of making illusion socially communicable. To the degree that Francis is successful at getting others to visualize a world in which it is preferable to be impoverished and outcast, he is a facilitator of a transformative lifestyle. Setting a new world view in this manner adjusts civilization by forcing it to adapt to a new series of rules, guidelines, and most of all, images. Pruyser also surmises that the new images are formed through illusion processing, the building of new images from aspects of existing images. At the heart of this process is one motivation that Francis is familiar with: desire. Change will be seen as well in its relationship with another driving force, the ideal of perfection.

Akin to Winnicott's view, Pruyser makes the connection between a change in the subject and a change in the subject's perception. Both Pruyser and Bollas note that there are specific internal objects that bring about change. Francis' object-image of the body and blood of Christ in the Eucharist and his various images of God are examples of such transformational and transcendent objects. McDargh identifies altering states of a sense of merger and then individuation as the individual moves toward a transcendence of the current state of self-being. It should be noted that Francis' advancement of a strong sense of individuality with attendant responsibilities has the effect of increasing the movement toward transcendence. McDargh and Rizzuto both add to this the impact of how one believes oneself to be perceived by others. At times this could be the state that one transcends, and at other times it is the objective state to be achieved through transcendence. Furthermore, Rizzuto concludes that, over time, one's God-images change in connection with a change of self.

Change

One of Francis' earliest writings verifies his awareness of the need for change in order to pursue the spiritual life. This exigency can be found in *The Prayer before the Crucifix*, where he cries to God: "enlighten the darkness of my heart and give me true faith, certain hope, perfect charity, sense and knowledge, Lord, that I may carry out Your holy and true command."[1] In the much later-dated *Letter to a General Chapter,* he expresses a similar idea: "cleansed and enlightened interiorly and fired with the ardour of the Holy Spirit, we may be able to follow in the footsteps of your Son, our Lord Jesus Christ, and so make our way to you."[2] These two passages point toward one of Francis' most prominent images of change, a journey involving a rite of passage. Like the concept of play described by Winnicott, there is a movement across space and time that leads to a transformative encounter of self with other. As a rite of passage this journey involves numerous challenges. In *The Rule of 1221* Francis uses a Scriptural image to advance the idea, saying: "They must strive to enter by the narrow gate, because in the words of the Gospel, How narrow the gate and close the way that leads to life! And few there are who find it."[3] Francis also captures the imagination with his description of a barrier in the path to communion with God. He commands that, "You should consider everything that makes it difficult for you to love God as a special favour, even if other persons, whether friars or not, are responsible for it, or even if they go so far as to do you physical violence."[4] Recalling that the solitude of an eremitical life in the wilderness was a typical source of transformation in medieval literature, it is only natural that Francis uses the image of a hermitage, not as a location but as an obstacle in one's path that must be embraced rather than avoided. He adds after the last passage: "You must love those who behave like this towards you.... This should be of greater benefit to you than the solitude of a hermitage."[5]

While offering such sound guidance for perseverance on the journey, Francis is acutely aware of the reality that spiritual change can be thwarted. In a *Letter to St Anthony*, he insists that Anthony should not allow academic study to "extinguish the spirit of prayer and devotedness...."[6] Nonetheless, Francis is certain that change is possible in one's relationship with God, and, therefore, others can and must be brought along on the journey. In the *Letter to a General Chapter* he claims that, "This is the very reason he has sent you all over the world, so that by word and deed you might bear witness to his message and convince everyone that there is no other almighty God besides him."[7]

References to time are a further indication that Francis associates change with imaginative conceptions, for time is an imaginatively derived means of measuring passing instances of experience. When describing the earlier-mentioned limit of death, Francis portrays the mystery-bound aspect of future-time. He remarks that, "You imagine that you will enjoy the worthless pleasures of this life indefinitely, but you are wrong. The day and the hour will come, the day and the hour for which you have no thought and of which you have no knowledge whatever. First sickness, then death, draws near."[8] Of course what Francis is trying to do is get his listener to imagine this moment in time as a very real and very significant juncture point at which everything changes, and yet, little else can change beyond that point. To add to the impact, he raises the notion of time, again, as a means of comparison. He conveys that the individual "loses both body and soul in this short life and goes to hell, where he will be tormented without end."[9] The distinction between time in this world and time afterward is important. The current time signifies the possibility of change, and the post-death time, time "without end," is the loss of this possibility.

In the *Letter to the Rulers of the People* the image of time takes on a kind of personification. Where Francis writes: "Consider and realize that the day of death is approaching," one might envision an advancing opponent, seeking to make a confrontation prior to one's attainment of a specified goal.[10] Here, Francis is attempting to alter memories by bringing God back into them. He adds, "I therefore beg of you with all the respect I am capable of that you do not forget God or swerve from his commandments because of the cares and anxieties of this world which you have to shoulder. For all who forget him and turn away from his commandments shall be forgotten by him."[11] It is time that breeds forgetfulness and finally delivers the fate of the forgetful. The symbolism of a time-expression, a day, takes on wider meaning as Francis uses it in a development of a Scriptural passage. He warns, "Take heed to yourselves, lest your hearts be overburdened with self-indulgence and drunkeness and the cares of this life, and that day come upon you suddenly as a snare."[12] It is the day, acting like a violent person, who will bring about change. Fortunately, not all of Francis' time imagery is connected with suffering a death. Later in *The Rule of 1221* he formulates a space and time-continuum that relates an on-going arrangement for praising God. He proclaims, "At all times and seasons, in every country and place, every day and all day, we must have a true and humble faith, and keep him in our hearts."[13] In a reversal of previous usage, time is now a stabilizing entity. It appears that Francis is using two images of time. The one conception occurs in the physical world and winds down to the moment of physical death. The other conception of time is less about change and more about continuity. In so far as one operates according to this latter time, by, for instance, believing, holding in our hearts, and loving God, one is also subject to the second, eternal, time. Francis uses other formulae of continuity to pass on the image of permanence in relationship to God, such as: "But deliver us from evil: present, past, or future," or the line that some renditions add subsequently: "Glory be to the Father, and to the Son, and to the Holy Spirit. As it was in the beginning, is now, and will be forever."[14] The second example seems to be a favorite of his since he repeats it elsewhere, although his use of the phrase may have also been an effort to adhere to custom.[15] In a final example of particular interest from an ORT perspective, Francis uses a woman as the model of constancy in a relationship with God. He writes of Mary: "On you descended and in you still remains all the fullness of grace and every good."[16] While this discussion on change has diverted to a discourse on continuity, it clearly serves to point out Francis' usage of time to reflect a physical world of change and a spiritual world where there is no change. His employment of both concepts in his writings is further indication of his ability to perceive the world according to both its physical and spiritual dimensions.

Transformation

Under the heading of transformation, change will be observed in terms of lifestyle in Francis' writings. Living according to the Spirit and living in penance are the operable terms that refer to a lifestyle redirected toward God. As such, change can be traced from its origins to its results. Following a brief consideration of states prior to and after transformation it will additionally be possible to consider the agency of change, specifically: who is able to bring one into or away from the penitential life? For Francis, change is predominantly something that occurs in reference to the condition of one's humanity as a result of the choices one makes. This is generally a clear-cut distinction; one either alters one's life for the better or for the worse. There is no in-process middle ground. The *Letter to All the Faithful* uses an individual's orientation to the light of God to express transformation in the wrong direction. People who become "slaves of the word and of the desires of their lower nature, with all the cares and anxieties of this life," are said to be "...blind, because they cannot see the true light."[17]

Most of the transformation imagery is related in some way to salvation. Francis uses a scriptural version of the light and darkness opposition in conjunction with a flavor description to indicate a choice against the lifestyle of someone earnestly seeking salvation. He notes in the *Letter to All the Faithful* that, "All those who refuse to taste and see how good the Lord is and who love the darkness rather than the light are under a curse."[18] This transformative orientation is also depicted as a downward movement in space. *The Rule of 1221* contains the idea briefly: "It was through our own fault that we fell."[19] Similar to this is the upward mobility which an individual seeks for him or herself. In *The Admonitions* Francis forewarns: "Woe to that religious who, after he has been put in a position of authority by others, is not anxious to leave it of his own free will."[20] A more acceptable upward movement is contained in a scriptural prayer for *Prime* where the movement involves raising praise toward God. Francis recalls Psalm 57: "Awake, O my soul; awake, lyre and harp! I will wake the dawn. I will give thanks to you among the peoples, O Lord, I will chant your praise among nations." (Ps 57:8-9).[21]

While most people brought up in the Catholic tradition think of penance as an action involved in the forgiveness of a sin, Francis' use of the term encompasses an entire lifestyle dedicated toward turning away from sin in favor of God. For those who do not embrace the transformative potential of this lifestyle Francis reveals their fate in *The Rule of 1221*: "Woe to those who die unrepentant; they shall be children of the devil whose work they do, and they shall go into everlasting fire."[22] Prior to this condemnation, however, he points toward the result of the preferred existence: "It is well for those who die repentant; they shall have a place in the kingdom of heaven."[23] Note that the final change is not so much taking up or neglecting the lifestyle; it is ultimately the salvation or damnation that ensues from this prior willful change. In the same text, Francis describes some of the actions that might precede the final transformation. He suggests that one should "put away every attachment, all care and solicitude, and serve, love, honour, and adore our Lord and God with a pure heart and mind; this is what he seeks above all else."[24] In *The Paraphrase of the Our Father,* Francis goes further in describing a complete transformation of one's spiritual orientation that might be involved in penance: "That we may love You with our whole heart by always thinking of you; with our whole mind by directing our whole intention towards you and seeking your glory in everything; and with all our strength by spending all our energies and affections of soul and body in the service of you alone."[25]

It is in the nature of a transformative lifestyle, as Francis depicts it, that there are three primary agents of change: the individual in question, another person, or an entity from the spiritual world, usually either God or the devil. A preponderance of the onus for transformation rests upon the individual since the denial or giving up of one's own will is a central trait of the kind of transformation Francis ultimately has in mind. In the *Letter to All the Faithful* he presents his vision of what a person must do in order to initiate the change of his or her orientation completely toward God. This text includes a lengthy prescription for change, but some of the highlights include: "We should praise him and pray to him day and night," and "We should confess all our sins to a priest and receive from him the Body and Blood of our Lord Jesus Christ," or "we must bring forth fruits befitting repentance."[26] Further examples include: "We must be charitable, too, and humble, and give alms, because they wash the stains of sin from our souls," and "We should visit churches often and show great reverence for the clergy."[27] The recurrent use of *habemus*, "let us," or "we should" and *debemus*, "we must," is fitting for the kind of text in which this prescription is found. As an admonition or exhortation, the purpose is to guide, goad, lead, or encourage an individual toward the transformation of his or her ways but not as a means of force. While "must" is stronger wording than "let," it is not commanding in the sense of "You will!"[28] The result of choosing to "endure to the last" in the lifestyle established by these various courses of action is that "the *Spirit of God...* will make his dwelling place in them and there he will stay, and they will be children of your Father in heaven whose work they do."[29] Using, now, familiar words in another passage, Francis describes what changes are necessary for an individual to gain a strong image of Jesus in his or her imagination. A *Letter to the Rulers of the Peoples* includes the lines: "Put away all worry and anxiety and receive the holy Body and Blood of our Lord Jesus Christ fervently in memory of him."[30]

Francis makes it clear that other people can have some role in the transformation of another person's lifestyle. In *The Letter to all the Superiors of the Friars Minor* he instructs the leaders of his order: "In all your sermons you shall tell the people of the need to do penance, impressing on them that no one can be saved unless he receives the Body and Blood of our Lord."[31] Francis also urges the use of admonition to redirect brothers, regardless of rank, back into the spiritual life of the order. He commands: "If they see that any of them [ministers and servants] is leading a worldly and not a religious life, as the perfection of our life demands, they should warn him three times. Then, if he has failed to amend, they must denounce him to the minister General, who is the servant of the whole order, at the Chapter of Pentecost..."[32] Under the same chapter heading Francis adds: "If a friar is clearly determined to live according to the flesh and not according to the spirit, no matter where he is, the others are bound to warn, instruct and correct him with humble charity."[33]

The individual's choice to follow or fall off the pathway of a lifestyle of penance is at the center of a heated struggle between God and the devil that is imaginatively expressed by Francis. Both participants in this fight seek to bring the traveler in their direction and on their preferred route. Francis provides several images in which either God or the devil stands out as an agent of change. In the *Letter to All Clerics,* Francis declares, "Surely we cannot be left unmoved by loving sorrow for all this; in his love, God gives himself into our hands; we touch him and receive him daily into our mouths."[34] Noting the rivaling tension, Francis writes, in *The Rule of 1221,* "All the friars, both the ministers, who are servants, and their subjects, should be careful not to be upset or angry when anyone falls into sin or gives bad example; the devil would be only too glad to ensnare many others through one man's sin."[35] The saint also points out that the devil would seek to alter the imagination of brothers who begin to slip from a penitential life. He explains that, "We should have no more use or regard for money in any of its forms than for dust. Those who think it is worth more or who are greedy for it, expose themselves to the danger of being deceived by the devil."[36] To fortify the brothers against this and similar challenges, Francis reveals an image of Jesus and Mary enduring the same difficulties, following the same path, as it were. Francis offers this advice for the brothers who must seek alms: "they should not be ashamed to beg alms, remembering that our Lord Jesus Christ, the Son of the living, all-powerful God set his face like a very hard rock and was not ashamed. He was poor and he had no home of his own and he lived on alms, he and the Blessed Virgin and his disciples."[37] Note the opposition of images used here: all powerful divinity versus poor beggar. This last paragraph, in particular, indicates the presence of strong images that are necessary to sustain a person throughout a life of penance. Next, the inner dynamic of a transformed life will be considered as a type of change called transcendence.

Transcendence

As the earlier discussions of imagination theories pointed out, transcendence, in its subjective dimension, is primarily concerned with a change in the way one perceives oneself in relationship to the way one perceives other aspects of reality. It is a matter of surpassing, for the better, the way a person visualizes things in relationship to him or herself. Normally it would be difficult to enter a historical consideration of a concept, like the self, which has so many contemporary developments and nuances, but this topic is no stranger to a long tradition of religious and philosophical inquiry into the nature and formation of the human person. Francis' strong distinction between the individual and God adds leverage to a look at this subject during the saint's time frame. To get at the heart of the inner dynamic that is occurring in the transcendence of a self-connected worldview, passages in Francis' texts will be analyzed that exhibit a range in self-awareness, including distorted perceptions of self, and intentionally altered perceptions of self. Then, the topic of obedience will be looked at as a form of discipline of the self. Finally, the shift in perception of the self will be aligned with the act of turning one's will over to a higher power, God.

Francis is clearly aware of how people manipulate the way they envision themselves, given the chance. In *The Rule of 1221* he writes: "as our Lord says, they must give no thought even to the slightest faults of others, but rather count over their own in the bitterness of their soul."[38] Although this insight has its origins in monastic formation and the Scriptures, Francis is able to use it to turn the consideration of spiritual condition back in upon oneself. The reader is, in effect, told to let go of the image of another as sinful and focus on the image of oneself as sinful and in need of change. From Pruyser's understanding of illusion processing, this would head off the danger of projecting features of a negative self-image onto another, resulting in burying the need to confront and overcome whatever is impeding a more realistic sense of self. Other features of Pruyser's notion of illusion processing may also come into play, especially introjection and incorporation, in which some external entity plays strongly in the formation of an image of self. Francis' stance against grasping for (necessarily external) material possessions is evident when he conveys that, "We must be firmly convinced that we have nothing of our own, except our vices and sins."[39] Since he precedes this exclamation with the warning "do not rejoice in this, that the spirits are subject to you," it seems clear that he is preparing people for a new basis of self perception.[40] He offers contrasting images that can be added into the soup of images found in the transitional sphere out of which a new, derivative image of the self will emerge. He instructs some missionary brothers to "be therefore wise as serpents, and guileless as doves."[41]

Beyond directing the attention of his followers away from the disparagement of other sinners, he also turns them from too much concern over those leading a soft lifestyle. In *The Rule of 1223* he writes: "I warn all the friars and exhort them not to condemn or look down on people whom they see wearing soft or gaudy clothes and enjoying luxuries in food and drink; each one should rather condemn and despise himself."[42] The kind of jealousy this guidance could unseat is the type that, today, might be associated with the erection of ego defense mechanisms, a constraint on both relationship and change. Francis' *Testament* contains other images that support his effort to put aside images of self that are dependent on a self-limiting series of relationships. He recalls quite plainly: "We made no claim to learning and we were submissive to everyone."[43] When advising against the acceptance of property, Francis insists: "they should occupy these places only as strangers and pilgrims."[44] Unlike the monastic way of life, there would be no tying of one's identity to a physical location.

Francis is also aware that a person can begin to assimilate elements of a divine personality to his or her own in such a fashion that the resultant image of self might begin to eclipse the necessarily over-riding perception of God as a distinct reality external to that person. Referring to people who believe that they "knew everything," or for whom "the things of heaven were an open book," or who "received from God a special revelation of the highest wisdom," he writes "you could not boast of it. But there is one thing of which we can all boast; we can boast of our humiliations."[45] By rightfully attributing all things that are good to God, Francis is sustaining the image of God as something worthy of relinquishing oneself to. He sets this distinction fairly clear when he explains: "We can be sure that a man is a true religious and has the spirit of God if his lower nature does not give way to pride when God accomplishes some good through him, and if he seems all the more worthless and inferior to others in his own eyes. Our lower nature is opposed to every good."[46] While these words might not resonate well with a generation bent on lifting popular esteem, they reveal a very important point that spans the ages. A healthy sense of self, one that can engage in meaningful relationships, cannot emerge from an empty background where self-supporting images are likely to collapse when put under a load. Good personal value is dependent on a solid structure of relatedness, and Francis is going to ensure that his followers don't build their identities with faulty material.

A final note on the general awareness of self touches on an idea that McDargh has raised. He indicated the connection between the formation of a good sense of self and being seen as one truly is in the eyes of another. Who we are, from an ORT standpoint, is highly dependent on the amalgamation of object representations formed from our perception of the way we perceive others perceiving us. Francis wishes to make one of these perceptions primary. He asserts that, "what a man is before God, that he is and no more."[47] This is the self perception that Francis seems to be guiding people toward.

Transcendence requires careful scrutiny of how one views oneself and the possibilities of other ways of envisioning who one could be. To make the move from present perception to potential perception is not an easy step. Francis uses a term, *obedientia*, obedience, that can be seen to refer to the discipline necessary to bring about change at the level of personal connectedness. He says, specifically, "Be well disciplined then and patient under holy obedience, keeping your promises to him generously and unflinchingly."[48] This discussion of obedience will consider two aspects of the subject as it is present in Francis' writings: what obedience is, and how it is carried out.

In *The Canticle of Exhortation for the Ladies of San Damiano*, Francis ties obedience to the way one goes about life. He writes: "Live always in truth, that you may die in obedience."[49] Francis avoids giving a strict definition of obedience, preferring to exemplify it in person and in word, but he offers some hints in this passage. It is tied to the way one *lives*, therefore, it is probably nearly synonymous with living in penance. This lifestyle should be maintained *always*, so obedience demands persistence and perseverance. Since this life has to be lived in *truth*, it involves clearing away one's vision of and relationship to all that is not real. Finally, obedience is a state that is preparatory to the final instance of change, *death*. Obedience is also a personal sacrifice that exposes an individual to various forms of suffering. Scarry's contributions should be brought to mind on this issue. She indicated that suffering fosters imaginative creativity, which can, in turn, propel change. In *The Rule of 1221* Francis reminds his brothers: "No matter where they are, the friars must always remember that they have given themselves up completely and handed over their whole selves to our Lord Jesus Christ, and so they should be prepared to expose themselves to every enemy, visible or invisible, for love of him."[50] This intentional vulnerability may work to overcome the absolutizing fear that can stunt the imagination and its motivation of change, as Lynch pointed out. Francis follows his reminder with a series of scriptural images of suffering and persecution, at the end of which he adds: "I say to you my friends: Do not be afraid of those who kill the body, and after that have nothing more they can do. Take care that you do not be alarmed. By your patience you will win your souls. He who has persevered to the end will be saved."[51] Obedience, it seems, is, in part, training against spirit-weakening fear. Francis is more direct on what obedience is not, noting that obedience is something that can be misused. He declares that, "A friar is not bound to obey if a minister commands anything that is contrary to our life or his own conscience, because there can be no obligation to obey if it means committing sin."[52]

Obedience is a matter of taking some control over desire and redirecting it toward something more worthy. Desire that is freely allowed to attach itself without careful deliberation is a danger to a clearer vision of reality and the ability to relate effectively within that reality. As the discussion of obedience moves into a consideration of how it is brought about, Francis offers more insights. It involves a shift in desire away from one's own personal interest, and it calls for seeing-as. In *The Rule of 1221* Francis writes that, "I beg the friar who is sick to thank God for everything; he should be content to be as God wishes him to be, in sickness or in health, because it is those who are destined for eternal life that God instructs by sickness and the spirit of compunction."[53] The suggestion that sickness be embraced as a pedagogical sign of God's favor is a case of seeing-as. In the same document, Francis explains why desire is meant to be redirected toward God. Using terms that might, more naturally apply to a maternal figure he describes God as: "kind, lovable, delightful and utterly desirable beyond all else for ever and ever."[54] There is, then, no more natural being to whom to attach desire.

In *A Letter to the Entire Order*, Francis brings together desire and a channeling of the will toward God for the purpose of retaining an image of Jesus. The saint exclaims: "With the help of God's grace, their whole intention should be fixed upon him, with a will to please the most high Lord alone, because it is he alone who accomplishes this marvel in his own way. He told us, Do this in remembrance of me."[55] The Eucharist, to which the words attributed to Jesus refer, becomes a conditioning device, enabling the consecrating priest and those who share his intentions to associate their desire with God's in an action that leads to a very visible manifestation of Christ's grace-endowed presence in their midst. This is also a situation of supportive reasoning which Francis gives for maintaining an attitude of obedience. The notion of placing one's desire at the pleasure of God is apparently so important to Francis that he includes it again in the prayer that concludes this text. He asks: "Almighty, eternal, just and merciful God, grant us in our misery that we may do for your sake alone what we know you want us to do, and always want what pleases you."[56]

The Rule of 1221 contains another example of disciplining the way one perceives things. Francis paradoxically remarks that, "our friends are those who for no reason cause us trouble and suffering, shame or injury, pain or torture, even martyrdom and death, but he goes on to clarify: "It is these we must love, and love very much, because for all they do to us we are given eternal life."[57] Seeing such people as a benefit to oneself certainly calls on a kind of end-game submission in which it is the final result that specifies and justifies the imaginatively-conceived prior relationship. It is the paradoxical world view of Jesus, filtered through Francis' eyes, that sets many of the rules and boundaries operating within obedience, according to an outlook of obedience. *The Admonitions* contain a similar situation that also serves to clarify that a life of obedience begins under the training of a religious superior. Francis observes: "A man takes leave of all that he possesses and loses both his body and his life when he gives himself up completely to obedience in the hands of his superior. Any good that he says or does which he knows is not against the will of his superior is true obedience."[58] Obedience entails the first state of detachment from physical possessions and images of self, as implied by the loss of body. In the following line, Francis adds the *seeing-as* feature of obedience: "A subject may realize that there are many courses of action that would be better and more profitable to his soul than what his superior commands. In that case he should make an offering of his own will to god, and do his best to carry out what the superior has enjoined. This is true and loving obedience which is pleasing to God and one's neighbor."[59]

While there is a certain amount of honor in seeing a personally challenging obedient act as a sacrifice offered to God, another image that Francis presents is less satisfying, and that may be his intent. Speaking of his superior, he writes in *The Testament of St. Francis*: "I want to be a captive in his hands so that I cannot travel about or do anything against his command or desire, because he is my superior."[60] This image of obedience, as imprisonment, does not just confine the body but also the desire. It is Francis' way of leading others to a last stage of relinquishment of their usual attachments.

A final reference to obedience, that traces its development in an individual, occurs in *The Admonitions*. Francis proclaims: "Blessed that religious who takes blame, accusation, or punishment from another patiently as if it were coming from himself."[61] Here he connects it with self-correction, a first step. Next, Francis adds: "Blessed the religious who obeys quietly when he is corrected, confesses his fault humbly and makes atonement cheerfully."[62] There is, now, a reduction of defenses against the imposition of an external will. The saint, then, concludes: "Blessed the religious who is in no hurry to make excuses, but accepts the embarrassment and blame for some fault he did not commit."[63] In this end stage, the life of obedience under the guidance of another has enabled a person to so fully release the attempt to control, protect, or manipulate his or her self perception such that justly and unjustly imposed criticism are accepted as one in the same. In parallel with this process of development is one or more of a series of changes in self-perception leading up to a final transformation that, when significant in nature and positively directed, might be called an experience of transcendence.

To observe this shift in self-perception it must be understood that there is a difference between a "let's make pretend" way of imagining something to be and a true seeing-as. In the first case there is the intention of retaining the former viewpoint in reserve in order to fall back upon it in short order when playfulness comes to an end. In the latter case, the investment in the new vision is more thorough. Something has changed on a very personal, very interior, level. The individual, so-to-speak, buys into the new perception. This occurs by a shift in the person's will, which is why the elements of obedience and desire are so significant. The will, with its closest associate and greatest nemesis, desire, becomes attached to and aligned with the central feature and/or source of the new way of seeing. The result is not a hallucination. All the same features of collective reality are still present; they are simply seen in a new light, and the altered outlook is not necessarily permanent. This is where the will comes in. The perception of reality, and one's relationship to it, after the transcendent experience, is governed by the attachment of the will to that central feature. This attachment and alignment can be strong, or it can be lost altogether, in which case, there will be change in the individual's outlook again.

Francis' writings very definitively recognize the importance of the alignment of the will to sustain the spiritual life and vision. He alludes to this fact in his very first recorded work, *The Prayer before the Crucifix*. He ends his petition for personal change with the words: "that I may carry out Your holy and true command."[64] In the *Letter to All the Faithful*, he provides the image of Jesus offering his will to God: "Yet he bowed to his Father's will and said, Father, thy will be done; yet not as I will, but as thou willest."[65] Francis immediately follows this line with a portrayal of Jesus' life and purpose as a sacrifice. He goes so far as to call this an "example" to "follow."[66] In this text, Francis links a transfer of will with a new basis of perception, and then urges others to follow suit. In *The Rule of 1221* Francis uses the idea of denying oneself in order to follow "the teaching and footprints of our Lord Jesus Christ," which is tantamount to sharing in his vision.[67] It can be supposed that denying oneself refers to a giving up one's will. This yields a perception of self associated with "perfection," since Francis includes the scriptural passage: "If you wish to be perfect, go, sell everything you have and give it to the poor," followed by the injunction to hate all one's relations and even one's own life (Mt 19:21; Lk 14:26). This is, in the end, a view of perfection free from the usual willful attachments to self.

At several points in his writings Francis attempts to form, for his readers, various types of images of a total transfer of will to God. In *The Rule of 1221* he places the image of this surrender against the emptiness that stands outside this relationship: "We should wish for nothing else and have no other desire; we should find no pleasure or delight in anything except in our Creator, Redeemer, and Saviour."[68] In *A Letter to a General Chapter*, Francis extends the idea that his followers will receive the will of God in exchange for giving up their own. He urges them to, "Keep nothing of yourselves, so that he who has given himself wholly to you may receive you wholly."[69] It is suspected that the total giving of self involves the will in both cases without the suggestion that anyone else gain control of God's will but merely gains access to it in the sense of a clearer perception of how God animates and intends the activity of creation. This conception is confirmed by another image in the same text. Referring to the saying of the Clerical Office, Francis urges his prelates not to concentrate "on the melody of the chant, but being careful that their hearts are in harmony so their words may be in harmony with their hearts and their hearts with God."[70] Although he is speaking about one small piece of reality, the musical image of an alignment of wills gives a good sense of his understanding that particulars (the melody) must be seen or heard in the context of the broader reality (God's score).

The idea of being in harmony with God makes a nice image, and images are great for fashioning the big picture, providing guiding perceptions, and sustaining relatedness, but they tend to be a little loose on exact details. If a brother was sent out on a journey with no other instruction than to walk in harmony with God, it might be a very interesting trip, but it is uncertain how a personal sense of harmony with God will advance the mission of Christ in the world. What exactly does it mean for a person to see and act from the perception of someone who has placed his or her will in order with God's will? Fortunately, Francis is very forthcoming on this point. In *The Testament of St. Francis* he claims: "When God gave me some friars, there was no one to tell me what I should do; but the Most High himself made it clear to me that I must live the life of the Gospel."[71] Note that Francis does not say: follow the Gospel as a step-by-step instruction guide; in another translation the word "pattern" is used, such that the Gospel offers a pattern for living.[72] Recalling Green's theory of a paradigmatic shift, visualizing the world according to the rhythm and weave, boundaries and pathways, images and prescriptions of the Gospel is just such a way of seeing the world through a new lens, or a lens that is finally wiped clear, and, when needed, can be used for finding insight into the will of God. When Francis mentions living by a pattern, he also uses another image related to God's will, but not defined by the Gospel. Recall that, in *The Canticle of Brother Sun*, it is one of the responsibilities of Sister Mother Earth, presumably also operating in accordance with the will of God, to govern us through her sovereignty.[73] Accepting that Natural Law was a greater part of most people's world view during Francis' time, the saint displays, here, two sources, taken together, that support and supply a transcendent perception of the world in consonance with the will of God. These sources are the Gospel and the dynamic yet cyclical action of God's creation.

A failure to accept or fully embrace the sources given for gaining a sense of the will of God is one reason many people today do not see the way Francis did. Francis' writings make it clear that attempting to perceive and follow God's will takes a powerful act of will in the first place. Additionally, he hints that there were some of his followers who were unable to make such an act. In *The Admonitions* he uses the image of Adam and Eve to make this point: "A man eats of the tree that brings knowledge of good when he claims that his good will comes from himself alone and prides himself on the good that God says and does in him."[74] There is a connection within this image between how one perceives reality and where one's will rests. Another important connection that is raised again later in the same document is the capacity to see all good things as originating in God even when the individual is the proximate agent. This is an elemental aspect of Francis' worldview. He adds another image when he raises the issue again: "Blessed the religious who refers all the good he has to his Lord and God. He who attributes anything to himself hides his master's money in himself, and even what he thinks he has shall be taken away."[75] This is an excellent passage to conclude a discussion of the relationship between the will, a transcendence of perception, and the imagination. Recall that the one disciple who held back the money belt, Judas, was the one who failed to shape his imagination to Jesus' vision, attached his will to personal gain instead of to God, and ended up, as the story goes, losing everything. As Francis sees it, much better off is the one in whose sight all good is attributed to God.

Change, in one or more of its variants, will be encountered on the spiritual journey. One does not offer oneself out of trust to another, seek a clearer image of God, or attempt to formulate meaning in a world that is static. As Winnicott posited, from birth on the human being is exposed to an onslaught of change in his or her perception of the world and self. Francis' writings unmistakably display the correlation between imaginative activity and a dynamic personal reality given momentum by change.

Faith and the Image of God

Two separate but clearly relatable topics are taken up in this section. For Francis, faith and God are indisputably related, such that faith can only be *in God.* Object Relations Theory, it must not be forgotten, is distinctly more neutral on this connection. Since the current analysis is of Francis' writings there will be overlaps between faith and God-images, but the two topics will be considered first in terms of the capacity to have faith, to believe in something, and, most of all, to trust. Then, the image of God and its formation will be studied in Francis' writings.

Faith

An ORT perspective on imagination can speak about faith because imaginative activity involves the perception of things that are not necessarily present to the senses. Since most people have some level of imaginative capacity that operates predominantly in an unconscious manner there is a widespread ignorance of the fact that trust is at the very base of all our imagining of things unseen. It is a trust that was developed with great effort as an infant and then all but forgotten as an adult. Earlier, Winnicott tied trust to the achievement of object constancy. While the mother is disrupting the child's sense of singular existence and self-sufficiency by her absence or delayed response, her timely return allows the child to discover her reliability and hence that there is reliability within the reality that exists beyond the microcosmic infant-self. This sense of trusted reliability, for an adult, could be discerned in images of care and concern, such as expressions of *holding* that hearken back to maternal empathy. Winnicott also suggested that trust enables a person to form and maintain good internal objects, such as the God objects that will be taken up in due course. Trust additionally sustains the capacity to be alone. Closely related to this is the ability to hold fear at bay, which would be suggested by some of Francis' references to anxiety and concern which have already been brought up. One observer of Winnicott's ideas went so far as to describe the potential space as a place of trust and reliability where one could engage in the difficult task of linking inner and outer reality.

Pruyser pointed out that a reliable image of the maternal figure stood behind a trusting attitude. Furthermore, the good internal objects formed as a result of adequate parenting enable a trusting relationship to the outside world. Francis' perception of the features of this world, found in *The Canticle of the Creatures,* is an indication of this relationship and the images that dwell behind it. Pruyser described several stages leading up to desire that each play a role in faith. In anticipation of some form of satisfaction, an individual might wait, pine, or have hope, which is a belief that the satisfaction will come to fruition. Francis' frequent mention of an eventual reward is one sign of his hope. A related point that Pruyser made is that if the image of God works as a type of transitional object, it is not only a drive object associated with the afore-mentioned desire; it is also related to ambivalence, which means that, as an object that can be both loved and hated or destroyed, it can consequently be disbelieved. Without the possibility of disbelief, it is difficult to completely conceptualize belief. Nonetheless, Francis will be seen to have an interesting take on this subject.

Where McDargh described faith in terms of a sense of self in relation to what is real, he found that a "fundamental faith" was needed to pursue an expansion of reality far beyond the self. He went on to describe faith as assurance that participation in a grander reality was both essential and worthwhile. Similar to his predecessors, he explained that trust is formed on the basis of parental availability, in which case, if Francis can be seen as a deeply trusting person, his positive maternal relationship is again affirmed. Where that trust is directed toward God, Jones' assertion, that idealized objects evoke trust, is substantiated. McDargh also took up the ability to be alone, but he tied it with the ability to be dependent. The latter requires the individual to advance beyond a strong maternal image since mature dependency, in a healthy or interdependent sense, eventually reaches beyond the maternal figure. McDargh went on to connect trust with the ability to play, and he found that playful trust led to the spontaneity needed to interact creatively with the external world by relating it to an internal vision as Francis so clearly does.

To move forward with an analysis of faith in the writings of Francis of Assisi three features of this topic will be considered. First, faith will be described as a way of living. Then, images of faith will be drawn from Francis' works in an effort to probe the workings of his imaginative activity. Finally, the certainty of faith will be explored through Francis' imaginative way of perceiving how reality operates.

A Life of Faith

Francis is very effective in upholding God as the primary object of faith, and his guiding images of God will be studied in the second half of the current section, but how Francis reveals or demonstrates his faith in God is the functional aspect that plays out in a life of faith. Francis indicates his ability to trust in the unseen but ever-present God, first of all, by penance as a lifestyle. To avoid excessive repetition, no images of this way of life will be given beyond those previously mentioned under the sub-headings for transformation. Certainly there must be an amazing depth of trust on the part of someone able to place his or her will in the hands of another. The capacity to embrace transformative pain and suffering and to allow it to have a meaningful end is another area rife with images of living a life structured on trust in God. The same can be said of voluntary poverty in which the apparent security of possessions is given up. Personal purity is a further feature that has a prominent place in Francis' life of faith, but this aspect quickly moves the discussion toward a sense of worthiness and away from trusting faith.

What, then, is left to consider as a life of faith? One insightful way to look at Francis' faith is not in terms of what to believe, but, rather, how to live in order to place one's trust in God. This is a kind of experiential faith wherein one carries on with the abiding sense that God will somehow render one's efforts meaningful. Pruyser's notion of an anticipated satisfaction is active here. In a give and take expression of charity Francis speaks of the end result that justifies any seeming loss to the charitable person: "We can bring with us only the right to a reward for our charity and the alms we have given. For these we shall receive a reward, a just retribution from God."[76] The saint is working with an image of the ultimate end-gain that could facilitate spiritual experiences of waiting, pining, hoping, and desiring. The life of faith, thus, has a *telos*, but it is first anchored in the present moment.

The life of faith also calls for the capacity for paradox. Francis consistently upturns commonly held notions of the nature of reality to reveal something more fundamentally real in which to place one's trust or toward which to direct one's trusting attitude. He discloses paradox as almost a God-given feature of reality when he exclaims: "Know that there are certain very lofty and sublime things in the sight of God that people sometimes think of as worthless and contemptible; there are others that are esteemed and remarkable to people that God considers extremely worthless and contemptible."[77]

In *The Rule of 1221* Francis explains that there are two ways to outwardly express the inner orientation of one's faith. He gives this explanation under the chapter heading: *Missionaries among the Saracens and other Unbelievers.* One means by which his missionaries could outwardly reveal their life of faith was to simply bear "witness to the fact that they are Christians."[78] This involves a determination not to deny one's faith in the face of personal danger. Where the danger is not so great, it means that one is willing to associate oneself with the faith when doing so would place oneself in the minority under conditions of shame, discomfort, or alienation. The other option Francis offers his missionaries is "to proclaim the word of God openly, when they see that is God's will, calling on their hearers to believe in God almighty, Father, Son, and Holy Spirit,... that they may be baptized and become Christians."[79] A guiding principal for a life of faith is found in this passage; it is to live and act so as to please God. Further down in the same document, Francis mentions another principal of a life of faith that links acknowledgement with a more extended expression of faith. He prays that we acknowledge "that all good belongs to him; and we must thank him for it all, because all good comes from him."[80]

Elsewhere in *The Rule of 1221* Francis ties verbal profession of faith to a more rounded description of the life of faith. He insists: "All the friars are bound to be Catholics, and live and speak as such."[81] It is interesting that he places the verbalization of belief last. In *The Rule of 1223*, within the chapter for receiving new brothers, which seems to be edited to meet certain ecclesiastical demands, the ministers are instructed to "carefully examine all candidates on the Catholic faith and the sacraments of the Church."[82] The implication, here, is that the life of faith is born out of assent to a series of propositions. *The Rule of 1221* has a different approach: "The minister, for his part, should receive him kindly and encourage him and tell him all about our way of life."[83] In this case, the life of faith begins with an understanding of the lifestyle and its challenges. Faith is not tested in words; it is tested in action. In the very next line the brother is asked to enter into a trusting relationship with God by abandoning any material source of security. This earlier option is a more purposeful means of entering the life of faith since it initiates the neophyte into the imagery of Francis' view of reality. In the concluding prayer of *The Rule of 1221,* the saint mentions persevering in the true faith, which reveals an image of this life as a great struggle, perhaps an arduous race to the finish.[84]

Images of Faith

The depiction of a life of faith as a race is just one way to portray Francis' perception of this path which is itself an image of living from the transitional sphere or "living creatively," as Winnicott puts it. The life of faith involves taking a selection of interior pictures of how life and one's participation in it should be, and struggling to transpose these images onto a broader perception of reality that is shared by others. The result does not necessarily have an immediate transformative effect on the collective reality, but it does move a person to perceive this aspect of reality differently. It is this alternate perception of reality, dwelling, often perilously, on the transitional border between inner and outer reality that is the more immediate cause of human-driven change in the world, spiritual action, or the external manifestation of the life of faith. One thing that sustains the individual's will to stay the course of faith and make the world a better place is the collection of images of faith that he or she forms and holds onto.

One particular image of faith involves taking the image of God, the object of faith, into some interior dimension and retaining it there as a constant reference. In *A Letter to the Entire Order,* Francis speaks of giving "proof in ourselves of the greatness of our Creator and of our subjection to him."[85] In another situation where the relationship that underlies faith is shown as a bond, Francis writes that, "A person is his bride when his faithful soul is united with Jesus Christ by the Holy Spirit."[86] This is an image of the wedding of faith. Particularly in Francis' time such a wedding is the start of a relationship in which a spouse, imaged as a woman in this case, comes to rely on her husband.[87] In another passage from *A Letter to a General Chapter* there is a possible maternal image that has been seen before, but it is also pertinent to a study of faith. In a prayerful section Francis proclaims: "Keep nothing for yourselves, so that he who has given himself wholly to you may receive you wholly."[88] This passage is both suggestive of the depth to which a mother gives over herself to the infant growing inside her, and it is also kenotic. The complete emptying of self-connectedness calls for trust that God will fill the void.

Both Pruyser and McDargh pointed out that a trusting kind of faith is required to relate, we might add, meaningfully, to the external world. Among the many relationships with external, physical reality that are provided in *The Canticle of Brother Sun,* there are several that bespeak a sign of Francis' trust in God. Most of the participants in this portrayal of creation, by their God-given functions, indicate God's intention to take care of and show concern for all of creation, and particularly humanity. Through the sun, God gives light and time, and by the sun and the moon one is drawn to an aesthetical experience of the beauty in the world. The wind does not just provide sustenance to people; it is trusted to provide this to "all that you have made."[89] The great value and usefulness of water are identified as gifts of God's solicitude. Fire, which is of little use to most creatures except to bring about destruction and then renewal, is a specific sign of God's trustworthy benevolence directed toward humans who can light up the night with it, dispel the fears of darkness, and find warmth in the strength of its heat. Then there is the earth, given to creatures for their home and as a place to find nourishment. Finally, Francis' image of God creating a system that creatures can rely upon for the needs of their existence is brought to its fullness. Sister Death is sent by the divine mediator of needs to "find" those who have trusted God and will be carried beyond all "harm" and also beyond all need except the need to be with God eternally.[90]

It should not be surprising that Francis uses vision images to depict faith, since he employs vision images for many of his religious expressions. Some of these images denote good faith and some point toward misplaced faith, such as the image of a blind person. Francis writes: "See, then, you who are blind, deceived by your enemies, the world, the flesh, and the devil."[91] A figural sight impairment causes a person to place ultimate trust in all the wrong or sub-ultimate entities. A failure to perceive the Eucharist with eyes of faith gives Francis cause for an additional image of faulty sight. He castigates people for not seeing the "difference between the bread which is Christ and other food."[92]

Francis favors another visual expression that he uses for various aspects of the life of faith. At the end of the *Letter to All the Faithful,* he implores his brothers to hear the words of Christ, "observing them perfectly. Those who cannot read should have them read to them often and keep them ever before their eyes."[93] In this occurrence, the word *observing,* with its connection to attentive seeing, is directed toward written guideposts of faith.[94] The vision-of-faith imagery is given more clarity in *The Admonitions.* Francis compares just seeing Jesus "in his humanity" with seeing and believing in his "Spirit in his Divinity, that He was the true Son of God."[95] He applies the same seeing and believing according to the Spirit" to the way one perceives the Eucharist.[96] Francis also prefaces a vivid description of Jesus on the altar with the visual term "behold."[97] Then, he goes on to write: "We too, with our own eyes, see only bread and wine, but we must see further and firmly believe that this is his most holy Body and Blood, living and true."[98] Francis ties such an image of seeing to Christ's constant presence with those who believe, both in this admonition and another one on purity. In the latter, Francis writes: a clean heart occurs by "never failing to keep God before his eyes and always adoring him with a pure heart and soul."[99]

Several of the vision images have touched on the sacraments. This is a natural connection since sacraments are visible manifestations of some unseen divine action. It is those features of a sacrament that cannot be discerned by the senses that call for faith and lead a person to see more deeply with the kind of vision Francis would recommend for a life of faith. In the *Letter to All Clerics,* Francis writes that, "We know his Body is not present unless the bread is first consecrated by these words."[100] In this instance, he is highlighting the mystery behind the Eucharist that relies on words in order to be effected. Francis adds his personal imagery to the words of consecration when he exclaims: "the whole world should tremble and heaven rejoice, when Christ the Son of the living God is present on the altar in the hands of the priest."[101]

Confession is another instance where a sacramental imagination comes into play. In the first place, faithful people bring to mind a litany of their individual sins in the form of images. Then, they confess these sins and "they should be convinced that once they have received penance and absolution from any Catholic priest their sins are forgiven, provided that they perform the penance enjoined upon them, humbly and faithfully."[102] In this stance against scruples, Francis reveals the importance of establishing an inner vision of one's soul in which former sins are no longer present. He follows this with an implied connection between having confessed one's sins and the ability to appropriately bring Jesus' words to mind as memory.[103]

Two related types of images from *The Testament of St. Francis* fall more into the category of sacramentals rather than sacraments. Sacramentals are visible signs of God's presence and action in the world that lack the procedural form and intentionality of true sacraments yet stand out every bit as much to remind believers that God is near. The first one to be considered is the image of churches. Francis makes clear that, "And God inspired me, too, and still inspires me with such faith in churches that I used to pray with all simplicity, saying, 'We adore you, Lord Jesus Christ, here and in all your churches in the whole world, and we bless you, because by your holy cross you have redeemed the world.'"[104] Three primary images come together in this statement. Francis is working with a vision of people gathered in designated locations all over creation to adore God. There is also the image of Christ present in each of these churches to accept and give meaning to that adoration, which leads to the final image, or perhaps mix of images. Francis pulls the image of redemption into the worship space as it is seen through the base images of Christ's passion, death, and resurrection. Francis could very well have been seated in a church when he came up with these lines, or he was thinking like an artist planning the various elements for an altar fresco or apse mosaic. His native land is filled with such imagery depicting the local faithful gathered in or around the community's church, participating in some feature of Christ's suffering that is played out in their midst as the hand of God, a host of angels, or the dove-like Spirit reaches down to reveal a greater drama simultaneously occurring. Meanwhile demons flee from the shadows in frustration and fear. Francis may not have included the many dramatic details in his rendering, but they are certainly suggested and likely based on the communal aspects of medieval imagining.

Immediately after describing his faith in churches, Francis goes to great lengths to explain his perception of priests. He writes: "God inspired me, too, and still inspires me with such great faith in priests who live according to the laws of the holy Church of Rome."[105] He adds that he would still see them through the eyes of faith even if they persecuted him, lacked his level of wisdom, or were outcasts among the poor. Then Francis writes that, "I refuse to consider their sins, because they are better than I. I do this because in this world I cannot see the most high Son of God with my own eyes, except for his most holy Body and Blood which they received and they alone administer to others."[106] This may be one of Francis' best lessons on the use of the imagination. He presents a variety of commonplace inadequacies of priests in his day that were widespread enough to instigate the reforms of the Fourth Lateran Council. The cumulative result of these shortcomings, in the minds of his readers, would have been the worst possible image of a prelate. He uses this image as a foil for his vision of God acting through the priest during the sacrifice of the altar. It could be that he hopes to change the perception of priests in the eyes of the faithful or he wants the priests to re-envision themselves according to the glory of God acting through them. At the same time, Francis is exemplifying his capacity for seeing reality according to two dimensions that are intertwined at various points. The very human limitations of a less than exemplary priest meet with the divine perfection of Christ on the altar. What is more, Francis verifies that seeing in this manner is not just for a latter-day prophet; it is for anyone who will strive to perceive the world with imaginative vision informed by faith. This is substantiated by his admission that the perception is intentional: "I do this because...."[107] His willingness to act-as or see-as is also an indication that there is no doubt in his mind and soul that God would be present through the minister.

Certitude

It could be said that one mark of a Christian spiritual life that is headed in the right direction is that the individual possesses a true and certain faith; but what is a *true and certain faith*? Does this mean that the list of one's beliefs mirrors an absolute standard, or does it mean that such belief has been confirmed by an inner voice, sensation, or intuition? The idea of certainty is a challenge when it comes to discussing faith since the latter concept, faith, generally includes elements of mystery, incomplete knowledge, and a transcendence of self, all of which call the would-be faithful to commit an act of trust in something that clearly involves exceeding a limit-of-experience. Maybe certitude in faith is actually measured by the degree to which one trusts in that which one trusts. Francis' writings portray a kind of certitude that sets trust, either subjective or objective, at the highest level. The certainty of his faith could be designated as *absolute* when the risks of the life it supports are taken into account. Several of his images that express certitude will be reviewed, ending with a consideration of the extreme opposite of certitude: faithlessness.

When Francis delivers *The Prayer before the Crucifix*, he asks God to give him "true faith, certain hope, and perfect charity, sense and knowledge."[108] Although, in this passage, certitude is linked with hope, each of the elements listed pertains to an active faith, and they all refer to the highest or most complete form, respectively. True faith counters belief or trust in anything false or not real. Certain hope rejects the possibility that there is no point in striving for the object of hope. Perfect charity hides behind nothing and holds nothing back for its own security. It is not clear whether perfect sense refers to wisdom or intuition, but in either case it goes hand in hand with perfect knowledge, which is understanding based on the data of experience. It is telling that Francis progresses from faith to knowledge, since the latter expresses its own trust and certainty that one's experiences adequately substantiate one's understanding. If faith, hope, charity, sense, and knowledge are taken together as advancing expressions of faith it is plausible that Francis' certitude is ultimately based on trust in his experiences of God, sustained by the images that these experiences actuate.

The *Letter to All the Faithful* contains one of Francis' scriptural selections that ties faith with a seemingly more certain knowledge. He writes: "And the words you have given me, I have given to them. And they have received them and have truly known that I have come forth from you, and they have believed that you have sent me."[109] This description of faith moves from acceptance of God's intentions, to trust that Jesus is a very real part of these intentions, to knowledge that God is actively engaged in fulfilling these intentions.[110] Referring, initially, to the apostles whose knowledge was based on first-hand experience of the humanity and divinity of Christ, Francis superimposes the image over his brothers to signify that their faith is not merely based on a nagging suspicion that God is still around. Rather, their faith exists on knowledge, definable as a definitive perceptual awareness gleaned from spiritual experience, that God is a vital presence in the world.

Other examples exist in Francis' writings where the certitude terminology of knowledge is used as an expression of imaginative awareness that symbolizes faith. In the *Letter to All the Faithful*, Francis declares: "We should realize, too, that no one can be saved except by the holy words of God, and it is the clergy who tell us his words and administer the Blessed Sacrament."[111] Here certainty is connected with knowledge through perceptual realization. In *A Letter to a General Chapter* there is further suggestion that knowledge of God's action is based on experience. The saint explains that, "This is the very reason he has sent you all over the world, so that by word and deed you might bear witness to his message and convince everyone that there is no other almighty God besides him."[112] This knowledge of God is built upon the testimony of those who have experienced the divine voice. An additional scriptural passage that ties faith to knowledge is found in *The Admonitions*. Francis reiterates that, "Our Lord Jesus told his disciples, I am the way, and the truth, and the life. No one comes to the Father but through me. If you had known me, you would also have known my father."[113] In this passage Francis finds an alignment between knowing God and the use of *seeing-as* imaginative activity. Propitiously, the connection bears Jesus' sanction. A scriptural prayer for *Matins* directly relates the assurance of faith suggested by the preceding passage. Francis recalls: "You are *God, my savior; I will act with confidence and have no fear.*"[114] Beginning with the knowledge that God exists and is God for him, Francis ties this awareness to a statement of confident action and fear-abating trust.

The Failure of Faith

Another imaginative approach to faith that Francis uses is memory. In *A Letter to the Rulers of the Peoples*, Francis asks the rulers to participate in the Eucharist "fervently in memory of him."[115] Remembering Jesus in this fashion implies that one retains an image of who and what Jesus is, but it also stands in opposition to one way that Francis expresses a failure of faith. Earlier in the same text he writes: "I therefore beg you with all the respect I am capable of that you do not forget God or swerve from his commandments because of the cares and anxieties of this world which you have to shoulder. For all who forget him and turn away from his commandments shall be forgotten by him."[116] Some scripture interpretations use *oblivion* in place of being forgotten by God. Using *oblivion* conjures up a host of its own images just to give it some sense. Francis steps around the notion that a person could ever simply stop believing in God. Instead, he allows for the possibility that one could forget God, or somehow misplace the image of God. The eternal loss of God's image and concern are apt descriptors of some theoretical approaches to hell, which is suggested in this passage. The use of forgetfulness and swerving from his commands in the same sentence points toward an instance of personal liability for the loss of God's image and the failure to be faithful.

While Francis uses the term "unbelievers," he is referring to people who do not believe in the Judaeo-Christian God, and probably more specifically God as revealed by Jesus Christ.[117] In this case he is not pointing toward people who give up their faith by making a willful choice not to place their trust in a higher power or toward people who lose the image of God.[118] Another word that Francis does employ to identify a failure of faith is ignorance. He proposes: "We clerics cannot overlook the sinful neglect and ignorance some people are guilty of with regard to the holy Body and Blood of our Lord Jesus Christ. They are careless, too, about his holy name and the writings which contain his words, the words that consecrate his Body."[119] Ignorance may not only mean a state of being uninformed about or unacquainted with the life altering and behavior changing experience of God. The Latin origins of the term also include the idea of disregard. The fact that ignorance is directly linked with sin indicates that this is the more likely and indicting meaning. The ignorant person sets his or her image of God out of view.

Refusal is another concept that Francis uses for a loss of faith. While still speaking about the Eucharist, he asks: "Have we forgotten that we must fall into his hands?"[120] The Latin text presents "forgotten" as more of a choice to not recognize the fact. With a word origin shared with *ignorance*, the refusal to *recognize* the image of oneself in the hands of Christ involves denying some condition that one has known previously.[121] The use of the concept of refusal suggests that the failure to know or--injecting a more modern definition--perceive the image of this relationship entails a willful rejection. Contrary to certitude of faith in God, for Francis, the loss of faith is never something that occurs because it is not sustained by sufficient experience. It falters because of a decision, made by the individual, not to nourish and care for his or her perceptions of God. On the other hand, faith endures because images of God persist as constant reminders of something real and meaningful to the individual. Francis' God images are certainly very real and very meaningful.

Images of God

Each of the ORT theorists mentioned earlier have something to add to an understanding of God images, but as their offerings are reviewed, it must be emphasized that images grow from experiences. ORT can shed light on some experiences that contribute to an individual's formulation of an image of God, but, being religiously neutral, the theory does not confirm any of Francis' actual encounters with God. The validity of such experiences is found in the arena of faith, Francis' and the many others who encounter God as they journey with Francis.

Winnicott has suggested that the process of bringing images together to form new images, such as those of God, involves imaginative play. Play is an activity that eases the tension of interaction. Further lowering instinct tension is the fact that this kind of play occurs in the transitional space, thus, in Francis' case, enabling him to mix negative paternal images with a wholly positive image of God. Winnicott identified the inclusion of youthful imaginative experience in response to new experiences that generate later-year imaginative activity. He has also driven home the point that an object that can be loved is not an object that exists solely to fulfill the demands of a supplicant. Francis' willingness to endure trial and tribulation for God backs his numerous expressions of love for God. Both Winnicott and Pruyser referred to object constancy at the service of the capacity to be alone with one's images and imaginative activity. Pruyser added that a reliable image of the mother stands behind this capacity, and thus also behind much of the maternal God imagery in Francis' writings.

The subject of trust was taken up prior to the formation of God images for good reason. Pruyser explained that an early trusting environment facilitates an expanded usage of the transitional space for imaginative activity in adulthood. One learns to place trust in a God, unseen but for imagery, by learning to trust in the first place. While aspects of desire like waiting, pining, and hoping support trust, Pruyser also indicated that when an image is lacking, the desire is frustrated or unsatisfied. On the other hand, when the image is apparent, it becomes the focus of desire. When speaking of the formation of images, he mentioned that one possible influence was *idealization,* in which a relationship of good versus bad or potential versus not-achieving-potential is set up. Francis' intense descriptions of God's unmatched characteristics are examples of this. Tied to idealization is name-ability. Pruyser found that this verifies the existence of something, at least in image if not also in independent existence. The combination of naming and idealization based on some version of good-bad, most probably *distress free* versus *distressing,* was described as the primary ordering principle. Francis displays this arrangement rightly by ordering all things to God as good.

Describing internalization as another source for image formation, Pruyser compared introjection, the application of features of an object image to oneself, with its opposite, projection. While Francis embraced certain features of Jesus' humanity that could be described as introjection, the second activity, projection, is equally present in Francis' images. Pruyser noted that projection involves taking features of an experience connected with one's sense of self and project-ing these onto the image of another. A final form of internalization, labeled identification, involves a complete cross-over between one's self image and the image of another. Hagiographic descriptions of Francis' encounter with the se-raph on Monte LaVerna evince a thorough identification of himself with the crucified Christ, but the saint's own writings do not corroborate it, whether or not Francis ever had such an experience.[122]

When McDargh referred to God images he took the capacity to be alone in a new direction by setting it side-by-side with the ability to be dependent. Both rely on trust in an object image able to substantiate this trust, and in either case, when the image does not uphold such trust, the individual can become over-whelmed by vulnerability. One of Francis' God images in particular works to mitigate this vulnerability. It is dubbed *The Defender*. McDargh also determined that a relationship with an image of God has very personal components: affects, images, and memories all go into the development of God images. He further exemplified the dynamic nature of God images by observing that certain ver-sions of an individual's God images increase and decrease as influences on cur-rent imaginative activity, and this is, in part, because the images are often formed in conjunction with self-images. Determining that parental estimation, from an individual's perspective, is a main ingredient of youthful self-perception, McDargh observed that God images eventually take over this role for many people. He additionally proposed that object images tend toward the transcendent as the world of experience expands in order to support a broader perspective on reality.

Rizzuto found that parental representations feature strongly in God image formation, and she also argued that imaginative activity becomes a memorial process once the image has formed. Even so, she is certain that an abiding mem-ory of a potent father figure does not deserve the credit Freud gives it as the sole source for the image of God. While noting that people never fully break away from early images, she explained that personal images do not replace God im-ages; they merely interact with them to alter the way God is imaged throughout life. This comes as the result of imaginative play in which one feels at liberty to bring different images together. Where Francis' God-images bear a paternal reflection, perhaps they are not based on direct images of his earthly father. Ra-ther, they could be the result of imagining himself as son of this particular fa-ther.

Looking at Francis' images of God, it quickly becomes apparent that he ex-emplifies the ORT position that throughout life people will form a number of God images which wax and wane in influence over their imaginative activity. Francis exhibits a number of interesting images in his writings that can all be traced to experiences in his earlier life, as well as written and depicted inspira-tions from his religious environment. Several of his images will be covered in brief, either because there is less detail about them, or, as in the case of the ma-ternal figure, much has already been said. Included in this limited grouping will be God as superlative, God as a fellow beggar, God in creation, God as love, and God as maternal. Images that find a more comprehensive expression in these pages include God as guild-master, God as defender, God as judge, and God as a fragrant flower. The first three of these observably point toward Francis' youth and adolescence for their origin. It should also be noted that, in most cases, the evidence for these images is found in more than one written work, suggesting that he carries his images with him, so to speak. They are not used as a one-time literary convenience and then set aside; instead, they settle back into Francis' transitional space, participating in imaginative play and waiting to reemerge as his imaginative activity demands.

A Passing Glimpse at Some Images

According to his writings, there are many ways that Francis comes to envision God. It might seem strange to begin considering a few examples by pointing out notions of God, or ideas. Nonetheless, Francis uses numerous conceptual expressions to reveal the way he imagines God. Most of these do not indicate a personified God; instead, they show a God who is encountered as some type of energy or force in the world. In the *Letter to All the Faithful*, the saint encourages people to praise God who "has borne so much for us and has done and will do so much good to us; he is our power and our strength, and he alone is good, he alone most high, he alone all-powerful, wonderful, and glorious; he alone is holy...."[123] In *The Rule of 1221* he begins with similar phrasing, and only after establishing the superlative nature of God does Francis turn to personified images: "Almighty, most high and supreme God, Father, holy and just, Lord, King of heaven and earth, we give thanks for yourself."[124] Francis first expresses the dimensions of God's divinity and then turns to add the image of a paternal and royal personage. If there were no other God images in Francis' inventory these two sets alone could justify Freud's exalted father figure theory, but this is not the case. Pruyser's point on desire is also well taken here since Francis is using concepts of supremacy to portray a God who is a worthy object of desire. At the same time, these expressions corroborate McDargh's position on images that tend toward the transcendent. Descriptions of God in the superlative are descriptions that reach for the transcendent.

The fact that both of the foregoing sets of imagery mention the goodness of God further backs Prusyer's view that idealization can be a powerful factor in image formation, and using a phrase like "Who alone is good," is also a way to name and, thus, endorse God's existence. Further evidence of the importance of naming God in Francis' spiritual view of the world is found in *Letter to All Clerics*. He declares: "God's name and his written words should be picked up, if they are found lying in the dirt, and put in a suitable place"[125]

In his writings Francis presents a very careful Trinitarian theology. This being the case, some of his images of God are found in references to Jesus Christ, both in his humanity and divinity. Francis remarks in *The Rule of 1221*: "They should not be ashamed to beg alms, remembering that our Lord Jesus Christ, the Son of the living, all-powerful God set his face like a very hard rock and was not ashamed. He was poor and had no home of his own and he lived on alms, he and the Blessed Virgin and his disciples."[126] There are four features in this already well-used passage that Francis associates with a divine personage even if he might not extend each of them to the fullness of God's divinity. First, Jesus was steadfast. He stood resilient against the challenges set before him. Second, he was not overcome with shame. Both of these features were the armor that enabled him to contend with the final two features, the experiences of deprivation and interpersonal alienation. Francis obviously employs these notions to give his followers a specific model of Jesus to follow, but it is conceivable that he drew from his own situation to format the model. By projecting onto Jesus a predictable negative reaction to suffering, in this case shame, he both created an image and gave new meaning to a feeling that he knew would otherwise be destructive in the life he had chosen. Of course, this is just loosely supported speculation. If, in his youth, Francis was introduced to Jesus as the great bearer of shame, then it is more likely that some form of introjection took place; Francis identifies with Jesus' shame, and he is introspective enough to reveal the source of his ability to put up with the humiliation encountered during a life of public voluntary poverty. Since the Gospels are more focused on the shame of Jesus' passion rather than that found in his itinerant lifestyle, projection onto Jesus is the more plausible activity.

Some analysis has already been presented on *The Canticle of Brother Sun* as a source of Francis' view of relationships, but this text also provides aspects of a few of his God-images, if not some of the direct images themselves. When Francis offers God praise through various elements of creation it is quite possible that he is associating his view of God with an image of each of the elements in turn. If he sees God in or as "my lord Brother Sun," "Sister Moon and Stars," "Brothers Wind and Air," "Sister Water," "Brother Fire," "Sister Earth, our Mother," or even "Sister Death," than these images are participating to a greater or lesser degree in his predominant God-image at that point in time.[127] If this is not the case, Francis is still going to great lengths to divulge aspects of his image of the divine. Through the functions that he ascribes to each element, he is displaying a view of the one God who has a concern in each area. For instance, this is seen when the sun "brings the day; and light you give to us through him;" through the wind "By which you cherish all that you have made;" through fire "through whom you brighten up the night;" and also through God's love people are moved to "grant pardon."[128] Francis' God works through creation to provide light, comfort, heat, and other essentials in a natural fashion. At the same time, Francis is signifying, using the active verb, that God is above all one who *gives*, which can be understood as the essential act of creation. Francis' God in the canticle is not the God who allows or permits; his is the God who gives, cherishes, brightens, moves, and provides.

Several of the foregoing analyses of imagery from *The Canticle of Brother Sun* indicate that an image is not just a depiction in the sense of a two dimensional picture. The way ORT understands the product of imaginative activity it seeks to grasp how something is, not how it looks in the narrow sense of the word as a visual reproduction. A conceptual image located in the *Letter to All the Faithful* demonstrates this point. Francis writes: "In the love which is God, I,

Brother Francis, the least of your servants and worthy only to kiss your feet, beg and implore all those to whom this letter comes to hear these words... putting them into practice... and observing them perfectly."[129] Using an image like "the love which is God" is a distinct attempt to exhibit something about who and what God is, not how God appears. Nevertheless, if a picture of God is still sought after, Francis proposes of Brother Sun: "How beautiful is he, how radiant in all his splendour! Of you, Most High, he bears the likeness."[130]

A final briefly presented God image found in Francis' writings is another reference to the maternal aspect of his perception of God. Recalling the hypothesis that Francis' relationship with his mother was over-all a positive one (one that could be deemed "good-enough"), it is likely that some qualities of this relationship slip into his view of God. Another of Francis' texts offers a comprehensive expression of this connection. The *Praises of God* was written immediately following his so-called stigmata event on Monte LaVerna which culminated a forty day retreat. As the idea of the stigmata suggests, this was a time when the saint identified very closely with Christ the crucified son of God; yet turning toward a parental image of the divine he does not reveal Aelred's Mary who failed to protect Jesus on the temple pilgrimage. Francis, on the contrary, emerges with an understanding of God who exhibits all the protective, nourishing, stress-abating characteristics of Winnicott's "good-enough mother." This text begins with many of the same superlative descriptions of God that have been seen elsewhere in Francis' works. According to one translation Francis then says of God: "You are endurance. You are rest, You are peace. You are joy and gladness. You are justice and moderation. You are all our riches, and you suffice for us," and another translation adds concepts like patience, beauty, and meekness."[131] While lauding God, Francis could just as easily be singing the praises of the mother who held her temper and eased the distress of his childhood traumas (patience, meekness, moderation), or returned his gaze with the radiant look of a new mother holding her child (beauty, gladness, joy). This mother image also provides him the confidence to close his eyes and enter the realm of sleep where images often play beyond the reach of the cognitive mind or memory (security-endurance, rest). Additionally, she gives order to the universe of reality that she is expanding for him (justice), while she meets his needs in the way that is most beneficial to his development (sufficiency).

The maternal image is reinforced in the following stanza of the *Praises of God* where many of the same concepts are reiterated before returning to a superlative and, perhaps, slightly more Christ-oriented image of God. He writes: "You are beauty. You are gentleness. You are our protector, You are our guardian and defender. You are courage. You are our haven and our hope. You are our faith, our consolation. You are our eternal life, great and wonderful Lord, God almighty, Merciful Saviour."[132] This final portion of the *Praises* emphasizes the protective facets of a maternal image, which is an appropriate segue into one of the more fully formulated images of God found in his writings: God the defender.

More Extensive Images: The Defender

Francis is known for living his life on the edge. He seeks out and embraces the vulnerability that centuries of social-cultural endeavors had sought to overcome. At stake is not only his life but his entire sense of being. This is one reason why his image of God as defender of the marginalized does not equate to many of the holy-protector images that were becoming commonplace in his time. For the most part, Francis does not entreat God to shatter the present moment with a miraculous spectacle meant to cut short the saint's discomfort or distress at the hands of man, beast, or nature. His is not the God who emerges from delusion by request—the kind that cannot be an object of love. Rather, Francis' God stands apart from a narrow perception of reality that limits possibility to an instant that is boxed in by a failure to see with eyes wide open. Francis' God does intercede, but it is the kind of intercession that shapes or guides meaning, not the kind of God that regularly defies and, therefore, undercuts meaning.

At first, the preceding description of God as a defender is difficult to see in Francis' writings. The works that depict this image are found in *The Office of the Passion*. Most of the imagery in these writings comes from his amalgamation of scriptural images, particularly the Psalms.[133] Many of the Psalms reflect the Old Testament view of a mighty warrior God able to smite the hordes that stand up against Israel. If there is any validity to the hagiographical mention of Francis' attempts to become a knight and his related dreams, a warrior figure for God would make sense.[134] However, these writings from the *Office* come at a later period in his life and conversion process when other images have softened the crudity of such a God-image. As an example, Francis reiterates the Psalmist's words: "Then do my enemies turn back, when I call upon you; now I know that God is with me." He adds a little later: "Holy Father, be not far from me; O my God, hasten to aid me. Make haste to help me, O Lord my salvation!"[135] While the language contained in these passages is suggestive of a God who wields military might, and there is a direct supplication to God to act on the speaker's behalf, there is no language specifying actual physical intervention such as violence, which might be expected from a warrior God. Instead, there is, finally, a call to aid, help, and salvation, which, as Francis arranges them, are neutral in regard to violence and miraculous intervention, with the possible exception of salvation.

In another scriptural prayer for *Matins* Francis despairs in the words of the Psalmist: "by day I cry out, at night I clamour in your presence. Let my prayer come before you; incline your ear to my call for help," and further down he reiterates: "Make haste to help me."[136] In this passage he begins by seeking an audience with God to air his needs, but nowhere in this collection of Psalms does he use a passage that requests a direct intervention against the enemies of which he speaks. Instead, he asks for a kind of liberty that is not a release from physical bondage. Because freedom is connected with the soul, Francis is drawing attention to an interior freedom that can only be initiated by seeing and responding to his situation in a new way. In the very next scriptural prayer, for *Prime*, Francis writes: "In the shadow of your wings I take refuge, till harm pass by."[137]

The weapon Francis envisions God using against this wickedness is not a cloud of death or a rain of fire; it is shame. The saint adds: "may he make those a reproach who trample upon me."[138] He then goes on to use the lines: "He rescued me from my mighty enemy and from my foes, who were too powerful for me."[139] Here Francis aligns the power of his enemies with hatred and not anything that could cause direct physical harm. Both the image of shadowing and snatching imply the presence of a bird of prey, ever watchful, and willing to somehow shelter Francis from imminent danger beneath the shadow of its wing.

Specific expressions of God as defender proliferate throughout the *Office*. In one expression presented for *Terce,* Francis exclaims: "Holy Father, be not far from me; hasten to my aid. Make haste to help me, O Lord my salvation!"[140] In another scriptural prayer for *Sext*, he points toward the interior nature of his need for God to defend him: "When my spirit is faint within me, you know my path."[141] A few lines after this, however, he does not avoid a description of physical violence, but it is directed toward him, and he does not ask God to return like for like: "they gathered together striking me unawares."[142] In a scriptural prayer for *None*, Francis indicates that God defends him by utilizing wisdom. After describing various kinds of suffering he declares: "Holy Father, with your counsel you guide me, and in the end you will receive me in glory."[143] A passage for *Compline* retains the standard opening for a reading of the office: "Deign, O God, to rescue me; O Lord, make haste to help me," and it ends with: "You are my help and my deliverer; O Lord, hold not back!" In the middle the scriptural prayer reiterates the idea of God using shame to fend off those who would stand against the writer.[144]

Recalling some of Francis' frequent discussions of cares, preoccupations, and anxieties of the world, it is not surprising to find him picking out scriptural passages that refer to distress as something with which God can help. An example for *Sext* begins with the petition: "The Lord answer you in time of distress; the name of the God of Jacob defend you."[145] It is not the hand of the Lord or the militant angel of the Lord that protects; it is simply the name of the Lord. Near the end of this same passage is a similar idea: "The Lord is a stronghold for the oppressed, a stronghold in time of distress."[146] In this case God is imaged as an edifice, or, better yet, as a secure space, one in which distress is alleviated, such as the mother-child ambience spoken of in ORT literature. If this connection seems far-fetched, the very next selection of scriptural prayers for *None* contains the idea: "On you I depend from birth; from my mother's womb you are my strength; constant has been my hope in you… Hide not your face from your servant."[147] As it turns out, the defender God-image that frees and protects Francis contains elements of a maternal figure, similar to the one in Celano's account, who released Francis from imprisonment by his father.[148]

The Guild-Master

There is a figure in medieval society who rose to the position of a leading townsman. He was not necessarily a skilled craftsman, but he was a businessman. His trade was the buying and selling of a valued commodity for which he had a monopoly or near monopoly in the local community, made possible by the advent of the guild system. As a powerful person in a carefully protected trade, young men might come to him in the hope of gaining access to some portion of his market. If the tradesman had few or no sons or there was much room to expand the business, other young men might be taken in to learn the secrets of the trade as an apprentice. They would pledge themselves to obedience and accountability under the guild-master with the prospect of some future gain. As Chiara Frugoni recounts, Peter Bernardone was just such a leading tradesman, and Francis might have experienced some or all of the relationship described above.[149] In any instance, features of this relationship emerge in his God-images.

A central characteristic of the relationship between an apprentice and a guild-master is subservience. At an early point, when Francis is presenting himself for God's service, he swears what could be called an oath: "that I may carry out Your holy and true command."[150] *The Rule of 1221* describes what happens when the oath is not upheld. Francis explains that those who "withdraw from obedience and disobey God's commandments, wandering about from place to place, can be sure that they are under a curse as long as they remain obstinately in their sin."[151] Offering more positive reinforcement, he suggests: "Be well disciplined then and patient under holy obedience, keeping your promise to him generously and unflinchingly."[152]

The *Letter to All the Faithful* clarifies that God is someone for whom others labor. Francis says of his brothers that "they will be children of your Father in heaven whose work they do."[153] A binding precept of the apprenticeship system was that an apprentice could not simply walk away from his current arrangement and enter a work agreement with any other master. When talking about people who do not live in penance, Francis reiterates the idea of the pledge. He refers to those who "indulge their vices and sins and follow their evil longings and desires, without thought for the promises they made."[154] Francis adds that these individuals, having failed to honor their obligation, go on to commit themselves to someone else, the devil, since they are "dedicated to doing his work."[155] Furthermore, by entering into an apprenticeship that has no legal standing since the guild-master never released them from the first agreement, these poor souls will never profit. Francis warns: "You have no good in this world and nothing to look forward to in the next. You imagine that you will enjoy the worthless pleasures of this life indefinitely, but you are wrong."[156] To further express the reality of their self-deception, Francis adds that, for those who do not fulfill their service to the master, "All talent and ability, all learning and wisdom which he thought his own, are taken away from him."[157] The control and influence of a successful guild was deep-reaching.

One way that Francis attempts to impress the image of God as guild-master upon his followers is to fully take on a subservient role. In the *Letter to All the Faithful*, he identifies himself to them as "Brother Francis, their servant and subject."[158] In this position, Francis joins in the cycle of productivity that will, hopefully, pay off in eventual, albeit delayed, profitability. He says: "We must bring forth therefore fruits befitting repentance."[159] Accentuating the notion that this situation is only for those willing to visualize and wait for the long-term return on their efforts, Francis proposes that, "We lose everything which we leave behind us in this world; we can bring with us only the right to a reward for our charity and the alms we have given. For these we shall receive a reward, a just retribution from God."[160] However, this opportunity to partake of the residual income of the business is only offered to those who have kept their balance sheets clean.

Francis clearly points out the responsibility that his followers have to carry out their part of the arrangement with God as trade-master. Using a Scriptural admonition, he maintains that, "Anyone who refuses to obey should realize that he will have to account for it before our Lord Jesus Christ on the day of judgment."[161] There is some indication that this issue with poor accountability is somewhat autobiographical for Francis. Celano conveys an incident in which Francis sold some of his father's expensive clothe and did not turn the profit over to Bernardone.[162] Realizing that personal use of the inventory was only for apprentices who advance to a higher status, Francis remarks that the friars "should avoid expensive clothes in this world in order that they may have something to wear in the kingdom of heaven."[163] Not only does God belong to a guild, it seems that God is a purveyor of fine clothe. In a final point that emphasizes the hierarchical nature of the master and apprentice relationship, Francis insists that, "The friars who are engaged in the service of lay people for whom they work should not be in charge of money or of the cellar."[164] In his view, there is only one treasurer and overseer, the one who has the best clothe to offer and to whom all accounts eventually come due.

The Judge

Guilt is certainly a feature of much religious writing, especially from the Middle Ages. Some theorists might find it convenient to claim that religion breeds guilt and guilt breeds religion's saints, but this reduction is not justified in Francis' case. Yes, his numerous allusions to humility suggest that he is working with a definite level of guilt, but guilt, often understood as a sense of unworthiness, must be seen in a specific context for Francis. In spite of his references to people who are "strangers to all good, willing and eager only to do evil," Francis does not seem to always express guilt in terms of being bad.[165] Rather, recalling that he views God as so very good, his expression of guilt, and thus judgment, could be understood as not being good enough. With this in mind, any discussion of a judge-type image cannot disregard the criterion or norm against which judgment is made. Francis' image of God as judge is inseparable from his view of God as the standard of all divine judgment, and that standard is goodness.

In the *Letter to All the Faithful*, Francis urges his followers to be sure that others are given the opportunity to know the good things about God. He asserts that neglecting to do so will set them before God in judgment. He writes: "Those who fail to do this shall be held to account for it before the judgment-seat of Christ on the last day."[166] This same document source contains an instance in which Francis asks the reader to imagine how they would like to envision God acting as a judge. He proposes: "Those who have been entrusted with the power of judging others should pass judgment mercifully, just as they themselves hope to obtain mercy from God. For judgment is without mercy to him who has not shown mercy."[167] If judgment is based on an orientation toward all that is good, than mercy entails reorienting the wayward. Someone who is not shown mercy is someone who is not pointed in the right direction, someone who continues to travel in opposition to goodness.

Francis clarifies the association between God as judge and God as the measure of judgment in the *Praises of God*. In a passage that has been used to point out the maternal features of a God-image, the saint uses various terms that hint at God as the norm and the manifestation of judgment. He observes that "You are justice and moderation. You are all our riches, and you suffice for us... You are our protector, You are our guardian and defender."[168] It should be noted that these terms are given shortly after one of Francis' acclamations of God's goodness.

Francis makes use of the term "condemn" in *Letter to a General Chapter*, but this must be understood in comparison with an example of condemnation given a paragraph earlier. Speaking of the consecration of the Eucharist, Francis observes: "He told us, Do this in remembrance of me, and so the man who acts otherwise is a traitor like Judas, and he will be guilty of the body and the blood of the Lord."[169] The example places someone who acts with a definite, good image of God in contrast with someone who made a significant choice based on a deficient standard, having lost his perception of God as all-good.

In light of his judge image, Francis confesses his sins before God and the court of heaven: "I confess all my sins to God, Father, Son, and Holy Spirit; to blessed Mary ever Virgin and all the saints in heaven and on earth."[170] The specific sins that he admits to are actually self-imposed duties, such as failing to follow the rule that he established or not reading the office that he put together. At the same time, these are activities that will help orient him to the goodness that is God. He explains that his failings are due to "carelessness or sickness, or because I am ignorant and have never studied."[171] Francis specifies how one of his areas for fault, the reading of the office, must be carried out so that it fits within the criterion of judgment. It should be read so "that their words may be in harmony with their hearts and their hearts with God."[172] The fact that this will "please" God, a judgment term by nature, suggests that Francis is talking about judgment as an effort to be consistent with a divine measure. The prayer he affixes to the end of this text begins: "Almighty, eternal, just and merciful God, grant us in our misery that we may do for your sake alone what we know you want us to do, and always want what pleases you."[173] That God bears the norm of divine judgment is also displayed in one of Francis' scripture selections for the *Office*. The saint writes: "He comes to rule the world with justice and the peoples with his constancy."[174] Another translation of this same passage reads: "He will judge the world with righteousness, and the peoples with his truth."[175] God judges according to the divine measure of what is true or real. Above all other measures, this seems to be goodness when Francis imagines God as judge.

A Fragrant Flower

The native flowers of Francis' homeland must have given him great consolation. To this day, the blood-red fields of poppies and the orchards blooming with snowy apricot buds symbolize a longstanding connection between the people and their land. Any familiarity with the sunflower that is now widely cultivated in Tuscany and Umbria might have driven Francis to make the connection between the plants of the earth and things of heaven. The modern term for sunflower in Italy is *girasole*, which translates as: turn to the sun. A lazy morning spent observing a field of these marvelous creations reveals the truth behind their Italian name, for they all stretch their faces in unison toward the source of their existence as it crosses the sky. Francis seems to have captured a similar sense of God in connection with the wonders of plant-life.

One instance where God is connected with flowers is found in the *Earlier Exhortation*. Francis commands his followers: "In the love which is God we beg all those whom these words reach to receive those fragrant words of our Lord Jesus Christ written above with divine love and kindness."[176] Of the two primary sources of fragrance, flowers and perfume, only the former is connected, via insemination, with the idea of the life of Christ growing within a person. Francis goes on to say that these words "are spirit and life," further accentuating the association between the living flower and the living God. In the *Letter to All the Faithful,* Francis writes: "I am the servant of all and so I am bound to wait upon everyone and make known to them the fragrant words of my Lord. ...I decided to send you a letter bringing a message with the words of our Lord Jesus Christ, who is the Word of the Father, and of the Holy Spirit, whose words are spirit and life."[177] Here the words, as fragrant flowers, are not just loosely tied to God; they are directly identified with a Trinitarian expression of the Godhead.

According to The *Canticle of Brother Sun*, flowers play a part in Mother Earth's activity: "All praise be yours, my Lord, through Sister Earth, our mother, Who feeds us in her sovereignty and produces various fruits with coloured flowers and herbs."[178] In this case, the flowers stand for God's effort to sustain life by marking the fruit. They also point toward God's effort to govern life by signifying the cycles of life.

If the connection between flowers and fruit is one that Francis carries with him, than his use of the scriptural discussion of ground quality adds to the floral image of God. Several Gospel passages are brought together to fashion Francis' reflection of the way God dwells in the soul of the human person.[179] In *The Rule of 1221*, Francis begins by asserting that, "The seed is the word of God."[180] The point Francis is trying to make is that in order for the word to flower and bear fruit it must be carefully planted in soil that is able to protect, nourish, and sustain the precious gift of God's life growing meaningfully in the human creature. Alternately, when the seed is scattered on the surface of the earth, "the devil comes and takes away the word from their heart, that they may not believe and be saved."[181] If the seed falls amidst rocks he says: "these have no root, but believe for a while, and in time of temptation fall away.[182] When seed attempts to grow among thorny weeds it cannot find the nourishment it needs to flower.[183] Of the seed that will survive he writes: "But that upon good ground, these are they who, with a right and good heart, having heard the word, hold it fast, and bear fruit in patience."[184] From Francis' various uses of seed, flower, and fruit analogies, it is apparent that he formulates an imagistic relationship between God on the one hand, a living entity in the midst of creation, who participates as the source of the life cycle, and, on the other hand, with creation's most beautiful, desirable, and purposeful product, the flower which bears the seed of the next generation in the cycle.

****

Throughout this chapter Francis' imaginative activity has been shown to be an active participant in his endeavor to fashion a spirituality based on how one perceives facets of reality. Since reality is understood in terms of the dynamic effort to link the internal and external features of an expanding world of experience, images of change were probed to identify the significance of this activity in Francis' rendering of the spiritual life. Using an ORT approach to the imagination, Francis' writings have yielded a multitude of images that guide and sustain the way one might grow in a life of faith, and turn one's self, heart and soul, over to God. His perception of this God, evolving from a series of experiences across his life, has been shown to include a lively and ever-changing mélange of imagery that reveals the saint's successful attempt to keep God as the fundamental source of meaning in his spiritual life. Since an ORT view of imagination is ever directed toward imaginatively formulating meaning from one's experiences in an evolving perception of reality, Francis' efforts to connect religious significance to several notable experiences will introduce the concluding chapter.

Notes

1. Francis of Assisi, *The Prayer Before the Crucifix, Francis of Assisi: Early Documents: The Saint,* 40.

2. Francis of Assisi, *Letter to a General Chapter,* 108.

3. Francis of Assisi, *The Rule of 1221,* 41.

4. Francis of Assisi, *Letter to a Minister,* 110.

5. Ibid.

6. Francis of Assisi, *Letter to St Anthony,* in Marion Habig, ed. *St. Francis of Assisi: Writings and Early Biographies: English Omnibus of Sources for the Life of St. Francis.* (Quincy, IL: Franciscan University Press, 1991), 164.

7. Francis of Assisi, *Letter to a General Chapter,* 104.

8. Francis of Assisi, *Letter to All the faithful,*97-98.

9. Ibid., 98.

10. Francis of Assisi, *Letter to the Peoples,* 116.

11. Ibid.

12. Francis of Assisi, *The Rule of 1221,* 40. The referred passage is Luke 21:34-35.

13. Ibid., 52.

14. Francis of Assisi, *The Paraphrase of the Our Father,* 160; Francis of Assisi, *A Prayer Inspired by the Our Father,* in Regis J. Armstrong, J.A. Wayne Hellman, and William J. Short, eds. *Francis of Assisi: The Early Documents.* Vol. 1, *The Saint* (New York: New City Press, 1999), 160.

15. See for example: Francis of Assisi, *The Praises To Be Said at All the Hours,* in Regis J. Armstrong, J.A. Wayne Hellman, and William J. Short, eds. *Francis of Assisi: The Early Documents.* Vol. 1, *The Saint* (New York: New City Press, 1999), 161.

16. Francis of Assisi, *Salutation of the Blessed Virgin,* in Marion Habig, ed. *St. Francis of Assisi: Writings and Early Biographies: English Omnibus of Sources for the Life of St. Francis.* (Quincy, IL: Franciscan University Press, 1991), 136.

17. Francis of Assisi, *Letter to All the Faithful,* 97.

18. Ibid., 96.

19. Francis of Assisi, *The Rule of 1221,* 50.

20. Francis of Assisi, *The Admonitions,* 84.

21. Francis of Assisi, *The Office of the Passion,* 144.

22. Francis of Assisi, *The Rule of 1221,* 47.

23. Ibid.

24. Ibid., 48-49.

25. Francis of Assisi, *The Paraphrase of the Our Father,* 160.

26. Francis of Assisi, *Letter to All the Faithful,* 94.

27. Ibid., 95.

28. An example of "you will" might be found in a derivative of *cŏgo* or *cŏactum* with the sense of compulsion or force that these terms suggest. Accept for a reference to being compelled to do something because of sickness, Francis seems to avoid such expressions of requirement.

29. Francis of Assisi, *Letter to All the Faithful,* 96.

30. Francis of Assisi, *Letter to All the Rulers of the People,* 116.

31. Francis of Assisi, *The Letter to all the Superiors of the Friars Minor,* 113.

32. Francis of Assisi, *The Rule of 1221,* 35.

33. Ibid., 35-36.

34. Francis of Assisi, *Letter to All Clerics,* 101.

35. Francis of Assisi, *The Rule of 1221,* 36.

36. Ibid., 38.

37. Ibid.,39.

38. Francis of Assisi, *The Rule of 1221*, 41.

39. Ibid., 45.

40. Ibid., 44.

41. Ibid., 43.

42. Francis of Assisi, *The Rule of 1223*, 59.

43. Francis of Assisi, *The Testament of St. Francis*, 68.

44. Ibid.

45. Francis of Assisi, *The Admonitions*, 80-81.

46. Ibid., 83.

47. Ibid., 84.

48. Francis of Assisi, *Letter to a General Chapter*, 104.

49. Francis of Assisi, *The Canticle of Exhortation for the Ladies of San Damiano*, in Regis J. Armstrong, J.A. Wayne Hellman, and William J. Short, eds. *Francis of Assisi: The Early Documents*. Vol. 1, *The Saint* (New York: New City Press, 1999),115.

50. Francis of Assisi, *The Rule of 1221*, 44.

51. Ibid.

52. Ibid., 35. A connection can be made here between the obligations of obedience and the obligations of spiritual friendship as Aelred describes it. In neither case do these concepts require taking a stance against what is right.

53. Ibid., 40.

54. Ibid., 52.

55. Francis of Assisi, *Letter to a General Chapter*, 104.

56. Ibid., 108

57. Francis of Assisi, *The Rule of 1221*, 47.

58. Francis of Assisi, *The Admonitions*, 79.

59. Ibid.

60. Francis of Assisi, *The Testament of St. Francis*, 69.

61. Francis of Assisi, *The Admonitions*, 85.

62. Ibid.

63. Ibid.

64. Francis of Assisi, *The Prayer before the Crucifix*, in Armstrong et al, 40.

65. Francis of Assisi, *Letter to All the Faithful*, 93.

66. Ibid., 94.

67. Francis of Assisi, *The Rule of 1221*, 31.

68. Ibid., 52.

69. Francis of Assisi, *A Letter to a General Chapter*, 106.

70. Ibid., 107.

71. Francis of Assisi, *The Testament of St. Francis*, 68.

72. Francis of Assisi, *The Testament*, in Regis J. Armstrong, J.A. Wayne Hellman, and William J. Short, eds. *Francis of Assisi: The Early Documents*. Vol. 1, *The Saint* (New York: New City Press, 1999), 125.

73. Francis of Assisi, *The Canticle of Brother Sun*, 131.

74. Francis of Assisi, *The Admonitions*, 79. Recall that the Tree of Knowledge was the forbidden tree.

75. Ibid., 84.

76. Francis of Assisi, *Letter to All the Faithful*, 95.

77. Francis of Assisi, *Exhortations to the Clergy: The Second Letter to the Custodians*, in Regis J. Armstrong, J.A. Wayne Hellmann, and William J. Short, eds. *Francis of Assisi: Early Documents*. Vol. 1, *The Saint* (New York: New City Press, 1999), 60.

78. Francis of Assisi, *The Rule of 1221*, 43.

79. Ibid.

80. Ibid., 45.

81. Ibid., 77.

82. Francis of Assisi, *The Rule of 1223*, 58.

83. Francis of Assisi, *The Rule of 1221*, 32.

84. Ibid., 59.

85. Francis of Assisi, *A Letter to the Entire Order*, 107.

86. Francis of Assisi, *Letter to All the Faithful*, 96.

87. I am not advocating marital relationships of inequality nor am I suggesting that Francis was in any sense an extreme advocate of such relationships. However, it seems from the text that he is describing a female role which, in his time, often involved a position of reliance upon the male role for security, shelter, and sustenance.

88. Francis of Assisi, *A Letter to a General Chapter*, 106..

89. Francis of Assisi, *The Canticle of Brother Sun*, 130.

90. Ibid., 131.

91. Francis of Assisi, *Letter to All the Faithful*, 97.

92. Francis of Assisi, *Letter to a General Chapter*, 105.

93. Francis of Assisi, *Letter to All the Faithful*, 99.

94. The Latin text uses a variant of *observo*: *recipere et operari et observare*. See Godet et Mailleux, *Corpus des Sources Franciscaines*, vol. 5, 166. Possible definitions for *observo* begin with: "to watch, observe, regard, attend to," and only later move to "guard" and then "obey." The Classic Latin Dicitonary, 1948, s.v. *observo*. The visual nature of the word clearly stands out.

95. Francis of Assisi, *The Admonitions*, 78.

96. Ibid.

97. Ibid., 79.

98. Ibid.

99. Ibid., 83-84.

100. Francis of Assisi, *Letter to All Clerics*, 101.

101. Francis of Assisi, *Letter to a General Chapter*, 105.

102. Francis of Assisi, *The Rule of 1221*, 46.

103. Ibid.

104. Francis of Assisi, *The Testament of St. Francis*, 167.

105. Ibid., 67.

106. Ibid.

107. Ibid.

108. Francis of Assisi, *The Prayer before the Crucifix*, in Armstrong et al, 40.

109. Francis of Assisi, *Letter to All the Faithful*, 96-97.

110. The Latin text for "they have known" is *cognoverunt*, a parsing of *cognosco*. See Godet et Mailleux, *Corpus des Sources Franciscaines*, vol. 5, 72. Definitions for *cognosco* include: "to become acquainted with, remark, notice, perceive, see," and also "to recognize." See The Classic Latin Dictionary, 1948, s.v. *cognosco*. For the most part, each of these senses for the word refers to an experiential encounter, past or present.

111. Francis of Assisi, *Letter to All the Faithful*, 95.

112. Francis of Assisi, *A Letter to a General Chapter*, 104.

113. Francis of Assisi, *The Admonitions*, 78-79.

114. Francis of Assisi, *The Office of the Passion*, 153.

115. Francis of Assisi, *Letter to the Rulers of the Peoples*, 115.

116. Ibid.

117. Francis of Assisi, *The Rule of 1221*, 43.

118. The modern concept of atheism does not seem to play a part in medieval thinking.

119. Francis of Assisi, *Letter to All Clerics, 100-101.*

120. Ibid., 101.

121. The Latin text actually uses *ignoramus.* See Godet et Mailleux, *Corpus des Sources Franciscaines,* vol. 5, 152.

122. Thomas of Celano, *Lives of St. Francis by Thomas of Celano: First Life, Book Two,* in Marion Habig, ed. *St. Francis of Assisi: Writings and Early Biographies: English Omnibus of Sources for the Life of St. Francis.* (Quincy, IL: Franciscan University Press, 1991), 308-311.

123. Francis of Assisi, *Letter to All the Faithful,* 97.

124. Francis of Assisi, *The Rule of 1221*, 50.

125. Francis of Assisi, *Letter to All Clerics,* 101. See also Francis of Assisi, *The Testament of St. Francis,* 67.

126. Francis of Assisi, *The Rule of 1221*, 39.

127. Francis of Assisi, *The Canticle of Brother Sun,* 130-131.

128. Ibid.

129. Francis of Assisi, *Letter to All the Faithful,* 98-99.

130. Francis of Assisi, *The Canticle of Brother Sun,* 130.

131. Francis of Assisi, *Praises of God,* 125; See also Francis of Assisi, *The Praises of God,* in Regis J. Armstrong, J.A. Wayne Hellman, and William J. Short, eds. *Francis of Assisi: The Early Documents.* Vol. 1, *The Saint* (New York: New City Press, 1999), 109; See also Francis of Assisi, *The Office of the Passion,* 143. In this text, Francis calls upon scriptural imagery to describe God as a foster mother: "To you I was committed at birth, from my mother's womb you are my God."

132. Francis of Assisi, *Praises of God,* 126. See also Armstrong et al, Francis of Assisi, *The Earlier Rule,* 85. A similar move from an expression of the superlative nature of God's goodness opens into a conceivably maternal description including the terms: "merciful, gentle, delightful, and sweet."

133. The plausibility of this image existing as a unique creation of Francis' rests heavily on the fact that most of the readings from the office are a compilation of intermixed Psalms and other biblical passages rather than single source readings, for example: all of Psalm 72. Since the writer was able to choose from amongst a broad spectrum of possible images, these texts reveal an intentional, or at least semi-intentional, effort to point toward a certain way of seeing God. The point that some of these texts appear to parallel events in the saint's life adds to the plausibility. While the editors of *Francis of Assisi: Early Documents* locate The Office of the Passion with Francis' writings, they describe it as a composition dependent at least in part on the earlier *Gallican* and *Roman Psalters.* However, it is in no way described as a copy of those works. See Armstrong et al, Francis of Assisi: Early Documents: The Saint, 139.

134. See for instance: Celano, *The Life of Saint Francis by Thomas Celano: First Life, The First Book,* 231-233.

135. Francis of Assisi, *The Office of the Passion,* 142.

136. Ibid., 142-143.

137. Ibid., 143.

138. Ibid.

139. Ibid.

140. Ibid., 144.

141. Ibid., 145.

142. Ibid., 145.

143. Ibid., 146.

144. Ibid., 148.

145. Ibid., 151.

146. Ibid.

147. Ibid., 152. There is one reading that contains the idea of God defending the suppli-cant by using violence. See Francis of Assisi, *The Office of the Passion, 153.* Here the writer of Exodus exclaims: "your right hand, O Lord, has struck the enemy," but a line later Francis uses a Psalm that goes: "See, you lowly ones, and be glad; you who seek God, may your hearts be merry!" As it turns out, God's defensive act comes in conjunc-tion with a visual act, an endeavor to see, on the part of a marginalized person.

148. Celano, *The Life of Saint Francis by Thomas Celano: First Life, The First Book,* 240. He writes: "She was moved by motherly compassion for him, and loosened the chains, she let him go free."

149. Chiara Frugoni, *Francis of Assisi: A Life,* 18-19. She indicates that Bernardone's influence was also extended through his willingness to lend money and reap the benefits in land taken through forfeiture of some debts. Little also describes the effects of this rising new class throughout his book. See: Little, Religious *Poverty and the Profit Econ-omy in Medieval Europe,* 23-24.

150. Francis of Assisi, *The Prayer before the Crucifix,* in Armstrong et al, 40.

151. Francis of Assisi, *The Rule of 1221,* 36-37. Wandering outside of obedience was a monastic concept regarding traveling monks who gave a bad name to those who fulfilled the vow of stability.

152. Francis of Assisi, *Letter to a General Chapter,* 104.

153. Francis of Assisi, *Letter to All the faithful,* 96.

154. Ibid., 97.

155. Ibid.

156. Ibid.

157. Ibid. 98.

158. Francis of Assisi, *Letter to All the Faithful,* 93. The editors of *Francis of Assisi: Early Documents: The Saint* make a point of the importance of servitude to Francis, 45.

159. Ibid., 94.

160. Ibid., 95.

161. Francis of Assisi, *Letter to All Clerics,* 101. The rendering of an account is a very popular theme for Francis who may have observed his father calling in debt obligations on a regular basis. See also Francis of Assisi, *Exhortations to the Clergy: A Letter to the Rulers of the Peoples,* in Armstrong et al, 59; Francis of Assisi, *The Earlier Rule, in Armstrong et al,* 67; and Ibid., 74.

162. Celano, *The Life of Saint Francis by Thomas of Celano: The First Book,* in Armstrong et al,188-189.

163. Francis of Assisi, *The Rule of 1221,* 33.

164. Ibid., 37.

165. Ibid., 47.

166. Francis of Assisi, *Letter to All the Faithful,* 99.

167. Ibid., 94-95.

168. Francis of Assisi, *Praises of God,* 125.

169. Francis of Assisi, *Letter to a General Chapter,* 104.

170. Ibid., 107.

171. Ibid.

172. Ibid.

173. Ibid., 108.

174. Francis of Assisi, *The Office of the Passion,* 146.
175. The New Oxford Annotated Bible: Psalm 96:13.
176. Francis of Assisi, *Earlier Exhortation,* in Armstrong et al, 45.
177. Francis of Assisi, *Letter to All the Faithful,* 93.
178. Francis of Assisi, *The Canticle of Brother Sun,*, 131.
179. See Luke 8; Matthew 13, Mark 4.
180. Francis of Assisi, *The Rule of 1221,* 48.
181. Ibid.
182. Ibid.
183. Ibid.
184. Ibid.

CHAPTER EIGHT
MEANING AND CONCLUSION

There is one focus area for the explication of an ORT perspective on imagination that has yet to be connected with Francis' writings. This area, the making of meaning, is a fitting part of the conclusion of a study of Francis' imaginative activity since it is the final purpose of the workings of his imagination. Francis imagines a two-dimensional world in which one can spiritually perceive the actions of God interpenetrating with one's physical view of God's natural creation. This is the basis of his experiencing, and it is also the basis of the meaning that he discovers, draws from, and crafts for his personal experience. His formulation of meaning, in turn, is the impetus to a life of self-giving, humility, gentleness toward others, and love of God, all in the face of personal suffering. With this in mind, the current chapter will peer at a few examples from Francis' writings where he uses imagery to make sense of an experience. Then, with the final piece of Francis' imaginative activity in place, it will be possible to look back over the path this work has taken to arrive at Francis' discovery of meaning through his imaginative effort to create a spiritual view of the world and pass this on to those who might want to see as he does.

Meaning

Object Relations Theory has shown that the seed of meaning is found in the first effort to put order to chaos. Meaning grows as one identifies relationships where relationships are commonly thought to exist, and, finally, it flowers where new relationships are formed where no one has yet considered them to be. Jonte-Pace pointed out the crossover between interior creativity and exterior discovery as the summit of meaningful imaginative activity while Winnicott tied meaning back to the earliest relationships. He observed that transitional objects are the first attempts to apply meaning. This is one reason why maternal and then God images feature so strongly in meaning-making. Another feature of this activity is the communication or transfer of meaning. Davis and Wallbridge found that it occurs almost wholly through implicit means, which is where Winnicott's interest in symbolism comes into consideration. The difference and similarity tension found in symbols is the hallmark of transitional phenomena. In this light, Biblical imagery can be seen as a form of symbolism in some of Francis' works.

Pruyser also associated meaning with the use of symbols. He determined that there is a process of symbolic attachment that comes across almost as a parallel activity to object relating. Studzinski added that certain symbolism contains surplus meaning that can be applied to more significant experience. Pruyser went on to indicate that the making of meaning is a complex procedure since the object about which meaning is forming evolves as the experiencing person does. He joined with Winnicott in conveying that a primary avenue for the communication of meaning is culture. A religious community, such as Francis established, is a culture in its own way. Pruyser and Studzinski emphasized that culture is an external matrix of meaning insofar as the imaginations of its participants are tutored according to a somewhat common way of seeing.

McDargh presented meaning in terms of an effort to grasp reality. He proposed that the track of object relations toward more transcendent objects is an indication of the human orientation toward a more profound sense of reality. McDargh also noted that one's primary images, such as those of God, parents, and other leading figures, affect who the individual senses him or herself to be, his or her self-meaning. Rizzuto described meaning as a new way of relating with old relationships. One example of this that she displayed was the interaction of personal God images with official God images. The earlier section on Francis' images of God certainly corroborates this. Rizzuto added that there will usually be several re-encounters between the individual and early primary images throughout a life of meaning-making.

Many of these listed features of meaning-making are found in Francis' writings, and several of them have been touched upon under other headings, such as the image of family that played so strongly in his conception of the relationship between himself and his brothers. Now a few general notions of meaning will be drawn from the writings of the saint after which two areas of Francis' experience will be explored to see how he formulated a meaningful understanding of them. In the first of these more detailed experiences Francis' yearning for nobility will be probed; then, his many confrontations with suffering will be taken into consideration. Recollecting previous discussions of suffering as chaotic or disordered experience, this latter area is a particularly fertile ground for an imaginative approach to meaning-making.

A Few General Comments on Meaning

The formation of a real, and therefore meaningful, world demands an imaginative expansion beyond the use of the senses. Sight is the fundamental sense that must be taken to a higher level through the imagination in order for meaning to follow. If a fragment of *The Earlier Rule* can be attributed to Francis, he makes the assertion that, "Wherever the brothers may be and in whatever place they may meet, they should see one another anew, spiritually and attentively, and honor one another without complaining."[1] The idea of seeing someone "anew, spiritually and attentively," requires the use of imaginative vision to set a relationship in a transformed and meaningful context.

In *The First Letter to the Custodians*, Francis reveals that a failure to perceive the importance of certain symbols or signs leads to the loss of important meaning. He writes: "Brother Francis... sends greetings, with new portents in heaven and on earth, which are very significant in the eyes of God, but are disregarded by the majority of people, including religious."[2] In an effort to get the clergy to uphold the meaning of the Eucharist he goes on to insist that "They should set the greatest value, too, on chalices, corporals, and all the ornaments of the altar that are related to the holy Sacrifice."[3] Regarding the accoutrements of the sacrifice as highly valued symbols is a gesture that encourages onlookers to see something occurring in a different light. Another gesture, which is itself a sign or symbol holding difference in tension, is the physical response made as the body and blood of Christ pass by. Francis comments that, "When the priest is offering sacrifice at the altar or the Blessed Sacrament is being carried about, everyone should kneel down and give praise, glory, and honour to our Lord and God, living and true."[4] He is attempting to accentuate the perceived reality of God's presence and action by connecting it with an intentional manifestation in the physical world. The image of an act of reverence typically directed toward a ruling figure is enmeshed with the Eucharistic image of the sacrificed Christ to yield, in meaning, the glorified risen Christ.

Francis carries the image of the earthly potentate a step further by linking it with the power of God which is both timeless and timely. He proposes: "When you are preaching, too, tell the people about the glory that is due to him, so that at every hour and when the bells are rung, praise and thanks may be offered to almighty God by everyone all over the world."[5] The bells may not directly carry out the symbolic value of God's power very well, but they could have the meaningful effect, once again, of bringing God's presence to mind.

It seems apparent that Francis understands the use of symbolic gesture to impart an implicit, meaningful level of understanding to people who would allow their imaginations to come into some degree of consonance with his imagination and that of others within the culture that is his order. He verifies this with a remark in *The Rule of 1221*: "All the friars, however, should preach by their example."[6] He is suggesting, with this statement, that the meaning of the Christ event can be safely passed on to other people by the symbolic expression of well-ordered action. In *A Letter to the Entire Order* Francis specifies the extreme lengths that are sometimes required to ensure that meaning is clearly transmitted through an action. He declares that, "At the sound of his name you should fall to the ground and adore him with fear and reverence; the Lord Jesus Christ, Son of the Most High, is his name, and he is blessed forever."[7]

Wanting Nobility

Francis' recognition of the application of imaginative activity to the formulation and communication of meaning was confirmed in the preceding pages. The great power of the imagination to create meaning from experience is even more distinctly revealed through some of the workings of Francis' own imagination that conceivably touch upon experiences for which he may have sought a more meaningful context. The first of these is a relationship with nobility.

Today there are a myriad of television programs, movies, travel opportunities, spas, automotive companies, and other lifestyle schemes that seek to put people in touch with a way of living that they could normally only aspire to achieve. The advertising industry is adept at playing with an inner desire of many people to be valued in a way that they do not feel themselves to be valued at present. This situation is often described as yearning for fame and fortune, even if only in the trappings. In light of the medieval countertrend of voluntary poverty, it is likely that a similar desire to be or have *more* was present in Francis' day. However, Francis fell into an interesting niche. As the son of a tradesman who was growing increasingly wealthier he was on the verge of becoming one of the rich and famous. Yet, he was unlikely to ever have fame in its quintessential medieval variety, the prestige of nobility. McDargh, more than any of the other ORT theorists, stressed the relationship between the individual's emerging sense of self and the kind of object images dwelling within his or her transitional space. In Francis' case, images associated with a noble and gallant lifestyle give some insight into how he might transform an experience of alienation into a unique and meaning-filled aspect of his maturing spiritual outlook.[8] As these images unfold from his writings it will become evident that he changes a type of social marginalization into a purposeful way of life.

The noble figure is a good example of the opposition in tension that is behind much imaginatively formulated meaning. Francis uses the character of a good nobleman, as a foil for the way of life that he and his followers have undertaken. It is no surprise that clothe has a function in the development of this imagery. If the noble person is seen as a knight, a reasonable possibility if Celano's depiction of Francis' youth is accurate, he would have gone through an investiture ceremony in which he receives some form of clothing or outer attire to mark his pledge of fidelity to his liege.[9] Along a similar vein Francis writes, in *The Rule of 1221*, that, "The friars who have already made their profession of obedience may have one habit with a hood and, if necessary, another without a hood. They may also have a cord and trousers."[10] This hardly sounds like a knighting ceremony taking place in some regal hall, but that is exactly where Francis places the oppositional tension. He makes the contrast plain. After declaring that: "All the friars must wear poor clothes," he follows with the Scriptural comment: "*Those who wear fine clothes and live in luxury are in the house of kings.*"[11] These two distinct situations appear to be worlds apart, but Francis brings them back together in a single composite image that sets the brothers' lifestyle choice in a new and more meaningful light. He writes: "And even though people may call them hypocrites, the friars should never cease doing good. They should avoid expensive clothes in this world in order that they may have something to wear in the kingdom of heaven."[12] He is asking them to re-envision an image of noble conduct in this world within another image of a noble eternity in the greater kingdom of heaven. *The Rule of 1223* has a different expression of the same idea. Here the writer speaks of the "pinnacle of the most exalted poverty, and it is this, my dearest brothers, that has made you heirs and the kings of the kingdom of heaven, poor in temporal things, but rich in virtue."[13] The sublime height of poverty is identified as begging alms.[14] A related portion of *The Rule of 1221* specifies that, "Alms are an inheritance and a right which is due to the poor because our lord Jesus Christ acquired this inheritance for us."[15] Like a lord's assignment of lands to support the lower nobles who offer him fidelity, Francis presents an equivalent benefit for Jesus' obedient followers.

The bond of new meaning surrounding the nobleman image is further set up by a series of distinctions and similarities. Francis expands the disparity between the earthly life of nobility and that of his brothers and himself by pointing out the potential for vanity in the former way of life. In *The Admonitions* he explains that, "If you were the most handsome and the richest man in the world..., all that would be something extrinsic to you; it would not belong to you, and you could not boast of it."[16] To hold the tension together, the saint raises a similarity between the two existences. Like a nobleman who can be stripped of the outer signs of his status and left in dishonor, Francis dictates a similar fate for a member of his order caught in a state of shame: "If a friar is tempted and commits fornication, he must be deprived of the habit. By his wickedness he has lost the right to wear it and so he must lay it aside completely and be dismissed from the order."[17] At another point the comparison diverges. An additional sign of nobility is the manner of their travel, traditionally by horse. On this matter Francis proclaims: "They are also forbidden to ride horseback, unless they are forced to it by sickness or real need."[18] Francis also presents another similarity. He indicates that a banquet has been set out for both the noble knights and his brothers, with the only difference being the host. For his brothers he says: "When we receive no recompense for our work, we can turn to God's table and beg alms from door to door."[19]

The final point of comparison between Francis and the nobleman is the presence of a virtuous woman toward whom they direct their attention. Frugoni makes much of this elusive female figure in Francis' story, and Joan Mowat Erikson identified this theme even earlier. Frugoni connects Francis' woman with the heroines of the troubadours, calling Francis' version "Lady Largesse" because of her self-giving.[20] Erikson sees this woman as a compilation of other female figures who have significant roles, in one way or another, within Francis' hagiographic story.[21] In some cases the compiled figures were based on living women such as his mother and female friends. A quick reading of the allegorical account of the saint's association with Lady Poverty in *The Sacred Exchange between Saint Francis and Lady Poverty* will indicate why so much attention is paid to the elusive woman in Francis' imaginative life.[22] In his words there is really only one good source for such a character, which actually reveals a family of such women. In *A Salutation of the Virtues*, Lady Poverty is one among several sisters under the guardianship of God. She can, with great care, be possessed in the sense that women were once said to be, but her hand can also be easily lost at the slightest offense to her dignity. Francis writes: "Hail, Queen Wisdom! The Lord save you, with your sister, pure, holy Simplicity. Lady Holy Poverty, God keep you, you're your sister, holy Humility. Lady Holy Love, God keep you, with your sister, holy Obedience. All holy virtues, God keep you, God, from whom you proceed and come."[23] The close identification between these women and God is evidenced by their capitalized pronouns in another, more exact translation of the passage, such as Francis only does for God, and by his statement that they "proceed" from God. Added to this is his comment that, "In all the world there is not a man who can possess any one of you without first dying to himself."[24] Regarding possession and offense, Francis also remarks that, "The man who offends against one, possesses none and violates all."[25]

Taking all the imagery of nobility under consideration, the idea that Francis rearranged images of nobility from his aspirations earlier in life to derive a meaningful new outlook from what may have otherwise been a source of endless frustration and even anger is well founded. Recalling Pruyser's ideas about projection as a source of imagery, Francis could have depicted all people of noble standing as the epitome of evil, but he did not. If he had any say in the development of *The Rule of 1223*, than the following could have been his words: "I warn all the friars and exhort them not to condemn or look down on people whom they see wearing soft or gaudy clothes and enjoying luxuries in food or drink; each one should rather condemn and despise himself."[26] In fact, Francis may have unwittingly instituted a type of introjection by including some positive features of the lifestyle of a noble knight into his spiritual view of the world. Examples of this are--1) attire: outer appearance should reflect inner condition, 2) oath: a pledge of loyalty, fidelity, and obedience to a higher authority, 3) fellowship: a banquet to commemorate the end of a great struggle, 4) motivation: a reputable woman who inspires the knight's courage and makes his sacrifice worthwhile. The coexistence of these positive characteristics alongside many less admirable qualities of nobility also substantiates the ORT conception that various images intermix in different ways as meaning is sought for a new experience.

Suffering

Francis is known for seeking a life of hardship. Living as a reflection of the Christ that he adores, he accepts so much of the pain that life offers simply because Jesus did not reject the suffering of the cross. In fact, an image of Christ experiencing this agony is behind the majority of his suffering imagery. The contemporary film, *The Passion of Christ*, allows viewers to visualize what Jesus went through in graphic detail.[27] What seems to take place for many of these vicarious onlookers is an act of sympathy. They have a felt response *for* the sufferer. When Francis contemplates his passion of Christ he is able to do so through an act of empathy in which similar experiences of suffering enable him to enter into a closer encounter *with* the sufferer.

It is difficult to know what it means to be cold unless you have felt the hostility of a bone chilling night of exposure without any expectation of near-term relief. The searing pain of wounded flesh means nothing unless you can connect it with your own memory-image of searing pain. The torment of hunger is just a phrase unless you recall the sensation that your hunger is finally abating not because you eat but because your body has stopped secreting the chemicals that tell it to feel hungry. And, it would be difficult to know what it feels like to be beaten and thrown down naked upon the cold hard ground unless that had happened to you like it happened to the Son of God.[28] While it is problematical to look in Francis' *vitae* for verification of his experience with the kind of suffering that makes for true empathy with Christ, his imaginative effort to apply meaning to suffering in his writings substantiates an encounter with these worst types of experience. It is also clear from his works that suffering falls into two dimensions: physical and emotional. A look at his ability to discover or create meaning from experiences of suffering will touch on each of these areas respectively, followed by a consideration of his unique linking of scriptural imagery with the series of painful run-ins he has with his father.

According to the dating of the *Letter to All the Faithful*, Francis, upon returning from a challenging journey to the Middle East, writes that, "because of my sickness and ill health I cannot personally visit each one individually."[29] Francis is a highly mobile individual. For him to avoid an otherwise intended trip to see some of his followers is a sign that his illness is quite debilitating. In *The Rule of 1221* he trains some of these individuals to see their own sickness in a new light, a light through which they can actually want to be sick. He proposes: "I beg the friar who is sick to thank God for everything; he should be content to be as God wishes him to be, in sickness or in health, because it is those who were destined for eternal life that God instructs by sickness and infliction and the spirit of compunction."[30] Although many people today might be un-inclined to believe that God intends suffering, Francis' idea that there is something to be learned from it demonstrates that he identifies suffering as a source of meaning. When he communicates with some of his sisters in *The Canticle of Exhortation for the Ladies of San Damiano*, he refers to the energy-sapping effects of sickness. He addresses: "Those weighed down by sickness and the others wearied because of them, all of you: bear it in peace. For you will sell this fatigue at a very high price and each one will be crowned queen in heaven with the Virgin Mary."[31] Using another paradoxical shift he turns something that any person would rather get rid of (fatigue) into a valued commodity that, in this situation, might be seen as the dowry that would obtain for them a royal spouse.

Looking again to Francis' own experience, Celano points out that Francis endures an excruciating operation in which parts of his face are cauterized to forestall the failure of his vision.[32] One line of *The Canticle of Bother Sun* might, in part, refer to this ordeal. Francis exclaims: "All praise be yours, my Lord, through Brother Fire, through whom you brighten up the night. How beautiful is he, how gay! Full of power and strength."[33] We can imagine Francis observing the fire by his bedside with the metal implements beginning to glow in the dancing flames. He gives meaning to the medium of his impending agony by calling the fire *brother* and linking its dreadful power with its more gentle qualities of beauty and playfulness as one might otherwise enjoy them while gathered around a warm fire in the company of good friends.

During Francis' time, other than a session in the hands of a surgeon, one of the most horrific forms of suffering is leprosy. As this disease progresses, wounds remain open, limbs are lost, and flesh rots on a live body. A human being begins to resemble a decaying corpse in all but breath and the remaining mobility he or she retains. Perhaps what is almost as bad as the physical suffering is the knowledge that one is abandoned in the hour of need. Lepers were shut out of contact with the rest of society, including their families. There was often no one to bandage their wounds or bring them the food that a charitable soul might leave at a safe distance. Francis admits to sharing the feeling of repulsion that accompanies any thought of people undergoing this torment, a torment that was easily ignored under the supposition that the leper had earned it for some grave personal fault. Francis admits that, "when I was in sin, the sight of lepers nauseated me beyond measure."[34] However, if his life as a whole was permeated with meaning, he clarifies that the path he took and the way that he was able to visualize reality is significantly attributable to his experience of suffering encountered with leprosy and its victims. He adds: "but then God himself led me into their company, and I had pity on them. When I had at once become acquainted with them what had previously nauseated me became a source of spiritual and physical consolation for me."[35]

While the experience of suffering with the lepers may have affected Francis' imagination and informed his spiritual outlook, it is quite possible that he did not leave the experience with the lepers behind him. Several theorists tout the idea that he actually suffered from the disease, at least later in life.[36] Francis never makes a direct reference to the stigmata that he is said to have, but perhaps wounds related to his suffering, wounds that affected his peripheral appendages, as is often the case with leprosy, give him cause to contemplate their meaning in connection with the image of the wounded Christ.[37] As Scarry pointed out, pain stimulates an imaginative effort to make some sense of it, to give it a context because pain lacks one otherwise.

The idea that Francis suffered along with the lepers is born out by his selection of related scriptural imagery for *The Office of the Passion*. In a *Matins* prayer he reiterates: "I am numbered with those who go down into the pit; I am a man without strength. My couch is among the dead."[38] Another scriptural prayer for *None* touches on the emotional impact of this departure: "To the dust of death you have brought me down. For they kept after him whom you smote, and added to the pain of him you wounded."[39] In a prayer for *Vespers* Francis makes a remark that comes closest to associating bodily suffering with the wounds of Christ. He orders his brothers to: "Prepare your hearts and take up his holy cross; live by his holy commandments to the last."[40] So it seems that physical suffering, whether it comes as a nagging cold or the feeling that burning steel is being forced into one's flesh, is a source for Francis' imaginative endeavor to set meaning to experience in light of other imagery held within his transitional space.

Much of the suffering that has been considered so far is physical in nature or at least in origin. It must be emphasized that mental or emotional suffering can be every bit as painful. The version of this kind of suffering that Francis attends to most closely is shame-related. In many situations shame or humiliation can be dehumanizing, yet, extremes of humility are a hallmark of Francis' order. Shame is, therefore, a particularly important experience that must be put into a meaningful context if the sufferer is ever going to move toward some form of wholeness in Christ. Returning to the rule on begging for alms, Francis allows that, "If they are in want, they should not be ashamed to beg alms, remembering that our Lord Jesus Christ, the Son of the living, all-powerful God set his face like a very hard rock and was not ashamed. He was poor and he had no home of his own and he lived on alms."[41] Francis dignifies a potential encounter with humiliation by co-imaging it with a vision of the dignified Christ engaged in the same situation. This image, the begging Christ, is a clear-cut product of the imaginative search for meaning. Jesus wears many titles throughout history, related to many of his official images, but Holy Beggar does not seem to be one of them.

To give added meaning to his followers' experience of humiliation, Francis adds: "If people insult them and refuse to give them alms, they should thank God for it, because they will be honoured before the judgment-seat of our Lord Jesus Christ for these insults."[42] Normally one might expect this scenario to play out with the reviler facing judgment before the tribunal, but Francis seems to understand that the image of someone else suffering for an offense he or she has given does not adequately fuel one's ability to persevere in the love of God under adversity. Francis does not allow his followers to forever project the blame for suffering outward where it can no longer be a source of spiritual edification. He suggests a similar turn inward in *The Admonitions*. He writes: "A man really loves his enemy when he is not offended by the injury done to himself, but for the love of God feels burning sorrow for the sin his enemy has brought on his own soul, and proves his love in a practical way."[43] The turn to contemplate personal shortcomings is not as inspiring as thinking about an eternal honor, but it can be supportive of a spiritual life.

Francis clearly reveals that suffering is a distinctive part of his meaning-making effort in *True and Perfect Joy*. To his chronicler he clarifies that joy is not a matter of having all one's desires fulfilled. He does this by declaring that the realization of many of his most well-known desires does not yield joy. Instead, he describes the end of an arduous journey on a piercing cold night. When he seeks entry into one of the friaries that he has founded he is told: "'Go away!... This is not a decent hour to be going about! You can't come in!'"[44] After further entreaty he is told: "'Go away! You are simple and uneducated fellow. From now on don't stay with us anymore. We are so many and so important that we don't need you.'"[45] In the end Francis shows that the meaning of this experience expands beyond joy. He says: "I tell you that if I kept patience and was not upset—that is true joy and true virtue and the salvation of the soul.'"[46] The editors of *Francis of Assisi: Early Documents* assert that this text cannot be accurately dated except that it originates with Francis.[47] Speculating that it was a later writing of his would allow for the possibility that he wrote it with another experience of humiliation in mind. The effort of various factions within the order to limit his influence and authority has certain parallels with the statements of the porter in Francis' story. The experience must be close to that of parents who raise a family only to find that they are not welcome at the homes of their offspring. It is an experience that for most people would defy meaning. For Francis, it is seen as an opportunity for God to accomplish his salvation.

For further expressions of emotional suffering, *The Office of the Passion* has an amazing sub-drama unfolding within it. Of course there is the drama of

Jesus' ordeal at the hands of the Jerusalem authorities, but this drama is arranged in a fashion that allows it to also be seen as Francis' effort to put a personal ordeal into a structure of meaning that would enable him to connect his experience with that of the Anointed One. The story of Francis' suffering at the hands of his father is found in Celano's accounts among other sources. Its level of particular detailing and the fact that it does not mirror the same situation in any of the common models of hagiography available in Francis' time suggests that it is highly authentic.

As Celano tells the narrative, Francis sells some of his father's wears in Foligno, after which he is moved to donate the proceeds for the restoration of the Church of San Damiano. Out of fear, the money is not accepted by the resident priest. Then, Francis' father "went around everywhere like a diligent spy, wanting to learn what had happened to his son."[48] "Calling together his friends and neighbors, he hurried to the place where the servant of God was staying."[49] This causes Francis to return to his chosen place of hiding in a hole or a covered pit. Eventually, while maintaining a state of serenity throughout the ordeal, "he left the pit and exposed himself openly to the curses of his persecutors."[50] "When those who knew him saw this, they compared what he was now with what he had been; and they began to revile him miserably. Shouting out that he was mad and demented, they threw the mud of the streets and stones at him."[51] Upon hearing of his sons' ridicule, Francis' father "immediately arose, not indeed to free him but rather to destroy him; and, with no regard for moderation, he rushed upon him like a wolf upon a sheep, and looking upon him with a fierce and savage countenance, he laid hands upon him and dragged him shamelessly and disgracefully home. Thus, without mercy, he shut him up in a dark place for several days, and thinking to bend his spirit to his own will, he first used words and then blows and chains."[52] After Francis' mother frees him, he returns to his place of solitude where he again encounters his father, who "ran to that place hoping that if he could not recall him from his ways, he might at least drive him from the province."[53] After this, Francis travels with his father to renounce his family relationships before the bishop where he relinquishes every attachment to his father including the clothes on his back.[54]

Celano makes a faintly visible attempt to transpose an image of Christ's passion on the details of Francis' difficulties with his father. There is even some similarity to the initial reaction of Bernard of Clairvaux's family upon hearing of his religious intentions, but these issues do not eclipse the fact that a young man and his father are at such odds that a public show of hostility ensues, involving the young man's shameful estrangement from the society in which he had been destined to have a significant place.[55] As a fellow friar, Celano would have been familiar with *The Office of the Passion*, so it is conceivable that he was influenced by the details about to be covered, but he also had contact with other brothers who could verify some of the events of Francis' paternal confrontation. In either case, both men are using available imagery to produce a meaningful context for an event that would be a psychological waypoint in any young man's life.

Near the beginning of the *Office* Francis uses scriptural words to recount: "All my foes whisper together against me and take counsel together. In return for my love they slandered me, but I prayed."[56] This idea of the community turning against Francis is used frequently. He repeats it again: "My friends and my companions stand back because of my affliction... I am imprisoned, and I cannot escape."[57] The last part of the quote might refer to the calmness with which Francis accompanied his father to the bishop. A scriptural prayer for *Matins* includes the exclamation: "O god, the haughty have risen up against me and the company of fierce men seeks my life, nor do they set you before their eyes."[58] He follows this with mention of going down into the pit and being among the dead. At *Prime* Francis would have his followers read that, "They have prepared a net for my feet; they have bowed me down; they have dug a pit before me, but they fall into it."[59] Most of the prayer *At Terce* retells a similar struggle with public humiliation. "Have pity on me, o God, for men trample upon me; all the day they press their attack against me. My adversaries trample upon me all the day; yes, many fight against me. All my foes whisper together against me; against me they imagine the worst. They who keep watch against my life take counsel together. When they leave they speak to the same purpose. All who see me scoff at me; they mock me with parted lips, they wag their heads... For all my foes I am an object of reproach, a laughingstock to my neighbours, and a dread to my friends."[60] The notion of exposure is easily linked with Celano's narrative, but the vulnerability at the hands of a guardian insinuates various interpretations. The guardians in question could be former friends in revelry who might be expected to stand at one's side in the event of a brawl. Alternately, the implication might be drawn toward Bernardone, or to both parents seeing as Francis' mother was at first a co-conspirator in his incarceration.

The theme of public confrontation and humiliation is also carried on in lines selected for *Sext*. Francis writes:

> In the way along which I walk they have hid a trap for me. I look to the right to see, but there is no one who pays heed... Since for your sake I bear insult, and shame covers my face, I have become an outcast to my brothers, a stranger to my mother's sons, because, Holy Father, zeal for your house consumes me, and the insults of those who blaspheme you fall upon me. Yet when I stumbled they were glad and gathered together; they gathered together striking me unawares... Must I restore what I did not steal?...They who repay evil for good harass me for pursuing good.[61]

In this passage Francis might be using the psalm to describe the estrangement he feels from his family, and there is a passing reference to his desire to use the money in question to rebuild a church. The reparation might point toward his return of all his garments to Bernardone. In a scriptural prayer for *None* he adds: "Indeed, many dogs surround me, a pack of evildoers closes in upon me.... They divide my garments among them, and for my vesture they cast lots... They opened their mouths against me like ravening and roaring lions."[62] The loss of Francis' clothing and the castigation by his father are mentioned again. After this, the confrontation imagery dwindles, but there is enough indication that Francis was doing what the evangelists did when they looked at Jesus' passion through the imagery of the Psalmists. Francis, and to an extent Celano after him, transposed a selection of sacred text images over a significant, traumatic experience that defies the order of a young man's reality until he imaginatively re-envisions it using images that inhabit his transitional space. Meaning is formed with imagery.

Concluding Appraisal

This work has been an effort to look at Francis of Assisi's writings that reflect a spiritual view of the world and to do this from a psychodynamic perspective of imagination. To that end the final few chapters have given ample evidence that Francis sees two worlds, the spiritual and the natural, intertwined, but with one having greater potential and meaning than the other. In his writings he demonstrates an astute use of the workings of his imagination to craft expressions that relate reality as it is commonly experienced with his perception of that reality, and more. This *more* can only be drawn from an inner landscape, called the transitional sphere, which is at the heart of Francis' imagination. Furthermore, he clearly understands the power of the imagination to bring others together into a more unified spiritual vision of the functioning and extent of reality as a whole.

The following pages will not seek to review and recount the analysis that has been applied to his writings. The analysis stands as it is, sometimes stretching an image or an idea, but on the whole giving ample testimony to the premise that there is much that can be gleaned from Francis' writings by employing a single-focus psychological lens: imagination. It is possible that there are a few imaginative expressions that were edited into these writings of Francis, but the sheer volume of imaginative expression uncovered in his writings affirms that we have a thoroughly plausible insight into the general activity of his imagination. Enough remains of the mosaic to sense the scope and beauty of the original artist's vision, and many people have shared in this vision.

A testimony to the claim that Francis was able to use his imagination, as described in this work, and to help others to craft their own spiritual views of the world, is found in various writings about his life. In his writings he made numerous statements that encouraged his readers to see in certain ways, in other words, to use their imaginations. He obviously made an impression on the imagination of Celano and other early chroniclers who were inspired to see Francis woven into the lineage of Christian holiness, but some of these people may have been moved as much by personal or near second-hand encounters with the saint than by his writings. The authors of the *Assisi Compilation* contend that Francis envisions himself as a work of artistry, projecting an image that has more meaning than the material from which it is constructed. They attribute to Francis the idea that, "God's servant is like a painting: a creature of God, through whom God is honored because of his blessings. He must not lay claim to any more merit than the wood and color do. Honor and glory must be given to God alone."[63] If these are the saint's words then he is also extending the notion of living as an image to others. However, it is the way Francis touches imaginations eight hundred some-odd-years later that is an enduring tribute to the far-reaching affect of his imaginative activity.

Lyn Scheuring observes of Francis that, "His universe was a huge forest of symbols redirecting the mind and heart to the creator."[64] She is among several scholars who find that Francis is a significant figure in the history of the imagination even if he did not add to the theoretical understanding of it. Calling Francis' spirituality "experiential," William Cook notes that, "Francis wants us not to remember the event so much as to experience it for ourselves."[65] This cannot happen without the imagination. Ewert Cousins points to a similar use of imagination. He claims that Francis engages in a "mysticism of the historic event," adding that, "In this type of consciousness, one recalls a significant event in the past, enters into its drama and draws from its spiritual energy, eventually moving beyond the event towards union with God."[66] Frugoni refers directly to Francis' imagination, but her statement appears to indicate that the saint's imagination did not fully resonate with that of his followers. She explains that the early brothers "would have liked to be fervent disciples, but they did not succeed in following Francis' bold imagination which unfolded endlessly, always a little beyond the common horizon."[67] Certainly these people are not transformed as much as Francis is by his imagination, but their choice to follow him is a sign that they are changed by the new vision of life he offers. At the same time, behind any communal manifestation of an individual imagination is the interior vision that shapes and drives it. Frugoni is right in pointing out that there is always something retained behind the imaginative expression that simply cannot find a shape, form, or relationship through which to participate in the public expression. A similar idea could reside with Trexler's notion that within Francis' story there is a "plasticity that allows each passing age to imagine Francis as its own."[68]

Various writers throughout recent times have sought to align their imaginations with the image of Francis and, by extension, the imagination that lies behind it. Amongst the previously mentioned spate of recent biographies written on the saint, each of the authors seeks to enter into his life by imagining their way into his setting in history.[69] In a less historically grounded but more moving biography, Julien Green uses his imagination to put readers in contact with a Francis who can be principally described as a singularly empathetic character.

Other than the general consideration of change through imagination, little else has been said about the impulse to action found in the initial description of imagination. But, an inspiration to action was and continues to result in imaginations touched by Francis'. Eric Doyle raises a call for concern over the effects of rapid technological advances in his book *Saint Francis and the Song of Brotherhood*. He is inspired to this action by Francis' *The Canticle of Brother Sun*, to which he adds a number of amendments, claiming: "Even as he said 'Brother Fire' we can learn to say 'Sister Nuclear Energy.'"[70] Amongst his other additions are Lady Sister Energy, Brother DNA, and Brothers Coal, Oil, and Gas, which all touch on areas of experience that still call upon creative imaginations to perceive their meaningful purpose in light of their often disordered applications. Leonardo Boff is similarly moved by Francis' imagination. In his book

Saint Francis: A Model for Human Liberation, he is able to weave Francis' view of a world on the brink of consumerism with the much more complex social and economic world that we have created today.[71] Boff uses his imagination to envision Francis' very simple approach to reality as a clue for a necessarily more elaborate and challenging response to an ever more complex world.

There are other examples of the reach of Francis' imagination that go beyond imagining with Francis. Some writers and artists seek to imagine as Francis did. In his *I, Francis,* Carlo Carretto writes of Francis' vision of the world in first person format, but from the time perspective of eight hundred years after the saint's death.[72] In this manner he attempts to project the saint's imagination into the future. Another first person account brings the written and depicted image together in an unexpected format. Marvel Comics Group's issue: *Francis: Brother of the Universe* contains first person dialogue and occasional scenes that are depicted from Francis' point-of-view.[73] Lauren Dunlap and Kathleen Frugé-Brown have put together a volume that reflects the use of Francis' imagination in its most complete form. Following after Carretto, their work *And I, Francis: The Life of Francis of Assisi in Word and Image* has Francis speaking in first person format while first person illustrations are made from conceptions of Francis' perspective.[74] The dust jacket synopsis goes so far as to call this a "creative but historically accurate 'autobiography.'"[75] How many other historical figures live on so fully in the imaginations of people from another generation in time and place?

Early on in this work, imagination was referred to as a description and not a definition. This remains the case. Much of what has been covered under the heading of *imagination* could be similarly set under the category of some other mental process like cognition. However, Warnock, for one, pointed out the fundamental versatility of using imagination as an approach to understanding human experience. The initial description of imagination as "the mental process that enables us to regard reality, ourselves, and God in such ways that invite or repel response, action, and connection," retains its value. It includes the full range of possible experience, the relational aspect, the correlation with change, the integral involvement of the self, and an ultimate reference to something beyond the self --God. Each of these features stands out, in varying amounts, in the general writings on the imagination, and in the imaginative perspective of ORT. What is most telling is that the same features also are thoroughly identifiable in Francis' writings from centuries prior. This, however, is not a claim for Francis' inclusion in the intellectual procession of imagination theory; rather, it is an assertion that in the proper hands there is a natural flowering of the imagination that is rightly distinguished by the elements listed above and throughout this work.

There is indication that Francis is influenced by some of the imaginative trends of his time. To some degree he shares in the apocryphal imagination. He makes frequent references to the judgment day, and one of his primary God images is as a judge. Francis appears to be a little less influenced by the courtly romances than some of his biographers infer.[76] In fact, it is more probable that Celano was the recipient of this influence. Pertinent elements, such as solitude in the forest, are most clearly presented in his account. One notable exception is the importance of clothing as a mark of transformation. This is included, in its own way, in the writings of both Celano and Francis.

The writings of Aelred of Rievaulx and Bernard of Clairvaux were scrutinized in order to provide a comparison between Francis' imaginative work and that of some near contemporaries. Throughout the forgoing pages a number of points of similarity and difference have been made. Much of the similarity rests with Bernard and the difference with Aelred. The link between good-enough mothers for Francis and Bernard is one plausible explanation for this correspondence, while Aelred's "absent mother" might account for the disparity. Francis and Bernard both have a penchant for seeking order in their experiences. For Bernard this was always in reference to an old or existing order. Francis sought to re-perceive reality according to a new order based on poverty and humility, but even this is ultimately constructed on an eternally existing order, the goodness of God. Both of these saints use flower imagery, and both of them ascribe a maternal role to themselves in relation to their confreres. By way of contrast, Bernard and Aelred's intense focus on person-to-person and person-to-God relationships leaves little room for a consideration of other relationships with reality as found in Francis' writings. Aelred also provides some very distressing maternal or female imagery that finds no significant equivalence in the writings of Francis or Bernard. On a very practical level, there is another marked contrast between the writings of Francis and the two monks. Spoto determines that the increased use of local dialect during Francis' time made the Latin writings from the monasteries significantly less accessible to the ordinary people.[77] Francis, on the other hand, was one of the ordinary people in many ways.

Beyond suggesting a framework for studying the potential application of the imagination to spiritual writings, the review of contemporary approaches to the imagination in Chapter Three also drew attention to imagination as a meaning-oriented activity. Furthermore, it identified many of the errant behaviors of an imagination that is not carefully tended. Primary among these is a failure to form relationships that bear some meaning for other people. Francis seems to have linked his imagination enough with various forms of collective imagination, particularly Scriptural imagination, to avoid this pitfall.

Several approaches to an Object Relations Theory perspective on imagination were given in Chapter Four and Chapter Five. The choice of using ORT to probe older spiritual writings is justified since it stands in continuity with the general trends in the intellectual expansion of imagination theory presented in Chapter Two and Chapter Three and the fact that Francis' imaginative activity, detailed in later chapters, so closely reflects the ORT perspective. No attempt was made to apply a contemporary psychological diagnosis to Francis. Instead, the products of his imagination were shown to reflect what today is considered to be a highly active and creative imagination in all the most positive senses of the word. In accordance with Object Relations Theory, Francis' writings indicate that he effectively seeks to envision the world in a manner that projects internal relationships onto the external screen that is reality as a whole. That he does this so effectively to the greater glory of God cannot be attributed solely to his imagination but to the grace acting therein.

Notes

1. Francis of Assisi, *Fragments (1209-1223): I. Fragments Found in a Manuscript in the Worchester Cathedral*, in Regis J. Armstrong, J.A. Wayne Hellman, and William J. Short, eds. *Francis of Assisi: The Early Documents*. Vol. 1, *The Saint* (New York: New City Press, 1999), 91. Note that the portion of the text following the bracket is identified by footnote as Kajetan Esser's interpolation.

2. Francis of Assisi, *Letter to all Superiors of the Friars Minor,* in Marion Habig, ed. *St. Francis of Assisi: Writings and Early Biographies: English Omnibus of Sources for the Life of St. Francis.* (Quincy, IL: Franciscan University Press, 1991), 113.

3. Ibid.

4. Ibid.

5. Ibid.

6. Francis of Assisi, *The Rule of 1221*, 44.

7. Francis of Assisi, *A Letter to the Entire Order*, 103-104.

8. Frugoni suggests that there is a very real possibility that Francis participated in the battle for La Rocca at the age of seventeen. La Rocca is the imposing fortress situated over the rest of Assisi where noble families took refuge during an uprising of the townspeople. Francis would have been among the townspeople. See Frugoni, *Francis of Assisi: A Life*, 6.

9. Celano makes several references to Francis' interest in becoming a knight. See: Celano, *The Life of Saint Francis by Thomas of Celano: The First Book*, in Armstrong, 185, 186, 189; or Celano, *The Life of Saint Francis by Thomas of Celano: The Second Book*, 263.

10. Francis of Assisi, *The Rule of 1221*, 33.

11. Ibid.

12. Ibid.

13. Francis of Assisi, *The Rule of 1223*, 61.

14. Ibid.

15. Francis of Assisi, *The Rule of 1221*, 39.

16. Francis of Assisi, *The Admonitions,* 81.

17. Francis of Assisi, *The Rule of 1221,* 42.

18. Ibid., 43.

19. Francis of Assisi, *The Testament of St. Francis*, 68.

20. Frugoni, 15.

21. Joan Mowat Erikson, 48.

22. Unknown, *The Sacred Exchange between Saint Francis and Lady Poverty*, in Regis J. Armstrong, J.A. Wayne Hellman, and William J. Short, eds. *Francis of Assisi: The Early Documents*. Vol. 1, *The Saint* (New York: New City Press, 1999).

23. Francis of Assisi, *A Salutation of the Virtues*, 132-133.

24. Ibid., 133. In the Armstrong et al translation capital letters are used for the pronouns. See Francis of Assisi, *A Salutation of the Virtues,* in Regis J. Armstrong, J.A. Wayne Hellman, and William J. Short, eds. *Francis of Assisi: The Early Documents*. Vol. 1, *The Saint* (New York: New City Press, 1999)164.

25. Francis of Assisi, *A Salutation of the Virtues, 133*. The idea of possessing another person in a romantic sense is often seen as a term of endearment suggesting that one is the sole recipient of his or her love. However, the concept can never be fully relieved of its negative connotation, wherein women (daughters and other young women under guardianship) were seen as a householder's property and were liable to be traded, through marriage, for the purposes of political, social, and financial gain. Is it possible that Fran-

cis' mother found herself married through just such an arrangement? If this is the case, it might explain Francis' comfort with using the idea of this kind of arrangement so lightly.

26. Francis of Assisi, *The Rule of 1223*, 59.

27. Mel Gibson, *The Passion of Christ* (New York: Newmarket Films, 2004).

28. Celano, *The Life of Saint Francis by Thomas of Celano: The First Book*, 241-242.

29. Francis of Assisi, *Letter to All the Faithful*, 93.

30. Francis of Assisi, *The Rule of 1221*, 40.

31. Francis of Assisi, *The Canticle of Exhortation for the Ladies of San Damiano*, in Regis J. Armstrong, J.A. Wayne Hellman, and William J. Short, eds. *Francis of Assisi: The Early Documents*. Vol. 1, *The Saint* (New York: New City Press, 1999), 115.

32. Celano, *The Life of Saint Francis by Thomas of Celano: The Second Book*, 270.

33. Francis of Assisi, *The Canticle of Brother Sun*, 130.

34. Francis of Assisi, *The Testament of St. Francis*, 67.

35. Ibid.

36. See for instance: Frugoni, 141; Spoto, 188, and J. Schatzlein and D.P. Sulmasy, "The Diagnosis of St. Francis: Evidence for Leprosy," *Franciscan Studies* 47 (1987): 181-217. House has a different take on the issue. He suggests the possibility of tuberculosis. See: House, 262.

37. I am not taking a stance against the miraculous nature of a stigmata event. Since Francis does not mention the stigmata in his writings, it is not within the purview of this work. What I would like to suggest is that Francis' ability to guide others in formulating meaning from unavoidable suffering is perhaps a greater sign of grace.

38. Francis of Assisi, *The Office of the Passion*, 143. See also Fortini, 208-210. His description of a ritual in which lepers are given their begging bowls and given a final blessing before departing from the healthy world is supportive of the way Francis may be linking imagery.

39. Francis of Assisi, *The Office of the Passion*, 146. The Armstrong et al translation has Francis iterating these words even more in the first person.

40. Francis of Assisi, *The Office of the Passion*, 147. He uses this phrase more than once.

41. Francis of Assisi, *The Rule of 1221*, 39.

42. Ibid.

43. Francis of Assisi, *The Admonitions*, 82.

44. Francis of Assisi, *True and Perfect Joy*, in Regis J. Armstrong, J.A. Wayne Hellman, and William J. Short, eds. *Francis of Assisi: The Early Documents*. Vol. 1, *The Saint* (New York: New City Press, 1999), 1501.

45. Ibid.

46. Ibid., 1502.

47. Regis J. Armstrong, J.A. Wayne Hellman, and William J. Short, eds. *Francis of Assisi: The Early Documents*. Vol. 1, *The Saint* (New York: New City Press, 1999), 166.

48. Thomas of Celano, *The First Book*, 237.

49. Ibid., 237.

50. Ibid., 238.

51. Ibid.

52. Ibid., 238.

53. Ibid., 240.

54. Ibid., 241.

55. See Thomas of Celano, *The First Book*, in Regis J. Armstrong, J.A. Wayne Hellman, and William J. Short, eds. *Francis of Assisi: The Early Documents*. Vol. 1, *The*

Saint (New York: New City Press, 1999) 191, note C, regarding opposition to Bernard's calling.

56. Francis of Assisi, *Office of the Passion*, 141.

57. Ibid., 142. In other scriptural translations there is an increased sense of the community turning against the speaker.

58. Ibid., 143.

59. Ibid.

60. Ibid., 144.

61. Ibid., 145.

62. Ibid.,146.

63. Unknown, *The Legend of Perugia*, 1080. Also known as *The Assisi Compilation.*

64. Lyn M. Falzon Scheuring, *Paradox of Poverty: Francis of Assisi and John of the Cross* (Quincy, IL: Franciscan Press, 2001), 69.

65. William M. Cook, "Francis of Assisi," in *The Way of the Christian Mystic*, 8 (Collegeville: The Liturgical Press, 1989), 88.

66. Ewert H. Cousins, "Francis of Assisi: Christian Mysticism at the Crossroads," in *Mysticism and Religious Traditions* (New York: Oxford University Press, 1983), 166.

67. Frugoni, 72.

68. Trexler, 2.

69. See Frugoni, House, Spoto, and Robson. Their specific approaches varied, but each utilized the current movement in historical studies to delve into the everyday life of communities in order to set Francis in context.

70. Eric Doyle, *Saint Francis and the Song of Brotherhood* (New York: Seabury Press, 1981), 116.

71. Leonardo Boff, *Saint Francis: A Model for Human Liberation*, trans. John W. Diercksmeier (New York: Crossroad, 1985).

72. Carlo Carretto, *I, Francis*, trans. Robert R. Barr (Maryknoll: Orbis Books, 1992).

73. Mary Jo Duffy and Roy Gasnick, *Francis: Brother of the Universe: His Complete Life's Story*, illustrated by John Buscema and Marie Severin (New York: Marvel Comics Group, 1982).

74. Lauren Glen Dunlap, *And I, Francis: The Life of Francis of Assisi in Word and Image*, illustrated by Kathleen Frugé-Brown (New York: Continuum, 1996).

75. Ibid., dust jacket.

76. See for instance Frugoni, 15; Julien Green, *God's Fool: The Life and Times of Francis of Assisi*, trans. Peter Heinegg (San Francisco: Harper San Francisco, 1985), 18; Joan Mowat Erikson, 54, 62-65.

77. Spoto, 17.

BIBLIOGRAPHY

PRIMARY SOURCES FOR FRANCIS OF ASSISI

Armstrong, Regis J., J.A. Wayne Hellmann, and William J. Short, eds. *Francis of Assisi: Early Documents.* Vol. 1, *The Saint.* Vol. 2, *The Founder.* Vol. 3, *The Prophet.* New York: New City Press, 1999-2001.

Legendae S. Francisci Assisiensis: Saeculis XIII et XIV Conscriptae. Analecta Franciscana sive Chronica aliaque varia documenta ad historiam fratrum minorum Spectantia, X. Ad Aquas Claras: Florentiae: Collegium S. Bonaventurae, 1895-1941.

Esser, Kajetan, ed. *Die Opuscula des hl. Franziskus von Assisi: Neue textkritische Edition.* Grottaferrata: Spicilegium Bonaventurianum XIII, 1976.

Habig, Marion A., ed. *St. Francis of Assisi: Writings and Early Biographies: English Omnibus of Sources for the Life of St. Francis.* Franciscan University Press: Quincy, IL, 1991.

Godet, Jean-Francois and Georges Mailleux, eds. *Corpus des Sources Franciscaines*, vol. 5, *Opuscula sancti Francisi, Scripta sanctae Clarae.* Louvain: Cetedoc, 1976.

OTHER PRIMARY SOURCES

Aelred of Rievaulx. *Aelred of Rievaulx: Spiritual Friendship.* Introduction by Douglas Roby. Translated by Mary Eugenia Laker. Kalamazoo: Cistercian Publications, 1977.

———. "The Commentary of the Venerable Aelred, Abbot of Rievaulx on the Passage from the Gospel: "When Jesus was Twelve Years Old." In *Aelred of Rievaulx: Treatises.* Translated by Theodore Berkeley. Spencer MA: Cistercian Publications, 1971.

———. *Dialogue on the Soul.* Translated by C.H. Talbot. Kalamazoo: Cistercian Publications, 1981.

———. "Pastoral Prayer." In *Aelred of Rievaulx: Treatises.* Transalted by R. Penelope Lawson. Spencer MA: Cistercian Publications, 1971.

———. "Sermon for the Assumption of Mary." In *Aelred of Rievaulx: The Liturgical Sermons.* Translated by Theodore Berkeley and M. Basil Pennington. Kalamazoo: Cistercian Publications, 2001.

———. "Sermon for the Coming of the Lord." In *Aelred of Rievaulx: The Liturgical Sermons.* Translated by Theodore Berkeley and M. Basil Pennington. Kalamazoo: Cistercian Publications, 2001.

———. "Sermon for the Nativity of the Lord." In *Aelred of Rievaulx: The Liturgical Sermons.* Translated by Theodore Berkeley and M. Basil Pennington. Kalamazoo: Cistercian Publications, 2001.

————. "Treatise Concerning a Rule for a Recluse." In *Aelred of Rievaulx: Treatises,* Translated by Mary Paul Macpherson. Spencer, MA: Cistercian Publications, 1971.

Bernard of Clairvaux. "Letter 64: To Alexander, Bishop of Lincoln." In *Bernard of Clairvaux: Selected Works.* Preface by Ewert H. Cousins. Introduction by Jean Le-Clercq, Translated by G.R. Evans. New York: Paulist Press, 1987.

————. "Letter 144: To the Brothers at Clairvaux." In *Bernard of Clairvaux: Selected Works.* Preface by Ewert H. Cousins. Introduction by Jean LeClercq, Translated by G.R. Evans. New York: Paulist Press, 1987.

————. *On Consideration.* Translated by George Lewis. Oxford: Clarendon Press, 1908.

————. *On Grace and Free Choice.* Translated by Daniel O'Donovan. Kalamazoo: Cistercian Publications, 1988.

————. "On Loving God." In *Bernard of Clairvaux: Selected Works.* Preface by Ewert H. Cousins. Introduction by Jean LeClercq, Translated by G.R. Evans. New York: Paulist Press, 1987.

————. "On Humility and Pride." In *Bernard of Clairvaux: Selected Works.* Preface by Ewert H. Cousins. Introduction by Jean LeClercq, Translated by G.R. Evans. New York: Paulist Press, 1987.

————. "Letter to Abbot Aelred." In *Aelred of Rievaulx: The Mirror of Charity.* Translated by Elizabeth Connor. Kalamazoo: Cistercian Publications, 1990.

SECONDARY SOURCES

Albin, Mel, ed. *New Directions in Psychohistory: The Adelphi Papers in Honor of Erik H. Erikson.* Lexington MA: Lexington Books, 1980.

Anderson, Luke. "The Rhetorical Epistemology in Saint Bernard's Super Cantica." In *Bernardus Magister: Papers Presented on the Nonacentenary of the Birth of Saint Bernard of Clairvaux,* ed. John R. Sommerfeldt, 95-128. Spencer MA: Cistercian Publications, 1992.

Archambault, Paul J. "Augustine's Confessiones: On the Uses and Limits of Psychobiography." In *Collectanea Augustiniana, 83-99.* New York: Peter Lang, 1990.

Barking, Leonard. "The Concept of the Transitional Object." In *Between Reality and Fantasy: Winnicott's Conception of Transitional Objects and Phenomena,* ed. Simon A. Grolnick and Leonard Barkin, 513-536. Northvale, NJ: Jason Aronson Inc., 1995.

Bergman, Anni. "From Mother to the World Outside: The Use of Space During the Separation-Individuation Phase." In *Between Reality and Fantasy: Winnicott's Conception of Transitional Objects and Phenomena,* ed. Simon A. Grolnick and Leonard Barkin, 147-165. Northvale, NJ: Jason Aronson Inc., 1995.

Bodo, Murray. *Francis: The Journey and the Dream.* Cincinnati: St. Anthony Messenger Press, 1988.

Boff, Leonardo. *Saint Francis: A Model for Human Liberation.* Translated by John W. Diercksmeier. New York: Crossroad, 1985.

Bollas, Christopher. *The Shadow of the Object: Psychoanalysis of the Unthought Known.* New York: Columbia University Press, 1987.

Bowker, John. *The Religious Imagination and the Sense of God.* Oxford: Clarendon Press, 1978.

Bredero, Adriaan. *Bernard of Clairvaux: Between Cult and History.* Edinburgh: T and T Clark, 1996.

Bryant, David. *Faith and the Play of Imagination.* Macon GA: Mercer University Press, 1989.

Bundy, Murray W. *The Theory of Imagination in Classical and Mediaeval Thought.* Urbana: University of Chicago Press, 1927. Reprints: Urbana: Folcroft Library, 1970, 1976, 1980; Norwood PA: Norwood Editions, 1976, 1978.

Capps, Donald, Walter H. Capps, and Gerald Bradford, eds. *Encounter with Erikson: Historical Interpretation and Religious Biography.* Santa Barbara: Scholars Press, 1977.

Carretto, Carlo. *I, Francis.* Translated by Robert R. Barr. Maryknoll: Orbis Books, 1992.

Cassirer, Ernst. *Language and Myth.* New York: Harper Brothers, 1946.

Charon, Jean Marc. "Psychohistoire et Religion: perspectives, defies et enjeux." *Religiologiques* 2 (Oct 1990): 67-76.

Coles, Robert. *Erik H. Erikson: The Growth of His Work.* Boston: Little Brown, 1970.

Cooey, Paula M. *Religious Imagination and the Body: A Feminist Analysis.* New York: Oxford University Press, 1994.

Cook, William M. "Francis of Assisi." In *The Way of the Christian Mystic, Vol. 8.* Collegeville: The Liturgical Press, 1989.

Copolillo, Henry P. "Maturational Aspects of the Transitional Phenomenon." *International Journal of Psycho-Analysis* 48 (1967): 237-246.

Coulton, G.G. *Two Saints: St. Bernard and St. Francis.* Cambridge: Cambridge University Press, 1932.

Cousins, Ewert. "Preface." In *Bernard of Clairvaux: Selected Works.* With an introduction by Jean Leclercq. Translated by G.R. Evans, 5-12. New York: Paulist Press, 1987.

Cousins, Ewert H. "Francis of Assisi: Christian Mysticism at the Crossroads." In *Mysticism and Religious Traditions* ,ed. Steven Katz, 63-190. New York: Oxford University Press, 1983.

Crowley, Paul G. "Ignatian Imagination and the Aesthetics of Liberation." In *Through a Glass Darkly: Essays in the Religious Imagination*, ed. John C. Hawley, 50-69. New York: Fordham University Press, 1996.

Davis, Madeleine, and David Wallbridge. *Boundary and Space: An Introduction to the Work of D.W. Winnicott.* New York: Brunner and Mazel, 1981.

Delehaye, Hippolyte. *The Legends of the Saints.* Translated by Donald Attwater. New York: Fordham University Press, 1962.

Deri, Susan. "Transitional Phenomena: Vicissitudes of Symbolization and Creativity." In *Between Reality and Fantasy: Winnicott's Conception of Transitional Objects and Phenomena*, ed. Simon A. Grolnick and Leonard Barkin, 44-60. Northvale, NJ: Jason Aronson Inc., 1995.

Dinnage, Rosemary. "A Bit of Light." In *Between Reality and Fantasy: Winnicott's Concepts of Transitional Objects and Phenomena*, ed. Simon A. Grolnick and Leonard Barkin, 365-378. Northvale, NJ: Jason Aronson Inc., 1995.

Dillon, John. "Plotinus and the Transcendental Imagination." In *Religious Imagination*, ed. James P. Mackey, 55-64. Edinburgh: Edinburgh University Press, 1986.

Doyle, Eric. *Saint Francis and the Song of Brotherhood.* New York: Seabury Press, 1981.

Duffy, Mary Jo, and Roy Gasnick. *Francis: Brother of the Universe: His Complete Life's Story.* Illustrated by John Buscema and Marie Severin. New York: Marvel Comics Group, 1982.

Dutton, Marsha. "Introduction." In *The Life of Aelred of Rievaulx*, by Walter Daniel. Translated by F.M. Powicke, 8- 43. Kalamazoo: Cistercian Publications, 1994.

Eigen, Michael. "The Area of Faith in Winnicott, Lacan and Bion." *International Journal of Psycho-analysis* 62 (1981): 413-433.

Emmerson, Richard K., and Ronald B. Herzman. *The Apocalyptic Imagination in Medieval Literature*. Philadelphia: University of Pennsylvania Press, 1992.

Erikson, Erik H. *Identity and the Life Cycle*. New York: WW Norton and Co., 1980.

———. *Young Man Luther: A Study in Psychoanalysis and History*. New York: Norton and Co., 1962.

Evans, G.R. *Bernard of Clairvaux*. New York: Oxford University Press, 2000.

———. *The Mind of St Bernard*. Oxford: Clarendon Press, 1983.

Falzon Scheuring, Lyn M. *Paradox of Poverty: Francis of Assisi and John of the Cross*. Quincy, IL: Franciscan Press, 2001.

Fisher, Kathleen R. *The Inner Rainbow: The Imagination in Christian Life*. Ramsey NJ: Paulist Press, 1983.

Forbes, Cheryl. *Imagination: Embracing a Theology of Wonder*. Portland OR: Multonomah Press, 1986.

Fortini, Arnoldo. *Francis of Assisi*. Translated by Helen Moak. New York: Crossroads, 1981.

Freud, Sigmund. *The Future of an Illusion*. New York: W.W. Norton and Co., 1961.

Frugoni, Chiara. *Francis of Assisi: A Life*. New York: Continuum, 1999.

Gadamer, Hans Georg. *Truth and Method*. New York: Seabury Press, 1975.

Gibson, Mel. *The Passion of Christ*. New York: Newmarket Films, 2004.

Glen Dunlap, Lauren. *And I, Francis: The Life of Francis of Assisi in Word and Image*. Illustrated by Kathleen Frugé-Brown. New York: Continuum, 1996.

Goodich, Michael. "Childhood and Adolescence Among Thirteenth-Century Saints." *History of Childhood Quarterly* 1 (1973): 285-309.

Greeley, Andrew M. *The Religious Imagination*. Los Angeles: Sadlier, 1981.

Green, Garrett. *Imagining God: Theology and the Religious Imagination*. Grand Rapids: Eerdmans, 1989.

Green, Julien. *God's Fool: The Life and Times of Francis of Assisi*. Translated by Peter Heinegg. San Francisco: Harper San Francisco, 1985.

Grolnick, Simon A. "Etruscan Burial Symbols and the Transitional Process." In *Between Reality and Fantasy: Winnicott's Conception of Transitional Objects and Phenomena*, ed. Simon A. Grolnick and Leonard Barkin, 381-410. Northvale, NJ: Jason Aronson Inc., 1995.

Grolnick, Simon A. and Leonard Barkin, eds. *Between Reality and Fantasy: Winnicott's Conception of Transitional Objects and Phenomena*. Northvale, NJ: Jason Aronson Inc., 1995.

Hallier, Amédée. *The Monastic Theology of Aelred of Rievaulx: An Experiential Theology*. Translated by Columban Heaney. Spencer MA: Cistercian Publications, 1969.

Harris, Maria. *Teaching and Religious Imagination: An Essay in the Theology of Teaching*. San Francisco: Harper, 1987.

Hart, Ray. *Unfinished Man and the Imagination: Toward and Ontology and Rhetoric of Revelation*. New York: Herder and Herder, 1968.

Herndon Steinhoff Smith, Roy. "The Denial of Mystery: Object Relations Theory and Religion." *Horizons* 16, no. 2 (1989): 243-265.

Hepburn, Ronald W. "Religious Imagination." In *Philosophy, Religion and the Spiritual Life*, ed. Michael McGhee, 127-143. Cambridge: Cambridge University Press, 1992.

Homans, Peter, ed. *Childhood and Selfhood: Essays on Tradition, Religion and Modernity in the Psychology of Erik H. Erikson*. Lewisburg PA: Bucknell University Press, 1978.

Hopper, Stanley Romaine. *The Way of Transfiguration: Religious Imagination as Theopoiesis*, eds. R. Melvin Keiser and Tony Stoneburner. Louisville: Westminster/John Knox Press, 1992.

House, Adrian. *Francis of Assisi: A Revolutionary Life.* Mahwah, NJ: Hidden Spring, 2001.

Jackelén, Antje. *Time and Eternity: The Question of Time in Church, Science, and Theology.* Philadelphia: Templeton Foundation Press, 2005.

Johnson, Luke Timothy. "Imagining the World Scripture Imagines." In *Theology and Scriptural Imagination,* ed. L. Gregory Jones and James L. Buckley, 3-15. Oxford: Blackwell Publishers LTD, 1998.

Jones, James W. *Terror and Transformation: The Ambiguity of Religion in Psychoanalytic Perspective.* New York: Taylor and Francis, 2002.

Jonte-Pace, Diane. "Object Relations Theory, Mothering, and Religion: Towards a Feminist Psychology of Religion." *Horizons* 14, no. 2 (1987): 310-327.

Jung, Carl. *Man and His Symbols.* New York: Doubleday and Co., 1964.

Kahne, Merton J. "On the Persistence of Transitional Phenomena into Adult Life." *International Journal of Psycho-Analysis* 48 (1967): 247-258.

Kant, Immanuel. *Critique of Pure Reason.* Translated by Norman Kemp Smith. New York: St. Martin's Press, 1965.

Kelly, Douglas. *Medieval Imagination: Rhetoric and the Poetry of Courtly Love.* Madison: University of Wisconsin Press, 1978.

Kestenberg, Judith S. and Joan Weinstein. "Transitional Objects and Body Image Formation." In *Between Reality and Fantasy: Winnicott's Conception of Transitional Objects and Phenomena,* ed. Simon A. Grolnick and Leonard Barkin, 75-95. Northvale, NJ: Jason Aronson Inc., 1995.

Knowles, Richard T. "Fantasy and Imagination." *Studies in Formative Spirituality* 4 (1985): 53-63.

Kohut, Thomas A. "Psychohistory as History." *American Historical Review* 91, no. 2 (Apr 1986): 336-354.

Krieger, Murray. *Theory of Criticism: A Tradition and its System.* Baltimore: John Hopkins University Press, 1976.

Kuhns, Thomas S. *The Structure of Scientific Revolutions.* Chicago: University of Chicago Press, 1970.

LeClerc, Eloi. *The Canticle of Creatures: Symbols of Union.* Translated by Matthew J. O'Connell. Chicago: Franciscan Herald Press, 1977.

Jean Leclercq. *A Second Look at Bernard of Clairvaux.* Translated by Marie-Bernard Saïd. Kalamazoo: Cistercian Publications, 1990.

————. "Introduction." In *Bernard of Clairvaux: Selected Works,* preface by Ewert H. Cousins, translated by G.R. Evans. New York: Paulist Press, 1987.

————. *Nouveau visage de Bernard de Clairvaux: approches psycho-historiques.* Paris: Editions du Cerf, 1976.

————. "Psycho-History and the Understanding of People." *The Hanoverian* 6 (1975): 6-9.

————. "Modern Psychology and the Interpretation of Medieval Texts." *Speculum: A Journal of Medieval Studies* 48 (1973): 476-490.

LeGoff, Jacques. *The Medieval Imagination.* Translated by Arthur Goldhammer. Chicago: University of Chicago Press, 1988.

Little, Lester K. *Religious Poverty and the Profit Economy in Medieval Europe.* Ithaca: Cornell University Press, 1978.

Lynch, William F. *Images of Hope: Imagination as Healer of the Hopeless.* Baltimore: Helicon, 1965.

Mackey, James P. "Introduction." In *Religious Imagination*, ed. James P. Mackey, 8- 28. Edinburgh: Edinburgh University Press, 1986.

Mahler, Margaret S., Fred Pine, and Anni Bergman. *The Psychological Birth of the Human Infant: Symbiosis and Individuation.* --: Basic Books, 1975.

Maier, Henry W. *Three Theories of Child Development: The Contributions of Erik H. Erikson, Jean Piaget and Robert R. Sears, and Their Application.* New York: Harper&Row, 1965.

Manselli, Raoul. "Gesture as Sermon in St. Francis of Assisi." *Greyfriars Review* 6, no. 1 (1992): 37-48.

McDargh, John. *Psychoanalytic Object Relations Theory and the Study of Religion: On Faith and the Imaging of God.* Lanham, MD: University Press of America, 1983.

McGuire, Brian Patrick. *Brother and Lover: Aelred of Rievaulx.* New York: Crossroad, 1994.

Meissner, W.W. *Ignatius of Loyola: The Psychology of a Saint.* New Haven: Yale U.P., 1992.

―――. *The Paranoid Process.* New York: Jason Aronson, 1978.

Miller, Ruth. "Poetry as Transitional Object." In *Between Reality and Fantasy: Winnicott's Conception of Transitional Objects and Phenomena*, ed. Simon A. Grolnick and Leonard Barkin, 449-468. Northvale, NJ: Jason Aronson Inc., 1995.

Mockler, Anthony. *Francis of Assisi: The Wandering Years.* New York: E.P. Dutton, 1976.

Modell, Arnold H. "The Transitional Object and the Creative Act." *Psychoanalytic Quarterly* 39 (1970): 240-250.

Mowat Erikson, Joan. *Saint Francis et His Four Ladies.* New York: W.W. Norton and Co., 1970.

Muensterberger, Werner. "Between Reality and Fantasy." In *Between Reality and Fantasy: Winnicott's Conception of Transitional Objects and Phenomena*, ed. Simon A. Grolnick and Leonard Barkin, 5-13. Northvale, NJ: Jason Aronson Inc., 1995.

Nguyên-Van-Khanh, Norbert. *The Teacher of his Heart: Jesus in the Thought and Writings of St. Francis.* Translated by Ed Hagman. St. Bonaventure, New York: Franciscan Pathways, 1994.

Oakes, Edward T. "A Life of Allegory: Type and Pattern in Historical Narratives." In *Through a Glass Darkly: Essays in the Religious Imagination*, ed. John C. Hawley, 134-150. New York: Fordham University Press, 1996.

Otto, Rudolph. *The Idea of the Holy: An Inquiry into the Non-rational Factor in the Idea of the Divine and its Relation to the Rational.* Translated by John W. Harvey. London: Oxford University Press, 1958.

Parker, Jo Ellen. "A Lesson in Reading: George Elliot and the Typological Imagination." In *Through a Glass Darkly: Essays in the Religious Imagination*, ed. John C. Hawley, 104-118. New York: Fordham University Press, 1996.

Pennington, M. Basil. "Introduction." In *Aelred of Rievaulx: The Liturgical Sermons,* translated by Theodore Berkeley and M. Basil Pennington. Kalamazoo: Cistercian Publications, 2001.

Pranger, Burcht. "The Concept of Death in Bernard's Sermons on the Song of Songs." In *Bernardus Magister: Papers Presented on the Nonacentenary of the Birth of Saint Bernard of Clairvaux*, ed. John R. Sommerfeldt, 85-93. Spencer MA: Cistercian Publications, 1992.

Pruyser, Paul W. "Forms and Functions of the Imagination in Religion." *Bulletin of the Menninger Clinic* 49, no. 4 (1985): 353-370.

―――. *The Play of the Imagination: Toward a Psycho-analysis of Culture.* New York: International University Press, 1983.

―――. *Between Belief and Unbelief.* New York: Harper and Row, 1974.

Riposa, Michael L. *Boredom and the Religious Imagination.* Charlottesville: University of Virginia Press, 1999.

Rizzuto, Ana-Maria. *Why Did Freud Reject God?: A Psychodynamic Interpretation.* New Haven: Yale University Press, 1998.

———. The *Birth of the Living God: A Psychoanalytic Study.* Chicago: University of Chicago Press, 1979.

Robinson, Edward. *The Language of Mystery.* Philadelphia: Trinity Press International, 1987.

Robson, Michael. *St. Francis of Assisi: The Legend and the Life.* New York: Continuum, 1997.

Roby, Douglas. "Introduction." In *Aelred of Rievaulx: Spiritual Friendship.* Kalamazoo: Cistercian Publications, 1977.

Rose, Gilbert J. "The Creativity of Everyday Life." In *Between Reality and Fantasy: Winnicott's Conception of Transitional Objects and Phenomena,* ed. Simon A. Grolnick and Leonard Barkin, 347-362. Northvale, NJ: Jason Aronson Inc., 1995.

Scarry, Elaine. *The Body in Pain: The Making and Unmaking of the World.* New York: Oxford University Press, 1985.

Schatzlein, J. and D.P. Sulmasy. "The Diagnosis of St. Francis: Evidence for Leprosy." *Franciscan Studies* 47 (1987): 181-217.

Schneiders, Sandra M. "Religion and Spirituality: Strangers, Rivals, or Partners?" *The Santa Clara Lectures* 6, No. 2 (2000).

———. "The study of Christian Spirituality: Contours and Dynamics of a Discipline." *Christian Spirituality Bulletin* 6, no. 1 (1998): 1-12.

———. "Theology and Spirituality: Strangers, Rivals, or Partners?" *Horizons* 13, no. 2 (1986): 253-274.

Sobel, Emilie. "Rhythm, Sound and Imagery in the Poetry of Gerard Manley Hopkins." In *Between Reality and Fantasy: Winnicott's Conception of Transitional Objects and Phenomena,* ed. Simon A. Grolnick and Leonard Barkin, 427-445. Northvale, NJ: Jason Aronson Inc., 1995.

Spoto, Donald. *Reluctant Saint: The Life of Francis of Assisi.* New York: Viking Compass, 2002.

Squire, Aelred. *Aelred of Rievaulx: A Study.* London: SPCK, 1969.

Stannard, David E. *Shrinking History: On Freud and the Failure of Psychohistory.* Oxford: Oxford University Press, 1980.

Studzinski, Raymond. "Tutoring the Religious Imagination." *Horizons* 14, no. 1 (1987): 24-38.

Stull, Bradford T. *Religious Dialectics of Pain and Imagination.* Albany: State University of New York Press, 1994.

Talbot, C.H. "Introduction." In *Dialogue on the Soul,* by Aelred of Rievaulx, 9-37. Kalamazoo: Cistercian Publications, 1981.

Tamburello, Dennis E., ed. *Bernard of Clairvaux: Essential Writings.* New York: Crossroad, 2000.

Tracy, David. *The Analogical Imagination: Christian Theology and the Culture of Pluralism.* New York: Crossroad, 1981.

Trexler, Richard C. *Naked Before the Father: The Renunciation of St. Francis of Assisi.* New York: Peter Lang, 1989.

Ulanov, Ann and Barry Ulanov. *The Healing Imagination: The Meeting of Psyche and Soul.* --: Daimon, 1999.

Warnock, Mary. *Imagination.* Berkeley: University of California Press, 1976.

Watson, Gerard. *Phantasia in Classical Thought*. Galway: Galway University Press, 1988.

―――. "Imagination and Religion in Classical Thought." In *Religious Imagination*, ed. James P. Mackey, 29-54. Edinburgh: Edinburgh University Press, 1986.

Welch, Martin J. "Transitional Language." In *Between Reality and Fantasy: Winnicott's Conception of Transitional Objects and Phenomena*, ed. Simon A. Grolnick and Leonard Barkin, 413-423. Northvale, NJ: Jason Aronson Inc., 1995.

Wheelwright, Philip. *The Burning Fountain: A Study in the Language of Symbolism*. Bloomington: Indiana University Press, 1954.

Winnicott, Clare. "DWW: A Reflection." In *Between Reality and Fantasy: Winnicott's Conception of Transitional Objects and Phenomena*, ed. Simon A. Grolnick and Leonard Barkin, 17-33. Northvale, NJ: Jason Aronson Inc., 1995.

Winnicott, D.W. "Living Creatively." In *Home is Where we Start from: Essays by a Psychoanalyst*, 35-50. New York: W.W. Norton, 1986.

―――. *Playing and Reality*. London: Tavistock, 1971.

―――. *The Family and Individual Development*. New York: Basic Books, Inc., 1965.

―――. *The Maturational Process and the Facilitating Environment: Studies in the Theory of Emotional Development*. Madison CT: International Universities Press, 1965.

―――. "Transitional Objects and Transitional Phenomenon: A Study of the First Not-me Possession." *The International Journal of Psycho-Analysis* 34 (1953): 89-97.

Wright, Eugene J. *Erikson, Identity and Religion*. New York: Seabury Press, 1982.

INDEX

ABOUT THE AUTHOR

Andrew McCarthy is an Assistant Professor of Humanities at Anna Maria College in Paxton, Massachusetts. He has degrees from the US Merchant Marine Academy (BS), Spring Hill College (MA), and the Catholic University of America (Ph.D.). His research interests include Spirituality, Franciscan Studies, Religion and Psychology, and Religion and Culture.

THE AWAKENING

NOTES

including
- *Life of the Author*
- *List of Characters*
- *Critical Commentaries*
- *Questions for Review*
- *Selected Bibliography*

by
Kay Carey, M.A.
University of Colorado

INCORPORATED

LINCOLN, NEBRASKA 68501

Editor	Consulting Editor
Gary Carey, M.A. *University of Colorado*	*James L. Roberts, Ph.D.* *Department of English* *University of Nebraska*

ISBN 0-8220-0218-3
© Copyright 1980
by
Cliffs Notes, Inc.
All Rights Reserved
Printed in U.S.A.

1997 Printing

Cliffs Notes, Inc.   Lincoln, Nebraska

CONTENTS

THE AWAKENING
Notes

LIFE OF THE AUTHOR

Kate Chopin was born in 1851 in St. Louis. The city was just beginning to gain a sense of commercial prominence in America, and Chopin's Irish father was ambitious to make a success for himself and his young family in this newly burgeoning American city on the Mississippi River. On Chopin's mother's side, the French influence matched Kate's father's Irish ambition and spirit; in fact, it was the unique combination of these two heritages which molded and fashioned Chopin's unique character.

Chopin's father was killed when she was four, and although his absence was a terrible, empty shock to the family, she was aware that her father had died in an attempt to unite an America that was daily becoming a great nation. His death occurred as the result of an unfortunate accident causing the deaths of several of the city's most influential civic leaders. A key link in the Pacific Railroad was being completed when a catastrophic collapse of a bridge brought the celebration ceremony to a sudden halt.

After her father's death, Chopin was reared by a family of strong women – her mother, her grandmother, and her great-grandmother. They were all iron-willed and capable women, and they all had a strain of the romantic and the raconteur in them; Chopin was often entertained nightly by their many and varied tales of people and adventures.

Chopin met Oscar, her future husband, when she was seventeen. She had just graduated from the St. Louis Academy of the Sacred Heart, and Oscar was eight years older than she; he had left New Orleans to become a clerk in a St. Louis bank. He was immediately fascinated by Chopin's striking beauty and individualism when they met, and the two were soon married.

Not much is known about Oscar, but it is clear that he was not at all Like Léonce Pontellier, the stuffy husband of the heroine of *The Awakening*. Oscar's childhood had not been a happy one (his father was a possessive and jealous man, especially contemptuous of women), and as a result, Chopin was given an immense amount of personal freedom. This was fortunate, for her personality contained a deep desire for liberty that needed fulfillment. She was alive, alert, and excited by the vast opportunities and experiences which life had to offer in her rapidly changing and growing country, and Oscar was always very supportive of his wife's many interests and allowed her even the luxury of solitude – an unheard of luxury in those days, but a necessity to Chopin. Even on her honeymoon, she recorded in her diary the many delights she found in simple walks alone; she enjoyed glimpsing into other people's homes, meeting strangers, and imagining all sorts of histories and intrigues about the people she met. Yet, even with the generous allowance of money and freedom which Oscar gave to her, Chopin constantly rankled at being a woman in what was undeniably a man's world.

The young couple returned from their European honeymoon and lived in New Orleans for their first nine years. Its influence on Chopin's life and her writings is indelible. She absorbed every flavor and every nuance of this exotic American city. And while she was accumulating memories, she was also accumulating a family at the same time. Before Chopin was thirty years old, she was the mother of six children, and she was regarded by all who knew her as a good, thorough, and conscientious mother. Oscar, meanwhile, was having increasing troubles with his job as a cotton commissioner and, in 1880, his business failed so miserably that he was forced to move his wife and family to the small village of Cloutierville in the western, Cajun area of Louisiana. There, he ran a general store and managed a few small plantations, and it was by helping her husband that Chopin grew to love and absorb even more of Louisiana's richly mixed heritage of French, Negro, Spanish, and English ways of living. In this new Cajun country, Chopin adapted rapidly to a society that was strikingly different from the exclusive Creole and aristocratic social worlds of New Orleans. And it was about these people, these Cajuns, or Acadians, that Chopin eventually wrote most of her stories and sketches. It was fertile, untapped literary ore, and Chopin was immediately recognized as a master of interpreting its local color and character. In fact, her early reputation as a "regional writer" is partly responsible for her being ignored as one of America's finest fictional writers. Primarily, however, her lack of lasting, national recognition is due to the reception of her second novel, *The Awakening*, published in 1899. Her earlier novel, *At Fault*, had gotten rather good reviews, though by no means did it receive the acclaim that her short stories had received. But it was *The Awakening* which brought her to the attention of all the major critics and to the general American reading public. Mrs. Kate Chopin had written a scandalous book. Its heroine was a woman who found her husband dull, her married life dreary and confining, and motherhood a bondage she refused to accept. Chopin was blunt about her subject matter, and her critics were equally candid. They were outraged that Chopin had written about a woman who not only had sexual urges and desires, but felt that it was her right to have those drives satisfied. Such novels with similar subjects had been published in Europe, of course, but that was different. A French author could raise literary eyebrows and be tolerated, but because Chopin was American and, moreover, because she was a woman, the critics pounced on both her and her heroine, Edna Pontellier, as being evil and debauched. One critic declared that the novel was "strong drink" and that it should be labeled "poison." Chopin knew that her novel was daring, but she dared to publish it, never dreaming of the extent of furor it would cause. Her friends wrote her many letters of encouragement after its publication, knowing that she would be hurt by the critics' harsh words, but Chopin was more concerned about the book's future than she was about the controversy that it was causing at the moment. When libraries began banning the novel, however, Chopin's spirits sank, and she wrote a note of apology in a local paper. Its tone is courageous and positive and, at the same time, it is wry and satiric. "Having a group of people at my disposal," she wrote, "I thought it might be entertaining (to myself) to throw them together and see what would happen. I never dreamed of Mrs. Pontellier making such a mess of things and working out her own damnation as she did. If I had had the slightest intimation of such a thing I would have excluded her from the company. But when I found out what she was up to, the play was half over and it was then too late." The mocking tone of this overly polite apology is delightful, but it hides Chopin's true disappointment, and when the reviewers continued to attack both her and her novel, she wrote little more;

yet she was never ashamed of the novel or of having written it. She simply felt that she had no further future as a writer. A widow by now, Chopin devoted the rest of her short life to her family.

The Awakening, a first-rate minor masterpiece, has only recently been rediscovered, and it and Chopin's other writings are at last receiving the long-neglected critical acclaim that they deserve. She has been compared to Lawrence, Gide, and Flaubert, yet all her writings and all her characters are distinctively American, remarkably contemporary, and have achieved prominence and recognition far beyond their initial status as romantic, local-color creations.

LIST OF CHARACTERS

Edna Pontellier

A handsome young woman of twenty-eight, she discovers during a summer vacation that she has led a pleasant, pampered married life, but that it has been a rigidly confined existence, and that her husband has always considered her to be his "property." She rebels and tries to find fulfillment for her psychological and social drives, as well as for her sexual drives. She is frustrated because no lifestyle in the 1890s offers her an alternative to the restrictions of motherhood and marriage; as a result, she commits suicide.

Léonce Pontellier

Edna's forty-year-old husband; he has a prosperous brokerage business in New Orleans, adheres strictly to the region's social conventions, and expects his wife to do likewise. All of the Pontelliers' friends consider Léonce to be "a perfect husband."

Robert Lebrun

A charming young man who spends his summers at his mother's resort on Grand Isle making the female guests feel "waited on." He begins an innocent intimacy with Edna Pontellier and flees to Mexico when he discovers that their friendship has turned to love.

Adèle Ratignolle

Edna's confidante at Grand Isle; she is Chopin's example of the perfect Creole "mother-woman." She is a well-organized, busy, home-loving mother of several children, and she thoroughly enjoys her role as a good wife and as a devoted and self-sacrificing mother.

Alcée Arobin

A young New Orleans "man of fashion." He is a good-looking, Casanova-type who is well known for his amorous affairs with vulnerable women. He hopes to make Edna one more of his conquests.

Mademoiselle Reisz

In contrast to Adèle Ratignolle, she offers Edna an alternative to the role of being yet another "mother-woman." The old, unmarried musician has devoted her life to music and is considered to be somewhat eccentric because of her outspoken and candid views. She is genuinely fond of Edna and concerned about her young friend's confused, frustrated dilemma.

Madame Lebrun

After her husband deserts her, she successfully manages to run their summer resort on Grand Isle and support herself and her two sons, Robert and Victor. She is always fresh-looking and pretty, a "bustling" woman – yelling commands to the servants, sewing rapidly at her noisy sewing machine, and clad always in white, her starched skirts crinkling as she comes and goes.

Victor Lebrun

Robert's darkly handsome, spoiled brother; he is also Madame Lebrun's favorite son. At Edna's dinner party, one of her guests garbs Victor in a wreath of roses, and to Edna's wine-heightened senses, he seems to suddenly become the "image of Desire." The vision upsets Edna so greatly that she shatters a wine glass, and her party comes to an early, unexpected conclusion.

Raoul and Etienne Pontellier

Edna and Léonce's children. Edna is criticized unfairly by her husband for neglecting them. Léonce's mother is always anxious for an opportunity to take the children to Iberville so that she can tell them tales of Creole lore and save them from becoming "children of the pavement."

Edna's Father

The old Kentucky colonel did not approve of his daughter's marrying a Catholic and a Creole, and although he and Edna have a good time at the races when he comes to New Orleans for a visit, he is still severely critical of Edna's independence. When he leaves, he instructs Léonce to be more firm with Edna and to treat her with "authority and coercion." His other two daughters, Janet and Margaret, are models of submissive southern womanhood.

Mariequita

A young, pretty Spanish "spitfire" who flirts with both Robert and Victor Lebrun. Robert once gave Victor a sound thrashing for being too familiar with her and for giving the impression that he had "some sort of claim" on her. The young girl usually goes barefoot and is not ashamed of her broad, coarse feet nor the sand between her toes.

Doctor Mandelet

A semi-retired physician in New Orleans whom Léonce consults about his wife's lack of interest in housekeeping and her notions about the "eternal rights of women." Doctor Mandelet, who has a "reputation for wisdom rather than skill," advises Léonce to be patient and not to worry. To him, Edna is going through a "mood" that will soon pass.

Montel

A friend of the Lebrun family and unofficial beau of Madame Lebrun; he hires Robert for a position in his firm in Vera Cruz, Mexico.

Madame Antoine

Robert brings Edna to her house to rest after Edna has to leave Mass because of the oppressive heat and Edna's emotional exhaustion; she lives with her son, Tonie.

Mrs. James Highcamp

A devotee of the races and friend of Alcée Arobin.

CRITICAL COMMENTARIES

CHAPTER 1

The novel opens on a Sunday in summer, in the late nineteenth century. A New Orleans businessman and his wife are vacationing on Grand Isle, a popular Creole resort, fifty miles south of New Orleans. Mr. Léonce Pontellier is irritated by the mid-morning chatter of birds, his landlady's shrill commands to her staff, and a particularly noisy piano duet played by two children; he is anxious to return to his brokerage business in the city. His wife is swimming.

This Sunday tableau is typical of many American and British novels of that era. In such novels, the setting was described, and after the main characters were introduced, the action began. Chopin's structure for *The Awakening* fits this scheme, but she embellishes her narrative skeleton with a multitude of details that her enthusiastic, early critics labeled as "local color." To the critics and readers not familiar with the region, New Orleans and its Creole trappings were mysterious and exotic. Chopin, for example, begins her novel with a stylistic flourish: "A green and yellow parrot, which hung in a cage outside the door, kept repeating over and over: *'Allez vous-en! Allez vous-en! Sapristi!'* " Put in a historical context, this was a rather bold stylistic stroke for a female novelist, especially one who wanted to be taken seriously and whose theme in this novel is the discontent and revolt of a woman who refuses to pay the price that matrimony and motherhood demand.

The caged parrot, however, is not merely "local color," nor is the caged mocking bird on the other side of the doorway mere decoration. Both are symbols of the novel's heroine, Edna Pontellier, who will "awaken" in the novel and discover that she is caged in a marriage that does not allow her to grow or to become a mature, self-critical woman with a mind of her own and a sexual body of her own. Interestingly, Edna Pontellier's husband is only mildly irritated by the noise of the caged parrot; later in the novel, he will be confused and furious when he finds himself threatened by a wife who tells him that she refuses, as it were, to parrot the "right" phrases and refuses to perform what is expected of the wife of a well-to-do businessman. For the present, the caged birds which hang on either side of the resort doorway seem only a part of Chopin's local color, and we should realize now that she will thread them and many other motifs throughout her novel to give it dimension and texture.

The other local color accents in this first chapter – in addition to the French- and Spanish-speaking parrot and the summer resort being south of New Orleans – are the Creole landlady dressed in starched, crinkled white (a contrast to the silent lady dressed in black, walking among the cabins and saying her rosary), the nearby island of Chênière Caminada, where Sunday mass is given, and the Pontellier's quadroon nurse, who follows the Pontelliers' two children around. Similar details frequently appear in Chopin's fiction; critics noted them and praised them. Yet it was not until *The Awakening* was published that they began to seriously consider the inner lives of the characters who lived in the midst of all this local color. Because Chopin was southern, and also a woman, critics read her short stories and pronounced them to be "finished," "charming," "delicious," and one even noted that she had "the dialect 'down fine.' " But *The Awakening* changed all that because the heroine is a woman who painfully comes to realize that many of the satisfactions of life are denied to her – precisely because she is a woman. Edna's awakening to the fact that she has no real identity and her subsequent revolt against this stifling southern status quo alarmed most of the readers and certainly all of the critics. The novel was said to be scandalous, and it was neglected and largely forgotten. Today, however, it has been recognized as a minor masterpiece, one of those small classics that is good literature and a joy to read and reread.

In Chapter 1, Chopin introduces us, first of all, to Edna's husband, and we hear about Edna from him before we see her for ourselves and are able to form our own impression. The man that Edna married is rather slender, has straight brown hair (parted neatly), a precisely trimmed beard, a slight stoop, and is forty years old. He is uncomfortable during this lazy summer weekend and is anxious to return to his business dealings in New Orleans. His first utterance is an "exclamation of disgust."

When we first see Edna through Mr. Pontellier's eyes, she is at a distance, and it is not precisely Edna whom we see. Far down on the beach we see only a white sunshade, or parasol, approaching. Under it are Edna and young Robert Lebrun, the landlady's son, whom Edna finds unusually fascinating. The mood of the lazy Sunday permeates this chapter as Chopin describes Edna's parasol approaching at a snail's pace, the gulf itself "melting hazily" into the horizon, and Edna and Robert seating themselves with "some appearance of fatigue," as they lean against the cottage posts. Mr. Pontellier says that it is "folly" to have gone swimming in such heat. His stuffy reaction reveals his characteristic indignation at his wife's childish and unladylike immaturity. He, of course, took a swim at the "proper" hour, at daybreak, and that is precisely why the morning has seemed long and never-ending to him. He feels out of place in this relaxed and peaceful pattern of his wife's Sunday morning, in the same way that he felt distracted by the early, noisy bustle around the Lebrun cottage.

"You are burnt beyond recognition," Léonce says to Edna. In other words, Edna has broken the social code which measures a woman's respectability by the cut of her dress, the length of her gloves, and in this case, by the color of her complexion. Edna is almost as dark as the racially mixed servants at the Lebruns' summer resort. Chopin then tells us precisely what Mr. Pontellier thinks of his wife: Léonce Pontellier regards Edna as "a valuable piece of personal property that has suffered some damage." Here is the key to Edna's predicament. Later in the novel, she will discover that she cannot be anyone's "personal property"; she cannot be the personal property of her husband or even of her children. She will refuse to be restricted by society, by her husband's code of confinement, or by the demands of her children.

Yet at this moment, when we first view Edna, she does not seem to feel particularly restricted by convention or by her husband's callous remark. She is enjoying the summer heat, the swimming, and she enjoys being the relaxed companion of young Robert Lebrun. When Edna is swimming, she is free of all bonds on her. She even takes off her wedding rings before she goes swimming—and she does this in an age when most married women superstitiously never removed their wedding rings. Here, she blithely takes them off, and she delights like a child when she asks for her rings back, slips them on, and watches them sparkle on her tanned fingers. Note here that when she wishes to have her rings, Edna and her husband do not exchange a word. They have lived together long enough to anticipate one another's requests and to respond to one another's gestures. Mr. Pontellier understands what Edna wants when she raises her hands; later, she understands what he means when he shrugs an answer to one of her questions.

In her husband's opinion, Edna is a good wife, if a bit irresponsible. He is so confident of her faithfulness that he is neither irritated nor jealous at the pleasure she finds in the company of Robert Lebrun. But instead of swimming and joking with the boyish Lebrun, Mr. Pontellier would much prefer to be playing billiards with other men.

The first scene closes with Edna asking her husband if he is coming to dinner. He doesn't give her an answer; he shrugs his shoulders, and Edna accepts his non-verbal communication and "understands." Again, her prescribed role does not seemingly bother her too much. Léonce allows her the freedom to go swimming, provides a nurse to look after their children, and gives her the freedom to enjoy Robert's company. Her husband's indifference doesn't bother her unduly. The prosaic reality of her marriage has become a habit, as has her passive response to it. As we might expect in any well-constructed novel entitled *The Awakening*, the heroine will first be viewed "asleep," as it were, before her "awakening" occurs. This is exactly what Chopin has done in this first chapter. She has shown us Edna Pontellier, and she has richly described Edna's two worlds – her exterior world (as a wife and mother) and her interior world (as a woman asleep – emotionally, intellectually, spiritually, and sexually), and the walls of both these worlds will topple before the novel is finished.

CHAPTERS 2-4

By choosing, first of all, to describe Edna's eyes (the "mirrors of the soul" in nineteenth century literature), Chopin tells us precisely what Edna looks like and *how* she looks: Edna is a handsome woman, rather than a beautiful one. Her eyebrows are thick and horizontal, and the eyes themselves are the same yellow-brown color of her hair; they fasten onto an object and hold it. Edna's gaze is candid and frank, yet contemplative, and Chopin's description here is direct and clear-cut, very much like Edna herself.

After Edna's husband leaves for his club, Chopin focuses on Edna and Robert Lebrun, the young man whom Edna finds engaging. From Chopin's details, we realize that although Robert is the landlady's son, he himself isn't particularly well-to-do. He rolls his own cigarettes, for instance, because he can't afford cigars; the cigar which he has in his pocket is a gift from Edna's husband, a treat he has reserved for himself after dinner. Robert's youth is accented by his clean-shaven face, in contrast to Mr. Pontellier's bearded features, which fashionably connote money and status. Robert has a boyish air, and as we learn later, he is not terribly ambitious. We also learn later that Robert has a modest job in New Orleans as a clerk; there, his fluency in English, French, and Spanish is highly valued. Robert seems to drift through life; he is drifting this summer, as he has done for many summers, hoping something will happen to make this summer interesting, and Edna's presence, it would seem, has just accomplished that.

Robert's most prominent feature is his facial *expression*: his is one of open contentment, where "there rested no shadow of care." Edna's eyes contemplate, Chopin tells us, "lost in an inward gaze"; Robert's eyes reflect "the light and languor of the summer day." Chopin inserts an abundance of description here in order to slowly create a mood. Earlier, her tempo was busily paced to catch our initial interest. We looked at, listened to, and noted Mr. Pontellier's impatience and his disgust at the noisy birds, the soprano cawings of his landlady, and the piano duet by the Farival twins. Now Chopin shifts this scene to an andante mood as she leisurely delineates two central characters—two people who value leisure, as they share the summer warmth of the Gulf and one another's presence. Edna plays with a palm-leaf fan, and she and Robert talk lightly about inconsequential things— the breeze, the pleasure they had while swimming, and the Pontellier children—all of the things that disgruntled Mr. Pontellier. The scene Chopin describes is a scene designed for lovers—which Edna and Robert are not, yet.

Throughout this novel, Chopin is never far from her narrative, and the early critics who charged her with "letting her stories tell themselves" or, on the other hand, of writing "analytical studies" failed to discern her particular style. One of the delights of reading Chopin's fiction is being suddenly aware, now and then, that we are hearing Chopin herself as she presents her characters and their problems. As an example, listen to her as she tells us about Robert: Robert "talked a good deal about himself. He was very young, and did not know any better. Mrs. Pontellier talked a little about herself for the same reason." The effect is dazzling. Chopin is being humorously intimate with us, while employing economy, conciseness, and a certain wise, wry humor. We have the feeling that she has a good understanding of her characters and knows and cares about the minor foibles of these young people. The effect is similar to Henry James' portraits, especially as she continues her description and tells us that Robert spoke of his intention of "going to Mexico in the summer, where fortune awaited him." Then Chopin offers us this neatly packed perception: Robert "was always intending to go to Mexico, but some way never got there." Succinct statements like this are electric with importance; we can predictably expect Robert either to continue his long-delayed daydream of seeking his fortune in Mexico, or else he may dramatically decide to stop his drifting and actually leave for Mexico. Already she has created suspense for us.

Edna and Robert's parting near dinnertime is casual; Chopin sustains the languid mood of the afternoon as Edna rises and goes to her room, and Robert joins Edna's children for a few last moments of play. There is a peaceful naivete in the simple pleasure that Robert and Edna find in one another. Neither of them, of course, is aware that they have begun an innocent intimacy.

The charm of Chopin's introduction to the Lebruns' summer resort on Grand Isle and to the typical upper-middle-class Pontelliers abruptly ends when Léonce Pontellier returns late from his club and loudly reproaches his wife for her "habitual neglect of the children." His loud anger is unjustified; his railing at Edna is not motivated by his concern for the boys or by young Raoul's questionable fever. In this scene, Léonce acts "like a child," a patronizing accusation which he frequently levels at Edna. He arrives home late, in high spirits, and expects Edna, "the sole object of his existence," as he likes to brag about her, to be awake and to adoringly listen to every word of his brusque joking about what happened at the club. He is angry that Edna is asleep, and he chooses to punish her with unwarranted charges that she is an irresponsible and negligent mother.

It is a temptation to make an easy villain of Léonce Pontellier. But he is no villain; in today's jargon, he is merely another example of a male chauvinist, a role not at all uncommon in his era. Léonce dramatically leaves the room of his allegedly sick child and orders his wife to tend to the child; meanwhile, he puffs on a cigar. His noisy concern for the child is enough responsibility for him in his role as a father and a husband. His responsibilities are practical; his duties include the brokerage business and making a living for the family. He has no time to either worry about his children's health or tend to their illnesses. Léonce believes both duties to be "a mother's place."

In this scene, it is significant that Chopin does not insert an editorial voice into the narrative. She presents the conflict between the Pontelliers quickly and cleanly. Instead of didactically denouncing Léonce's unjust actions, Chopin focuses more on Edna; she explores Edna's feelings after Léonce has finished his cigar and has fallen asleep. Edna is bewildered—and not merely about her husband's unjust outburst. She does not understand why she is suddenly crying; the fact that she is crying disturbs her more than her husband's angry insults. She feels lost but she is not absolutely lost; in particular, she is aware that she is allowing herself to succumb to a strange, deep mood. This is the first time that such heavy emotion has overwhelmed her and that she has let herself be *aware* that she is dissatisfied with her marriage and with Léonce. Her confusion dissolves her. She is slowly awakening in this sense. Until now, Léonce's upbraidings have never mattered particularly; Léonce has always been abundantly kind and devoted, as a generous recompense for her service to him as a wife and as a mother to his children. But tonight something new and different has suddenly happened, and Edna cannot fathom her strange sense of oppression nor does she even try to. It comes from "some unfamiliar part of her consciousness"; its anguish is vague, "strange and unfamiliar," and it consumes her. Of central importance is the fact that she *allows* herself to be engulfed in emotion.

Next morning, Mr. Pontellier leaves punctually in his carriage to catch the steamer to New Orleans; he will not return to Grand Isle until the following Saturday. Chopin, therefore, neatly concludes this chapter with a tableau of his leaving. Léonce's excitement builds as he anticipates a lively business week ahead of him, and he gives Edna half of his night's winnings as he leaves.

The effect of Léonce's leaving is liberating to Edna. Yet this feeling vanishes in a few days; Edna receives a box of candies from him, and the values of her mother and her grandmother and long generations of women before her cause her to graciously acknowledge that Léonce *is* a good man. Léonce gives Edna things; he is overly generous with presents to her. Edna is envied; people say that Mr. Pontellier is the best husband in the world. Not surprisingly, Edna decides that perhaps, after all, Léonce is a fine husband. Chopin's final comment here is that Edna "was forced to admit that she knew of none better" – that is, Edna knew of no better husband than Léonce. Perhaps this is true; perhaps Edna does not know of a better husband, but earlier in this scene we witnessed Edna beginning to feel the possibility that there *might* be something more to marriage than what she and Léonce share, something deeper in the relationship between a man and a woman than that which exists between her and Léonce. A sense of dissatisfaction, undefined and indistinct as of yet, has taken root unconsciously within her.

Perhaps some of this has to do with the setting. Compared to the rest of the women on Grand Isle, Edna is different. On the surface, Edna is a "good" mother and a "good" wife, but not in the way that Léonce, for example, is a "perfect" husband. Edna is not what Léonce expects her to be – that is, she is not like the "mother-women" here at Grand Isle. This term that Chopin uses to describe the Creole women is superlative, and its concept is central to the novel's theme. In the following chapters, we see Edna mingling with the other women and, as she does so, we measure her against them. Grand Isle, it is clear, is a summer nesting place for mother-women while their husbands are working in New Orleans. One can see them fluttering about the resort, their protective wings protecting their brood of children. But not Edna. Her boys fight their own battles, overseen by their quadroon nurse who, when need be, buttons trousers for the boys and makes sure that their hair is parted on the proper side – all the little things that the mother-women do for their children.

As a perfect example of this mother-woman, there is none better than Edna's good friend, Adèle Ratignolle. Whereas Edna is handsome, Adèle is strikingly beautiful. Edna's yellow-brown hair contrasts with Adèle's spun-gold hair that neither "comb nor confining pin" can restrain. Mothering, like her golden good looks, comes as easily and as regularly to Adèle as her continual birthing of babies. Nor does mothering seem to drain her energy. Adèle radiates gifted capability, whether she is tending her children or mending one of their bibs. Chopin captures the essence of Adèle as the mother-woman marvels over a pattern for a baby's winter drawers. Edna, in contrast, could not be less interested. She has never felt an impromptu, bubbling joy over the intricacies of a baby's winter drawers. She is capable of joy, but not about next season's baby clothes, and it bothers her that she feels that she should at least feign an interest in such things simply because she is a mother.

Although Edna has never taken the time to analyze her thoughts, she is aware that it is impolite to act uninterested in a friend's enthusiasms. But Adèle's passion for motherhood is only one of many things which Edna cannot explain or feel comfortable with. Equally puzzling is the Creole temperament. Edna Pontellier is the only non-Creole at Grand Isle, and she is not used to the community bond that exists among them – in particular, their "entire absence of prudery" and their "freedom of expression." These people have grand emotions – real and feigned – and share their feelings with the community; Edna does not. Her joys and her disappointments in life have been brief and certainly never tumultuous; usually she is evenly felicitious and somewhat guarded. Adèle can talk easily about a woman's "condition"; Edna is not even at ease when using this euphemism to describe a woman's pregnancy. Edna is bored with Adèle's patterns and she is shy about sexual matters. In contrast to the mother-women, Edna is a lady-child. But this summer, Edna is changing – a bit. She is astonished at the Creoles' frankness and their freedom of expression; the risque books and stories which make the rounds of the guests amaze her sense of privacy. But she slowly begins to realize that their world is not a threat to her own and that their world is made up of wonders "which never cease." To a certain degree, all of this fascinates her.

But what Edna does not realize – yet – is that these women, while being free to discuss sexual matters, have given up their own unique identities. Their freedom to talk about sexual matters is natural to them because of its being relevant to marriage and children. They *seem* free, yet all of them have willingly conformed to the prescribed role pattern for the Creole wife and mother. Their frankness is not unusual to them; it is something they grew up with. And this frankness is not synonymous with freedom. Their frankness about sex and sexuality is merely a part of their evolving into mother-women; moreover, they have all conformed willingly. Edna feels alien because she could never conform so willingly to their role. She has conformed, certainly, for she has a prudish side; she was reared to be a "lady." But Edna is also somewhat of an innocent, childlike rebel. She is most *un*ladylike, at times, because she swims at whatever hour of the day she wants to, doesn't worry about how brown her skin becomes, and she is more than willing to let a quadroon nurse look after her children. In fact, it is her very individuality which is most striking about her, compared with the other women of Grand Isle.

CHAPTERS 5–6

Because Edna is not one of the Creoles, she often watches them with a sense of fascinated detachment; for example, she thoroughly enjoys young Robert Lebrun's company, but her friendship with Robert is not as open nor as close as is Adèle's friendship with him. Adèle and Robert share a playful, spirited camaraderie. They joke, in Edna's presence, about Robert's "role" at Grand Isle; for the last two summers, Robert was Mademoiselle Duvigne's "knight" of sorts – that is, he pretended to be ready to serve her every whim, and he pretended to be inconsolable if her temper darkened. After Mademoiselle Duvigne died, Robert posed as the very figure of despair at the feet of Adèle, grateful for any crumbs of sympathy she might toss to him in his depression. It was a game of fantasy and romance for Robert and Adèle, fraught with gestures of grand emotions and grand passions – sensations which are alien to Edna. She sits on the edge of their mirth as they delight in teasing one another about broken hearts and tragic sufferings.

This scene helps us to better understand the "exotic" Creoles. Chopin wanted to show us the light and easy familiarity that existed between married Creole women and single men. The mere idea of jealousy makes Adèle and Robert laugh; the community shares its joys and its sorrows with all its members. And sexual jealousy for the Creoles, Chopin tells us, is virtually unknown. Jealousy, she says, is that "gangrene passion . . . which has become dwarfed by disuse." Chopin's comment here reminds us of Léonce Pontellier's attitude toward Robert; he feels absolutely no jealousy toward the young man. Likewise, Adèle's husband is not jealous of Robert and, therefore, this particular scene between Adèle and Robert should be compared to the scenes between Robert and Edna. The relationship between the young Creole man and Edna, the outsider, is "different." Robert does not feel free to exaggerate and boldly joke with her about "passions" which burn within him until "the very sea sizzled when he took his daily plunge." Throughout this novel, we must be continually aware that Edna is not a Creole; she has never experienced passion – real or imagined – nor has she ever discussed it nor joked lightheartedly with anyone about it, especially the "hopeless passion" which Robert describes himself as being a tragic victim of.

This light bantering about "hopeless passion" is important to note here, for it is not wholly comic nor merely a part of Chopin's "local color"; it is an element which will play a pivotal role later in the novel when Edna becomes a victim of a passion that is, as it turns out, hopeless. Yet, at this moment, passion is a subject of romantic comedy, and while Adèle can laugh gaily at Robert's rich inventiveness, Edna cannot; she has never tossed through sleepless nights because of "consuming flames." She soon will, however, and thus, Chopin is preparing us for the change that is about to occur within Edna by showing us how foreign these feelings are to her at present so that we can compare them with her later emotions, after she has begun to "awaken."

Edna has always kept her distance from strong emotions. So far in this novel, she has been largely an observer. She is not sure how much of Robert's bravado she can believe. More important, however, she is sure that she is absolutely incapable of such intense feelings as her friends joke about, and she is even a little annoyed when Robert touches her casually while she is sketching a portrait of Adèle.

Chopin's tableau of this trio begins to close as Edna breaks off sketching for the day and fills the open hands of her children with bon-bons. Chopin tells us that "the sun was low in the west, and the breeze soft and languorous." Edna notices that Adèle, the ideal mother-woman, is a bit flushed; she wonders if Adèle's lively imagination is responsible. Edna is extremely curious about this mother-woman. As she did earlier, she watches this mother-woman as she greets her children, showering them with endearments. The mother-woman leaves, and Edna is left feeling free from the pressing duties of all of the Creole mother-women. For this reason, she is coaxed by Robert into taking an evening swim.

Chopin accompanies the scene with words that are very much like ones she used earlier: "The sun was low," she tells us, "and the breeze was soft and warm."

Chopin speaks of the sea and the sea's waves and the waves of wonder that Edna feels as she tries to fathom the mysterious Creole nature and as she tries to understand her feelings toward the sea. Edna is slowly awakening to the fact that the sea is beginning to speak to her, making her aware of its caressing quality and the embrace of its solitude. This will signal the dawn of one of several of Edna's "awakenings." Chopin describes the feeling on this particular night as "a certain light . . . beginning to dawn dimly with [Edna] – the light which, showing the way, forbids it." Edna is a stranger to the bewildering symptoms of troubled dreams, anguish, and uncontrolled sobbing, just as she is a stranger to the sensuous, delicious delight of feeling the sea fold around her body.

But Chopin does not leave us with merely metaphors. She wants her readers to clearly understand what her novel will deal with – the ecstasy and pain of sensuality and of romantic and sexual passion, subjects which were revolutionary in her time, especially for women writers. Chopin states clearly that Edna was "beginning to realize her position in the universe as a human being, and to recognize her relation as an individual to the world *within* and *about* her" (emphasis mine). She also makes it clear that Edna is not undergoing a mere, or brief, sudden, shadowy insight into life, or even vaguely sensing a simple lesson in maturity. Chopin will be challenging Edna with complex ideas and with "a ponderous weight of wisdom." At twenty-eight, Edna will receive "perhaps more wisdom than the Holy Ghost is usually pleased to vouchsafe to any woman." This is a strong comment; obviously men of the late nineteenth century granted little wisdom to women. But here Chopin accuses even God Himself of neglecting to grant women unusual wisdom. Edna, however, is to be an exception and, as Chopin's readers, we are curious and interested to see how Edna will receive and cope with this "ponderous weight of wisdom."

The voice of the sea ends the chapter. Chopin calls it "seductive; never ceasing, whispering, clamoring, murmuring; inviting the soul to wander for a spell in abysses of solitude; to lose itself in mazes of inward contemplation." This passage could have come directly from Walt Whitman's "Out of the Cradle Endlessly Rocking," a poem published some forty years before *The Awakening*. In his poem, Whitman speaks of the rocking rhythms of the sea, its powerful call, and its ability to "soothe, soothe, soothe!" Chopin, like Whitman, is aware that the sea invites the soul to wander, as it pulses with its sensual, caressing wetness. For Whitman, the sea was a symbol of rebirth. It will offer Edna a retreat, for awhile, away from life, an opportunity to rock her body and soul into a peace that will prelude her awakening so that she will emerge freshened, strengthened, and reborn.

When Robert asks her to accompany him for a swim, she declines, then reconsiders. Convention rather forbids it—swimming at evening time—yet Edna rather wants to swim, and so she accepts Robert's offer. After all, why not? Swimming, to Edna, is frankly sensuous, and its sensuality is enhanced by the handsome young man beside her. A healthy *man* would not hesitate to respond to the sea, and Edna is beginning to question why she, simply because she is a woman, should deny herself this gratification or why she should let society deny it to her. Edna, as we noted, is beginning "to recognize her relation as an individual to the world within and about her." She is aware that she is a separate, unique individual; she is *not* a mother-woman and, at twenty-eight, she is beginning to view herself in an entirely new perspective this summer as she lives among the Creole mother-women on Grand Isle.

Initially, Edna simply enjoyed swimming in the sea, but now something new is beginning to happen; her moments are no ordinary moments. Edna is allowing herself to become part of an unconscious fusion with the sea, feeling the echoes and the restless pull of the sea's waves within her body. In Edna's body, remember, there was a sea itself, one in which each of her children was rocked; the waves and the pull of this Gulf sea invite Edna back to it, just as it has invited generations of beings who left it long ago. The sea has always held a certain mystery and mystique; men have always been fascinated by it, but perhaps no man can fully feel the magic of it as a woman can. Edna cannot explain nor fathom the lure she feels. She only knows that she enjoys allowing herself to respond to it.

This is a moment of epiphany for Edna. She realizes innocently, without intellectually analyzing her feelings, that this seemingly quite ordinary moment—her deciding to swim in the sea and to freely enjoy her new emotional feelings about the sea—is more than a simple "swim." She is aware of the intense cleansing and renewing sense of this moment. Chopin applauds Edna's frankly sexual and spiritual response to the sea. She does not caution her readers against its seductive hold; on the contrary, she urges her readers to listen to the cadence of her prose as she attempts to evoke the feeling of this moment as Edna steps into the sea, succumbing to its strength as it speaks to her soul and to her body, "enfolding [her] in its soft, close embrace." Edna will soon be awakened to a new and fragile sexuality within herself. At the same time this happens, she will begin to sense within the sea the vast solitude that is within her and within humanity. Her awakening, then, will be double-edged: it will delight her and it will open new depths for her, and finally it will become her consolation.

CHAPTERS 7–10

After Chopin shows us Edna's mystical and sensuous immersion in the late evening sea, we witness Edna's relaxing her body and slowly releasing herself to new emotions and feelings. Then Chopin pulls back her narrative perspective and gives us some straightforward background exposition about the change that is to occur within Edna Pontellier. She tells us, for instance, that up to now Edna has always been a very private person, never given to confidences; even as a child, Edna had "her own small life all within herself." This small, private inner world, we realize, has continued to be characteristic of Edna throughout her adult life. She has whole dimensions of herself that she has not shared even with Léonce – nor with anyone else – until now. Now, a vague, undefined possibility of change occurring in her life has presented itself to Edna. This summer, she senses, will change the course of her life, and she is correct; neither she nor Léonce will ever be the same again.

At Grand Isle, she has allowed herself to be friendly with Robert – but only to a certain degree; it is therefore natural that she turns first to Adèle Ratignolle, another woman, when she feels the need to talk about herself. Adèle's unusual beauty so fascinates Edna that she believes that Adèle might perhaps be sympathetic to Edna's new, ambivalent feelings about discovering a new sense of beauty in living and, at the same time, a sense of confusion within herself.

As the two women walk along the beach, Chopin again contrasts them; their bodies seem parallels of their personalities. Adèle is "the more feminine and matronly"; Edna has "no suggestion of the trim, stereotyped fashion-plate . . ." Chopin adds that "a casual . . . observer . . . might not cast a second glance [at Edna]." Chopin is cautioning her readers not to label Edna as a stereotype who will be "awakened" in this novel and suddenly "bloom." Her "awakening" is far more important than a cliched, romantic, physical change. Edna is *not* the usual nineteenth-century heroine; Chopin stresses this point continually. She is, in Chopin's words, "different from the crowd."

In yet another of Chopin's tableaus, the two women are sitting by the sea, and its force and boundless freedom strengthens Edna's resolve to talk about herself. Symbolically, she removes her collar and "opens her dress at the throat" before she begins to speak. The lady in black is in the background, Chopin's ever-present symbol of death and danger, as are the two lovers, the antithetical symbols of a secure life and love.

Adèle instinctively senses that Edna needs to confess, and so she listens quietly as her friend reveals that sometimes as a young girl she could not resist reacting unexplainably to nature. One time, she remembers, she suddenly threw her arms outward, "swimming when she walked, beating the tall grass," and feeling as though she could walk on forever. She remembers that this was done on impulse. Usually she was not so spontaneous; she did not grow up that way. She grew up "driven by habit" and only now, this summer, have those feelings of childhood, those days when she wandered "idly, aimlessly, unthinking and unguided," returned to entice her. Adèle is clearly aware of how important this confession is to Edna and how different these new feelings are to her in contrast to her many years of living "by habit." Adèle is also aware that Edna does *not* withdraw her hand when Adèle covers it protectively; ordinarily, Edna avoids any sudden physical contact, as she did when Robert accidentally touched her while she was sketching. Adèle even strokes her friend's hand reassuringly, freely allowing her mother-woman instinct to comfort this woman who feels troubled here among the Creoles; she realizes that Edna feels unable to share in the Creole community of familiarities and is deeply confused by what is happening within her.

Chopin then removes us from this scene again; to help us understand Edna more fully (Edna will allow herself to tell Adèle only so much about her past), Chopin speaks directly to us. She tells us that Edna was not altogether comfortable with her young romantic feelings when she developed a schoolgirl crush on "a dignified and sad-eyed cavalry officer"; later, when her family moved from Kentucky to Mississippi, she developed a romantic crush on a young man, but the infatuation was brief and he was already engaged; as a grown woman, she fell in love with the face and figure and photograph of "a great tragedian." Her first romantic kisses were given to the cold glass that contained his photograph. It is no oversimplification: Edna has never known real love or real passion.

Chopin tells us frankly that Edna's marriage to Léonce Pontellier was "purely an accident." Léonce fell in love with Edna, he pressed for an answer, and Edna was flattered by his "absolute devotion." She imagined that there was "a sympathy of thought and taste between them." But despite the fact that there was no romance between herself and Léonce, Edna could *not* be convinced to reject this Creole Catholic man. She married Léonce despite the violent oppositions of both her father and her sister Margaret. Edna had been proposed to by a man who worshipped her, and if she married him, she felt that she would have a "certain dignity in the world of reality"; thus she consciously chose to close the door on a young woman's "realm of romance and dreams," and that door has remained closed until this summer when, by accident, she discovered it open, exposing old memories and old feelings, but more important, revealing fresh new concepts about herself and her emotional and physical needs.

Until now, Edna has been "fond" of Léonce; similarly, "in an uneven, impulsive way," she has been "fond" of her children. But nowhere does Chopin mention that Edna has a deep love for either Léonce or for the children. In fact, the months which her children spent with Léonce's mother granted Edna "a sort of relief." But, as was noted earlier, Edna cannot tell all of this to Adèle; she has lived too long encased in years of inner privacy. Of necessity, Chopin must tell this to us.

Talking so candidly with Adèle is almost traumatic for Edna, and Adèle understands this. She understands that Edna's sudden decision to confide in her has "muddled her like wine, or like a first breath of freedom." Edna is suddenly weak when Robert appears with "a troop of children," and she must gather up the loose ends of her thoughts, her reveries, and rearrange her composure. Adèle is keenly sensitive to the pain and confusion that has been laced throughout Edna's confessions, and it is for this reason that she feigns having such aching legs that Robert must assist her while they walk back to the cottage. She senses that Edna is beginning to fall in love for the first time, and she knows that she must warn Robert. Adèle and Robert have an old comradeship, and being old friends, they can seemingly discuss anything, and the mother-woman within Adèle is as protective of

Edna's tender new emotional awakenings as if Edna were one of Adèle's own children.

Adèle's request that Robert "let Mrs. Pontellier alone" is not received well. Robert realizes that his old friend is deadly serious, and he is momentarily disarmed; he is caught off-guard by Adèle's somber directness and, moreover, his pride is wounded when Adèle warns him that Edna "might make the unfortunate blunder of taking you seriously." Adèle's words sting because Robert has playfully toyed with married women for many summers, but until now he has not thought much about it; now Adèle has given Robert new insight into the emptiness of the "role" he has played and replayed in a long-running, trivial summer game. Before he leaves Adèle, Robert says with seriousness, softened by a smile, that she should not have warned him about Edna; rather, she should have warned him about himself, against *his* taking himself seriously. He leaves her then, and in the background are Chopin's familiar woman in black, looking even more ominously jaded, and the two lovers, seeming to be even more in love than ever. They are symbols, obviously, and are inserted here to prelude what is about to follow.

Robert's confusion, distraction, and irritation are apparent as soon as he enters his mother's house and hears the clacking noise of her sewing machine. Imaginatively, we can also hear the monotonous, mechanical clacking and parallel it with the monotonous, mechanical summer pattern that has been pivotal to Robert's summer years on Grand Isle. Yet it was a pattern which Robert enjoyed until Adèle made him realize how insignificant it was.

Robert inquires about the whereabouts of Mrs. Pontellier, and he reminds his mother that he promised to lend Edna the Goncourt. It is Robert now, not just Edna, who seems to be floundering. Ironically, Robert's life of simple spontaneity has been "driven by habit," just as Edna's life of bland sterility has been "driven by habit." And neither Robert nor Edna can fully understand nor grasp the changes that each of them instinctively feels is necessary for them. But Robert, however, seems far more alarmed and frantic than Edna, and when he remembers Adèle's capsule analysis of himself, it seems almost more than he can bear. It is easy to understand his thinking of Edna immediately; if no one takes him seriously, Adèle has said that Mrs. Pontellier might do so. The realization that he has been valued as no more than amusing summer entertainment is frightening to him. Like Edna, who is just beginning to discover how barren her life has been, Robert has suddenly viewed the deep void of his own life.

By accident that evening, he learns that Montel, an admirer of his mother, is in Vera Cruz, Mexico, and has inquired about Robert's joining him in a business venture. By chance, Robert suddenly realizes that two people, for the first time in years, are considering taking him seriously—Mrs. Pontellier and Montel. Mrs. Pontellier finds him romantic and Montel considers him mature enough to be a business partner. The temptation to suddenly prove himself and establish a sense of his own manhood is overwhelming. He chides his mother for not telling him sooner of Montel's offer, and he searches for the Goncourt to take to Mrs. Pontellier.

After Adèle warns Robert about the danger of Edna's susceptibility to his charms, Chopin allows a few weeks to pass. It is now Sunday and an impromptu party of sorts is underway; there is music, dancing, an unusual number of people, and even the children are allowed to stay up later than usual. The Farival twins who once irritated Léonce Pontellier with their piano playing are at the piano again, and even the parrot is once again shrieking outside the Lebrun doorway. Recitations are being given, as well as a performance by a young, amateur ballet dancer.

Edna joins the ballroom dancing for awhile, but soon prefers sitting outside on the gallery in the Gulf moonlight, watching the "mystic shimmer" on the "distant, restless water." Her revery is short-lived. Robert is determined to tempt her and please her, and he does so in a way that makes her the focus of the evening. Robert promises to have old Mademoiselle Reisz play the piano especially for Edna; he knows that he can charm the quarrelsome, eccentric old woman into performing, and he does. Entering the hall with Robert, Mademoiselle Reisz requests of Edna what music the lady would like to hear. Robert carries off his role of summer cavalier well, providing Edna with a gift of music and assuring himself that Adèle was right: Edna does take him seriously, and she is romantically fascinated by him; she is not like the Creole women with whom he played empty games during the past summers. Edna, of course, is ignorant of Robert's motives, and she is embarrassed and overwhelmed by what he does, and she begs that Mademoiselle Reisz choose suitable music. The old woman is intuitive about Robert's motives and about Edna's feelings toward Robert.

What Edna hears unnerves her. Chopin tells us that Edna has responded to piano music before, conjuring up vague moods of solitude, moods of longing and despair as embodiments of her own confused emotions, but Edna is totally unprepared for the raw passion that Mademoiselle Reisz sets ablaze within her, sending tremors down her spine, invading her soul and, sea-like, "swaying it, lashing it." Edna seems, we feel, almost ready to faint, feeling the music beating against her. She trembles and chokes, and tears blind her. Significantly, old Mademoiselle Reisz is aware of how successfully she has accomplished magic with her Slavic, romantic music.

Yet while Edna is the most visibly shaken, the entire company is moved by the music, and suddenly it is as though Robert "arranges" yet another bit of evening entertainment in yet another attempt to be taken seriously. Chopin tells us that Robert proposed that they all go for a swim "at that mystic hour under that mystic moon" and that "there was not a dissenting voice."

Robert is definitely assuming a new, commanding role in the novel, and while he does not "lead the way" to the beach, Chopin tells us that he "directed the way." Yet even he is not sure of the rules of his new role, for he finds himself "whether with malicious or mischievous intent" parting the two lovers that Chopin has included in various scenes and dividing them, as he walks between them.

Edna can hear Robert's voice from afar, but she is confused as to why he does not join her. She does not understand his new attitude. Once they were comfortable companions, and suddenly he has become unpredictable, absenting himself for a day, then redoubling what almost seems to be a kind of devotion to her the next day. It seems as though he is deliberately choosing to tease Edna, for Chopin tells us that Edna has begun to miss him, "just as one misses the sun on a cloudy day . . ." Clearly, Edna is falling in love with Robert, and he obviously is aware that she is doing so – becoming, in fact, seriously enamored of him. This is no longer the usual summer game of charade for him. Robert's attentions are being taken seriously by a monied, married woman, and he is enjoying his "seduction" of her; after all, he is a past master at such games.

It is now that we learn that Edna – all during the summer – despite all of her attempts, has never learned to actually swim. Despite her affection for the sea, she has never mastered it and while it lures her daily, it fills her with a "certain ungovernable dread." Tonight, however, all alone, she finds herself actually swimming for the first time in her life. The realization is overwhelming. Scarcely has she had time to adjust to Robert's generous attentions toward her than she was swept up by the power of Mademoiselle Reisz' romantic music, and now she discovers that she no longer has to "play" or "bathe" in the sea. Her emotions have been drained, yet she is giddy; she has gained a small bit of mastery—of herself and of the sea. It is almost as magical for her as Chopin has described the night as being.

Aware that she can actually swim gives Edna a new sense of freedom. She no longer needs a nearby hand. Her intoxication with her discovery makes her dramatically assertive; she wants to swim "where no woman had swum before," and she tries, swimming out alone, seaward, letting herself meet and melt with the pulsings she feels deep in the moonlit sea. Yet while she does not go any real distance, she goes far enough that she becomes frightened when she realizes that she might not be able to swim back. This is Edna's first encounter with the fear of death—yet another "awakening." But there is no one with whom she can share this terrible new discovery. Léonce is certainly not impressed that she can swim or that she is frightened. Not surprisingly, Edna chooses to leave him and return home alone. She is strongly affected by the rich magic of the music, by suddenly discovering the power of her swimming, and by the powerful fear that drowning is a possibility if one swims too far, alone.

Her senses are still swimming when Robert overtakes her; she is able to tell him, impulsively, exactly how she feels—of her exhaustion, of her joy, of her confusion, and of this night's being like a dream. She confesses that she feels possibly bewitched or enchanted.

Robert's response is dramatically on cue. He assumes the pose of a raconteur of Creole lore and interrupts her to explain that she has been singled out by a spirit that has "haunted these shores for ages." He fills Edna with romantic fancy, teasing her that perhaps the "spirit" that has found her may never release her. But he overplays his role; he gilds his fancy with too much embellishment, and Edna is finally hurt by his flippancy. Not being a Creole, she cannot respond with sufficient light wit and dash.

In the silence, Edna takes Robert's arm, then allows him to help her into a hammock. Both are aware that they are alone; she asks for her shawl, but she does not put it around her. Twice, Robert asks if he should stay until Mr. Pontellier returns and twice she says that he must decide. He smokes, they do not speak, yet she watches him, and in the silence, there are, Chopin tells us, "moments of silence . . . pregnant with the first felt throbbings of desire."

Robert leaves when the other bathers begin to approach, and when Edna says nothing, he believes that she is probably asleep. He could not be, ironically, more mistaken. Edna is fully awake, more awake than she has ever been in her life, aware of his body passing in and out of the strips of moonlight and, metaphorically, of his passing in and out of her body's desire for him.

Fittingly, Edna lies suspended in a hammock; she has learned to swim alone in the sea which she loves and which she now fears; she can almost joyously control this fierce natural power, yet she cannot wholly dominate it, for it fills her with a certain dread. Similarly, she has learned that her body has unloosened itself and she has let her emotions flow outward, unbounded; she has responded sexually to Robert's physical presence, yet, like the mysterious awe she has for the sea's power, she feels threatened by this new discovery of her sexuality because she cannot control what she does not understand. This night has engulfed her in multitudes of new emotions and discoveries. It is no accident that Chopin closes the chapter with Edna Pontellier suspended in a hammock, literally and symbolically suspended between a new reality and a night of magical awakenings.

CHAPTERS 11–14

It is a combination of exhilaration, a surge of new courage, a trace of fear, but most of all it is a sense of new peace that fills Edna Pontellier as she lies alone in her hammock. She does not even speak to Léonce when he returns home. In fact, she does not even answer him initially when he questions her, and note here how Chopin's style parallels Edna's inward transformation; in her narrative, Chopin tells us that Edna's eyes "gleamed," suggesting clear, direct sight and, further, Chopin says that Edna's eyes, despite the late hour, had "no sleepy shadows, as they looked into his." This descriptive phrase is doubly significant. It underscores Edna's newly awakened state, and it stresses Edna's looking directly at her husband, facing him as an equal and even as an opponent. Her voice rings with new authority as she tells him *no* – she is not asleep. Edna is absolutely awake and newly aware of her aroused physical feelings and emotions. Her "Don't wait for me" is symbolic of her new sense of life's enormous potential. Edna is no longer Léonce Pontellier's childlike lady-wife; she is no longer in need of a man's presence before she can begin readying herself for bed. She has awakened to a new confidence and to a new assertiveness within herself. Chopin emphasizes the seriousness of the metamorphosis that we are witnessing by telling us that ordinarily Edna would have obeyed her husband "through habit," would have "yielded . . . unthinkingly . . . [like] a daily treadmill of . . . life." Understandably, Léonce is puzzled by his wife's "whimsical" defiance, especially when she repeats once again that *no*, she is not going to bed; she is "going to stay out here."

At this point, one must turn backward toward a time long past and consider not only the courage it took for Edna to defy her husband, but also the courage it took for Chopin herself to envision such a scene as this and create the character of a "dutiful, submissive" wife suddenly asserting heretofore latent, unrealized willpower. For Léonce Pontellier, it must seem as though his wife is possessed and, to a degree, even Edna herself must feel a bit "possessed" as she realizes that "she could not at that moment have done other than denied and resisted" the force that she feels within her. The effect of Léonce's threat not to "permit" her to stay outside on the veranda is impotent, as is his derisive judgment that Edna's actions are more than "folly."

Léonce cannot comprehend the new voice he hears within his wife, a voice which has begun to articulate a new and independent identity. Heretofore, it has always been Léonce who has made all decisions, even minor ones. Now Edna has discovered the courage to hold her own nebulous future within her own two hands and, without rationally considering the consequences, she tells Léonce not to "speak to me like that again."

The silence is heavy. Léonce's preparations for bed are overly self-consciousness and nervous; he slips on "an extra garment," drinks two glasses of wine, and smokes several cigars. And all this time we are not even sure that Edna is conscious of her husband's puttering preparations for bed; she is experiencing a mildly chaotic ecstasy – "a delicious, grotesque, impossible dream." Truly, it must seem "grotesque" – Chopin's adjective is not too extravagant – for Edna Pontellier has come to the realization that it is *unnatural* for her to be dominated any longer by her husband. Chopin speaks of the "realities pressing into her soul" and of the "exuberance" exulting within her. Her words are suggestive of an intellectual, an emotional, and even a sexual climax within Edna; she has cut herself loose from the moorings of a life of attendance on monied, middle-class mores. Instead of stagnating in Léonce Pontellier's shallow marital confines, she has swum out and felt the cleansing power of new, fresh perceptions. She has never before sensed her own strength nor imagined that she could escape from an oppression which had always seemed a necessary dimension of a woman's lot.

After a few hours of feverish sleep, Edna's physical actions are not entirely strong. Chopin says that the cool morning air "steadied somewhat her faculties," but Chopin does not let her readers worry that Edna's "folly" (so termed by Léonce) was only momentary. Edna is as triumphantly awake in these morning hours as she was in the dark hours of the night and particularly this morning "she [is] not seeking refreshment or help from any source . . ." To describe Edna's new sense of herself, Chopin uses such words as "blindly following . . . alien hands . . . [which] freed her soul of responsibility."

This is a Sunday morning, and Chopin's Sabbath tableau includes once again the symbolic young lovers, strolling toward the wharf and also the lady in black. Edna, having passed through a night saying things to herself and to Léonce she has never said before, thinking things she has never thought before, and certainly doing things she has never done before, does something else this morning which she has never done before: she tells a little Negro girl who is sweeping the galleries to go and awaken Robert and tell him that she has decided to go to the Chênière, the nearby island where Sunday mass is held; moreover, Edna adds an afterthought of urgency: she says that the young girl should "tell him to hurry," and her impulsive decision to include an injunction to Robert contains three parallel phrases: "She had never . . . She had never . . . She had never . . ." All this must have seemed frighteningly revolutionary to women (and men) readers of 1899; revolt was a fearsome thing for those who had the abundance of leisure to read "novels," themselves things of "folly," according to many male intellectuals. Female independence was threatening; any modicum of liberty allowed to women was a dangerous risk. But Edna's defiance of her husband was clearly no whim that surfaced and disappeared during a night that Robert Lebrun mischievously termed as being "enchanted." Edna Pontellier is just as firmly assertive this morning as she was when she was lying in the hammock, and she is putting her new-found sense of liberty to a test. She commands Robert's presence, and he comes to her. Her future is dim and still vague, obscured by a present that is overpowering in its potential, but Edna is happy as she starts out on this small voyage to Sunday mass and on a much larger voyage out toward the fulfillment of her womanhood.

In addition to the collection of summer vacationers on the wharf, including the lovers and the lady in black, double-edged symbols of Edna's obscure new destiny as an independent woman, Chopin includes a new character in her Sunday tableau – a young Spanish girl, Mariequita. Mariequita is a pretty girl, and she and Robert speak Spanish briefly, a language that no one else understands. Edna notices the girl's feet: Mariequita is barefoot, her feet are broad, and there is "sand and slime between her brown toes." The girl is a flirt, openly "making 'eyes' at Robert," and tossing saucy comments to the man in charge of the boatload of passengers.

Although no one else understands what Robert and Mariequita are saying, Chopin reveals their conversation to us. Mariequita wants to know more about Robert's relationship with Edna; the fact that Edna is married is of no consequence to the young Spanish girl – marriage is no barrier to sexual satisfaction between two lovers, but she wants to know because she is interested in Robert herself: is Robert the lover of Mrs. Pontellier? Robert does not answer her directly; he teases and hushes her with a light jest. Meanwhile, Edna is dreamily intoxicated by the fierce new tenacity she feels within herself. As the boat's sails swell and become full-blown, Edna feels "borne away"; she feels "chains . . . loosening," and she feels "free to drift whithersoever *she* chose to set her sails" (emphasis mine). Her horizons are no longer limited. As the Sunday morning air strikes Edna's face, she is aware that she has been confined too long by social convention and marital muzzles.

Robert's spur-of-the-moment suggestion to Edna that they go to Grand Terre the next day excites Edna's new taste for boldness. She likes the idea of going and of being "alone there with Robert." Chopin stresses the physical satisfaction that Edna hopes will be hers when she imagines herself and Robert "in the sun, listening to the ocean roar and watching the slimy lizards writhe in and out among the ruins of the old fort." It is the seductive earthiness of the adventure that excites her, the pounding power of the ocean that fills her sense of adventure, and there is also a sexual suggestion when Chopin mentions the lizards writhing among the "ruins" of an old fort – symbolically, Edna's old fortress of middle-class security that she has been locked in until now. Neither Léonce nor even Robert fully comprehends this new woman; Robert asks if Edna won't be afraid of crossing the sea in a canoe, and Edna's "no " is sure and assertive. This causes Robert to promise her other trips, at night; then he slips into his jester's role, teasing her again about the "Gulf spirit" and warning her that it will whisper to her where hidden treasures can be found. Spontaneously, Edna matches Robert's imaginative caprices, saying extravagantly that she will squander any pirate gold they might find and throw it to the four winds, just "for the fun of seeing the golden specks fly." Edna is rich already; she has unearthed her own hidden treasure – herself, and the sureness of herself; it is exciting to see her laughing so freely and fancifully about imaginary hidden treasures.

Significantly, the oppressiveness of the church service becomes so restrictive and stifling that Edna is forced to leave the service. The ritual of the circumscribed dogma filling the tiny enclosure begins to suffocate Edna's new, bursting spirit. To be imprisoned so soon after she has experienced a breath of freedom is impossible for her. Robert solicitiously follows her out of the church and instinctively, perhaps, takes her where she can hear "the voice of the sea." She takes a drink from a rusty cistern and is "greatly revived"; this is Chopin's symbolic mass for Edna – a baptism with water that is holy not because it is divinely sanctified but because it comes from the earth and is naturally cool and refreshing to Edna's *physical* body, as well as to her spiritual body.

At Madame Antoine's, where Robert takes Edna, notice the freedom which Edna feels when she decides to loosen and remove her clothes, how responsive she is to the feel of the sheets and to the odor of laurel in the air; there is a sensuousness within her as she stretches her body to its full length. Edna is discovering the pleasure of physical self-awareness, how delicious her own body can feel. This is part of the "ponderous weight of wisdom" that Chopin spoke of earlier. Edna is claiming, as well as discovering, her own sensuality: "she saw for the first time, the fine, firm quality and texture of her flesh."

After she sleeps long and soundly and awakens late in the afternoon, her first words to Robert strike him as somewhat fey, but they are symbolically full of great significance: "How many years have I slept?" Robert's playful joking about her sleeping one hundred years seems romantically the right kind of response from this young man who has, summer after summer, assumed the role of a knight errant, attending some fair lady at his mother's summer resort. But Edna's question, if exaggerated, is weighty. She has metaphorically been asleep a very long time. And as she awakens from her late afternoon nap, she is also just beginning to awaken to the reality of an identity crisis. Of course, at this moment it is no crisis – that will come later – but the immediacy of her new identity is of concern and that concern now is with her resolve to commit herself fully to the new identity that she conceives is possible for her – whatever that illusive, unformed, unimaginable identity might be.

Among Edna's many thoughts, she considers whether or not Léonce will be "uneasy," but note that this is only a "consideration" for her; it is not a concern that he might be worried about her. We must realize that Edna no longer fears a possible reproach from him for her "folly," as Léonce will no doubt declare her actions to be.

When Robert and Edna sit down to eat at Madame Antoine's, Robert notices the "relish" with which Edna eats; she is discovering new and satisfying sensations in even such commonplace acts as eating. Her appetite for food and, more important, her appetite for living has been whetted and sharpened. She allows herself the freedom to sit under the orange trees, watch the shadows lengthen, and listen to the Creole tales and fancies of Madame Antoine until "the night came on." She is severing herself, freeing herself to absorb what is offered to her – the food, the cooling air from the sea, and the compelling, storytelling voice of Madame Antoine. These moments are not dictated by "habit" or directed by a mindless adherence to duty or by any other consideration, save one: herself. Feeling freed from a past of repression, Edna allows herself to linger fully in the luxuriousness of this moment.

This long Sunday afternoon has not been satisfying for the rest of Edna's family. Adèle Ratignolle, however, Edna's mother-woman confidante, has been able to coddle and pacify the younger of Edna's children, as well as Edna's husband, who has gone off to discuss the latest happenings of the cotton exchange. Now that Edna has returned, Adèle admits to suffering from the heat, and she refuses to remain even for a moment with her friend, even to hear about Edna's afternoon adventures. Monsieur Ratignolle is "alone, and he detested above all things to be left alone." The contrast between Edna's new sense of herself and her role as a wife and mother is in bold contrast to Adèle's life, governed wholly by domestic duties and demands; she must take charge of and take care of a multitude of mother-woman things—food, children, and a husband. She satisfies herself by being useful to them; she knows of no other possible pleasure for herself. Her value lies in her devotion to her utility—to the man she married and to their children.

When Robert leaves Edna finally, after both children are in bed, Edna asks him with the wonder of a child who realizes that something very special has happened, if *he* realizes that they have been together "the whole livelong day." His answer is serious, despite his surface joking: "all but the hundred years when you were sleeping," and when he leaves, Chopin tells us that he goes not to join the others, but that he walks alone toward the Gulf. This afternoon has touched Robert also.

Alone, Edna breathes deeply and her sense of solitude swells; she allows her mind to billow backward over the long day's length, trying to discover "wherein" this summer has become suddenly different from "every other summer of her life." Softly, she sings a song to herself that Robert sang earlier, the refrain returning after each verse, "*si tu savais*": "if you only knew . . ." There is little doubt that she is falling in love with her fresh sense of freedom, in love with the sense of adventure she has discovered in life and in herself, and in love with Robert.

CHAPTERS 15-16

Time passes—we cannot be sure how long—and Chopin begins this chapter with startling news: Edna comes to dinner and is told simultaneously by several guests that Robert has decided to go to Mexico. What has happened between the two of them since we left them on that Sunday evening and this moment we can measure only by Edna's genuine confusion. For example, they spent the entire morning together, and Robert did not mention Mexico. His leaving Grand Isle so rashly seems unreal, and as Edna sits across from him at dinner, she allows him—and everyone else—to see her undisguised bewilderment. Robert looks both embarrassed and uneasy when Edna asks "of everybody in general" when he is going. When she learns that he intends to leave this very evening, her voice rises in astonishment at the utter impossibility of such an unexpected exodus. Even Robert's voice begins to rise, Chopin tells us, as he defensively explains that he has said "all along" that he was going to Mexico. Only the two high-pitched voices are haranguing, and yet Madame Lebrun must finally knock on the table with her knife handle and declare that her table is becoming a bedlam.

It is an awkward scene as Robert is forced to admit that his decision was made only this afternoon. As he explains his actions to Edna, Chopin describes him as feeling as though he is "defending himself against a swarm of stinging insects"; explaining his leaving to the other guests, Robert is characterized as feeling like a "criminal in a court of justice." Edna senses that his answers are too lofty and that he is posturing; we feel this too. It is as though Robert is trying to make his decision to go to Mexico seem like a mature decision made after long months of weighing and mulling over the alternatives and advantages—instead of the hasty escape from Grand Isle that Edna half-fears and half-believes that it may be.

Later, Adèle Ratignolle's mother-woman instincts try to comfort Edna; what Adèle feared at the beginning of the summer has happened: Edna has fallen in love with Robert Lebrun. Adèle assures Edna that Robert was wrong to say nothing about his leaving until only moments before he was due to leave, but she thinks that Edna should, for manners' sake, join her and the others in seeing Robert off; otherwise, it won't "look friendly." Here, she reveals how thoroughly imprisoned and confined she is in her prescribed role as a perfect and proper mother, wife, and woman. Adèle cautions Edna not to expose her emotions, especially her wounded feelings toward Robert; even if Edna's heart is broken, she should camouflage her shattered dreams and submissively join the rest of the guests. Edna's pride, however, refuses to yield to her friend's pleadings, and it is Robert who finally seeks out Edna, instead of the traditional frantic female pursuing the departing male.

Bluntly, Edna asks Robert how long he will be gone; she admits that she is unhappy and doesn't understand him or his silence. Edna plays no games. Her love for Robert has no coy edges; she admits to having daydreamed of seeing him often in New Orleans after the summer was over. Robert half-confesses to having had the same hopes, then breaks off, assuming the manners of a gentleman, extending his hand, and addressing her as "Mrs. Pontellier." Edna cannot, or will not, conceal her hurt and disappointment; clinging to his hand, she asks him to at least write to her, and he promises to do so. Then he is gone. Edna struggles to keep from crying, from lapsing into silly, adolescent feelings of desertion. She realizes all too well what has happened; she allowed herself to take Robert's presence for granted, just as she allowed herself to joyously take for granted her newly discovered feelings of independence and the knowledge that she was in love with young Robert Lebrun. There is, however, nothing to be done now. Robert will be gone in a few minutes.

Edna's suffering and pain in this scene is another of her awakenings; when she opened herself to the possibility of passion for a man, she should also have included the possibility of great pain. It seems a simple enough equation, but Edna was still a naive woman, even though she was twenty eight years old when she fell in love for the first time. Yet once she accepted the profound delights of love, she should also have realized the possibility of profound pain as being the probable denouement of love between a married woman and a single man in the restricted, patriarchal southern society of 1899. Edna, however, is an innocent and she committed emotional adultery without forethought and without guilt because of her loveless marriage.

In contrast, Robert—a role-oriented and role-defined Creole—cannot break his community's mores. We sense that he has fallen in love with Edna, but that he is unwilling to risk an affair with her—out of respect for her and out of respect for a code which forbids it. Thus he flees to Mexico rather than confront his feelings for her; he refuses to resolve or cope with what seems to be an unsolvable dilemma. Throughout this summer, he has been Edna's teacher; he opened her soul to spiritual and physical delights, but when he realized that he was falling in love with his married, adoring pupil, he could not deal with his desire for her. His long-time fantasy of going to Mexico and finding success and happiness abruptly became an instantaneous destination for him. To remain in Grand Isle and become Edna's lover would make him a cad; to exit to Mexico is the way of a coward, yet he sees no alternative for himself. He is too weak to stay, and his weakness accentuates Edna's emotional heroism.

Seemingly, she would be willing to risk everything; Robert cannot commit himself to such a decision.

After Robert's departure, Chopin tells us that Edna spent much time in a "diversion which afforded her the only pleasurable moments she knew"—that is, swimming in the sea. Edna belongs to no "community" here, in the way that Adèle belongs to her community of mother-women. Without Robert's companionship, Edna feels her closest kinship with the sea, especially now that she has learned to swim. Remember that the sea once offered her the soothing company of its solitude. Now she returns to it.

The Creole community misses Robert's vivacious presence; they naturally assume that Edna does also. Certainly Léonce is aware that his wife greatly misses her young friend. Yet no one guesses the extent to which Edna is pained by Robert's absence. Chopin speaks of Edna's unconsciously looking for him, seeking out others to talk about him, and gazing at old photographs of Robert in Madame Lebrun's sewing room, taken when he was a young boy. One photograph in particular amuses her—a picture of Robert, looking "full of fire, ambition and great intentions." It is a positive sign of Edna's growing maturity that she is able to smile at that picture. Despite her pain of missing him, she knows full well that she is infatuated with a man who is sorely lacking "fire, ambition and great intentions." Robert is, by nature, gentle, sensuous, and a dreamer; it was these qualities that first attracted Edna to him. And because he is basically a gentle young man, his abrupt severing of their relationship is all the more painful.

We now encounter a passage in the novel that probably shocked Chopin's readers far more than the notion of Edna's romantic need for an "affair." We learn that Edna and Adèle Ratignolle once had a rather heated argument during which Edna told her mother-woman confidante that she "would give [up her] money, I would give my life for my children, but I wouldn't give myself"—that is, Edna would *not* sacrifice day after day of living an empty, unfulfilled life for her children's sake—"or for anyone." She would, if ever such a drastic choice were necessary, sacrifice her life so that her children might live, but she would *never* live an empty life, devoted solely to her children, dedicated to them, doing everything for *their* sakes. She could never define herself in terms of them, nor would she use their lives as a surrogate for her own life.

Surely this was the fullest declaration of independence uttered by a heroine in a novel that Chopin's readers had ever encountered. Many novels prior to *The Awakening* had contained episodes in which married heroines left their husbands for another man, or had an affair with a young lover, but here was a woman who defied the whole concept of the family unit. Edna would give her life, if necessary, for her children, but she would not live an empty life dedicated to anyone – save herself and what *she* considered essential for herself. This is as shockingly revolutionary to Adèle Ratignolle as it must have been to Chopin's readers and early critics. The whole masculine-conceived, family-oriented universe is being suddenly defied by young Edna Pontellier. Edna is protesting against a woman's living vicariously through the lives of her husband, her children, or anyone else. Edna demands full responsibility for herself – and to herself. She refuses to dedicate her life to a role that she does not fashion, define, and fulfill.

CHAPTERS 17–19

Within two weeks, the Pontelliers are reestablished in their large house in New Orleans. Seemingly, they are the happy master and mistress of the charming, many-columned, broad verandaed home, and Chopin details for us its dazzling white exterior, contrasting it with the serenity of the inner furnishings – the soft carpets, the damask draperies, the cut glass, the silver, and the rich paintings – all presents from Mr. Pontellier to Edna, "the envy of many women whose husbands were less generous than Mr. Pontellier." Mr. Pontellier takes great pride while walking through his house, surveying its sumptuous details. "He greatly valued his possessions," Chopin states, and we recall a sentence near the beginning of the novel when he irritably commented on his wife's sun-bronzed body. He scolded that she was "burnt beyond recognition . . . looking at his wife as one looks at a valuable piece of personal property which has suffered some damage." Léonce Pontellier esteems "his possessions, chiefly because they [are] *his*" (emphasis mine). Among his possessions, he obviously and unthinkingly includes his wife because he lives in an era when he and his men friends conceive of their wives in terms of their being personal possessions.

The lazy summer days of the Gulf resort seem remote as Chopin describes the Tuesdays which are Edna's official "reception days," when "a constant stream" (an ironic image here) of lady callers alight from carriages or stoll up to the front door, greet the mulatto houseboy, who holds a tiny silver tray for their calling cards, and are offered liqueur, coffee, or chocolate before they are finally allowed to greet the mistress of this elegant mansion: "Mrs. Léonce Pontellier, attired in a handsome reception gown." This role has occupied and embodied Edna's existence ever since she became Mrs. Pontellier, six years ago. Certain evenings are designated for the opera, and others are for plays; days are scheduled very much alike – Mr. Pontellier leaving between nine and ten o'clock and returning between six and seven in the evenings, and dinner is always at half past seven.

It is on one of these Tuesdays when Léonce returns home and notices, much as he might detect an unexpected crack in an expensive china bowl, that his wife is not wearing a reception gown; she is wearing an ordinary housedress. Léonce comments that no doubt she is overly tired after her many callers, and Edna confirms that there were indeed many callers – at least there were many cards in the silver tray when she returned. Deliberately, she does not say from where she had returned. Edna has broken a long-established pattern: she was not a "hostess" today.

Léonce is almost, but not quite, angry with her. He is busy adding condiments to his soup, scolding her softly: "people don't do such things" – unless they have a good excuse. Edna has no excuse, nor did she leave any explanation for her callers, nor does she offer any to Léonce.

Mr. Pontellier explains to his wife, much as he would to an absent-minded maid or a socially backward daughter, that they both must observe "les convenances" (the conventions). That his chiding is done in French is an added affront of smug male superiority, as is his cranky complaining about the tastelessness of the soup, as though he were a culinary authority. He requests that the silver tray of cards be brought to him; social callers musn't be snubbed – especially the monied ones, he comments, as he discovers that a certain Mrs. Belthrop found his wife not at home this afternoon. He tries to humor Edna and make her realize that these niceties *are* important, and he insists that she must apologize to a certain caller and that she must avoid another. Just as he has *his* business duties, Edna has *her* social duties, which are an important extension of his business world.

Mr. Pontellier's critical evaluations continue and include each of the food courses, all of which he finds fault with. "Cooks are only human," he says, implying that hired help must be constantly kept on guard lest they become lazy. He adds that hired help, if not watched carefully, will soon "run things their own way." The phrase is intense with significance. Mrs. Pontellier's refusing to perform the social pattern of her Tuesdays, as she has for six years, is an example of someone deciding to do "things their own way." And while Edna cannot literally be considered an employee of Mr. Pontellier, he certainly considers her a functionary in the house. His comment is purposely pointed. Of course, he rewards Edna generously for performing her duties, but that means that she is duty-bound to repeat on each Tuesday a succession of mindless greetings and chatter to insure and further the Pontelliers' social status. Edna is symbolically and, in fact, a costly, performing puppetlike possession of Mr. Pontellier. Their marriage ceremony decreed it, he identifies her as such, and he expects *her* to do likewise. As a reward, he bestows every possible material thing of value upon her so that she will further enhance him and be satisfied with being defined as "Mrs. Léonce Pontellier." She is envied. He knows it, and other people know it, and being envied is of much importance to Mr. Pontellier.

There were times, Chopin tells us, when Edna attempted to plan a menu or when she studied cookbooks, trying to please her husband's highly critical expectations, but those days are over. Tonight, after Edna finishes dinner, she goes to her room and stands in front of an open window. At this point in the novel, one can't even imagine Edna's standing in front of a *closed* window; she has finally felt the satisfaction of independent judgments and actions, and the open window is symbolic of the free flowing, fresh air of freedom. Edna is not terribly unhappy tonight; she is frustrated. She recognizes the mystery of the night beyond the window. It revives old memories, but she is not soothed by them. She paces, she tears a tiny handkerchief to ribbons, then flings her wedding ring onto the carpet, and stamps the heel of her shoe upon it as though she could crush it. The strength of the tiny gold band, however, mocks her frustration and causes her to grab up a glass vase and fling it onto the tiles of the hearth. The crash and clatter are welcome sounds of destruction – until a well-trained maid hurries in and begins cleaning up the mess. When the maid returns the ring to Edna, she slips it on, slipping uncomfortably once again into the tightly restricted role of being Mrs. Léonce Pontellier.

The following morning, the Pontelliers quarrel briefly about new fixtures for the library. Edna thinks that her husband is excessively extravagant for wanting to buy them; he regrets that she doesn't feel like selecting them. Cautioning her to rest and take care of herself, he takes his leave and Edna is left alone. The world beyond the Pontellier veranda is fragrant with flowers and noisy with street vendors and young children. Edna, however, feels alienated from them, alienated from everything and everyone around her. Chopin has built up a good deal of tension and suspense. Edna is about to do something. Her frustration will not allow her to return to a world where she ignorantly and innocently half-lived for six years as her husband's charming hostess and wife and the dutiful mother of his children.

Edna leaves the house, and as she walks we learn that "she [is] still under the spell of her infatuation." She has tried to forget Robert, but has been unsuccessful. As she did on Grand Isle, Edna has decided to seek out Adèle Ratignolle and try to talk about her problems. The two women are confidantes, even though the Ratignolles are certainly less well off, materially and socially, than the Pontelliers. They live above their drug store, prosperous though its trade is, in an apartment, commodious though it might be. Adèle does not have a "receiving day"; she has, instead, once every two weeks, *soirees musicales*, evenings of musical entertainment which are very popular and considered a privilege to be invited to.

The mother-woman is unsurprisingly busy, sorting the family laundry; she says that it is really the maid's work, but she enjoys doing it, yet stops to chat with Edna. Once again, Chopin contrasts the two women. The domestic harmony that Edna sees is pleasing but she does not and cannot belong to that world. Edna can never find full, true contentment folding laundry, preparing meals, and listening with honest interest to her husband's dinner talk. That world is colorless, boring, and confining to Edna. It contains no measure of exhilaration and nothing of what Edna suddenly voices in her inner thoughts as "the taste of life's delirium." Chopin comments that "Edna vaguely wondered what she meant by 'life's delirium.'"

Chopin's readers were also probably puzzled by that phrase. Modern readers, however, do not find the term puzzling at all; it seems antiquated in its articulation perhaps, but we do not "vaguely wonder" about the meaning of the term. We realize that Edna is beginning to demand for herself no more or no less than the right to experience the fullness of her emotional spectrum. The solidarity of the Ratignolles' lifestyle is too mechanical and unimaginative; it is constructed on routine and precludes all possibility of unbounded pleasure and passion, as well as violent pain. Edna finds no consolation in Adèle's maternal security and happiness. Adèle has traded her identity and her independence for serenity and security. Adèle's life is centered on her utilitarianism, just as Léonce's world is centered on material possessions and social position. A free existence for a woman – devoid of her being equated with husband, children, and household chores – was unheard of in 1899, unless one were an "artist." And this seems to be at least a possibility for Edna. She lives in New Orleans, a city filled with writers, painters, and artistic types; Edna is beginning to envision that perhaps this lifestyle is her only alternative. The position of being sovereign of the Pontellier mansion that Léonce offers to her is repugnant. Léonce places Edna on a pedestal, yet at the same time he shackles her there. Edna wants to break these chains. It is a dangerous, nebulous ideal that Edna desires; years later, a modern Greek writer, Nikos Kazantsakis, articulated precisely the yearnings of this frustrated Victorian woman in his novel *Zorba the Greek*. The hero, speaking to a rather prudish young Englishman, tells his friend that one "must, sometimes, cut the rope [of rationality]; a man needs a little madness in his life." Zorba, of course, would (like Léonce Pontellier) deny such freedom to a woman. But not Chopin. She created a heroine who, like Zorba, wanted "a little madness" in her life, something besides the dull and conventional and stifling role that was forced on her by generations of men and by their submissive wives, as well. Edna is beginning to distrust the value of permanence and is beginning to trust the value of her instincts. She was awakened on Grand Isle to feel that there was a possiblity for her to be more than a wife and more than a mother; she is not sure *what*, but she is certain of the possibility.

Unfortunately, Léonce Pontellier is not aware of this change within his wife. He expected her to begin once again the patterned ritual of their New Orleans social life once they returned to the city for the winter. Edna cannot; she is struggling with her deliverance from that role, and she feels within her a force superior to Léonce's drive for power and position and also superior to Adèle's happy security within the four walls of Monsieur Ratignolle's home.

It was childish to stamp on her wedding ring; it was childish to smash a vase. Edna realizes that she was acting exactly like a frustrated child. Yet Léonce conceives of his wife as childlike; he assumes that she will accept docility and dependence as her natural lot. Ironically, she behaved exactly like Léonce's child-wife, the person whom she desperately tries *not* to be. And in order "to do as she liked and to *feel* as she liked" (emphasis mine), Edna realizes that she must control her emotions, as well as her actions. As long as she is smashing vases and raging, she is denying herself moments of self-declared and self-defined control. She can complain as loudly as she wishes, but unless she begins to act upon her own convictions, she will be doomed to the futile, cliched role of being yet another woman moaning about the injustice of the world and blaming men for her misery. Her violence was spontaneous, but it ultimately solved nothing. It left her as powerless as before. But she will *not* be bought or compromised by the promise of new library furnishings or the threats of social disapproval.

Thus Edna decides to completely abandon her "Tuesdays at home" – an act of social revolution that was unheard of in the Pontelliers' New Orleans social circle. Nor does Edna explain her decision – just as she refuses to return the visits of her lady callers.

Mr. Pontellier is at first bewildered, then shocked, and is finally angered that his wife means to exchange the role of being "head of a household" for being a painter in an atelier. Her lack of logic confuses him, but it does not confuse or even frighten Edna. For the moment, she *feels* like painting; "perhaps I shan't always feel like it," she says, knowing and admitting to Léonce that she is "not a painter." She does not know *why* she is doing what she is doing, but it is what she *must* do. Edna is hearing and responding to the beat of what Thoreau calls "a different drummer," and she is following it without being overly concerned about her final destination. A man in her time could have been able to do the same thing and no one would have questioned his gambling with life. Nor would they have been shocked by his admission that his ultimate goals were undefined; after all, Robert was able to pack up and suddenly leave for Mexico, and the only consternation concerned his sudden departure – not his actual leaving. Such things are possible – if one is a man. Edna wants that same choice for herself; it is her only hope of release from years of habitual submission.

When she was on Grand Isle, swimming in the sea, listening to its soothing music of freedom, feeling it surround her – all this intoxicated her. It relieved her from the heavy weight of nineteenth-century New Orleans convention. Her exultation unlocked her; Edna is shedding a fictional self that Léonce and even she herself created for her, dressed her in, and taught her to perform as.

Léonce allows her this "whim"; like a restless child, his wife will tire of dabbling in painting and dawdling in obscure, transient "folly"; he is sure of this. He could not be more mistaken. Edna knows that she is no great painter; she never intends to turn out great masterpieces of art. She simply needs to paint at the present and, most important, she needs *not* to entertain boring streams of women callers every Tuesday.

Edna works, then, with great energy – "without accomplishing anything" – but as she draws and paints, she sings to herself the refrain that Robert sang after they had spent the day on the island of Chênière Caminada. The memory of the rippling water and the flapping sails are sensual memories, preludes to her body's remembering "a subtle current of desire." This is not simple romantic revery; this is richly sexual, a yearning to have the desire consummated. Chopin is boldly stating that a woman experiences the same sexual excitement and needs that a man does when she is aroused by certain smells and certain sounds and memories. The memories of the brief hours spent with Robert exude the heat of an aphrodisiac for Edna, a concept considered unhealthy and akin to heresy in Chopin's time.

Edna's desires must, of necessity, remain unsatisfied, but she accepts the inevitable – for the present. She knows that she can recreate and rekindle the fire within herself, even if she cannot satisfy it. This is part of the breadth of the emotional spectrum that Edna claims for herself in exchange for her former role as wife and possession of the well-to-do Léonce Pontellier.

CHAPTERS 20-24

Although Edna is not completely satisfied with being an "artist," she continues to paint; being a painter frees her to a great extent, and it causes her to seek out another woman who is also an artist, a character from the past—old Mademoiselle Reisz, the pianist who played the powerfully passionate music the night Edna discovered that she could actually swim; it was also on that night that she discovered the courage to defy her husband's demands that she obey something as insignificant as "coming to bed" because of the possibility of being "devoured by mosquitoes." Edna cannot easily locate the old woman's address, but her impetuous decision to find the old woman becomes a challenge for Edna. She follows suggestions from strangers, is led to new neighborhoods, hears disagreeable gossip from those who claim to have known her, but Mademoiselle Reisz herself remains illusive until Edna remembers that if anyone would know the whereabouts of the eccentric musician, it would probably be her summer landlady, Madame Lebrun, now living in New Orleans for the winter months.

Ironically, it is while Edna is on this capricious, independent adventure that she hears a quarrel within the Lebrun house before the door is opened. A black servant is demanding of Victor, Robert's brother, that *she* be allowed to open the door; it is her duty. This is sharply symbolic. Chopin is contrasting Edna's new independence with the actions of a servile, submissive black servant; it is inserted inobtrusively, yet very naturally, into the scene, as Chopin quietly denounces pride in what is ultimately an abject role.

It is Victor, Robert's handsome, nineteen-year-old brother, who greets Edna with undisguised delight, and he allows Edna to sit on the side porch instead of "properly" guiding her into the parlor. Impetuously, he begins to tell the handsome older woman about a romantic escapade he had the night before when he followed the flirtatious lead of a girl who was taken by his good looks. This is obviously something he would never tell his mother, but he feels—after the summer that he observed Edna on Grand Isle—that Edna is "different," even if she is older than he is, and a wife and a mother.

Edna indulges Victor's imaginative, male bravado-embroidered storytelling until Madame Lebrun enters. The family, she learns, has received two letters from Robert, letters which Victor declares to be of little value and glibly recites the contents of. Futilely, of course, Edna had hoped for some greeting to her; instead, Robert simply asked that his mother remember him affectionately to "all his friends."

Edna's mood darkens briefly, but because the Lebruns know old Mademoiselle Reisz' address, Edna leaves the Lebrun house in good spirits. Not only Madame Lebrun notices how "handsome" Edna looks, but Edna's beauty has not escaped Victor; "ravishing" is how he describes her, commenting that ". . . she doesn't seem like the same woman."

Mademoiselle Reisz also comments on Edna's handsome, healthy looks. She prides herself on a candor that she can afford because of her old age and "artistic" eccentricity. Edna, however, is also direct—because she *chooses* to be. When the old pianist says that she feared that Edna would not come to see her in New Orleans, she is told candidly that Edna herself has not been sure whether or not she likes the woman—a frankness that pleases the old woman. She therefore quickly reveals the fact that she has had a letter from Robert, written in Mexico City. But she refuses to let Edna read the letter, even though she says that it contains nothing but questions about, and recollections of, Edna. In particular, Robert asks Mademoiselle Reisz to play the Polish composer Chopin's "Impromptu" for Edna, should Edna pay a call on Mademoiselle Reisz. According to Mademoiselle Reisz, Robert wants to know, afterward, how the music affects Edna.

The old woman is teasing Edna. We sense that she is trying to measure Edna's passion for young Robert, trying to determine whether or not Edna is merely a dilettantish, frivolous, bored wife of the well-to-do Mr. Pontellier. She is trying to decide whether or not Edna is merely dabbling in painting and pretending passion for a young man who is living in an exotic, faraway country. Therefore, she does not play merely the Chopin "Impromptu"; she combines it with one of Wagner's love themes, hoping that her background mood music will expose the truth of Edna's emotions as she reads Robert's letter. The music, the deep shadows in the little room, the night air, and Mademoiselle Reisz' music all cause Edna to begin sobbing—something she has not done since a night long ago on Grand Isle.

Léonce Pontellier decides to call up his old friend Doctor Mandelet, a "semiretired physician . . . [who has] a reputation for wisdom rather than skill," and it must have given Chopin much secret delight to write an entire chapter, short though it is, devoted to "man talk" about women. Mr. Pontellier boasts of his own manly good health and his healthy Creole genes—in contrast to his wife who, while not sick, is "not like herself." The two men agree that women are moody, delicate creatures, not to be fully understood. Of course, however, Mr. Pontellier assures the old doctor that Edna's *heredity* has nothing to do with her problems. He *chose* her from "sound old Presbyterian Kentucky stock"; Chopin's satire is especially keen here. In particular, Mr. Pontellier is puzzled about Edna's notions that she has recently acquired "concerning the eternal rights of women." This also causes the old doctor some concern as he lifts "his shaggy eyebrows," protrudes "his thick nether lip," and taps "the arms of his chair . . ." Chopin's portrait is magnificent. Léonce continues: Edna isn't interested in attending her younger sister's wedding; she says that "a wedding is one of the most lamentable spectacles on earth." The doctor nods; Edna is another woman "going through a phase." He assures Mr. Pontellier that "the mood will pass . . . it will pass; have patience." Secretly, the old doctor wonders if another man might be involved in Edna's personality change, but he knows better than insult Mr. Pontellier with such a question.

The introduction of Edna's father into the narrative is unexpected; he was mentioned at the beginning of the novel, when we learned that he had once owned a Mississippi plantation before he settled in the bluegrass country of Kentucky, and we recall that he was not merely opposed to Edna's marriage to Léonce, a Catholic Creole, but that he was "violently opposed." Edna is "not warmly or deeply attached" to her father, but most of their antagonism seems to have faded; she welcomes his coming to New Orleans as a distraction from her own indecision about what she must ultimately do with her life.

Adèle Ratignolle, Edna's confidante, urges Edna to encourage Léonce to spend more time at home and less time at his men's club. Edna does not understand how this would solve anything; "What should I do if he stayed home? We wouldn't have anything to say to each other," she counters. And frequently while reading this novel, one needs to go back almost a century and imagine the readers of this novel and the critics who were suddenly confronted with such intimate, honest declarations as this. It is little wonder that they were puzzled, shocked, and offended. Yet Chopin is not being racy. She is simply allowing Edna to speak openly about the emptiness of her marriage. Almost a hundred years later, the problems of such marital voids are the subject of many monthly articles in magazines in the supermarkets and drugstores, but in Chopin's day, such indiscretions were considered, if not sinful, at least a defect on the part of a negligent, willful wife. It was a wife's duty to keep her marriage harmonious – at any cost – sincerely, as well as superficially. Edna will not permit any of this mindless convention, especially now that she realizes what thoroughly different people she and Léonce are. Her moments of anguish may be painful, but she plumbs them and exhausts them, and she does not harbor them morbidly or romantically. And when they are finished, she opens herself to new experiences, just as she does in this chapter when she and her father share rare moments of excitement and thrills at the racetrack. Doctor Mandelet is particularly struck by Edna's radiance when he sees her; there is none of the mysterious moodiness that Léonce was worried about. Yet the old doctor is not pleased to learn that Edna encountered Alcée Arobin, a man we heard about earlier, in Chapter 8, when tongues clucked about his affair with the consul's wife at Biloxi. The old doctor fears that a rich (and bored – if Léonce's assessment can be relied on) wife might be an easy target for the notorious heartbreaker; in addition, the doctor notices that Edna has a new "animal" vitality; Léonce Pontellier's wife seems "palpitant with the forces of life . . . [like] some beautiful sleek animal waking up in the sun" – an even more dangerous ingredient in the possibility that she and Arobin find one another attractive, fascinating, and each with ample time to spend together.

Chopin ends the chapter with four stories, one told by each of her principal characters. Each of the characters has been warmed by wine, made comfortable by each other's company, and each reminisces about particularly telling episodes. Mr. Pontellier's story is about himself and is humorous and mischievous; the Colonel's likewise concerns himself, although more solemnly; and the doctor's tale concerns an "old, ever new" story about a woman, lured briefly away from her husband, but returning sensibly after a few days. Edna's tale is quite different. She tells about a pair of young lovers who drift away in a canoe into the southern night, "drifting into the unknown," never to be heard of again. She tells it with such purity and passion that everyone present is moved; its aftermath is strangely akin to the way the summer vacationers on Grand Isle felt after old Mademoiselle Reisz played Chopin's powerful piano music.

The leave-taking of Edna's father is not pleasant. He insists that Edna attend her sister's wedding, and she refuses to do so; he threatens that neither of her sisters will probably speak to her, and he is certain that the bride-to-be will not accept "any excuse." It is at this point that Chopin inserts one of her stylistic gems; still speaking about the outrage of Edna's father, Chopin notes that he assumes that Edna has given an excuse as to why she isn't coming back to Kentucky; the old Colonel is "forgetting that Edna had offered none." This has been characteristic of Edna ever since she decided to have no more "Tuesdays at home." She offers no excuses; Edna is straightforward and frank in her reactions. For that reason, she is often terribly disarming, but she refuses to let herself be compromised by coercion or convention.

Edna's husband, in turn, treats the old Colonel with excessive courtesy; he himself will attend the wedding, hoping that his presence, his "money and love will atone" for what he, we assume, considers to be his childish wife's "mood." Edna's father is as direct as his daughter; he advises Léonce to use authority and coercion on Edna. According to him, they're the "only way to manage a wife" – a subject that has long been just beneath the surface of this novel.

Mr. Pontellier's leaving, which we have been alerted to for some time, occurs shortly after Edna's father departs. While she is packing Léonce's clothing, Edna fears briefly that she may be lonely, but she feels a "radiant peace" when she is at last alone in the house. Even the children are gone, we are told; Léonce's mother has taken them, fearful of her daughter-in-law's lack of maternal indulgence and anxious for their young company, anxious to keep alive in them the Creole ways and temperament.

When Chopin describes Edna's feelings and actions after Léonce leaves, it is as though she were describing the inner thoughts of a person who has just been released from prison. Edna, after "a big, genuine sigh of relief," tours the house, sitting in various chairs and lounges; the house, without Léonce, is like a new acquaintance. She immediately brings in big bouquets of bright flowers and plays with the children's small dog. Edna fills her solitude with the satisfaction she feels within herself. We feel that there is a sense of beginning over, of a new awakening. Edna is enjoying, for the first time, talking with the cook and dining alone, comfortably, in a peignoir. Even the dog seems to be aware of the change within Edna, who is delighted and astonished by her new joy. As the chapter ends, Edna has a long refreshing bath and washes herself clean of old frustrations, of Léonce's interference, and her father's demands. She is "determined to start anew . . . now that her time was completely her own . . . a sense of restfulness invaded her, such as she had not known before."

CHAPTERS 25-32

This section contains many of the novel's most revealing revelations about Edna Pontellier. Following Léonce's departure and her own initial exuberance, Edna becomes restless and moody – filled not with despair, but with boredom, with a sense that "life was passing [her] by." She is a woman who has recently been awakened by romance and love and has declared her independence to paint, but her "art" is not enough to fill her long days; she is aware that she has no real artistic ambitions and that she is not driven by a need for accomplishment.

She fills this void by going again and again to the races; she knows horses and likes the thrill of gambling, the excitement and tenseness of the crowd, and the nostalgic memories of Kentucky horses and paddocks. She is as knowledgeable as most of the men at the track about horses, and she knows it. It is this aura of unusual knowledge and power, in addition to Edna's high-colored handsomeness, that arouses the interest of Alcée Arobin when they attend the races by coincidence together, in the company of one of Edna's friends, a Mrs. Highcamp. Arobin catches "the contagion of excitement," Chopin comments, and is drawn to Edna "like a magnet."

Edna is not unaware of this fact, and she does not flirt with Arobin. On the contrary, it is Arobin, the "young man of fashion" who flirts coquettishly with Edna. Edna's conduct is remarkably cool and contained, even though she feels a fever burning within her. After their first day at the races, and after Arobin has driven her home, she is unusually hungry. She munches on some Gruyere cheese and sips from a bottle of beer, while she pokes "at the wood embers on the hearth"; this is as symbolic to Edna as it is to us. Arobin has stirred the embers of passion within Edna, embers from the summer that were kindled within Edna by Robert Lebrun. There is a restlessness within Edna that wants a release from the bounds of the Pontellier garden and from the four walls of her painting atelier. For this reason, Edna decides to allow herself to go to the races with Arobin alone, to invite him for dinner, and to linger afterward. Yet she cannot allow herself to become merely one more of Arobin's conquests, even though his intimate, confessional tone does tempt her.

When Edna is finally alone, she ponders the possibility of having an affair with Arobin – but on her terms. Chopin is not so blunt as this, but then she could not be in her time. Edna cold-bloodedly considers the consequences of having an affair with this "young man of fashion," and it is significant that it is not herself that she worries about. She doesn't worry about her feelings or even her reputation; it would be easy for her, for "Arobin was absolutely nothing to her." Nor does Edna consider Léonce. It is Robert whom she thinks about; her love for him disturbs her, and an affair with Arobin would seem cheap, a little like adultery. She did not marry Léonce because of love, but she does love Robert, and she cannot reconcile these feelings with the temptation to satisfy her physical craving for a sexual affair with young Arobin. She has sent him away, saying that she no longer likes him, but she is sure that she is as much a narcotic to him as he is to her. Her passion is a need she no longer fears fulfilling, but if she chooses to fill its demands, she must be the one to do the choosing.

Later, after Arobin's polite, elaborate note of apology for acting overly bold so soon after they met, the matter of his kissing her hand seems trivial. Of course, he may see her art studio. Edna is convinced that electric though his charm may be, Arobin is no threat to her. Arobin responds on cue, Chopin tells us "with all his disarming naivete." He is aware that beneath Edna's maturity is raw passion — and he is correct. Chopin tells us that Arobin, despite his rather silly subservience and wide-eyed adoration, pleased the "animalism that stirred impatiently within" Edna.

Feeling a need to talk with someone, it is to old Mademoiselle Reisz that Edna now turns; Edna feels a freedom with her that she can express with few other people. Nothing shocks the old pianist. She is not embarrassed that Edna finds her ailing, her neck wrapped in flannel and that Edna did not ask for an invitation. Nor is Edna embarrassed to drink from the old woman's brandy "as a man would have done." There are no ridiculous, "lady-like" preludes to Edna's reason for coming; she announces immediately that she is moving out of Léonce's house and into a small, four-room house around the corner from Léonce. She wants — and needs — a house of her own. Once uttered aloud, however, the fact of Edna's leaving Léonce's house seems too severe, but old Mademoiselle Reisz will not let Edna make any feeble excuses — such as the Pontelliers' house being too large, the servants too much trouble, etc. She makes Edna state aloud that Léonce's house is not *hers*; it is his. Edna says that she has a little money of her own, the promise of more, and she does want a place of her own in addition to a "feeling of freedom and independence."

That afternoon, over a roaring fire in the old lady's stove, over chocolate, Edna resolves "never again to belong to another than herself." This is one half of this section's climax; the other half concerns another letter that Mademoiselle Reisz has received from Robert Lebrun. Even though the old lady knows that it is painful for Edna to read letters that Robert has written to someone else, she shares them with Edna. She is convinced that Robert is in love with Edna and that he is trying to forget her; that is the reason he left so abruptly for Mexico and why he has not written Edna, something he would have done had he considered Edna merely a casual "friend." Mademoiselle Reisz is sure that Robert saw the social consequences, as well as the futility, of his falling in love with Edna. Thus the old woman gives Edna the letter, one that is unlike any of his other ones. In this letter, Robert writes that he is returning to New Orleans – very soon.

The old woman then forces Edna to admit aloud what she has admitted to no one else: that she is indeed in love with Robert Lebrun and that a woman cannot say *why* she loves whomever it is that she loves. Moreover, she does *not* select the man she falls in love with; love is unreasonable because of its very nature. Edna does not know what she will do when Robert returns. For the present, the mere fact that he is returning is enough. Irrationally, generously, she orders a huge box of bonbons for the children in Iberville. Likewise, her exuberance causes her to write to Léonce; because of Robert's welcome news, Edna is able to break the news of her impending move in a letter to her husband, including her plans for a large "farewell dinner." Edna believes that her letter is charming, and Chopin assures us that it is; it is "brilliant and brimming with cheerfulness."

That night Edna allows herself to be kissed, by firelight, by Arobin; "it was the first kiss of her life to which her nature had really responded." She is as intoxicated as a child before Christmas who cannot wait to open the packages. She allows Arobin's charms to be a surrogate for Robert, for what she imagines will happen when Robert returns. Passion, like an effervescence, builds within Edna. She is choking with the emotions of anticipation, and she allows Arobin to touch her. She follows her instincts instead of thinking about them. But she does not wholly abandon her rationality. When she kisses Arobin, she *decides* to kiss him, "[clasping] his head, [holding] his lips to hers." The promise of Robert's anticipated passion is tumultuous. Edna satisfies her craving, and even Arobin is probably aware that

Edna's thoughts are not about him, for he told her earlier in the evening that he felt as though her thoughts were "wandering, as if they were not here with me." He was far more accurate than he would ever have believed, or than his ego would have allowed him to believe.

Inserted into this short scene is an observation made by old Mademoiselle Reisz; touching Edna's shoulder blades, she explained to her that she was feeling to see if "the little bird would soar above the level plain of tradition and prejudice." Such a bird would need "strong wings," she said, adding that it was a "sad spectacle to see the weaklings bruised, exhausted, fluttering back to earth." The old woman senses Edna's strong determination to become something more than Léonce Pontellier's "property," but the old woman cannot imagine how a married woman and a mother of two young children can successfully cope — even in New Orleans — merely because she is in love with a man other than her husband.

Irresponsibility, perhaps, is the first feeling which troubles Edna after Arobin leaves. She can be sure of Léonce's reproach, were he to find out about her passionate evening with Arobin; but as we have seen, Léonce has reproached Edna before. Robert's reproach — that can be matched and overcome by love and understanding. Significantly, Edna feels no shame nor remorse for letting Arobin kiss her and for her taking his head and kissing him deeply. It was an act of passion that she shared with Arobin, not an act of love — and that makes a vast difference to Edna. She needed Arobin's passion and regrets that it could not have been, simultaneously, love, but it was not. It was only that: passion — no more or no less — and Edna felt better afterward: ". . . as if a mist had been lifted from her eyes, enabling her to look upon and comprehend the significance of life." Passion is a part of life, and Edna has satisfied her body's need for passion. Life is not just love — beautiful, lovely romantic love. Life is a "monster made up of beauty and brutality" — for women, as well as for men.

Chopin must have enjoyed creating the character of Arobin, the Casanova. She makes him thoroughly charming, certainly handsome, kind, well-mannered, but, without caricature, she makes him a man who is rather shallow, who satisfies himself on the sighs and bodies of married women until they become uninteresting and a new prospect appears before him. His "conquest" of Edna contains all the little things that might cause him to believe that Edna is yet another lonely, idle rich wife who is so captivated by him that she dares convention to make love with him—for awhile—until he replaces her with another. Edna's unusually lively conversation with him, the fever burning in her cheeks and eyes at the races, her going to the races with him alone, their sitting beside the fire together, her responsiveness to his boyish frankness and boastings, her allowing him to kiss her hand, and then her boldly making love to him—all these things have convinced him that *he* has "stolen her heart" and that when he appears next, he will find her "indulging in sentimental tears."

Arobin could not be more surprised than he is the next day when he finds Edna high atop a ladder, a kerchief knotted around her head, her sleeves rolled to her elbows, looking "splendid and robust," helping a housemaid prepare to take down and pack "everything which she had acquired aside from her husband's bounty." Arobin implores Edna to come down, anxious that she will fall and hurt herself. But Edna refuses. She can barely wait to move to the "pigeon house," as she calls it. There is no recourse for the confused Arobin, since he is a proper gentleman, other than offer to climb up on the ladder himself and unhook the paintings. Edna lets him do this; the offer is convenient. She even makes him don one of her dust caps, which sends the housemaid into "contortions of mirth." The short scene is a brief masterpiece of male-female reversal, filled with the joy of poetic revenge and justice.

Chopin took great care to create interest and suspense about Edna's making one last, grand gesture—a magnificent farewell dinner party. It would be visual, social proof, accompanied by approval and joy, that Edna was "moving out," an artist on her own, maintaining her own lifestyle and her affairs in what she humorously calls the pigeon house. Not surprisingly, however, the party is not the grand affair which Edna fantasized about. We know that Edna has sundered most of her New Orleans social relationships and that she has abandoned her "Tuesdays at home"; logically, New Orleans' social world will not be rocked. The party, as it turns out, is a comfortable group of ten people. Yet Edna has furnished even this small number of people with grandeur and sumptuous magnificence, including a group of hired mandolin players to serenade her guests softly and discretely at a distance from the dining room.

Chopin herself is present, discretely slipping in brief comments about the guests and making us aware that this is a rather odd assemblage of people. For example, we have never heard of the Merrimans until now; we learn that Mr. Merriman is "something of a shallow-pate" and that, because he laughs at other people's witticisms, he is "extremely popular." Arobin is there, of course, over-indulging in flattery for his hostess, and there is also Mrs. Highcamp, a fellow enthusiast of the races. Old Mademoiselle Reisz is wearing fresh violets in her hair, and she is seated, because of her diminutive size, atop a number of plump cushions. Monsieur Ratignolle is alone (his wife fears that she will soon begin labor pains). The aging Miss Mayblunt inspects her food and the other guests through a lorgnette and is said to be intellectual. There is also a "gentleman by the name of Gouvernail . . . of whom nothing special could be said"—in short, a motley lot. Representing the Lebrun family is young and handsome Victor Lebrun, who unexpectedly becomes the center of attention at the party and the reason for the party's coming to a quick conclusion.

Edna, of course, looks magnificant as the hostess in a dazzling gold satin gown, with a fall of flesh-colored lace at the shoulders and a cluster of diamonds atop her forehead. Chopin comments on her regal bearing, her sense of being "alone"; Edna, it seems, stands alone, outside the assemblage of her party and is aware that one person is missing—the person she desires most to be there: Robert. Her love for Robert overpowers her precisely when it should not. The party—if it is to be a true celebration of her independence demands that she retain—despite any mishap—a regal air and command as a hostess, but as it turns out, she cannot bear the sight of the handsome Victor, slightly drunk, garbed and garlanded by Mrs. Highcamp as (in Gouvernail's murmured words) ". . . the image of Desire." She cannot bear the sight of him as the embodiment of pagan desire, and neither can she bear to have him begin to sing the "*si tu savais*" (if you only knew) refrain of the song which Robert once sang to her, the song she sings softly to herself for rhapsodic and romantic comfort.

The party's tableau, with Victor as its focus, is shattered almost in slow motion. The wine has lulled the party into semi-drowsiness and no one is unduly alarmed when Edna cries out for Victor to stop his song, nor when she accidentally shatters her wine glass and its contents across Arobin's legs, nor when she rushes to Victor and places her hand over his mouth. The guests make charming small talk and, like the mandolin players, slowly steal away, and Edna is lost amid a "profound stillness."

The "little bird" that Mademoiselle Reisz spoke of earlier is emotionally – and perhaps physically – exhausted. Her nervous energy caused her to do a good deal of preparation for the party herself. But, for the most part, Edna's exhaustion is due to the coinciding of the monumental decision to move out of her husband's house and the unexpected news that Robert Lebrun is returning to New Orleans. Arobin, of course, thinks that it is his overwhelming charm which is preying upon her sensibilities; her passion is afire for him. Edna lets him think whatever he pleases; she does not concern herself unduly with Arobin. For example, he has filled her pigeon house with large bouquets of fresh flowers and, with old Celestine's help, distributed them everywhere as a surprise for Edna. Edna does not even comment on the flowers. She sits and rests her head on a table and asks Arobin to leave. Instead, he comes to her and smoothes her hair, his hand caressing her bare shoulders, kissing her lightly there, and continuing to caress her until "she had become supple to his gentle, seductive entreaties." Once again, he imagines that it is he and his touch that are causing Edna's anguish. He imagines that he is irresistible and that he can have any woman he chooses. Edna, however, allows him to caress her because she lets herself enjoy what he is a master of.

Emotionally, Edna knows that Arobin is nothing to her. With her head on her arm, her eyes closed, Arobin is simply a stimulus to ease and arouse and please her; her nerves are tense and his touch is tender. Besides, Edna is confident that if Arobin were to become too aggressive, she could tell him to leave and he would do so. She can handle young Arobin – if she chooses to. As noted, she allows him to caress her because her body enjoys – and needs – being touched and soothed. Arobin leaves, feeling triumphant that he has satisfied Edna's passion; little does he fully realize that Edna let herself be aroused by his anonymous, trained touch. With her eyes closed, Edna was scarcely aware of Arobin himself. Her thoughts were with Robert Lebrun.

Léonce Pontellier proves to be far more clever than one might have imagined. When he realizes that his wife seriously means to move out of their house, he invents a ruse of their having their already grand mansion remodeled. The idea is certainly original and certainly ingenious. It is also a surprise when we discover that he does not worry about Edna's moving out causing a personal scandal. On the contrary, Léonce is alarmed about what people might think concerning their "finances." The idea that others might gossip about Edna's moving out being a prelude to Léonce's joining her in the pigeon house almost undoes him. Thus he hires a well-known architect and, within days, the Pontellier house is cluttered with packers, movers, and carpenters – all in an effort to disguise any hint of instability in the Pontellier *fortune*. Léonce's entire concern is with financial scandal; his "unqualified disapproval and remonstrance" are related to the possibility that Edna's latest "whim" might do "incalculable mischief to his business prospects." Chopin's satire on Pontellier's material vanity is superb when she tells us about a brief notice in one of the daily papers (inserted, we can be sure, by Léonce himself) about the possibility that the Pontelliers might spend the summer abroad. Chopin, in her own small way, repays in kind the many years of male laughter over the vanity of women. To be sure, she tips her hand by not suppressing her impulse to include an exclamation point, but who can blame her for summing up Léonce's reaction with ". . . Mr. Pontellier had saved appearances!"

Edna is satisfied with her small house so completely that she soon feels ready to leave it and go see her children, and the week that she spends there is described by Chopin in detail; the paragraphs are full of the "local color" that her critics – prior to the publication of *The Awakening* – were so quick to praise. Edna listens to her little boys' tales of mule riding, fishing, picking pecans, and hauling chips. Even Edna herself enjoys going with them to see the pigs and the cows and also the black servants – laying the cane, thrashing the pecan tree, and catching fish in the back lake. Edna thoroughly enjoys being with the children, answering their questions about the new house – where everyone will sleep and where their favorite toys are. For the entire week, Chopin tells us, Edna gave "all of herself" to her children – unreservedly and happily. And when she has to leave, it is with a sense of regret. All the way home, "their presence lingered with her like the memory of a delicious song." But once Edna returns to New Orleans, her thoughts are not on her children.

This joyous scene of Edna with her children and of her leaving them and returning to New Orleans helps us understand what Edna meant when she told her friend Adèle Ratignolle that she would die for her children, but that she would not give up a life of her own in exchange for a daily devotion to them. Edna loves her children; of that there is no doubt, but she cannot make her family the focus of her life. She admires Adèle's beautiful embodiment of the mother-woman role, but she herself cannot compromise for the stifling demands of the role. Edna does not want a predefined role, and her options seem to be either a mother-woman like Adèle or an eccentric, living only for her art, like old Mademoiselle Reisz. Like her children, Edna's art can richly consume her time, but Edna has no ambition to be a great artist. She doesn't want to be a "dedicated artist," in the same way that she defies being a "dedicated mother" and, especially, a "dedicated wife." The allegiance to the world of "art" is ultimately as unacceptable as the world of "mother, wife, and housekeeper." When Edna decides to move out of the big house into a house of her own, she has no role model to follow. She is aware of the solitude that accompanies her decisions and actions. She has no man to talk with that might offer understanding or direction, nor does she have any other woman – save Adèle and Mademoiselle Reisz – to share her feelings with. Chopin's ending Chapter 32 with the simple sentence "She was again alone" is a clear, direct summing up of Edna's predicament. She is very much alone. Not only now, but ever since her first moments of her awakening, solitude has accompanied her growth. On Grand Isle, she especially felt the embodiment of this solitude in the sea. For that reason, she was supremely happy when she learned to swim in it and no longer had to fear it and have a "hand nearby"; she could freely share in its abundant solitude.

CHAPTERS 33–39

Robert Lebrun's actual return to New Orleans is as surprising to us as it is to Edna. During Edna's dinner party, Victor mentioned nothing about his brother's leaving his job in Mexico; Madame Lebrun has said nothing definite to Edna, nor has Adèle Ratignolle. We know from his letter that Robert plans to return, but we are as shocked as Edna is when she is sitting alone in Mademoiselle Reisz' apartment one evening, waiting for her to come home, and Robert suddenly opens the door.

Coincidentally, one of the reasons that Edna has come to see Mademoiselle Reisz is to talk about Robert. Even though Robert has been gone for almost a year, he has not written to Edna – not even once. As a result, he has become somewhat of a fantasy lover to Edna. She has no certain hope for his returning permanently to New Orleans, so she has filled her stray moments by romantically imagining his returning for a brief visit. Always in her fantasies, Robert has come to her and declared his love for her; or else, in another fantasy, he has accidentally revealed his love for her. Either way, his love for Edna has matched her deep love for him.

Now, however, he is suddenly, physically, before her, and the situation evokes a phrase that Edna used not long ago to describe life; she called it a "monster of beauty and brutality." Reality has come crashing down upon fantasy; the rendezvous she fantasized has occurred and it is the antithesis of how Edna hoped it would be. Robert is as handsome as ever, but he is ill at ease and awkward. When he sits on the piano stool, one of his arms crashes discordantly across the piano keys. The noise is brutal, as is his confession that he has been in New Orleans for two days. Edna's movements in this scene are mechanical, awkward, and unsteady. She has been caught completely off-guard; this is not the way it should have happened. She came to Mademoiselle Reisz' apartment for peace and some solace after a boring, irritating morning, and Robert (her fantasy of peace) has broken her quiet revery.

In the midst of this sudden "brutality" of life, the shattering of all her romantic daydreams, there is also beauty, however, for in spite of Robert's not writing to her, Edna finds in his eyes the tenderness she saw long ago on Grand Isle. Now she finds "added warmth and entreaty," qualities that were not there before. In his eyes, she sees the warmth that kept alive her love for him, the love she sensed was shared between them. Here is the proof—in his eyes.

Yet even this discovery becomes ultimately painful because Robert refuses to acknowledge his feelings for her. Instead, he speaks about settling in with his old firm and ambiguously excuses his not writing by saying that there "have been so many things . . ." Robert has obviously asked a great many questions about Edna. He knows, for example, that the Pontelliers might spend the summer abroad and that Edna has moved into her small house. He seems as shy as Edna is bold. He dares not to do what she has done—that is, face herself and life, with all its "beauty and brutality" and cope with, if not solve, life's problems. Robert has committed himself to the role of becoming a proper New Orleans gentleman and businessman, as Adèle Ratignolle and Mademoiselle Reisz have committed themselves to their prescribed roles. Edna cannot bear the fraudulence she finds in Robert. When he says that his letters would not have been "of any interest" to Edna, the lie is too painful and too insulting. ". . . it isn't the truth," Edna says, and prepares to go. She has waited too long, anticipated too much, fantasized too freely, and now when she is confronted with the man she loves most, she cannot and will not listen to lies or excuses. She has become a fervent disciple of a new integrity, and she will not abide hypocrisy, especially from Robert.

When Robert insists on accompanying her home, she allows him to do so because, after all, Edna is human. She loves him and she has missed him. He begs to stay a bit if Edna will "let" him. The tension between them is broken, and Edna is able to laugh and relax and put her hand on his shoulder and tell him that he is beginning to seem like the old Robert she once knew.

This intimate mood is broken almost immediately, however, when Robert finds a picture of Arobin and is jealous that Edna has it. Edna is neither ashamed nor embarrassed by the picture. Arobin is nothing to her; we know that. Edna tried to make a sketch of Arobin, and he brought the photograph, hoping that it might help her sketching. The photograph is no "lover's gift," no memento. Edna tells Robert no more or no less than the truth: she finds Arobin's head worth drawing, he is a friend of hers, and of late she's come to know him better. Robert calls Edna "cruel" for being so blunt. Edna is not cruel; quite simply, she can play games no longer. Robert grew up playing games; the Creoles all play games. When Edna met Robert, he was playing the role of a knight in search for a fair lady to serve during the summer. In fact, everyone Edna knows plays role games – speaking and acting predictably – and no one questions the role or varies from its prescribed actions. Yet Edna was "awakened," and she questioned her role as wife and mother; afterward, she began to try and fashion a life that would be uniquely hers – something no one she knows has ever done before. Where it will end, she cannot imagine, but she will not compromise – not now, not even with Robert, the man she loves. If Edna is cruel, it is because she has recognized and accepted the fact that life is beautiful and that it is also cruel. If Robert is ever to mature, he too must make his own odyssey, searching for his own truths as thoroughly as Edna has done.

A certain coolness comes between Edna and Robert; Chopin terms it "a certain degree of ceremony." Edna is not able to penetrate Robert's reserve and his reluctance to admit his emotional feelings toward her.

He admits to forgetting "nothing at Grand Isle," but this statement is cautious and non-commital. In contrast, Edna says that being with Robert "never tires" her. He does not comment on this. During the dinner and afterward, Edna is patient with Robert's aloofness until she notices a strikingly embroidered tobacco pouch that Robert lays upon the table. She admires the needlework, and when Robert reveals that the pouch was given to him by a Mexican girl, Edna becomes uncharacteristically jealous. Her questions are uncharacteristically indirect and bitter, and Robert's answers are taunting and ambiguous; behind all of Edna's questions is one single, unasked question: did you love the Mexican girl who gave you the tobacco pouch?

As Robert is pocketing the pouch, Arobin enters. The scene is already bristling with intensity, and Arobin's entrance multiplies that tenseness. When Arobin discovers Robert with Edna, he and Edna perform an impromptu charade of camaraderie, ridiculing Robert's romantic luck with women. Robert's demeanor is seemingly unruffled; he shakes hands with both Edna and Arobin, asks to be remembered to Mr. Pontellier, and leaves. His mentioning Mr. Pontellier is only proper good manners, of course, but it is Robert's subtle way of reminding Edna and Arobin that Edna is a *married* woman.

The next morning's sunlight cheers Edna; after the previous night's confusion and brooding, Edna feels that she was foolish to have been so introspective and jealous. Robert loves her; she was certain of that yesterday and she is just as certain of that today. It is only a matter of time before Robert's reserve is broken – for two reasons: first, because he does love her; and second, because of her passion for him. Edna is convinced that Robert knows that she loves him; soon, he will also realize that she desires him, that he has awakened sexual passion within her. She confronts the possibility of his remaining cool and distant for awhile, but she can live with that possibility. The important thing now is that he *has* returned, that he lives in New Orleans, and is not almost a continent away. Time will awaken Robert; Edna can wait.

Because of her decision to allow Robert his freedom to adjust once again to the business of living in New Orleans and to adjust to the new circumstances of her freedom, Edna is able to deal decisively with the morning's mail. To her son who asks for bonbons, she promises treats; to Léonce, Edna is diplomatic and friendly, though evasive;

she has made no plans to go abroad. In fact, she has made no plans whatsoever. She is absolutely open to whatever Fate offers.

Edna burns Arobin's love note; his professed concern for her is of no consequence. She does allow him, however, to fill her empty hours when days go by and Robert does not call or even send a note. Arobin is allowed to be a surrogate. He possesses a sense of danger and romance and fulfills her need for male companionship. Arobin, meanwhile, preys on Edna's "latent sensuality." And whereas earlier, she often went to bed despondent because Robert had not called, at least now, when Arobin fills her evenings, there is no despondency when she falls alseep, but neither is there a freshness and joy when she awakens in the morning.

Thus Edna lives on the periphery of hope, longing to see Robert and compromising for Arobin's ready, romantic companionship. For that reason, she often goes alone to a small enclosed garden cafe, where she can be alone, can read quietly, and dream idly of Robert. Yet, quite by accident, Robert walks into the garden one day and interrupts her reverie. They are awkward, apologetic, and then distant. Edna attempts to explain why all of her questions to him must seem "unwomanly": she has changed. She says what she thinks now, and she asks questions, and she is prepared to face the consequences. Robert is obviously attracted to her, but he is cautious before this new woman he has discovered. He follows her home, although she does not ask him to do so, and he stays, sitting in the shadows while she goes to bathe her face. When she returns, she leans down and kisses him.

Edna continues to satisfy her passion, putting her hand to his face and pressing her cheek against his. They kiss and he confesses to having wanted to kiss her many times. It was his love for her that drove him away from Grand Isle. He had no other choice.

Edna tries to explain that it makes no difference to her if she is married to Léonce Pontellier. She jokes that Léonce is generous; perhaps he might "give" her to Robert, an offer she finds absurd. No one can "give her away." Edna already *is* free. She belongs to no one except herself. When Robert mentions wanting her to be his wife, she is affronted; she scoffs at "religion, loyalty, everything . . ." Kissing Robert on the eyes, the cheeks, and the lips, she chides him for imagining that someone must "set her free" in order for them to be able to make love.

At that moment a message is delivered, and fate interrupts their passionate avowals. Long ago, Edna promised Adèle to help her when her labor pains began; now Edna must go to her friend. The two lovers kiss goodbye, and Edna feels that Robert's passion matches her own. She promises him that *nothing* is of consequence now – except their love for each other. She leaves him precisely when he needs her most. Robert is weak; he needs Edna's strength. He fully realizes how thoroughly he loves this married woman who promises herself, who promises to defy all convention for him.

Witnessing Adèle in the throes of childbirth is painful for Edna. The physical pain she sees is symbolic of the psychological pain she feels is inherent in motherhood. This scene of birth is ugly and bloody and preludes, for Edna, Adèle's never-ending bondage to a child who will overpower her will and identity. And Adèle will allow it to happen. Edna cannot. The scene causes Edna to remember her own painful scenes of childbirth and her "awakening to find a little new life she had been given." But Edna has awakened now as an adult and found a new little life that she herself created – and this new life is liberating. It does not limit; being a mother limits one, and the pain Edna sees before her is not as painful as the fact that once one has decided to become a mother-woman, one gives up everything for the children. Despite the torture that Edna sees Adèle enduring, torture and pain which Edna finds repulsive, Edna stays – in revolt and as a witness against nature for its cruel demands. She stays so long, in fact, that Adèle is able to whisper, exhaustedly, that Edna should "think of the children . . . think of the children! Remember them!" Adèle, even in her great pain, is thinking of Edna, afraid that Edna is about to abandon her husband and children in exchange for a romantic whim. She appeals to what she, as a mother, holds most sacred: the children, even as she suffers the pains of birth.

For Adèle, this new baby is new evidence of her worth as a mother-woman; for Edna, it is yet another burden; it is a reminder of a woman's powerlessness, of how her liberty is checked by men, family, and society.

When Edna is free at last of the confines of the Ratignolle's apartment, she feels dazed; the trauma of seeing her friend give birth has unnerved her. Even Doctor Mandelet thinks it was cruel for Adèle to insist that Edna witness the childbirth scene in order that she might recall that she too had once given birth, that she too had brought forth children from her body, and that they were, by definition, physical extensions of herself. They grew within her body and despite their being severed, they are still part of her flesh and blood.

The object lesson was not wholly lost on Edna. Before she left for Adèle's house, she was convinced that no one would, or could, or should, demand that she do anything she did not wish to do. Now she is not sure. She *is* sure that Léonce cannot force her to go abroad, but she is unable to say, unreservedly, that no one has the right to force her to do anything that she does not wish to do "except children, perhaps . . ." Her thoughts are incoherent.

Yet of one thing she is sure; she has awakened to new visions and new perspectives and new possibilities, and she can never return to a life of dreaming and illusions or of being Mrs. Léonce Pontellier. Motherhood, in contrast, has become nebulous; *her* life should come first; she should be able to live her life her way—regardless of whom she must "trample upon," and yet, ultimately, she realizes that she cannot "trample upon the little lives."

We have never seen Edna, for any length of time, exhibit maternal feelings. Her children and her love for them have been vague and on the periphery of this novel, except for the week spent at their grandmother's home. Yet witnessing Adèle give birth has made Edna realize anew that her children were created within her own body and that a mother must, ultimately, be responsible for them.

At the same time, she can envision no greater bliss than that which she shared with Robert—their embracing, their kissing and expressing their love for one another. He almost gave himself to her. She resolves to think of the children tomorrow. She will awaken Robert's passion again tonight with her kisses and arouse him with her caresses. There will be time to think of the children tomorrow. Tonight she will awaken Robert and claim him.

But Robert is not waiting for her. He has left a note saying goodbye. He leaves her because he loves her. She has been willing to sacrifice everything—even the little ones—for him, but he is afraid to risk anything.

The final chapter of the novel is set once again on Grand Isle. Robert's brother, Victor, is patching up one of the cottages and the feisty, flirtatious Mariequita is sitting in the sun watching him, handing him nails and dangling her legs. Victor has talked for an hour of nothing but the fabulous party at Edna's; he has described in exaggerated detail the party, embroidering his memories with romantic fancy, especially his memory of Edna, resplendent in sparkling diamonds. Both young people are struck dumb with amazement when Edna suddenly appears and begins to chatter about hearing the hammering and being glad to know that the loose planking is being mended, complaining how dreary and deserted everything looks. She has come to rest, she says; any little corner will do. She is alone and simply needs to get away and rest.

The young people continue to chat and argue, while Edna walks toward the beach; she does not hear them. The sun is hot and she lets its heat penetrate her. Edna has reached a crisis, one which she must solve alone. She has no man she can relate to; Robert is gone. Léonce does not matter. She has no woman she can relate to: Adèle's role of mother-woman is as oppressive and limited as old Mademoiselle Reisz's role as an artist. Edna's priorities demand that she cannot compromise her newly awakened life for anyone. All of her friends have safe, well-defined niches, but those niches have walls; the old-fashioned, rosy ideals of marriage and motherhood are rank to Edna. The absurdity of condemning herself to such tyranny is too much to ask.

As she enters the sea, she cuts cleanly through the waves and begins to swim out farther than any woman has ever gone before. Here, there are no goals, no roles, no boundaries; there is only the solitude that whispered to her long ago. There is a freshness in the sea that is denied her in the Pontellier house; as a wife and mother, she would stagnate, losing all self-confidence and direction; thus she chooses to swim out to her death. Already, of course, metaphorically she has swum out further than any woman has done when she risked enticing Robert to a romance that would preclude her roles of wife and mother. Edna knows what she is rejecting. Never again will she be bound into a role that she does not choose for herself.

She hears the sea and its murmurs; they seem to be "inviting the soul to wander in abysses of solitude." Edna's solitude is her own companion. Robert, especially, has abandoned her. Above, a bird with a broken wing, beats the air, fluttering, circling, until it reels down the water." Mademoiselle Reisz warned Edna once, using the symbol of a little bird, about having the strength and courage to be able to fly if one were to "soar above the level plain and prejudice . . ." At that time, the old woman felt Edna's shoulder blades to see if Edna's "wings were strong." It was a sad spectacle, she said, to see the weaklings "bruised, exhausted, fluttering back to earth."

Yet the bird Edna watches does not fall to the earth; it falls into the sea. And Edna does not die "bruised" and "fluttering." She enters the water naked, swimming where "the waves . . . invited her." There is no sense of melodrama and hysteria here. Edna lets the sea "caress her, enfold her" in its "soft, close embrace." These are words of love and passion. Edna listens to its voice, and she understands its depths of solitude. She knows that this is no shallow haven of simple calm. This is a deep, restless sea of change and currents. She is not afraid, even though her arms and legs are tiring. No one can claim her now; she can give herself to the sea. And she does, freely joining her solitude with its own solitude. She had to choose and decide whether or not life was worth being lived on terms other than her own, and she decided that it was not. She confronted life's most fundamental philosophical question. That act was an "awakening" in itself. She acts in revolt against the tyranny she finds in social myths that would limit her growth as a free woman. She cannot find meanings in the family unit as it exists and to accept the sacred connotations that generations have given to it would be living fraudulently. The quality of short experience that Edna finds swimming out to her death is measureless, compared to the endless years of robot-like role playing which she would be condemned to were she to return to Léonce Pontellier and her family. Edna's awakening on Grand Isle gives her no alternative. Swimming out to her death gives Edna a sense of dignity because the choice is hers. She has grasped the full reality of the hollow life that would be hers if she condemned herself to living "for the little ones." By choosing death, she frees herself from continuing an existence that would be miserably mechanical. She cuts off all hope for herself by choosing death, but she can conceive of no real hope otherwise. Freedom is more important, even in these few short minutes that she swims out. It is a strange, new clarity that Edna possesses. Her last thoughts are of her youth, the time prior to her awakening. She returns to this state of purity, free of a world that would encase her and consume her. Edna's strokes in the sea are "long, sweeping"; they are not "frantic beatings." We must, of necessity, imagine her as happy and free at last.

QUESTIONS FOR REVIEW

1. What is Grand Isle? Where is it, geographically, in relation to New Orleans?

2. How much older is Mr. Pontellier than Edna? How long have they been married, and what is the significance of their age difference?

3. Describe Edna's physical appearance and her character at the beginning of the novel.

4. What are the circumstances of Edna's first "awakening"? Would you describe Edna's "awakening" as happy or unhappy? Explain.

5. Describe Robert Lebrun's charm early in the novel. Why does he finally decide to leave Edna?

6. Characterize the Creole women, in contrast to Edna.

7. Why does Robert decide to go to Mexico?

8. Mademoiselle Reisz' lifestyle is one of the choices Edna considers after her "awakening." Describe this particular lifestyle.

9. What kind of a mother is Edna? What kind of a hostess is she for her husband?

10. Is Chopin sympathetic to Alcée Arobin? Why or why not?

11. What is Mr. Pontellier's reaction to Edna's announcement that she is moving into the pigeon house?

12. Describe Edna's relationship with Arobin.

13. Briefly comment on the conclusion and the consequences of Edna's grand party.

14. How does Edna finally come to view life? How is this viewpoint different from her viewpoint at the beginning of the novel? Explain the term "life's delirium."

15. How does Adèle's childbirth scene affect Edna?

16. What importance does Chopin assign to the sea in this novel?

17. In your own words, paraphrase Edna's reasons for committing suicide. Do you agree or disagree with her? Explain.

SELECTED BIBLIOGRAPHY

BERTHOFF, WARNER. *The Ferment of Realism: American Literature 1884-1919.* New York: Free Press, 1965.

BUTCHER, PHILIP. "Two Early Southern Realists in Revival," *College Language Association Journal*, 14 (1970), 91-95.

EATON, CLEMENT. "Breaking a Path for the Liberation of Women in the South," *Georgia Review*, 28 (Summer, 1974), 187-99.

EBLE, KENNETH. "A Forgotten Novel: Kate Chopin's *The Awakening*," *Western Humanities Review*, X (Summer 1956), 261-69.

FLETCHER, MARIE. "Kate Chopin's Other Novel," *Southern Literary Journal*, 1 (August 1966), 60-74.

_____. "The Southern Women in the Fiction of Kate Chopin," Louisiana Historical Quarterly, 7 (Spring, 1966), 117-32.

MAY, JOHN R. "Local Color in *The Awakening*," *Southern Review*, 6 (1970) 1031-40.

LEARY, LEWIS. "Introduction," *The Awakening and Other Stories.* New York: Holt, Rinehart and Winston, Inc., 1970.

_____. "Kate Chopin and Walt Whitman," *Walt Whitman Review*, XVI (December 1970), 120-21.

_____. "Kate Chopin, Liberationist?" *Southern Literary Journal*, III (Fall 1970), 138-44.

MILLINER, GLADYS W. "The Tragic Imperative: *The Awakening* and *The Bell Jar*," *Mary Wollstonecraft Newsletter*, II (December 1973), 21-26.

OBERBECK, S.K. "St. Louis Woman," *Newsweek*, LXXV (February 23, 1970), 103-04.

POTTER, RICHARD H. "Kate Chopin and Her Critics: An Annotated Checklist," *Missouri Historical Society Bulletin*, XXVI (July 1970), 306-17.

RINGO, DONALD A. "Romantic Imagery in Kate Chopin's *The Awakening*," *American Literature*, 43 (January 1972), 580-88.

ROCKS, JAMES E. "Kate Chopin's Ironic Vision," *Louisiana Review*, I (Winter 1972), 110-20.

ROSEN, KENNETH M. "Kate Chopin's *The Awakening*: Ambiguity as Art," *Journal of American Studies*, 5 (August 1971), 197-200.

SCHUYLER, WILLIAM. "Kate Chopin," *The Writer*, VIII (August 1894), 115-17.

SEYERSTED, PER. *Kate Chopin: A Critical Biography*. Baton Rouge: Louisiana State University Press, 1969.

SKAGGS, MERRILL M. *The Folk of Southern Fiction*. Athens: University of Georgia Press, 1972.

SPANGLER, GEORGE. "Kate Chopin's *The Awakening*: A Partial Dissent." *Novel*, 3 (1970), 249-55.

SULLIVAN, RUTH AND STEWART SMITH. "Narrative Stance in Kate Chopin's *The Awakening*," *Studies in American Fiction*, I (1973), 62-75.

WILSON, EDMUND. *Patriotic Gore: Studies in the Literature of the American Civil War*. New York: Oxford University Press, 1962.

WOLFF, CYNTHIA. "Thanatos and Eros: Kate Chopin's *The Awakening*," *American Quarterly*, XXV (October 1973), 449-71.

ZIFF, LARZER. *The American 1890s: Life and Times of a Lost Generation*. New York: The Viking Press, 1966.

ZLOTNICK, JOAN. "A Woman's Will: Kate Chopin on Selfhood, Wifehood, and Motherhood," *Markham Review*, III (October 1968), 1-5.

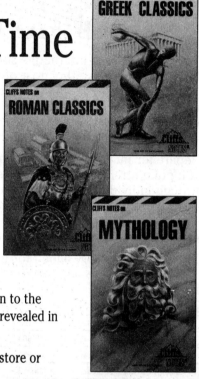

Your Guides to Successful Test Preparation.

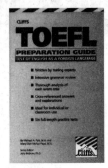

Cliffs Test Preparation Guides

• *Complete* • *Concise* • *Functional* • *In-depth*

Efficient preparation means better test scores. Go with the experts and use *Cliffs Test Preparation Guides*. They focus on helping you know what to expect from each test, and their test-taking techniques have been proven in classroom programs nationwide. Recommended for individual use or as a part of a formal test preparation program.

Publisher's ISBN Prefix 0-8220

Qty.	ISBN	Title	Price	Qty.	ISBN	Title	Price
	2078-5	ACT	8.95		2044-0	Police Sergeant Exam	9.95
	2069-6	CBEST	8.95		2047-5	Police Officer Exam	14.95
	2056-4	CLAST	9.95		2049-1	Police Management Exam	17.95
	2071-8	ELM Review	8.95		2076-9	Praxis I: PPST	9.95
	2077-7	GED	11.95		2017-3	Praxis II: NTE Core Battery	14.95
	2061-0	GMAT	9.95		2074-2	SAT*	9.95
	2073-4	GRE	9.95		2325-3	SAT II*	14.95
	2066-1	LSAT	9.95		2072-6	TASP	8.95
	2046-7	MAT	12.95		2079-3	TOEFL w/cassettes	29.95
	2033-5	Math Review	8.95		2080-7	TOEFL Adv. Prac. (w/cass.)	24.95
	2048-3	MSAT	24.95		2034-3	Verbal Review	7.95
	2020-3	Memory Power for Exams	5.95		2043-2	Writing Proficiency Exam	8.95

Prices subject to change without notice.

Available at your
booksellers, or send
this form with your
check or money order
to **Cliffs Notes, Inc.,**
P.O. Box 80728,
Lincoln, NE 68501
http://www.cliffs.com

☐ Money order ☐ Check payable to Cliffs Notes, Inc.

☐ Visa ☐ Mastercard   Signature_____

Card no. _____ Exp. date_____

Signature _____

Name _____

Address _____

City _____ State_____ Zip_____

*GRE, MSAT, Praxis PPST, NTE, TOEFL and Adv. Practice are registered trademarks of ETS.
 SAT is a registered trademark of CEEB.

Get the Cliffs Edge!

TEST PREPARATION GUIDES

- Enhanced ACT
- AP Biology
- AP Chemistry
- AP English Language and Composition
- AP English Literature and Composition
- AP U.S. History
- CBEST
- CLAST
- ELM Review
- GMAT
- GRE
- LSAT
- MAT
- Math Review for Standardized Tests

- Memory Power
- NTE Core Battery
- Police Officer Examination
- Police Sergeant Examination
- Postal Examinations
- PPST
- SAT I
- TASP™
- TOEFL
- Advanced Practice for the TOEFL
- Verbal Review for Standardized Tests
- WPE
- You Can Pass the GED

CLIFFS NOTES

More than 200 titles are available. Each provides expert
analysis and background of plot, characters and author
to make it easier to understand literary masterpieces.

Get the Cliffs Edge!